GAME CHANGER

GAME CHANGER

The Impact of 9/11 on North American Security

Edited by Jonathan Paquin and Patrick James

UBCPress · Vancouver · Toronto

22 21 20 19 18 17 16 15 14   5 4 3 2 1

Printed in Canada on FSC-certified ancient-forest-free paper (100% post-consumer recycled) that is processed chlorine- and acid-free.

Library and Archives Canada Cataloguing in Publication

Game changer : the impact of 9/11 on North American security / edited by Jonathan Paquin and Patrick James.
Includes bibliographical references and index.
Issued in print and electronic formats.
ISBN 978-0-7748-2706-5 (bound).– ISBN 978-0-7748-2707-2 (pbk.)
ISBN 978-0-7748-2708-9 (pdf).– ISBN 978-0-7748-2709-6 (epub)

1. September 11 Terrorist Attacks, 2001–Influence. 2. National security–North America. 3. North America–Foreign relations. I. Paquin, Jonathan, 1975-, author, editor of compilation II. James, Patrick, 1957-, author, editor of compilation

HV6432.7.G33 2014   355'.03307   C2013-907717-0
                                               C2013-907718-9

Canadä

UBC Press gratefully acknowledges the financial support for our publishing program of the Government of Canada (through the Canada Book Fund), the Canada Council for the Arts, and the British Columbia Arts Council.

This book has been published with the help of a grant from the Canadian Federation for the Humanities and Social Sciences, through the Awards to Scholarly Publications Program, using funds provided by the Social Sciences and Humanities Research Council of Canada.

UBC Press
The University of British Columbia
2029 West Mall
Vancouver, BC V6T 1Z2
www.ubcpress.ca

Contents

Acknowledgments

In this book, a group of distinguished scholars assess the state of North American relations more than a decade after the September 11, 2001, terrorist attacks on New York and Washington, DC. Their contributions highlight the fact that 9/11 was a "game changer" in North American relations.

The completion of this book would not have been possible without the financial support of several agencies. We are grateful to the Consulate General of the United States in Quebec City, the United States Embassy in Ottawa, the Canadian Department of Foreign Affairs and International Trade, the Canadian Department of National Defence, the Canadian Security Intelligence Service, the Quebec Ministry of International Relations, the Quebec Ministry of Public Safety, the Faculty of Social Sciences at Laval University, and the Hautes études internationales (HEI) at Laval University for their generous financial support. We would also like to thank Daniel Navarro Castano, Joanie Trudel, Anne-Christine Poulin, Marion Guay-Arcand, Philippe Beauregard, and Catherine Thomassin for their assistance with this project.

GAME CHANGER

Introduction

The Changing Contours of North American Security

JONATHAN PAQUIN AND PATRICK JAMES

The traumatic events of September 11, 2001, caused a security upheaval in North America. The process by which the North American Free Trade Agreement (NAFTA) partners had been coordinating their economic integration in the 1990s came to an abrupt halt as border security and sovereignty issues reappeared in the national political agendas. It is therefore fair to argue that 9/11 was a game changer – "a newly introduced element or factor that changes an existing situation or activity in a significant way."[1]

In response to the attacks, the US government rapidly implemented a series of security transformations that impacted its bureaucracy, defence apparatus, and border security system. Within a year, the Bush administration had created a massive Department of Homeland Security from several federal agencies, the Department of Defense had established a US Northern Command (NorthCom) to protect the homeland and provide military support to the US government, and new bilateral border security agreements were signed with Canada and Mexico. The main objectives of these agreements were to facilitate policy coordination at the Canada-US and Mexico-US borders and to keep North American borders closed to security threats while open to the legitimate movement of people and goods. These changes inevitably affected Washington's relations with Ottawa and Mexico City and compelled the Canadian and Mexican governments to adapt to new American security requirements in order to minimize the effects of 9/11 on transborder trade and commerce.

These security transformations led to intense cooperation as well as obvious political tensions among the three North American partners. The fact that Canada, the United States, and Mexico operate in an asymmetrical interdependent environment, and tend to arrive at different assessments of the issues at stake, explains the simultaneously sweet and sour aspects of their mutual relations. In this respect, one question at the centre of discussions throughout the 2000s was how to reconcile two North American requirements: the reality of economic interdependence and the timeless Westphalian notion of national security and territorial protection.

In that context, this volume provides a better understanding of the increasingly important domain of twenty-first-century hemispheric security integration. While also focusing on important points of continuity in North American relations, it investigates how and why security transformations have occurred since 9/11. Hence, its main objective is not to provide a normative assessment of continental integration or to generate a macro-historical analysis of its political evolution. Rather, the essays in this collection identify the grounds for further cooperation as well as the sensitive issues that should be handled with care to improve the future of North American security relations.

Collectively speaking, the contributors to this volume write with authority on the subject at hand. Most of them are Canadian scholars pursuing their career in North American universities across the continent, and, given this reality, the book reflects, to a certain extent, a Canadian perspective on hemispheric security relations and offers a unique take on the complex issues discussed. More specifically, the chapters in this volume constitute an important addition to the growing literature on North American politics, making a theoretical and empirical contribution to the study of core security issues that have challenged North American governments since 9/11. Among the overarching themes are variations in the perception of threat among Canada, the United States, and Mexico, and consequently differences in the interests and priorities of their respective governments. Most of the specific issues addressed here are derived from these general themes. For instance, the failure to establish a trilateral approach to dealing with security integration in the aftermath of 9/11, or the bargaining situation in which Canada's and Mexico's economic benefits depended on the success of security negotiations with the United States, directly related to these states' different security perceptions and priorities.

Thus, *Game Changer* builds upon recent scholarly contributions that address a variety of issues on North American relations, including *North America in Question,* edited by Jeffrey Ayres and Laura Macdonald; "Sharing the Burden of the Border," by Stéfanie von Hlatky and Jessica Trisko; *Does North America Exist?* by Stephen Clarkson; and *Politics in North America,* edited by Yasmeen Abu-Laban, Radha Jhappan, and François Rocher[2] – titles that foreshadow some of the priorities adopted by this book.

Each of the experts contributing to *Game Changer,* having knowledge of a wide range of substantive issues in the domain of security, was asked to address a number of questions, including the following:

- Given the nature of the regional context, how do international relations theories help to explain the behaviour of the North American states toward one another in the post-9/11 era?
- How can the tension between state autonomy and the search for greater regional cooperation be reconciled for the sake of better security relations?
- To what degree is the perception of threat uniform versus unique to each respective state and society?
- Did the intense nature of 9/11 induce linkage between issues among the three North American states?
- To what extent did 9/11 set the stage for trilateralism, perhaps in the form of a security perimeter?
- What combinations of factors – monadic, dyadic, or triadic – have played the most significant role in shaping policy after 9/11?

Hence, the chapters provide answers to various subsets of these queries. The book is organized into two parts, followed by a conclusion that integrates the insights from the overall study into comprehensive answers.

Part 1 focuses on a range of theoretical explanations of state behaviour in the post-9/11 continental environment. This is significant because the literature in international relations has largely ignored this important topic. Hence, the chapters rely on international relations theories to debate North American security relations and shed light on the behaviour of the United States, Canada, and, to a certain extent, Mexico in the current regional context. The authors all agree that 9/11 caused political discontinuity in the integration process that had been initiated by NAFTA.

Charles Doran opens the discussion with a multilevel analysis of the different impacts of 9/11 on North America. He sees 9/11 as having ushered in a form of countervailing power through a dramatically increased sense of vulnerability at home for the United States. Whereas the trend on the continent had been toward continental integration, the new security imperatives in Washington reversed that momentum. It is in this way that Doran sees 9/11 as a game changer. In his view, the enhancement of security measures has dampened the idea of a North American community. At the same time, he wonders whether the tensions over security and border issues experienced in the last decade may simply have provoked a return to normality – that is, to the pre-NAFTA context, when differences and diverging political interests sometimes caused disagreements between North American neighbours. Whether or not this is the case, Doran characterizes 9/11 as a highly prominent event, with an important short-term impact on security and economic cooperation that overshadowed the ongoing effects of more important structural trends. He regards the shift in power away from North America and toward Asia – less visible than the loss of life and destruction of property on 9/11 – as likely to impact much more significantly on foreign policy strategies over the long term. Thus, more thought needs to be given to how North America as a whole ought to react to this structural change in capabilities, as opposed to continuing to focus on more superficial policy aspects related to terrorism.

Chapter 2, by Frank Harvey, offers a dramatic answer to the question of how much things have changed by focusing on the causes of public fears about terrorism in the United States. He identifies a seemingly insatiable need for security among the American public, a need not based on any kind of rational calculation of probability regarding the danger from terrorism. Instead, the US reaction is fundamentally emotive and tends to exaggerate the importance of terrorism because it is a menace that seems beyond control. It is crucial for the leaders of Canada and Mexico to grasp this belief among many Americans in order to identify policies that may help to reduce US pressure to close off the borders. Harvey offers an approach to policy that might be implemented by the different governments to minimize damage to trade relations in particular. Given the likelihood that the American public will continue to demand very strict border security even under conditions of objectively minimal dangers from terrorism, it would be prudent for Canadians and Mexicans to accept this psychological reality and pursue adaptive strategies and tactics.

In Chapter 3, Justin Massie looks closely at Canadian policy toward the United States. Based on terminology from the realist school of international relations, he identifies two phases in Canadian policy after 9/11. In the years immediately following 9/11, the Canadian government adopted a hybrid position. Canadian strategy and tactics featured some degree of balancing against US interests while simultaneously bandwagoning with its much more powerful neighbour when convenient. These policies, in the language of realism, can be referred to as "soft" balancing and bandwagoning; the decisions to adopt one or the other of these low-intensity options were quite pragmatic and circumstantial. By contrast, in more recent years, the government of Stephen Harper has revealed what Massie sees as a more programmatic commitment to hard bandwagoning. Canada, in seeking favour with the United States, has shown convergence with the latter's security policy with regard to both means and ends. Pro-US positions, along with a shift toward military procurement and deployment, represent the key features of Ottawa's current approach to Washington in the domain of security policy.

In Chapter 4, Mark Paradis and Patrick James apply a political psychology framework to decision making to obtain insights about Canadian foreign policy after 9/11. Canada has supported the United States on some occasions but not others. Attribution theory can help solve the puzzle of varying Canadian reactions to US requests for security cooperation. This theory focuses on whether actions can be traced to the disposition or situation of a given actor. Thus, Canada, for example, might be more sympathetic to the use of force by the United States if Washington appeared to have no choice (situation) as opposed to having rejected viable alternatives (disposition). Attribution theory is well confirmed by evidence from the memoirs of Canadian prime ministers. As predicted by the theory, Canada supported the US-led overthrow of the Taliban (a situation in which the United States appeared to have no choice but to act as it did) but reacted in the opposite way when Washington initiated a war against Iraq on the basis of what appeared to be rather flimsy evidence.

In the last chapter of Part 1, Jonathan Paquin and Louis Bélanger examine the creation and downfall of one of the key North American security coordination initiatives of the last decade, the North American Security and Prosperity Partnership (SPP). The SPP brought together the three North American states in a flexible intergovernmental forum with the goal of addressing trade and security needs in a coherent process of common regulatory norms. The partnership did not last, however, and was abandoned after four years of irregular negotiations. Paquin and Bélanger test several theoretical explanations for its demise. The end of the SPP ultimately serves as a reminder of the limits of trilateral cooperation among such a diverse collection of states.

Part 2 offers a series of analyses of the principal developments in continental security and defence since 2001. President George W. Bush's post-9/11 statement that "security trumps trade" heralded Washington's policy shift from a free trade to a national security emphasis, and foreshadowed a new set of priorities for Washington's negotiations with its neighbours. Part 2 examines how this security priority has been embodied in North American relations, and the impacts of this transformation on the North American dynamic. This policy shift has also had an impact on the continental defence integration process and leads us to wonder whether 9/11 has resulted in a deeper level of defence integration.

In Chapter 6, Stephen Clarkson assesses the impact of US policies since 9/11 upon relations between Mexico and Canada. In his judgment, Washington's intense pursuit of security has had a deleterious effect on the two countries' relationship. On the surface, Canada and Mexico should have joined forces in trying to cope with the United States' heightened demands regarding border security. Instead of demonstrating enhanced cooperation, however, Canada and Mexico have drifted apart as a by-product of Washington's continued pressure on both countries to enhance security across the board. In fact, Clarkson's review of Canada-Mexico relations shows a movement toward competition as each state attempts to prove its worth to the United States in particular.

Chapter 7, by Athanasios Hristoulas, focuses on the foreign policy challenges experienced by Mexico. Given a series of problems, some of which predate 9/11, the Mexican government is moving toward a more pragmatic and less nationalistic stance toward North America. This is true especially of Mexico City's relationship with Washington. Interesting to ponder, as the Mexican government tries to work out compromises with the United States over border security in particular, is the role of the domestic setting as a constraint on action. Concerns about sovereignty and excessive linkage to the United States pervade the Mexican state and society, and act as an impediment to interstate coordination of policy.

In Chapter 8, Isabelle Vagnoux concentrates on US relations with Mexico. Of paramount importance to this relationship after 9/11 was Washington's movement toward a more encompassing sense of security, with concomitant challenges to Mexico City regarding its northwest border. A much greater fear of terrorism in the country put massive pressure on US leaders to act on border security after 9/11. This has increased tension with Mexico, whose border with the United States is one of the most heavily transited in the world. The US decision to build a border fence as well as the greatly increased deployment of security personnel reflect the fact that issues such as drug and human trafficking have merged with the terrorist threat to create a "thickening" of the border. All of this points toward deteriorating relations between the United States and Mexico, which takes offence at the imposition of measures that appear to link it, in the US mind, with dangerous intrusions.

In Chapter 9, Donald Abelson focuses on the world of ideas, most notably the role played by think tanks. He finds that, in the wake of September 11, these research institutes followed government priorities in producing their reports. The agenda of the White House is a good predictor for what will be conveyed by think tanks in terms of both content and recommendations. Abelson notes that, among neglected items, the economic effects of border restrictions are of particular importance. Little is understood about this topic because the various think tanks have generally embraced rather than criticized the security-oriented narratives coming out of Ottawa and Washington. Abelson concludes that efforts on the part of think tanks to consider policy options above and beyond the standard government positions would be most welcome at this point.

Philippe Lagassé explains in Chapter 10 that whereas Ottawa and Washington cooperated extensively on border security and counterterrorism during the decade following 9/11, they failed to achieve full cooperation in the area of bilateral defence, although defence cooperation did intensify after 2001. According to Lagassé, this was partly due to the fact that, for reasons related to domestic politics and managerial concerns, the Canadian government was not interested in further integrating Canada's defence with the United States. Canada's main interest throughout the decade lay with keeping trade flowing across the border; in this context, a deeper bilateral defence architecture was unattractive to Ottawa. Moreover, Canada's refusal to join the coalition against Iraq in 2003 and to integrate the ballistic missile defence system rendered political discussions on continental defence more difficult. In sum, during the first decade of the twenty-first century, Canada and the United States were unable to create a truly binational approach to North American defence.

The impact of 9/11 on the military-industrial complex is assessed by Yan Cimon in Chapter 11. He focuses on the Canadian and American aerospace and defence industries to infer the degree to which expansion occurred in response to the greater sense of threat from terrorism. In terms of employment, the data are quite revealing, with the number of people working in the military-industrial sector increasing consistently over the last decade, which witnessed a transition into a period of consolidation and adaptability. In other words, the uncertain environment resulting from 9/11 produced both quantitative and qualitative changes in the military-industrial sector for Canada and the United States.

David Haglund concludes Part 2 by asking whether there is room for Mexico in Canada-US defence cooperation. He answers this question in the affirmative, proposing a rather novel idea. According to Haglund, the three North American states could reduce their "irritants" and increase cooperation on the continent by institutionalizing their security and defence partnership through the transatlantic alliance, that is, by integrating Mexico into NATO. Haglund demonstrates that objections based on intuition regarding Mexican eligibility are off base. Mexico, it turns out, would fit into NATO better than some states that have achieved membership with little or no controversy. This original and unconventional idea would, according to Haglund, boost military cooperation between the United States and Mexico and could have a positive effect on democratic and security reforms in Mexico, although NATO's security sector reform capabilities would not eliminate the problem of corruption in Mexico.

This volume concludes with an assessment by Jonathan Paquin and Patrick James of the contribution made by these reflections on North American security after 9/11. The questions posed at the outset of this introductory chapter will be answered at least tentatively. It is our hope that this book will stimulate further efforts to appraise the meaning of 9/11 and apply its lessons to a more effective pursuit of North American security in the future.

NOTES

1 Merriam-Webster, http://www.merriam-webster.com/dictionary/game changer.
2 Jeffrey Ayres and Laura Macdonald, eds., *North America in Question: Regional Integration in an Era of Political Economic Turbulence* (Toronto: University of Toronto Press, 2012); Stéfanie von Hlatky and Jessica Trisko, "Sharing the Burden of the Border: Layered Security Cooperation and the Canada-US Frontier," *Canadian Journal of Political Science* 45, 1 (2012): 63-88; Stephen Clarkson, *Does North America Exist? Governing the Continent after NAFTA and 9/11* (Toronto: University of Toronto Press, 2008); Yasmeen Abu-Laban, Radha Jhappan, and François Rocher, eds., *Politics in North America: Redefining Continental Relations* (Toronto: University of Toronto Press, 2007).

PART I

THEORETICAL EXPLANATIONS OF POST-9/11 SECURITY RELATIONS

1

Was 9/11 a Watershed?

CHARLES F. DORAN

Without question, the events of September 11, 2001, inadvertently and without forewarning introduced a new tension in relations among the United States, Canada, and Mexico.[1] Terrorism and the effort to quench it became a preoccupation for the United States, and therefore for the other two North American polities as well, to varying degrees.[2] Security concerns re-established the border between the United States and its neighbours, reversing the trend toward greater openness since the signing of the Canada-US Free Trade Agreement (CUFTA) and the North American Free Trade Agreement (NAFTA). Although the argument was made that border security and trade openness were compatible, border security appeared to have a higher priority than trade and investment, at least for the United States.[3]

According to proponents of enhanced border protection, border security and trade are compatible because new techniques of interdiction, monitoring, and surveillance using new technologies and procedures interfere less with the flow of commerce and trade. The notion of a "smart border" becomes coterminous with border security. Yet firms, especially small firms without sophisticated ways of managing risk, especially on the Canadian side of the border, continue to complain about delays and the cost of border security and regulation. Despite good faith on both sides of the northern and southern borders to make them easier to cross legally, the fear of terrorism at the Canada-US border, along with the problem of drugs and illegal immigration at the Mexico-US border, seem to erect all kinds of new barriers to the free flow of goods and services between these countries.

The real problem with the impact of border security on the overall relations among these countries was that secondary economic and political effects of surveillance began to impinge on the respective relationships.[4] The borders began to diverge as to purpose and problem despite an American attempt to treat the two borders in the same way. The US border with Mexico became increasingly dominated by the flow of drugs and of illegal workers from one side and the illegal flow of guns from the other side. Its border with Canada, on the other hand, became part of an effort to create a foolproof barrier to hypothetical terrorists entering from the north. This divergence in terms of problem and objective began to wear at the edges of NAFTA, which was designed for coequality in terms of country participation.[5] Security matters tore at the very heart of the notion that North America could be a single community.

The United States suspected that it defended "its" borders more rigorously than either Mexico or Canada. Mexico and Canada feared that border security disadvantaged them more seriously than it did the United States.[6] For example, the decision by foreign as well as Canadian firms to locate in a US market that was ten times larger rather than in the smaller Canadian market appeared, because of increased border risk, to disadvantage Canada. Why, asked Americans, did the opening morning passenger line at the Calgary Airport stretch so far that it extended through the front door of the airport? Was there a problem of resource application here in terms of the number of gates available and the number of immigration and customs officials on duty? Why, asked Canadians, did it take just one hour for Canadian border officials to process passengers on Amtrak at the Niagara border crossing, but two hours for American border officials to process passengers going in the opposite direction? Were asymmetries creeping into the enforcement of procedures that no one desired but that everyone had to contend with, though not always proportionately?

But the real question regarding the impact of 9/11 on relations among the three North American countries is whether security concerns will create an irreversibly thickened border and result in a loss of commitment to the future enhancement of regional trade, financial, and commercial relations that have benefited each country so much.[7] In an age of globalization, this question is hard to answer not only, for example, because of the attractiveness of China as a platform for manufacture but also because of the difficulty of assessing all of the costs and risks necessary to decide whether even without the security issue North America remains competitive globally for many goods and services that previously originated from one of its three countries. Security is essential, but is the effort to enhance security adversely influencing North American capacity to compete in world markets? If the answer is yes, then 9/11 would truly be a watershed in North American international political economy, unless the lack of competitiveness in certain industries had long predated 2002.

What is the origin of the lack of North American competitiveness in certain industries, especially in manufacturing, when did this lack of competitiveness begin, and how much additional burden on competitiveness does a "thickened" border impose? These are central questions for additional empirical research. The events of 9/11 provide a kind of natural experiment to reinforce the test. Is added security a meaningful source of the problem of North American competitiveness, or much of an additional burden at all?

From the opposite side of the discussion, regarding the efficacy of walls, higher walls, or thicker walls on both the Mexican and Canadian borders, we are reminded of the famous poem by Robert Frost about the annual spring mending of a stone wall between him and his neighbour. The neighbour confidently quotes the expression passed down to him by his father: "Good fences make good neighbors." Frost is not so sure. At the very least, he reminds the reader, "*Why* do they make good neighbors?"

> Before I built a wall I'd asked to know,
> What I was walling in or walling out,
> And to whom I was like to give offence.

Frost wants to be certain that the purpose (and the actual unilateral capacity to achieve this purpose) justifies the means. And so should we. A stone wall to keep out cows is one thing; one to keep out squirrels is quite another.

Foreign Policy Change and Continuity

Underlying the question of whether 9/11 was actually a watershed for foreign policy in North America is the larger issue of whether foreign policy change or continuity is more pronounced among the United States, Canada, and Mexico.[8] Perhaps, for example, the real discontinuity lay in the signing of the North American Free Trade Agreement, which was perhaps unequalled by any other treaty or mode of association in the linkage it brought about among the three countries. Indeed, perhaps the NAFTA signing was even more momentous in that it was the first time a developing country had entered into a multilateral trade agreement on equal terms with two advanced industrial countries. So the novelty may not have been the impact of 9/11 leading to greater dissociation among governments in North America – perhaps 9/11 merely precipitated a return to the normality of comparative *dissociation* among North American governments.[9] Perhaps the true novelty was the prior break with the long-standing pattern of independence among North American governments in the final decade of the twentieth century.

To try to answer these questions more definitively, we must consider developments affecting the United States, Canada, and Mexico at three different levels of foreign policy conceptualization. First, we will examine world politics to determine whether international political developments at the global level signalled any kind of profound structural change circa 2002. North American relations do not operate in a global vacuum. What is happening on the world stage is crucial to the understanding of politics within North America. Too often in the discussion of North American relations the global perspective is brought in only tangentially and implicitly.

Second, we will consider foreign policy relations among the United States, Canada, and Mexico per se. To do this, we will look at three dimensions of analysis: (1) the trade-commercial dimension, (2) the political strategic and security dimension, and (3) the psycho-cultural dimension.[10] In examining change in each of these dimensions simultaneously, we will seek to discover breaks with the past that are definitive for the entire set of relations among these countries. Moreover, individual countries will weigh these dimensions differently, providing an even richer canvas of comparison and contrast.

Third, we will delve into the domestic politics of each country to determine the extent to which party politics, institutional change, electoral factors, and regional difference affect the conduct of foreign policy. It is at this level that we will explore how Quebec has shaped the foreign policy of Canada in important ways, and how federal/state and federal/provincial relations have been factors in the manner in which the three governments have articulated their respective foreign policies toward each other.[11] For North America, domestic politics may be a more important precursor of policy initiative externally than the impact of global politics on the region or the interaction among the three governments within North America as a whole.[12]

In any case, to answer the question of whether 9/11 signified a true break with past policies, all three levels of analysis must carefully be examined. We do not expect to find comparability at each level, but by assessing change at each level of analysis, we will be in a better position to make judgments about whether continuity or change tends to predominate in the overall foreign relations among the governments of North America.

How World Politics Affects North America

As explained in terms of power cycle theory, after rising on its power cycle for over a century and three-quarters, the United States "peaked" in relative terms somewhere around 1970.[13] But because its level of relative power was so great and its decline so gradual, the peaking was experienced more like a plateau, and the downward trajectory of the United States was scarcely noticeable until a decade into the twenty-first century. The information revolution, which occurred in the United States first, combined with both the Reagan military buildup financed on borrowed money and the remaking of the American corporation, concealed from view American decline in its proper proportion. Some writers exaggerated this decline by not looking carefully at or misreading the numbers. Other writers and polemicists claimed for the United States "hegemony" in the interval of unipolarity, without defining the notion of hegemony precisely or recognizing the constraints on American power, great though it was.[14] For the more prudent analyst, however, the United States, although its trajectory in relative power terms was downward, remained the pre-eminent military and economic power in the international system able to carry out a principal leadership role.[15] Nevertheless, together with reinvigorated postwar Europe, Japan had been rising rapidly since the middle of the twentieth century, taking away a share of power from the United States so that when the latter peaked, it was incapable of sustaining such a role.

In the 1980s, some writers were claiming that Japan would be the new Number One, despite signs that the Japanese economy was beginning to sputter and Japanese military capability was minuscule compared with Washington's. Only the Soviet Union could rival the United States militarily, in terms of its nuclear deterrent and its second-strike nuclear capability. Yet it was also very easy to exaggerate the military prowess of the United States in terms of actual capacity to control outcomes politically. Careful thinkers did not exaggerate either the rate of American decline or the level of American ascendancy, while noting that only one country within the international system – the United States – possessed a global reach.

Canada and Mexico were affected by the American provision of security in North America as well as by its involvement in wars abroad. Canada chose to stay out of the Iraq fray but to participate with NATO in the Afghanistan operation. Both of these choices, resulting from global international political threats, affected relations between the United States and Canada profoundly. Only those observing the relations between Washington and Ottawa from afar would have mistaken the impact of these events on the capacity of each government to make policy, not just in a multilateral context but also in terms of bilateral cooperation.

During the Cold War, Canada and the United States were driven closer together for three reasons. First, particularly in the Stalinist period, the fragile security of Greece and the political vise around Eastern Europe put the democracies at risk in security terms. Second, polarization caused the two countries to coordinate their security policies closely in both a multilateral and a bilateral sense.[16] Third, the multilateral freedom that Canada found within NATO gave it the confidence to act independently when it chose to do so, such as during the Vietnam War. Paradoxically, this sense of confidence also enabled Canada to cooperate with the United States in a host of other international situations, such as the Suez Crisis (1956) and the Canada-US Free Trade Agreement (1988).

Whether this cooperation between the two nations in security terms was an example of bandwagoning or of balancing is a mystery perhaps better left unsolved.[17] From the US perspective, Canada joined the United States in an effort to offset Soviet power in both its rising and its declining phases. This joint policy coordination required a closer monitoring of Soviet air power in the nuclear age within the North American Aerospace Defence Command (NORAD) than the United States undertook with virtually any other government, with the possible exception of the United Kingdom.[18] On the other hand, from the perspective of Canada, the mutual interaction between the two nations, especially in its trade and economic dimension, looked very much like bandwagoning.[19] Canada felt that it could not and did not balance the Soviet Union in a meaningful sense. But the economic benefits that it obtained from the United States during the Cold War, such as those stemming from the Auto Pact (1965), corresponded to the expected gains on a visible scale from bandwagoning. In Chapter 3, Justin Massie looks in detail at the role of bandwagoning and balancing in shaping Canadian foreign policy toward the United States.

The difference of opinion regarding whether bandwagoning or balancing was the valid perspective reveals the importance of the psycho-cultural dimension of relations between Canada and the United States. It was not quite a case of "don't ask, don't tell" at the international level, but the United States never sought to discover the true motivation for Canada's collaboration with it, and Canada never volunteered any answers. That such a complexity of understanding could exist for so many years on the part of two governments that had as much at stake as Canada and the United States is a tribute to the centrality of the psycho-cultural dimension for the relationship of trust that prevailed. The United States learned not to press too hard. Canada learned where the limits of disagreement lay.[20] The United States called this practice "taking the long view." Canada was always sensitive to where vital interests began and ended.

In the aftermath of the Great Recession of 2008-09 and its lingering employment, housing, and investment consequences in the United States, the rise of China came into focus more sharply than ever. Mexico felt the presence of China in its export markets for labour-intensive goods to the United States and elsewhere, in part because of the former's success in raising its standard of living and therefore of its wage rates; however, Mexico did not enjoy an educational advantage vis-à-vis China sufficient to offset this growing wage disparity.

Much like Australia, Canada sought to increase its sales of commodities and raw materials to China without alienating the United States. It also welcomed Chinese investment in – where else? – its raw material industries, such as the oil sands development, and in pipeline construction, although there were limits to its acceptance of such investments (for example, regarding potash acquisition). Canada worried about alienating China, but it may as well not have worried. Chinese neomercantilists could take all such reactions in stride as long as Chinese companies could make inroads into resource acquisition elsewhere, under the very nose of the United States.

It is difficult to say whether the levelling out of the shares of total trade among Mexico, Canada, and the United States a decade after the signing of NAFTA contributed to the rise of trade between China and each of the North American trading partners, or whether spiralling trade between China and each of these states led to the plateauing of trade among the NAFTA partners.[21] Perhaps these effects are two sides of the same coin. In any case, China became a growing factor in the trade and commercial policy of the three North American countries.

Correspondingly, barely a decade and a half after the NAFTA treaty was signed, the NAFTA idea appeared to move to the back burner for each of the partners. One of the motivations for NAFTA was to make North America competitive with Asia in trade matters.[22] Some genuine progress was made in each of the three economies, but only further trade liberalization could bring about truly effective responses to the strains of globalization. Politically, such a move toward enhanced North American trade liberalization did not seem to be on the agenda of Ottawa, Washington, or Mexico City.

Many Western governments find it convenient to omit this fact, but China, although a capitalist state, is also governed by a communist party. One of the conceptual issues emerging in multilateral diplomacy with respect to China's ascendancy in the world system is whether the increase in trade and commercial interaction with China will impact the security dimension of the interaction. Would China insist on such a linkage? Would any of the North American trading partners try to "bribe" China into an enhanced trading and commercial interaction by offering to soft-pedal human rights criticisms or to downplay the importance of security ties with third parties? Or would China try to "extort" such behaviour? If China did so, how successful would the attempt be? This issue is etched even more starkly in Asia, as seen, for example, in South Korea's relations with China vis-à-vis South Korea's third-party interactions with Japan and the United States. Evidence regarding either of these potential tendencies for political bribery or extortion is still very conjectural.

It is indisputable, however, that China is having an impact on the relations between the three North American partners. For example, in the strategic-military dimension, the response of each country to events in the South China Sea – a long way from North American shores – shows marked differences. The jockeying and pushing and shoving that goes on between Chinese fishing trawlers and Vietnamese, Philippine, Taiwanese, Japanese, Indian, and South Korean vessels is virtually ignored by Mexico.[23] Canada has chosen to reserve judgment. The United States, on the other hand, has actively indicated its disapproval of the repeated Chinese actions to intimidate the maritime and naval fleets of its neighbours and to lay claim to virtually all of the South China Sea. The US navy has engaged in joint naval exercises with Japan and with South Korea to demonstrate solidarity with these governments. Although the three North American governments have responded differently to the Chinese provocations, China has not driven a wedge between them in terms of their attitude toward it. Nor has any of these governments dropped its support for a peaceful resolution of these disputes that recognizes the interests of all parties.

Viewed in terms of power cycle theory, however, the rise of China has important consequences for North America. According to power cycle theory applied to structural change in the modern state system since its origin, when structural change accelerates or decelerates, the increase in the probability of war becomes statistically significant.[24] Soon (the exact temporal point cannot be predicted with precision) China will pass through such a critical point in its power cycle where everything changes for state and system, and uncertainty will replace the normal degree of certainty in statecraft. That is, China will reach the first inflection point in its power cycle, where the prolonged acceleration in the growth of Chinese relative power will abruptly give way to deceleration. Although China will continue to grow in relative power (albeit at an ever-decreasing rate), it is not psychologically prepared for this loss of momentum in the expansion of its foreign policy role. It is not prepared for the loss of face that will accompany this abrupt change in its prospects for a continued high rate of growth in visibility and material capacity for development. Under these circumstances of abrupt, massive structural change, the events in the South China Sea that presently amount to mere annoyance could suddenly escalate into war-prone behaviour.

Hence, North America, scarcely having recovered from the long bout with terrorism and instability in the Middle East, is now likely to have to contend with a much more earnest set of challenges associated with systems transformation. Systems transformation is structural change that is massive. Systems transformation has its origin in Asia but is not restricted to Asia. Systems transformation will involve all of the leading states in the system, hence it is likely to be upsetting to world politics. North America will not be able to escape the draft generated by these events.

Canada would like to operate in a trade and commercial sphere free of these larger international political complications, but this will not be possible. Just as power cycle theory looks at the world in terms of a "single dynamic" composed of state and system and of changing relative power and foreign policy role, so Canada must recognize how interrelated the economic-commercial and the strategic-military dimensions of statecraft really are.[25] Canada would like to concentrate on a world in which a loss of economic momentum in North America can easily be offset by new trade and commercial ties to China, but the problem with this idyllic conception of foreign policy is that it is likely to be confronted by all kinds of political and security complications that extend well beyond North America and yet entangle North America in their grasp.

Although more gradual, the ascent of China and eventually of India is likely to be more consequential for North America than the horrendous events of 9/11 and their policy aftermath. The ascent of China and India has the potential to de-industrialize large parts of North America for the very simple reason that the enormous disparity between productivity and cost of labour in these countries acts as a magnet for all goods and services production that is labour-intensive. Similarly, unlike the exchanges between the United States and Mexico and the United States and Canada regarding trade, in which the value added is very substantial for the smaller countries and the employment benefits very real, China and India, because of the size of their markets, will have the ability to push North America into a situation where it is principally a food and commodity exporter to the two manufacturing giants.

The principle of comparative advantage guarantees that, in terms of cost, relative advantage, not absolute advantage, enables a trading nation with high-cost labour to find something to produce that is competitive in world markets. For the North American partners to escape the food/commodity production trap, they will need to specialize in high-tech output. This need to specialize will test the educational system in North America to the limit, in an age when literacy is a worldwide phenomenon and science and technology are broadly available to any firm willing to pay for them. Nevertheless, through a combination of entrepreneurship and technological sophistication, North America must find the niches and specializations that push the frontiers of manufacturing and services outward.

An open trading system in which comparative advantage is permitted to flourish is crucial. If neomercantilism is allowed to predominate, and if China is able to enforce a new worldwide trading and investment regime in which unilateral deals are cut for access to the Chinese market in exchange for the sale of a firm's latest technology, this "beggar thy neighbour" regime will undermine the principle of free trade. Firms in the import-competing industries struggling for a share of the Chinese market will be the first to feel this pressure for a new set of rules with a neomercantilist bent: witness the experience of the insurance industry in attempting to carve out a tiny share of the Chinese market. The liberal trading order is not doomed, but North America, Europe, and like-minded countries in Asia will need to defend it in the face of very determined neomercantilist opposition.[26] By the end of the twenty-first century, 9/11 may be all but forgotten but the century-long fight to preserve the rules of a liberal trade order will remain salient. To the extent that North America can help preserve this order and international trade thrives in open and uncontrolled fashion, the wealth of North America will continue to grow, undiminished. The United States, Mexico, and Canada must keep this vision of the engine of their prosperity ever before the eyes of their hard-pressed and sometimes fearful electorates.

Interactions among North American Countries

Toynbee once said that the key to American prosperity and power is that the United States was the first truly large, integrated market. Because the United States is so large, North America as a whole appears quite integrated, at least by world standards, and the European Union, despite its success and its motivation to unite, is not as integrated in economic terms. When one considers political integration and its importance for economic integration, the answer is even clearer: North America has an edge. The paradox is that a North America that does not want an overriding set of supranational institutions is technically more integrated than a Europe with such institutions and that aspires to still greater political integration.

On the other hand, North America has made impressive progress toward greater economic integration across national borders through the great bilateral and multilateral treaties.[27] Beginning with the Canada-US Auto Pact in 1965, which was much like the European Coal and Steel Community of 1951 but with a somewhat different motivation (unlike Germany and France, Canada and the United States were not trying to prevent a resurgence of war between their countries), North American integration proceeded from an industrial agreement to a framework at the governmental level. The progression from the Auto Pact, to the Canada-US Free Trade Agreement, to the North American Free Trade Agreement paralleled the roughly similar progression from the European Coal and Steel Community, to the European Economic Community, to the European Community, and finally to the European Union.

What the North American governments wanted, however, was the benefits of economic integration without any of the costs of further political integration. Indeed, electorates in Canada and the United States were persuaded to accept the huge step to the Canada-US Free Trade Agreement only with the implicit guarantee that no movement toward supranational political institutions would ever occur. Each country – Mexico, Canada, and the United States – has jealously guarded its notion of sovereignty, even as their governments have busily helped erode some of that sovereignty in economic terms. Rather than touting the benefits of economic integration, the governments had to emphasize the fact that they were not considering political integration in order to gain acceptability for the treaties.

In recent years, the study of international political economy has revealed that, notwithstanding trade liberalization, national economic sovereignty remains widespread. Based on so-called gravity trade models that measure trade intensity, it has been calculated that ten to twelve times as much trade intensity exists in Canada as is involved in cross-border trade with the United States.[28] Economists call this "home bias," but they could equally call the amount of trade with a foreign country, expressed as a percentage of a country's total foreign trade, "international bias." In any case, the intensity of trade within each of the three North American countries far exceeds that of trade between each of these countries, and always will. Each national economy is far from dissolving into some kind of larger, homogeneous North American amalgam. The same is true for the countries in the European Union.

It can be argued that each North American country values its interactions with the others in different ways. Mexico and Canada emphasize the trade-commercial dimension.[29] The United States emphasizes the security dimension. It has been claimed that the psycho-cultural dimension is still the most important, particularly because when the interests of the various countries diverge somewhat, as they have, the burden is on diplomacy to smooth differences and coordinate policy. Even before 9/11, the United States saw its relationship with Mexico in terms of the security problems related to drugs first and then to illegal immigration. For the United States, therefore, security trumped trade in its relationship with Mexico. After 9/11, security trumped trade with Canada. Why is the United States so paranoid?

In fact, the United States is *not* paranoid, vis-à-vis either of its near neighbours or the global system. In fairness to Canada and Mexico, however, the security problems with which the United States must contend stem from forces well beyond their borders. Drugs come from Colombia and other countries worldwide. The drug lords use Mexico largely as a conduit, but a conduit that has become so corrosive for Mexican civil society that the "drug problem" is far worse for Mexico than for the United States, as former president Felipe Calderón has repeatedly said. Regarding the problem of terrorism, the United States because of its worldwide responsibilities and presence is the primary target, not Canada and not Mexico.[30] Hence the United States, although by no means ignoring the importance of trade and commerce, especially in an era of considerable financial stringency, must continue to give priority, even though perhaps just by a slender margin, to security matters over economic matters.

At the intergovernmental level, the greatest novelty in diplomatic approach was introduced by Canada in the first years of the Obama administration. This novelty involved a new diplomatic focus. Instead of attempting to deal with its North American partners in terms of annual trilateral meetings, Ottawa made the argument that relations between the United States and Canada and between the United States and Mexico were so different from each other that each set of relations should be handled separately and on its own terms. In effect, this was the death knell for the NAFTA process. It signalled a return to bilateralism with the United States, instigated, ironically, not by the United States in some implicit plan to "divide and rule" or in terms of some "hub and spokes" notion of imperium, but by one of the two smaller partners, Canada. The Harper government took the lead and the Obama administration reluctantly acceded. Mexico, with its hands full on the US border because of the out-of-control drug problem, quietly followed. In North America, Canada jettisoned multilateralism on the grounds that it was not working.

Canada took this distancing from Mexico a step further. Worried about an apparent loophole in its admittedly extremely generous asylum policy through which dissidents and possibly criminal elements in Mexico could claim asylum in Canada, Canada abruptly altered its immigration policy toward Mexico. Rather than alter the law governing its asylum policy, it instead demanded visas of Mexican nationals travelling to Canada. Despite protests from the Mexican government, this change was not entirely unanticipated in Mexico City. Once again, however, the policies of Canada and the policies of the United States were somewhat at odds with regard to Mexico. The NAFTA accord was intended to increase openness and multilateral cooperation, but on another issue, immigration policy, it was fragmenting and coming apart.

In the summer of 2011, driven in part by Canadian business leaders, the newly elected Harper government appeared to be staking out new territory with implications for North American relations, boldly inviting China to open a new partnership with Canada in trade and commerce. Gone were the anxieties over human rights policies in China and the concern over faltering efforts at democratic governance. In their place was a new enthusiasm for Chinese foreign investment in Canada and the prospect of new joint projects, particularly in the field of energy. China was even becoming a player in oil sands development. Who can predict where these promising initiatives might lead? What they suggest, however, is that frustration with the expansion of trade and investment in North America is contributing to more offshoring of jobs and more global substitution of trade priority.[31] Will China someday replace the United States as Canada's largest trading partner? Some Canadian analysts seem to think so.

How Change in Domestic Politics Affects Foreign Policy

Regarding the impact of domestic politics on foreign policy, three momentous events occurred in North America in the past decade, one in each country. First, Vicente Fox and his National Action Party (Partido Acción Nacional, or PAN) were elected to government in Mexico City in 2000, replacing the Institutional Revolutionary Party (Partido Revolucionario Institucional, or PRI) and bringing democracy back to Mexico. For more than seventy years, the PRI had reigned without interruption. For an orderly change of political leadership to occur according to democratic principles, democracy must have deep roots. Democracy triumphed in Mexico with the 2000 election, making many things possible in foreign policy, including a subtle reorientation away from the rest of Latin America toward North America.[32] Elites gave up some of their European, soft-left bias in favour of more educational, cultural, political, and especially business ties with the rest of the continent, especially the United States.[33] The promise of democracy made NAFTA possible; for its part, NAFTA encouraged the further development of the democratic process in Mexico through the press and through corporate support.[34] Mexico kept the PAN in power for more than eleven consecutive years. With the return of the PRI to power in late 2012, Mexico established itself for the first time as a conventional democracy in which political parties alternate successfully.

Second, an African American, Barack Obama, was elected to the presidency of the United States in 2008. War-weary and worried about its social programs and economy, the United States sought change, particularly generational change, in 2008. Without the support of the sixteen-to-thirty generation, President Obama would probably never have been elected, but the onset of the Great Recession was also genuinely responsible for his victory. Highly popular in both Canada and Mexico, he raised expectations in each country. Each country expected more of the United States because they could identify with its president. In many respects, however, Obama has been a middle-of-the-road president, and his foreign policy has reflected as much. He has been prudent and realistic, open but not deeply committed to change in foreign policy toward either Canada or Mexico. Indeed, public opinion in each of the three countries has perhaps not been supportive of any grand new schemes for North American economic initiatives. In his second term, President Obama has promised a strong liberal program of reform. What impact, if any, this political orientation will have on America's neighbours, especially regarding environmental protection, remains to be seen.

Finally, in the 2011 federal election, political change also struck Canada. Never since Confederation had the Liberal Party of Canada failed to win an election or fill the role of official opposition, to which the New Democratic Party (NDP) was elevated for the first time ever. Moreover, the Bloc Québécois, a federal political party that had promoted Quebec's secession from Canada since 1993, virtually disappeared. And, after a number of years as a minority governing party, the Conservative Party of Canada formed a majority government for the first time.

What does all of this mean for Canadian foreign policy and Canada's relations with its neighbours? First, as a majority party, the Conservative Party will mostly set the agenda, determine legislation, and make foreign policy decisions. However, the very fact that the NDP is so well situated electorally means that the Conservative Party will be forced to craft its foreign policy with an eye to that party. What is Prime Minister Stephen Harper likely to see?

In the coming years, Harper is likely to adopt foreign policy positions designed to block further NDP gains. This means that he will be more aware of Quebec and of Quebec's positions on different issues. He will try to address the NDP's type of issues before they arise politically. Since the NDP is the most nationalistic of Canadian federal parties, the Conservative Party will have more leeway to distance itself from the United States than if the Liberal Party had been the official opposition. For instance, the shift toward China has a business foundation, but it is also the case that dissociating Canada from the US position regarding Chinese behaviour in the South China Sea, for example, is not likely to result in much of an electoral penalty. Adopting distinctively Canadian positions on issues even when these are at cross-purposes with US policy will not cause much of a backlash from the NDP. In terms of Canadian attitudes toward foreign affairs, the Conservative Party has a virtual free hand with regard to its foreign policy choices.

Second, as a unified polity, Canada is likely to be able to craft its foreign policy more boldly than in the past. When the Liberal Party was in power, it always worried about what the Quebec wing would think about its formulation and conduct of foreign policy. National unity was always a concern. But with the official opposition assuming a very pro-Quebec position, the Conservatives can respond to the NDP and not to some fear that a particular policy is likely to jeopardize Canadian national unity. It is clear that this new orientation will put even more pressure on the NDP's leadership to adopt policies that can unify the party. No longer composed of just its Toronto base and its western, more free trade–oriented wing, the NDP with its strong Quebec foundation will now find challenge in diversity.

Third, as long as the Conservatives are in power, the kinds of issues that appealed to the Canadian electorate under the Liberals may diminish. Liberal think tanks, liberal news outlets, and liberal spokesmen are likely to find less financial support or opportunity for expression. It is not that the Conservatives will reach toward the right, just that the Conservatives have no reason to favour Liberal Party–type issues.

Canada could well become more polarized on issues that profoundly divide the NDP and the Conservative Party. The latter will still possess all the levers for making foreign policy and shaping public opinion that any majority government enjoys. Harper is a master of strategy and tactics and is not likely to overreach; nor is he likely to allow backbenchers to embarrass him in the face of provocations by the NDP. Still, major foreign policy debates could emerge around issues that have less of a growth and more of a distributional quality, and more of an ideational character. For instance, moral debates could absorb Canadian energies and, combined with Canadian desire to appease China for commercial and trade reasons, could create greater distance between Canada and the United States on some important global issues.

In the end, the emergence of the PAN and the reaffirmation of democracy in Mexico did have profound consequences for the interaction among the North American countries. The election of President Obama has reoriented American foreign policy toward a realist outlook expressed by both former Secretary of Defense Robert Gates and former Secretary of State Hillary Clinton.[35] It is only reasonable to assume that the new alignment of political forces in Canada will have some impact on the way Canada makes its foreign policy, and therefore also on the interaction among the governments in North America.[36]

Conclusion

This chapter began with a simple question: Was 9/11 a watershed for interstate relations in North America? Certainly the impact was undeniable. A trend toward closer economic and political relations among the United States, Canada, and Mexico was halted. Efforts to keep the borders open to the flow of people and goods paralleled the efforts to make them secure in a time of high tension over terrorism worldwide. Governments succeeded in counterterrorism but at high cost globally and to some extent in North America. The infrastructure personnel, training, and delays necessary to safeguard the airlines are only one example of the cost imposed on ordinary people by the scourge of terrorism.

To examine this question in the larger context of historical events, however, we examined the situation in North America at three levels. First, we looked at the impact of world developments on politics in the United States, Mexico, and Canada. Next, we examined the relations among the three governments, especially economic relations. Finally, we examined the impact of domestic politics on the making of foreign policy. Several striking conclusions emerged.

First, notwithstanding the evident impact of 9/11 on relations in North America, other events have had an equal or even greater impact, but not necessarily in the same direction or in the same fashion. To some degree, technology has dampened the negative consequence of 9/11 on border procedures. And surely the coming of democracy to Mexico and the changes of government in the United States and Canada have huge consequence as well for North American relations.

Second, the rise of China and its significance for both economic relations and world politics may eclipse anything experienced after 9/11 in North America, especially regarding the nature and expansion of trade and commercial relations. To confuse the effects is to misunderstand the dynamic of globalization.

Third, the task of coordinating policy among three governments with differing emphases is a continuing challenge. Canada and Mexico stress business and trade relations. Although scarcely ignoring the trade-commercial dimension, the United States focuses on security and defence matters. The psycho-cultural dimension remains pre-eminent as these governments attempt to coordinate policy across these divergent dimensions of interest and role in world politics.

NOTES

1 Three excellent compendiums on relations in North America are: Patrick James and Mark Kasoff, eds., *Canadian Studies in the New Millennium* (Toronto: University of Toronto Press, 2008); Patrick James, Nelson Michaud, and Marc J. O'Reilly, eds., *Handbook of Canadian Foreign Policy* (Lanham, MD: Lexington Books, 2006); and Greg Anderson and Chris Sands, eds., *Forgotten Partnership Redux* (Amherst, NY: Cambria Press, 2011).

2 Thomas Homer-Dixon, "The Rise of Terrorism," *Foreign Policy* 128 (January-February 2002): 52-62; Walter Laqueur, *The New Terrorism: Fanaticism and the Arms of Mass Destruction* (Oxford: Oxford University Press, 1999); Ian Lesser et al., *Countering the New Terrorism* (Santa Monica, CA: Rand Corporation, 1999).

3 Nelson Michaud, "Souveraineté et sécurité: Le dilemme de la politique étrangère dans l'après 11 septembre," *Études internationales* 33, 4 (December 2002) : 647-65.

4 D.K. Alper, "Trans-Boundary Environmental Relations in British Columbia and the Pacific Northwest," *American Review of Canadian Studies* 27, 3 (Autumn 1997): 359-83.

5 Greg Anderson, "The Compromise of Embedded Liberalism, American Trade Remedy Law, and Canadian Softwood Lumber: Can't We All Just Get Along?" *Canadian Foreign Policy* 10, 2 (Winter 2003): 87-108.

6 Louis Bélanger et al., "Most Safely on the Fence? A Roundtable of a 'Canadian' Foreign Policy after 9/11," *Canadian Foreign Policy* 11, 1 (Spring 2004): 97-118.

7 Raising some of the central questions is Kim Richard Nossal, "Canadian Foreign Policy after 9/11: Realignment, Reorientation, or Reinforcement," in *Foreign Policy Realignment in the Age of Terror,* ed. Leonard Cohen, Brian Job, and Alexander Moens (Toronto: Canadian Institute of Strategic Studies, 2002).

8 Maxwell A. Cameron and Brian Tomlin, *The Making of NAFTA: How the Deal Was Done* (Ithaca, NY: Cornell University Press, 2000); Elizabeth Smythe, *Multilateralism or Bilateralism in the Negotiation of Trade-Related Investment Measures*, Canadian-American Public Policy (Orono: Canadian-American Center, University of Maine, 1995).

9 Stephen Clarkson, *Uncle Sam and Us: Globalization, Neoconservatism, and the Canadian State* (Toronto: University of Toronto Press, 2002).

10 Charles F. Doran, *Forgotten Partnership: US-Canada Relations Today* (Baltimore: Johns Hopkins University Press, 1984).

11 Louis Balthazar, Guy Laforest, and Vincent Lemieux, eds., *Le Québec et la reconstruction du Canada, 1980-1992: Enjeux et perspectives* (Québec: Septentrion, 1991).

12 Louis Bélanger, Ivan Bernier, and Gordon Mace, "Canadian Foreign Policy and Quebec," in *Canada among Nations 1995: Democracy and Foreign Policy*, ed. Maureen Appel Molot and Maxwell A. Cameron (Ottawa: Carleton University Press, 1995).

13 Charles F. Doran, *Systems in Crisis* (Cambridge: Cambridge University Press, 1991).

14 Charles Krauthammer, "The Unipolar Moment," *Foreign Affairs* 70, 1 (1990/1991): 23-33.

15 Joseph S. Nye, *The Future of Power* (New York: Public Affairs, 2011), 153-206.

16 Robert Bothwell, *Canada and the United States: The Politics of Partnership* (Toronto: University of Toronto Press, 1992).

17 Stephen Walt, "Alliance Formation and the Balance of Power," *International Security* 4, 9 (Spring 1985): 3-43.

18 Joseph T. Jockel, *No Boundaries Upstairs: Canada and the United States, and the Origins of North American Air Defence, 1945-1958* (Vancouver: UBC Press, 1987); D.F. Hollman, *NORAD in the New Millennium* (Toronto: Canadian Institute of International Affairs, 2000).

19 Andrew F. Cooper, *Canadian Foreign Policy: Old Habits and New Directions* (Scarborough, ON: Prentice-Hall Allyn and Bacon Canada, 1997); Charles-Philippe David, ed., "De la SDN à l'ONU: Raoul Dandurand et la vision idéaliste des relations internationales," *Études Internationales* 31, 4 (December 2000): 641-762.

20 David Dewitt and John Kirton, *Canada as a Principal Power* (Toronto: John Wiley and Sons, 1983).

21 Michael Lusztig, *The Limits of Protectionism: Building Coalitions for Free Trade* (Pittsburgh, PA: University of Pittsburgh Press, 2004); Laura Macdonald, *Adapting to a New Playing Field? Civil Society Inclusion in the Hemisphere's Multilateral Processes* (Ottawa: FOCAL Policy Paper, 2000).

22 Eric M. Uslaner, "The Democratic Party and Free Trade: An Old Romance Restored," *NAFTA: Law and Business Review of the Americas* 6 (Summer 2000): 347-62.

23 Ben Bland and Girlfa Shivakumar, "Beijing Flexes Muscles with South China Sea Challenge to Indian Ship," *Financial Times*, 2 September 2011; Richard C. Bush, *The Perils of Proximity: China-Japan Security Relations* (Washington, DC: Brookings Institution Press, 2010).

24 Charles F. Doran, "Power Cycle Theory and Global Politics," *International Political Science Review* 24, 1 (January 2003): 13-49.

25 David G. Haglund, ed., *Over Here and Over There: Canada-US Defence Cooperation in an Era of Interoperability* (Kingston, ON: Queen's Centre for International Relations, 2001); Jack Granatstein, *Who Killed the Canadian Military?* (Toronto: HarperCollins, 2003).

26 Michael Hart, *A Trading Nation: Canadian Trade Policy from Colonialism to Globalization* (Vancouver: UBC Press, 2002); Axel Heulsemeyer, *Globalization in the Twenty-First Century: Convergence or Divergence?* (Basingstoke, UK: Palgrave Macmillan, 2003).

27 T.V. Paul and Norrin Ripsman, *Globalization and the National Security State* (Oxford: Oxford University Press, 2010); Bruce Doern and Brian Tomlin, *Faith and Fear: The Free Trade Story* (Toronto: Stoddart, 1991).

28 John J. Helliwell, *How Much Do Borders Matter?* (Washington, DC: Brookings Institution Press, 1998).

29 Consider the prescience of this book: Louis W. Pauly, *Who Elected the Bankers? Surveillance and Control in the World Economy* (Ithaca, NY: Cornell University Press, 1997).

30 Stéphane Roussel, "The Blueprint of Fortress North America," in *Fortress North America? What Continental Security Means for Canada,* ed. David Rudd and Nicholas Furneaux (Toronto: Canadian Institute of Strategic Studies, 2002).

31 Jagdish Bhagwati and Alan S. Blinder, *Offshoring of Jobs: What Response from US Economic Policy?* (Cambridge, MA: MIT Press, 2009).

32 Robert A. Pastor, "North America's Second Decade," *Foreign Affairs* 83, 1 (January/February 2004): 124-35.

33 Bernard Patry, *Partners in North America: Advancing Canada's Relations with the United States and Mexico. A Report of the Standing Committee on Foreign Affairs and International Trade* (Ottawa: House of Commons, December 2002).

34 Isabel Studer-Noguez, *Ford and the Global Strategies of Multinationals: The North American Auto Industry* (New York: Routledge, 2002).

35 For the Canadian version of realism, see Joel J. Sokolsky, "Realism Canadian Style: National Security Policy and the Chrétien Legacy," *Policy Matters* 5, 2 (June 2004): 1-44.

36 Janice G. Stein, *Choosing to Cooperate: How States Avoid Loss* (Baltimore: Johns Hopkins University Press, 1993); Evan H. Potter, "Canada and the World: Continuity and Change in Public Opinion on Aid, Trade, and International Security: 1993-2002," *Études internationales* 33, 4 (December 2002): 697-722.

2

The Homeland Security Dilemma

Assessing the Implications for Canada-US
Border Security Negotiations

FRANK P. HARVEY

This chapter addresses two important questions concerning the state of North American security relations in the decade since the terrorist attacks of September 11, 2001: (1) Given the nature of the regional context of Canada-US cooperation, how do international relations theories explain the behaviour of North American states toward one another in the post-9/11 era? (2) How can Canada and the United States avoid irritants for the sake of greater and better security relations? The main objective is to highlight the primary social and psychological pressures that will continue to shape security priorities in the United States and Canada for the foreseeable future.

Specifically, this chapter focuses on an important dimension of the homeland security dilemma, namely, public (mis)perceptions of the probability of terrorist threats and the effects of these overestimations on the government's security policies and practices.[1] The discussion begins with a review of conventional (but mistaken) wisdom on the origins of public fear. Contrary to standard accounts, heightened fears of terrorism are not the product of successful risk entrepreneurs (the media, security companies, government officials involved in public safety) who stand to gain by convincing the public that terrorism constitutes an existential threat. The generally held assumption that public fear is the product of these exogenous factors and pressures is derived from correspondingly weak theories of fear. Extensive research indicates that public fears of terrorism are largely driven by endogenous factors, internal to the individual and associated with *probability neglect* – a much stronger account of high levels of public fear that explains exaggerated threat perceptions based on the almost primordial tendency we all have to consistently underestimate the probability of some threats while overestimating the probability of others. Terrorism falls into the latter category, and security policies are strongly influenced by policy makers' expectations about typical trends in public perceptions of threats, particularly following security failures (e.g., the Boston Marathon bombings in April 2013). The statistical probabilities and associated risks of successful terrorist attacks are far less relevant to the government's calculations and priorities.

Understanding the causal mechanisms associated with these patterns is essential to understanding the dilemma policy makers face when designing cost-effective and successful security programs. The implications are not only relevant to appreciating the predicament facing those responsible for US security but also directly relevant to evaluating the strengths and weaknesses of common assessments of Canada-US security-trade relations and related correctives. These are discussed in more detail in the final sections of the chapter, which ends with policy recommendations on Canada-US relations going forward.

Conventional Wisdom: Threat Entrepreneurs and the Inflation of Public Fear

The most recent and widely cited version of the conventional wisdom is offered by John Mueller in his book *Overblown:* "The monied response to 9/11 has created a vast and often well-funded coterie of risk entrepreneurs. Its members would be out of business if terrorism were to be back-burnered, and accordingly they have every competitive incentive (and they are nothing if not competitive) to conclude it to be their civic duty to keep the pot boiling."[2] Mueller goes on to make the following widely shared argument:

> International terrorism generally kills a few hundred people a year worldwide – not much more, usually, than the number who drown yearly in bathtubs in the United States. Americans worry intensely about another 9/11, but if one of these were to occur every three months for the next five years, the chance of being killed in one of them is 0.02 percent ... (and) the lifetime probability that a resident of the globe will die at the hands of international terrorists is 1 in 80,000, about the same likelihood that one would die over the same interval from the impact on earth of an especially ill-directed asteroid or comet.[3]

To effectively manage pubic fears of terrorism, therefore, Mueller believes government officials should simply make note of the following whenever the subject comes up: "coconuts kill far more people each year, and that (outside of 2001) international terrorism isn't that much out of the coconut class." Todd Litman offers a similar list of statistical facts that optimists could use to minimize the threat from terrorism:

> On an average day, nine people die and more than 800 are injured in British road accidents. The July 7 (2005) London terrorist deaths represent about six days of normal traffic fatalities.
>
> In Israel, the annual road traffic death toll was two or three times higher than civilian deaths by Palestinian terrorists during the violent years of 2000 through 2003.
>
> The Sept. 11, 2001, terrorist attacks killed about the same number of people as a typical month of U.S. traffic accidents.[4]

The reality of exaggerated public threat perceptions is widely acknowledged in the literature. In a relatively benign security environment in which the government has arguably experienced an almost perfect homeland security record over the last ten years (with a few relatively minor exceptions tied to domestic terrorism, such as the Boston Marathon attacks), there is no question that fears of terrorism remain considerably higher than they should be.[5] In fact, the odds that any US citizen would be directly affected by a terrorist attack of any kind are virtually nil. In response to these inflated threat perceptions, Mueller repeats the same sage advice: just look at the numbers and related probabilities, understand the real threats and associated risks, relax, and get a life.

An irrational fear of terrorism is only one in an expanding list of overreactions listed by Barry Glassner: youth crime, road rage, airline safety, teen pregnancy, pedophile priests, crack babies, rare illnesses, cyberporn, mercury in the water, radon, pesticides, tainted or poisoned Halloween candy, shark attacks, skin cancer, calcium deficiency, SARS, the shortage of flu vaccine, and so on.[6] Like terrorism, none of these threats warrants the kind of serious concerns they usually raise, and yet all have been consistently overestimated by the public and media. Each case reveals a serious disconnect between statistically more probable risks and those we mistakenly perceive to be more deserving of serious concern. The solution, according to purveyors of this standard view, is for the government to develop effective mechanisms for critical risk communication; the more information the public has (such as comparative statistics and probabilities of various risks and threats), the more likely it is that the public will have a considerably more balanced assessment of real as distinct from imagined risks.[7]

But here is the main problem with these relatively straightforward diagnoses and related cures: the public tends to consistently overestimate some threats (such as terrorism) despite knowledge of the facts and evidence to the contrary – especially after relatively minor failures. Political officials are compelled to implement security measures on the basis of their expectations regarding the public's emotional reaction to a terrorist attack. The statistical probability of a terrorist attack, or the relatively minor effects these security failures typically have on a state's overall security, are considerably less relevant to policy makers' calculations. As I have argued elsewhere,

> Lack of knowledge about comparative risks, statistics, and probabilities is not the problem. Repeating the extremely low statistical odds of dying in a plane crash will not change the fact that air travel will be misperceived by most people, most of the time, as posing a significantly greater risk than driving a car. If facts, statistics, and rational probabilities alone were sufficient to guide perceptions and choices, then insurance companies, lotteries, and the tobacco, fast food, and gambling industries would not be among the most profitable businesses in the world.[8]

Although Mueller and many others correctly identify the very common tendency to exaggerate fears, they spend considerably less time explaining *why* this pattern recurs, and almost no time addressing the policy implications of these pathologies when contemplating the pressures associated with designing and implementing counterterrorism, critical infrastructure, and border security policies. Disseminating the facts about comparative threats, risks, and probabilities will never be enough to resolve this part of the homeland security dilemma.

The pathology in question is associated with *probability neglect*. A clearer appreciation of the effects of probability neglect exposes serious deficiencies with standard interpretations of the dilemma and reveals several logical and practical problems with the "solutions" offered by those who subscribe to the conventional wisdom espoused by Mueller and other optimists.

Probability Neglect

Excellent research on probability neglect has emerged from a variety of subfields, including behavioural economics, social and cognitive psychology, decision making and learning, evolutionary biology, and neuroscience.[9] Each of these authors approaches the same basic question from a slightly different perspective – specifically, how and why do individuals interpret risks and uncertainty in ways that deviate from rational choice? Why are we so consistently bad at performing relatively straightforward calculations of probability based on common sense or observable data? "We pride ourselves on being the only species that understands the concept of risk," Jeffrey Kluger notes, "yet we have a confounding habit of worrying about mere possibilities while ignoring probabilities, building barricades against perceived dangers while leaving ourselves exposed to real ones."[10] Paul Slovic explains the patterns with reference to two systems for analyzing risks: "an automatic, intuitive system and a more thoughtful analysis. Our perception of risk lives largely in our feelings, so most of the time we're operating on system No. 1."[11]

The consensus in the literature on probability neglect is clear: humans predictably overestimate some risks and underestimate others in relation to the nature of the risks and threats in question. The level of risk people assign to specific events (or behaviour) is a function of, among other things, *familiarity* and *controllability;* it is almost never a function of facts, statistics, or probabilities.[12] Easily controllable risks associated with personal choices or habits are usually perceived as less serious than those over which we have no real control. As noted by Harvey, these tendencies explain why familiar and controllable risks related to smoking, drinking, or driving a car are typically underestimated, despite the fact that each of these activities virtually guarantees thousands of deaths each year. Terrorist attacks are rare, unfamiliar, uncontrollable, spectacular, and dreaded, so a large segment of the population consistently overestimates the real risks.[13] In sum, probability neglect provides a much stronger foundation for understanding the origins of public fear levels. The explanatory model goes well beyond blaming risk entrepreneurs in the security industry, an exploitive media, or self-interested politicians pushing false alarms.

The more complex theory of fear derived from probability neglect also reveals serious problems with standard accounts and associated policy recommendations. Consider the following examples. Commenting on the Arab Spring during a recent airing of his CNN talk show, *Fareed Zakaria GPS,* Zakaria made the following observations:

> Since 9/11, al Qaeda has been unable to launch a single attack in the United States. Small groups of people inspired by it have managed a few smaller attacks in some cities in Europe and the Middle East and Asia, but even these have been getting fewer and fewer and further and further between … Political support for al Qaeda, Islamic terrorism and suicide bombings has been dropping in every Muslim country in the world on which we have polling data. If the Arab world becomes more Democratic, those numbers will continue to

fall. So can we all take a deep breath, stop cowering in fear of the impending caliphate, and put the problem of Islamic terrorism in perspective? It's real. But it is not going to take over the world any time soon.[14]

Of course, Zakaria's assessment of the numbers is largely correct. The problem with his advice, however, is that security *failures*, not *successes*, dominate perceptions of progress in the war on terrorism. Our emotional (experiential) reaction to the thought of security failures determines how we interpret risks; our reactions are almost never a product of rational assessments of the statistical probability of many more successes. With respect to our exaggerated fears of terrorism, therefore, the number of people who successfully escaped the Twin Towers on 9/11, or the very positive outlook on al-Qaeda portrayed by Zakaria, does not determine our fears of terrorism or the counterterrorism policies the government implements to address them. Inevitably, it is the failures, the casualties from al-Qaeda's suicide bombings, collapsed buildings, crashed planes, falling bodies, and so on that create and sustain our suspicions, anxieties, doubts, fears, and policies. Security measures are designed to deal with the infinitesimal number of criminals who might break the law, not the billions who don't.

Weak Policy Recommendations Derived from Conventional Wisdom

Like Zakaria, James Fallows has argued that manufactured or exaggerated threats can be defeated "*simply* by a refusal to overreact" (emphasis added).[15] The United States, Fallows recommends, "can declare victory by saying that what is controllable has been controlled: Al-Qaeda Central has been broken up. Then the country can move to its real work."[16] Mueller agrees with both Zakaria and Fallows: "Terrorists can be defeated *simply* by not becoming terrified – that is, anything that enhances fear effectively gives in to them" (emphasis added).[17] But there is nothing about the relationship between terrorism and fear that is simple. In fact, far from defeating terrorism, many of the policy recommendations that flow from Zakaria, Fallows, and Mueller threaten to raise rather than lower fear, for reasons tied to probability neglect. If a significant segment of the American public remains overly concerned about terrorism, despite large numbers of successes and very few security failures over the past decade, and continues to overestimate the probability that it will be directly affected by an act of terrorism, fears would *increase* following public pronouncements by government officials that we've won the war.[18]

Fallows does go on to clarify his position: "What it suffered five [now twelve] years ago on 9/11 was terrible and unprecedented and paradigm-changing. But it does not mean, as current political discourse seems to assume, that we need to live in fear and assume the worst forever."[19] But Fallows provides no answers to the questions policy officials will be compelled to address, and admits to being "agnostic" about the actual terrorist threats facing the United States today. What level of threat does Fallows suggest we live with, and what specific programs and policies should we retain or implement, at what cost and with what probability of success or failure? The absence of specific answers renders any declaration of victory highly suspect.

Clearly, weak theories of fear derived from standard accounts of risk entrepreneurs selling exaggerated threats to the public can also lead to unrealistic or counterproductive policy recommendations. Consider the following examples of bad advice emerging from conventional wisdom. One solution, according to Mueller, is "to reduce terrorism's principal costs – fear, anxiety, and overreaction – not to aggravate them."[20] But the *absence* of fear is not a panacea for well-reasoned and informed policy analysis. In fact, the absence of fear consistently leads to the deaths of hundreds of thousands of people each year who ignore the risks of smoking, drinking, and heart disease at a cost of billions in health care. With respect to international politics, the absence of fear can lead to dangerous levels of complacency and/or hostility. In fact, almost every security failure is preceded by some underestimation of an impending threat; an absence of fear set the stage for 9/11. It was the absence of fear of a direct homeland attack that prevented Washington from addressing threats from al-Qaeda. Fear can simultaneously motivate us to do the right or wrong things. The real issue, therefore, has never been about whether fear is (or should be) absent or present, but when and under what conditions it produces positive or negative outcomes.

Mueller's second recommendation is to avoid becoming excessively worried or anxious by subscribing to the "just relax" aphorism. All we desperately need are more pronouncements like Senator John McCain's:

> Get on the damn elevator! Fly on the damn plane! Calculate the odds of being harmed by a terrorist! It's still about as likely as being swept out to sea by a tidal wave ... Suck it up, for crying out loud. You're almost certainly going to be okay. And in the unlikely event you're not, do you really want to spend your last days cowering behind plastic sheets and duct tape? That's not a life worth living, is it?[21]

Mueller expands on this advice by imploring officials to "stress that some degree of risk is an inevitable fact of life, that the country can, however grimly, absorb just about any damage terrorism can inflict (it now absorbs

40,000 traffic deaths per year), and that seeking to protect every imaginable terrorist target is impossible and absurd."[22] As Mueller recommends:

> There should at least be some efforts to try to put the threat in context – to indicate how few people are ordinarily killed by terrorism and to convey some sense of the probability that any individual will become a victim ... Since September 11 those voices rarely emphasize the possibility that the phenomenon they are analyzing may prove to be quite a minor one, and they are vastly outweighed by the cries of alarm and the visions of apocalypse and Armageddon promulgated so regularly by the terrorism industry.[23]

Again, although the low statistical odds of dying from a terrorist attack are perfectly sound, Mueller's policy guidelines underestimate the negative consequences of following them. First, probability neglect (rather than probabilities) explains why the public remains fearful of terrorism – these fears have everything to do with qualities intrinsic to the threats themselves. By implication, comparing terrorist casualties to those caused by coconuts, bathtubs, or car accidents will raise (not lower) fears about the government's minimalist commitment to public security. Some deaths are not the same as others. Deaths from highly probable car accidents will never be as disturbing as the far fewer deaths from a low-probability terrorist attack. People will always demand more from governments to stop terrorism but usually care very little about fatal bathroom and coconut accidents.

A third recommendation is to establish a policy of restraint, which will fail for three important reasons. First, "Optimists ... who recommend a policy of restraint have no real way of knowing whether the application of that policy on any given day makes any sense, or what constitutes restraint in the first place – restraint in comparison to what? Restraint seemed to make perfect sense on 10 September 2001, because at that point the threat was seriously underestimated. But the policy of restraint the day before 9/11 was clearly shown to be a terrible mistake when the Twin Towers fell."[24] When should we stop worrying about (or preparing for) an anthrax attack, a liquid or shoe bomber, a pocket knife, or a terrorist attack on the US mass transit system? Optimists rarely have any clear answers to this important policy-relevant question.

Second, "The fact that extreme events do not necessarily repeat is irrelevant to political officials who, in the midst of crisis, have no way of knowing whether this is the one case that does. If it's impossible to know during the crisis what type of case you're dealing with, and if the default assumption is that it might happen again, then Mueller's sage advice is not very useful in practical policy terms."[25] US post offices, for example, rationally spent hundreds of millions of dollars to implement what turned out to be unnecessary overreactions to the 2001 anthrax threat, because they had few, if any, acceptable options at the time. Once a threat is imagined, it becomes embedded and institutionalized in security infrastructure. Any backtracking will inevitably increase fear because it logically elevates the probability that terrorists will see this as another opening.

Third, the US intelligence community was arguably responsible for underestimating the pre-9/11 threat from al-Qaeda and overestimating Iraq's "weapons of mass destruction" threat prior to the war. With these failures in mind, how certain *should* any political official claim to be about the various threats he or she is obligated to address, and how much faith will the public have in pronouncements that prioritize a policy of restraint? Policy makers are constantly faced with the difficult challenge of implementing a range of programs and policies to avoid the high social, political, and economic costs of failures. And once a security policy or public safety program is implemented, any change will predictably generate an immediate pushback by Congress (consider, for example, the recent failed attempt to reverse the ban on carrying small pocket knives on airplanes). The typical response to all security failures illustrates the impact of policy momentum. Governments will be seized by uncertainty following an attack and will inevitably implement costly policies and regulations that become permanent. It is difficult to reverse these programs once they are in place.

In sum, optimists seem to overlook the fact that security policies are based on political calculations of anticipated public or media reactions to security failures. If some risks and threats are more relevant than others to inducing public fear and anxiety, then it follows that some risk or threat assessments are likely to be more relevant to government officials. Of course, Mueller is right when he states: "If a small portion of the excess spending on airline security had been spent instead on enforcing automobile seat belt laws, the number of lives saved would have been considerable."[26] And yet Washington officials are still compelled to spend more to prevent or mitigate the effects of terrorist attacks on airlines than they are to lower the number of road accidents, simply because the political costs of a terrorist attack are so much higher than the political costs associated with thousands of fatal road accidents.

Canada-US Security-Trade Relations: Challenging Conventional Wisdom

The purpose of the preceding analysis was to provide a clearer, theoretically informed explanation for the imperatives that continue to drive US security policies, and the barriers that continue to plague Canada-US security-trade negotiations (see Chapter 5). The analysis reveals several ongoing hurdles confounding efforts to reverse the standard operating procedures, disruptive security measures, and regulations that continue to cause delays costing billions in two-way trade.

Unfortunately, several current and former Canadian diplomats and trade experts remain entrenched in the conventional wisdom described earlier. Terrorist threats are obviously exaggerated, they argue, so the obvious solution to enhancing two-way trade across the border should simply focus on changing, reversing, or cancelling wasteful security measures. Again, simple theories of fear, tied to mistaken assumptions about the origins of exaggerated threats, inevitably lead to weak, superficial interpretations of what are actually very complex problems. Critics in Canada who continue to point to wasteful Canada-US border security measures find it hard to understand why officials in Washington cannot implement policies based exclusively on the statistical probabilities of specific terrorist attacks or the limited (non-existential damage) they can cause. If these perspectives continue to dominate the current round of Beyond the Border talks, Canadian negotiators will continue to fail in their efforts to resolve the border problems.

There have been dozens of academic reports and policy directives published by Canadian experts designed to address the impediments to Canada-US cross-border trade. Consider the large number of initiatives, policies, and programs introduced over the last ten years.[27] But the most interesting (and theoretically relevant) point emerging from all of that activity is this: we have compiled crystal-clear evidence of significant economic losses on both sides over the last ten years, all tied to an increasingly rigid, entrenched, and complex set of regulations and security arrangements that result in costly delays at the border. These losses have continued under the watch of three prime ministers, two presidents, and administrations on the right and left of the political spectrum. All of these decisions have unfolded in the midst of an almost perfect homeland security record since 9/11, with only one recent exception – the domestic terrorist attack during the 2013 Boston Marathon. Obviously, the serious challenges facing Canada-US border security and trade negotiations pre-date the most recent security failure and occur in the context of several major counterterrorist successes since 2001, *including the capture and death of Osama bin Laden.*

Moreover, these significant economic losses continue notwithstanding Zakaria's insightful observations about al-Qaeda's impending demise, sage policy advice by Mueller, Fallows, and many others to stop overreacting, and hundreds of books and articles outlining concrete facts about the statistically low probability of experiencing (or being harmed by) a catastrophic terrorist attack. Why, then, do we continue to be affected by so many entrenched and obviously counterproductive practices?

Counterproductive Recommendations on Canada-US Security-Trade Relations

To illustrate the problems with conventional Canadian wisdom, let us focus on one of the more recent reports on the subject, written by former Canadian ambassador to the United States Derek Burney. His report is representative of many similar studies published by individuals, organizations, and think tanks in Canada over the past ten years. Like other reports, Burney's analysis and recommendations do not appear to fully grasp the nature of post-9/11 realities from Washington's point of view.

The report does an excellent job of outlining the costs to the Canadian economy of post-9/11 border security measures, and provides a long list of regulatory, border infrastructure, redundancy, visa, immigration, and other impediments to the free flow of goods and services that need to be addressed. However, for a former senior diplomat with extensive experience working with American officials, it is surprising how little time Burney spends discussing the complex collection of domestic political, social, bureaucratic, psychological, and international pressures that account for the continuity in US behaviour and priorities since 9/11, *despite* the obvious effects on both economies, and *despite* the low probability of a catastrophic terrorist attack. By focusing exclusively on Canadian perspectives and a related list of complaints, and by failing to engage reality from the US point of view, the analysis misses half of the problem and a large part of the solution to the puzzle.

The problem, of course, is that most Canadian observers tend to believe (without being able to prove it) that the security threats facing Canada and the US are largely overblown. For instance, the series of interviews conducted by Jonathan Paquin and Louis Bélanger and discussed in Chapter 5 shows that American officials believe (without being able to prove it) that these measures have contributed to public safety. Canadian observers can't quite grasp why the debate between these two positions is inevitably won by (1) those who emphasize the positive effects of enhanced security measures, and (2) those who exaggerate the negative consequences of security failures; this, they believe, is why the status quo prevails. Security entrepreneurs can make their argument more plausible because American citizens will always be more inclined to believe that terrorism is a serious problem, far more serious than delays at the border. Security entrepreneurs win because political officials are more inclined to cater to those perceptions than to dismiss or downplay the threat – regardless of how economically irrational this approach appears to folks in Ottawa. The constant refrain from Canadian officials that we need a little more common sense and rationality to resolve the issue says more about Ottawa's misunderstanding of the problem.

Consider this account of the problem by Derek Burney, former Canadian ambassador to the United States: "The forces of globalization oblige countries like Canada and the U.S. to revitalize trade flows and break down regulatory barriers. The new majority government in Ottawa should help embolden attention to the twin challenge." But this is a typical Canadian perspective highlighting Canadian interests that focuses almost exclusively on the "economic" effects of globalization. Obviously, a globalizing world facilitates the expansion of trade flows by accelerating the pace (and sources) of product manufacturing, transportation, and tracking, and governments should take advantage of these forces to promote free trade and profits. For many large countries, however, these same forces also exacerbate the scope, nature, and probability of security threats, risks, and failures (for example, democratization of WMD technology, proliferation of intelligence and information on WMD, miniaturization of weaponry, the free flow of black market trade in WMD components, and so on). Globalization multiplies the threats and the consequences of terrorist attacks as quickly as it facilitates trade.

Burney also states:

> U.S. mindsets have been rigidly shaped by the horror of 9/11. Among these officials, interest in smoother access to boost the benefits of free trade or the advantages of economic integration is minuscule. The overriding objective for the U.S. will be to strengthen border security whereas Canada's priority will be easier access for goods and services. That is why striking a healthy balance between the two objectives may prove to be the most daunting task of all for the negotiators.[28]

He repeatedly invokes America's security interests without really exploring what those interests are, or how profoundly powerful they are in determining US preferences. Canadian officials need to understand that there are few "political" costs to overestimating or exaggerating the threats, but there are significant costs to getting this wrong. Canadian and American officials have different interpretations of "legitimate" security concerns. We claim to understand the risks and threats from terrorism, but we really only see these things as outsiders looking in. We've never experienced this kind of trauma – the Air India bombing doesn't come close. The problem is not that American negotiators don't get the economics behind security; they just don't (and never will) care as much. That's why it's been so difficult to convey the "Canadian" point of view despite dozens of major reports by the business community extolling the virtues of streamlined regulations and perimeter security. Unless Canadian negotiators acknowledge the biases affecting their interpretation of "legitimate" security measures, their bargaining strategies in this round of talks will fail again. And constant references to the success of free trade negotiations miss the point: the free trade agreement was not negotiated after 9/11.

Burney also argues that we should "seek to establish a better balance between legitimate concerns about security and the need to strengthen the competitiveness of our economies"; that "there are no guarantees of success and much hard negotiation lies ahead"; and that "the Joint Action Plan represents a refreshing outbreak of common sense." Again, he appears to be missing the point: US security measures *are* about protecting important parts of the US economy, despite the economic consequences to Canada-US trade. The report's simplistic bifurcation dichotomization of security versus trade misses the significant "economic" and "financial" incentives tied to US security measures. Consider, for example, the global economic impact of the 9/11 security failure, combined with the immediate and lingering effects on the US stock market, oil prices, the airline, insurance, and tourism industries, and the city of New York. These losses constitute the economic impact of failed security measures that arguably far outweigh in magnitude the costs to Canada-US trade.

Conclusion and Policy Recommendations

Instead of following the same unsuccessful strategy, Canadian negotiators should consider a little "outside-the-box" thinking when negotiating. As Thomas d'Aquino noted in his assessment of the potential for progress, "achieving transformative change in the relationship will require a fresh vision, brilliant strategies, the unprecedented deployment of resources, and boundless tenacity in execution."[29] Similarly, Colin Robertson argues that any progress in this round will require a clear commitment to learn from several important *lessons* acquired from years of doing business with the Americans:

1 Understand the American system
2 Know your "Ask" and frame it as an American issue
3 All politics is local
4 "Think big" and play by American rules
5 It starts with trust and relationships

   6   Bringing value to the table
   7   Institutions work
   8   Canada Inc.
   9   A permanent campaign
10   Tending the garden.[30]

It is beyond the scope of this chapter to address each lesson in detail, but it does help to highlight the relationship between the findings and observations emerging from this chapter (and other excellent historical overviews; see Chapter 1) and the first six lessons noted in Robertson's insightful report (italicized above).

One obvious suggestion that flows directly from the preceding analysis is for Canadian negotiators to adopt a proactive security agenda designed to protect our economic interests, rather than a proactive economic agenda that will come across as competing with US security interests. Early reports on the outcome of Beyond the Border negotiations indicate that officials in Ottawa have essentially adopted this strategy; Canadian officials have made significant concessions on US security measures and procedures. The key was to avoid the impression that negotiations were over two competing interests, economics versus security. Instead, the strategy focused on bargaining over different strategies/options in defence of common security interests. Three key observations (guiding principles) emerge from the latest, and arguably most productive, round of Canada-US security-trade negotiations in February 2011.

First, American officials will always be willing to accept the economic risks and costs of enhanced security. Canadian officials, on the other hand, have always been more willing to accept the security risks of enhanced trade, because we don't see the same threats, and because we typically assume that American officials are overestimating the risks. These perceived differences need to be marginalized. Coming to the table with a trade rather than a security agenda will reinforce the perceptions and divisions that have prevented significant movement on these issues in the past. Canadian officials need to be viewed by their American counterparts as credible partners who are equally concerned about the political and economic fallout of security failures, not the economic fallout of tighter border security.

Second, what we need in Canada are security entrepreneurs, not another collection of Canadian trade experts reminding their counterparts in Washington, again, that the statistical probability of a serious terrorist attack is diminishing, and that freer trade across the border would be very lucrative to both sides. By co-opting US concerns for security, and by taking the lead in identifying, investing in, and developing the right (trade-friendly) kinds of security measures, Canadian negotiators will have a much more effective impact on managing mutually beneficial economic prosperity. The focus should be on "managing" the relationship rather than "resolving" or lifting the impediments to trade. The goal is essentially the same but the former approach is more likely to succeed.

Third, Canadian negotiators should exploit Washington's security addiction in a way that protects Canadian economic interests. Instead of complaining about the irrational increase in the number of border guards since 9/11, or arguing for a cut in those numbers, Canadian negotiators should demonstrate to the Americans why retaining current levels is a better alternative than raising them. Our arguments should be based on the negative impact of additional bureaucracy on security, not the effects on our economy. In other words, if the expansion of US security measures is inevitable, then Canada should promote solutions that cause the least harm to our economy over time.

Canadian negotiators should consider the real problem in relative terms: if the pressures to expand security infrastructure and regulations are still so powerful after ten years of a relatively benign homeland security environment (and despite the enormous costs), imagine how much more pressure Washington will experience (and Canada will suffer from) after the next terrorist attack on US soil. This is the context in which a discussion of Canadian interests and values (economic-, security-, and sovereignty-related) becomes most relevant. Our economic interests will always be directly tied to maintaining a perfect US homeland security record.

NOTES

1 Frank Harvey, "The Homeland Security Dilemma: Imagination, Failure and the Escalating Costs of Perfecting Security," *Canadian Journal of Political Science* 40, 2 (2007): 283-316; Frank Harvey, *The Homeland Security Dilemma: Fear, Failure, and the Future of American Insecurity* (New York/London: Routledge, 2008).

2 John Mueller, *Overblown: How Politicians and the Terrorism Industry Inflate National Security Threats, and Why We Believe Them* (New York: Free Press, 2006), 41-42.

3 Ibid., 2.

4 Todd Litman, "Terrorism, Transit and Safety," *Toronto Star*, 27 July 2005.

5 Harvey, *Homeland Security Dilemma*.

6 Barry Glassner, *The Culture of Fear: Why Americans Are Afraid of the Wrong Things* (New York: Basic Books, 1999), 30.

7 In addition to Mueller's work, see Glassner, *The Culture of Fear*; Baruch Fischhoff, Roxana Gonzalez, Deborah A. Small, and Jennifer S. Lerner, "Judged Terror Risk and

Proximity to the World Trade Center," *Journal of Risk and Uncertainty* 26, 2-3 (2003):
137-51; Bruce Schneier, *Beyond Fear: Thinking Sensibly about Security in an Uncertain
World* (New York: Copernicus Books, 2003); Bruce Schneier, "The Psychology of
Security," 18 January 2008, http://www.schneier.com/.

8   Harvey, *Homeland Security Dilemma*, 55.

9   Cass R. Sunstein, *The Laws of Fear: Beyond the Precautionary Principle* (New York:
Cambridge University Press, 2005); Cass R. Sunstein, "Probability Neglect: Emotions,
Worst Cases, and Law," *Yale Law Journal* 112, 1 (October 2002): 61-107; Cass R. Sunstein,
"Terrorism and Probability Neglect," *Journal of Risk and Uncertainty* 26, 2-3 (2003):
121-36; Cass R. Sunstein, "Fear and Liberty," *Social Research* 71, 4 (2004): 967-96;
Christine Gorman, "The Science of Anxiety," *Time* 159, 23 (10 June 2002),
http://www.time.com/ (a great source of information on the biology of stress and
anxiety); Daniel Gilbert, "If Only Gay Sex Caused Global Warming: Why We're More
Scared of Gay Marriage and Terrorism than a Much Deadlier Threat," *Los Angeles
Times,* 2 July 2006; Daniel Gilbert, *Stumbling on Happiness* (New York: Vintage Books,
2007); Daniel Kahneman, Paul Slovic, and Amos Tversky, eds., *Judgment under
Uncertainty: Heuristics and Biases* (London: Cambridge University Press, 1982); David
Ropeik and George Gray, *Risk: A Practical Guide for Deciding What's Really Dangerous in
the World around You* (New York: Harvard University Center for Risk Analysis/
Houghton Mifflin Company, 2002) (the authors explore fifty public health risks and
evaluate the real as opposed to publicly perceived risks and consequences); Frederick
F. Schauer, *Profiles, Probabilities and Stereotypes* (Cambridge, MA: Belknap Press of
Harvard University Press, 2003); Julian Morris, ed., *Rethinking Risk and the
Precautionary Principle* (Oxford and Boston: Butterworth-Heinemann, 2000); Kenneth
Foster, David Bernstein, and Peter Huber, eds., *Phantom Risk: Scientific Inference and the
Law* (Cambridge, MA: MIT Press, 1993); Michael Fumento, *Science under Siege:
Balancing Technology and the Environment* (New York: William Morrow, 1996). For
additional excellent work on real versus perceived risks, see Paul Slovic, "Perception
of Risk," *Science* 236 (1987): 280-85; Paul Slovic, *The Perception of Risk* (London:
Earthscan Publications, 2000).

10 Jeffrey Kluger, "How Americans Are Living Dangerously," *Time,* 26 November 2006,
http://www.time.com/.

11 Quoted in ibid.

12 Several other factors are cited in the literature to explain why certain risks are over-
and under-estimated, although "controllability" and "familiarity" are commonly
accepted as instrumental. For an excellent treatment of these issues, see Vincent T.
Covello, Peter M. Sandman, and Paul Slovic, *Risk Communication, Risk Statistics, and Risk
Comparisons: A Manual for Plant* Managers (Washington, DC: Chemical Manufacturers
Association, 1988), http://www.psandman.com/. In addition to "controllability" and
"familiarity," for example, Covello and colleagues list the following factors to explain
why risks are overestimated (all of which apply to the post-9/11 experience):

catastrophic potential, lack of understanding, uncertainty, voluntary exposure, effects on children, effects on future generations, victim identity, effects dreaded, absence of trust in institutions, media attention, costs/benefits, reversibility.

13   Harvey, *Homeland Security Dilemma*, 55.

14   Fareed Zakaria, "Transcript: Unrest in the Arab World; US Budget Battles," CNN, 6 March 2011, http://transcripts.cnn.com/.

15   James Fallows, "Declaring Victory," *Atlantic Monthly*, September 2006, http://www.theatlantic.com/.

16   Ibid.

17   John Mueller, "A False Sense of Insecurity?" *Regulation* 27, 3 (Fall 2004): 42-46.

18   Harvey, *Homeland Security Dilemma*.

19   Fallows, "Declaring Victory."

20   Mueller, *Overblown*, 7.

21   Quoted in ibid., 151.

22   Ibid., 7.

23   John Mueller, "Response," *Terrorism and Political Violence* 17, 4 (2005): 526-27 (a response to Richard Betts, Daniel Byman, and Martha Crenshaw's assessment of Mueller). See also John Mueller, "Six Rather Unusual Propositions about Terrorism," *Terrorism and Political Violence* 17, 4 (2005): 487-505.

24   Harvey, *Homeland Security Dilemma*, 144.

25   Ibid., 141.

26   Mueller, *Overblown*, 31.

27   Security and Prosperity Partnership; Western Hemisphere Travel Initiative; Smart Border Agreement; Integrated Border Enforcement Teams; Canadian Air Transport Security Authority (April 2002); Financial Transactions and Reports Analysis Centre of Canada; Container Security Initiative; International Ship and Port Facility Security Code; migration integrity officers; Integrated National Security Enforcement Teams (INSETs); Integrated Threat Assessment Programs; Bilateral Intelligence Sharing Agreements; expansion of NORAD's mandate to include maritime security; creation of Canada Command (CanadaCom) and NorthCom; several major policy statements by Liberal and Conservative governments (National Security Policy under Paul Martin; International Policy Statement, Canada First Defence Strategy under Stephen Harper); Harper-Obama "Beyond the Border" Memorandum of Understanding and Working Group; North American Competitiveness Council recommendations; Regulatory Cooperation Council recommendations; North American Perimeter.

28   David Burney, "A Fresh Start on Improving Economic Competitiveness and Perimeter Security," *The School of Public Policy, SPP Research Papers* 4, 8 (2011): http://policyschool.ucalgary.ca/sites/default/files/research/dburney_0.pdf.

29   Thomas d'Aquino, "Security and Prosperity in the Canada–United States Relationship: Two Sides of the Same Coin," address to the Conference of Defence Associations and the CDA Institute Conference on Defence and Security, March 2011 (Calgary:

Canadian Defence and Foreign Affairs Institute, 2011), http://www.cdfai.org/PDF/ Security and Prosperity in the Canada-United States Relationship.pdf.

30   Colin Robertson, *"Now for the Hard Part": A User's Guide to Renewing the Canadian-American Partnership* (Strategic Studies Working Group, Canadian International Council and Canadian Defence and Foreign Affairs Institute, February 2011), http://www.cdfai.org/PDF/Now for the Hard Part.pdf.

3 Toward Greater Opportunism

Balancing and Bandwagoning in Canada-US Relations

JUSTIN MASSIE

Have Canada-US relations changed since 9/11? This chapter examines the evolution of the Canadian government's international security policy strategy toward the United States. It does so by using the increasingly popular concepts of "soft" and "hard" bandwagoning and balancing to make sense of states' post–Cold War security behaviour vis-à-vis the United States. It argues that hard bandwagoning has gained prominence under the Harper government, and has the potential to supplant the traditional twin pillars of Canada's security policy: continental soft bandwagoning and transatlantic soft balancing.[1] The shift appears less to illustrate a pragmatic adjustment to the continental and international security environments since 9/11 than to reflect a neoconservative ideology underpinning the Harper government's foreign policy.

Balancing and Bandwagoning

Faced with the absence of a counterbalancing force to the United States' power in the decade following the end of the Cold War, neorealists abrogated their research paradigm to make it fit with reality.[2] Some destructuralized neorealism by emphasizing the importance of domestic (public opinion, legislative system, etc.) and ideational (ideology, identity, culture, etc.) determinants of foreign policy to help explain the unexpected fact of "underbalancing."[3] Others widened the range of policies available for realpolitik statecraft, most notably to include non-military (economic, diplomatic, and institutional) balancing strategies. In addition to what is now known as "hard" balancing (which realists had previously referred to simply as "balancing"), "soft" balancing gained notoriety. It is even said to have replaced traditional hard balancing as the preferred foreign policy of states in the face of US unipolarity.[4]

Contrary to hard balancing, soft balancing does not directly seek to overthrow US hegemony. Rather, it comprises non-military policies aimed at delaying, frustrating, constraining, or undermining the unilateral exercise of power by the United States, through "territorial denial, entangling diplomacy, economic strengthening, and signalling of resolve to participate in a balancing coalition." Traditional hard balancing, on the other hand, includes measures such as "military buildups, warfighting alliances, and transfers of military technology to U.S. opponents."[5] Two dimensions are thus central to identifying soft balancing: intentions (resistance short of seeking to overthrow US hegemony) and means (non-military).

Soft balancing not only restrains states' exercise of power but also influences their policies "by using institutional mechanisms, rules, norms, and procedures of mutual regulation ... This allows them to influence the dominant power's policies and increase their bargaining position within the institution."[6] Weaker or more vulnerable states are "thereby rendering asymmetric power relations less exploitive and commitment more certain."[7] In other words, Canada may exercise soft balancing against the United States within common institutions, such as NATO and the United Nations Security Council (UNSC), by binding the hegemon to institutionalized norms and rules and by restraining its potential unilateralism.

The choice to bandwagon with US preponderance is also attributable to the relative benevolence/belligerence of the United States' power. Indeed, the United States is said to generally adopt policies benefiting other states. It provides public goods such as a stable reserve currency; it enforces the rules and institutions that govern the international political and economic systems; it protects the "global commons" as well as many states from their rivals; it mostly exercises its power through multilateral institutions; and it accepts domestic and external restraints on its power.[8] In addition to the benignity of US hegemony, the United States' sheer size also explains why states prefer to bandwagon with rather than balance against it. The state of unipolarity, argues William Wohlforth, "is a structure in which one state's capabilities are too great to be counterbalanced."[9] The United States has reached a concentration of power that renders counterbalancing futile, as it is prohibitively costly and could lead to the balancer's annihilation.[10]

The varying degrees of cooperation with the United States open the door to distinguishing "soft" from "hard" bandwagoning.[11] Understood as the opposite of balancing, bandwagoning can take two forms: modest and indirect or full and open alignment with a more powerful or threatening state.[12] As Walt suggests, the bandwagoning state "makes asymmetrical concessions to the dominant power and accepts a subordinate role."[13] It freely chooses, or (given its geostrategic predicament) resigns itself to, accommodation of a more powerful or threatening state by accepting its dominance in exchange for greater security and/or autonomy, or other coveted gains.[14] Bandwagoning thus involves a defensive (soft) and an opportunistic (hard) dimension: states may soft bandwagon with the dominant power for fear of being forced into obedience, or hard bandwagon to profit from it.[15] In Canada's case, according to Walt, it is because of the United States' benign policy toward it and because of its own weakness and isolation that Canada has "chosen" to bandwagon with the United States.[16]

In sum, the debate over balancing and bandwagoning vis-à-vis the United States emphasizes a wide spectrum of responses to, and explanation of, enduring US hegemony. States adopting realist foreign policies may choose, or be forced to choose, from among the following strategies:

- hard balancing – direct military opposition to the most powerful state in order to overthrow its hegemony
- soft balancing – non-offensive resistance to a threatening power's policies in order to constrain and/or influence it
- soft bandwagoning – modest or indirect support of a threatening or powerful state in order to optimize its security or profit from it
- hard bandwagoning – full and open support of the most powerful state in order to profit materially or ideationally from it.

Counterweights in Canada's Transatlantic Security Policy

Is Canada bandwagoning with or balancing against the United States? As a country sharing a bilateral and a multilateral military alliance with the United States, Canada is often portrayed by non-Canadians as a bandwagoning state.[17] But Canadian scholars describe and/or explain their country's international security policy as one involving a long-standing quest for "counterweights" to the United States, most notably through NATO. So much has been written about the transatlantic "counterweight" in Canadian academia, and so many times has it been cited as a crucial rationale for joining (and continuing to support) the Atlantic Alliance that it can indeed be regarded as a significant component of Canada's strategic culture.[18]

This apparent contradiction is merely one of definition. Galia Press-Barnathan, according to whom balancing within a common alliance is an oxymoron, nevertheless argues that NATO members advance two strategies to manage their relations with the United States. "First, they may create a pact of restraint to try to restrain the hegemon and influence its policies from within the alliance. Second, they may create a division of labour that allows them to offer meaningful contributions to their hegemonic partner ... to enhance their bargaining and restraining capability vis-à-vis the hegemon on other issues."[19] Both strategies therefore entail a desire to restrain the United States while not seeking to overthrow its hegemony, and both involve non-military means of doing so. In other words, what is labelled bandwagoning may in fact represent instances of soft balancing.

A case in point is Canada's traditional NATO policy. For most Canadian decision makers, NATO holds the potential to constrain US military interventions and elevate Canada's status and rank as a prominent and meaningful world actor.[20] Because of its geographic proximity to the United States, its "economic and military vulnerability to rapacious great powers, the United States in particular," and its "inability to defy continentalist tendencies alone," argues Michael Tucker, Canada has had need of "counterweights" – Great Britain prior to 1949, and NATO Europe thereafter.[21] This is not out of fear of abandonment, as "soft bandwagoning" implies; on the contrary, Canada benefits from the United States' involuntary security guarantee. It is rather the result of a perceived need to "exert a moderating influence" on US policies, as Lester B. Pearson put it in 1948. Indeed, despite the hegemon's perceived benevolence, Pearson feared that the "United States may press the Russians too hard and too fast and not leave them a way out which would save their faces. To lessen this danger, the Western European powers will have to exert a steady and constructive influence on Washington ... The establishment of a North Atlantic Union will give them additional channels through which to exert this moderating influence."[22] For Pearson, preventing US unilateralism was indeed "the first principle of Canadian diplomacy."[23]

While restricted to collective defence during the Cold War, NATO quickly expanded its security roles and mandates to include peace operations following the collapse of the Soviet Union. It further expanded the scope of its ambition by taking counterinsurgency, counterterrorism, and capacity-building roles following the attacks of 9/11. This offered Canada new opportunities to attempt to influence US international security policy, for the principles that had pushed Canada to intervene in Korea in the 1950s and in the Persian Gulf in the early 1990s – active participation in US-led military interventions within a multilateral coalition – could now be undertaken under NATO command. For Canada, this meant the need to significantly contribute to NATO-led operations in order to be able to exert a moderating influence on US policies. The Chrétien government did just that in the former Yugoslavia throughout the 1990s.

The prevalence of such strategic thinking was evident in the early aftermaths of the attacks of 9/11. On the very day the terrorists struck, the Canadian permanent representative to the North Atlantic Council proposed that, for the first time in its history, the NATO Charter's Article 5 on collective defence be invoked. The next day, Prime Minister Chrétien declared that Canada would fully support the United States when action would be taken. A month later, despite the absence of any explicit authorization from the UNSC, Canada announced its participation in the US-led operation to overthrow the Taliban regime. In early 2002, it became the fourth-largest military contributor to the operation. Months later, Minister of National Defence John McCallum responded positively to a US request to send troops to Kabul. The Canadian government sought, as expected, to bring the ongoing military operations in Afghanistan under NATO command, just as it would again do in 2005 by redeploying troops to Kandahar in order to expand NATO's authority throughout the country.

Soft balancing helps make sense of these decisions. Indeed, they indicate a desire to restrain US unilateralism through the establishment and expansion of a multilateral and institutional command, despite the initial reluctance of some European allies.[24] Jean Chrétien and Paul Martin sought, with some success, to influence the war in Afghanistan by contributing troops and institutionalizing it within NATO.[25] One may therefore conclude, as former Canadian ambassador to NATO David Wright did earlier regarding Canadian participation in the war against Serbia, that "Ottawa's influence on Washington was ensured because of US support for NATO and the need to maintain unity."[26] Maintaining the relevance and unity of the Atlantic Alliance remained essential to achieving the first principle of Canadian diplomacy following 9/11, for without Western European "counterweights," Canada could not dream of effectively curbing the potential excesses of US foreign policy.

The war against Iraq represents a further case in point. Because the Chrétien government was not successful in finding a compromise between Western Europe (mostly Germany and France) and the United States, it chose not to support its southern neighbour's decision to invade Iraq. As Chrétien's policy adviser Eddie Goldenberg put it: "The circumstances with respect to Kosovo were very different in 1999 than they were in Iraq in 2003. Then the Clinton Administration was not pursuing a unilateralist foreign policy; it insisted on the serious participation of Europe and NATO in a military operation."[27] One may therefore be tempted to conclude that, had Canada's soft balancing strategy been successful – if a compromise had been reached among its trusted allies – Canada would probably have gone off to battle in March 2003.[28]

Continental Soft Bandwagoning

The most attractive alternative to soft balancing is soft bandwagoning, that is, modest or indirect support of the United States in order to optimize Canadian security or profit from US preponderance. In its defensive variant, this strategy has been pursued by Canadian decision makers since at least the late 1930s, through a policy conventionally labelled "continentalism." It refers to a vision of Canadian foreign policy based on the vast and multifaceted network of exchanges (goods, people, capital, ideas, and so on) between Canadian and American societies, and a positive appreciation of its consequences for both societies and governments.[29] Although better known in its economic version, which promotes deeper integration with the United States, in terms of defence, continentalism also rests on the paramountcy of the United States, as well as Canada's supposed ability to leverage a close relationship with the US government in order to "collateralize [its] bilateral assets" and enjoy greater influence beyond North America.[30]

Rather than seeking to multilaterally constrain US power, as in transatlantic soft balancing, Canada should embrace, contribute, and hence bandwagon (softly or heavily) with US hegemony, according to continentalists. Such policy is perceived as a necessity arising from Canada's unique geographical position, favourably located next to the world's sole liberal and benevolent hegemon. Canada-US relations should therefore be recognized as "the indispensable foundation of Canadian foreign policy in all its dimensions ... The principal foreign policy challenge for Canada is to manage the forces of silent integration drawing us ever closer to our giant neighbour and to obtain maximum benefit from that integration."[31] In other words, bandwagoning appears to represent the foreign policy recommended by many continentalists.

Atlanticists disagree, mostly because they do not share continentalists' assessment of US benign intentions and policies. They fear that the "natural" pull toward ever greater North American integration may marginalize Canada's autonomy to the point of making Canada a mere satellite to the United States.[32] Limiting Canadian foreign policy to its bilateral relationship, no matter how important that relationship is, would undermine the country's sovereignty, as it would not benefit from the help of its allies and of multilateral institutions in restraining US excesses. Even during the bipolar era of the Cold War, writes historian Desmond Morton, "The Soviet Union was the ultimate threat but the United States was the imminent danger."[33] Indeed, successive violations of Canadian sovereignty by the United States during and following the Second World War altered Ottawa's threat analysis in ways favourable to the establishment of a multilateral institution that would manage transatlantic defence relations. For Pearson, "under such a [North Atlantic] treaty the joint planning of the defence of North America would fall into place as part of a larger whole and the difficulties arising in Canada from the fear of invasion of Canadian sovereignty by the United States would be diminished."[34]

Yet the inevitable forces underlying North American continentalism have worked against the pursuit of the soft balancing strategy espoused by Pearson. Instead, Canada's continental defence policy has been institutionalized in a solely bilateral – and even binational, through the North American Aerospace Defence Command (NORAD) – relationship. This strict compartmentalization between bilateral and multilateral defence has "satisfied Washington's desire to prevent its European allies from interfering in the management of the systems for defending US soil ... But more curiously, it has satisfied some Canadian desires as well."[35] The most important examples of the bilateral (as opposed to multilateral) institutionalization of US-Canadian defence are the 1940 Ogdensburg Agreement and NORAD (its creation, renewals, and functional expansions), both of which significantly tied Canadian and American security exclusively to each other.

Contrary to the opportunistic bandwagoning strategy advocated by some continentalists, it is a mostly defensive variant that characterizes the Canada-US continental security relationship. By bandwagoning with the United States, Canada seeks to optimize its security – defined in terms of autonomy and sovereignty protection – rather than to profit from its neighbour's power (although it does). This is the result not only of long-standing US pressures on Canadian sovereignty but also of a fundamental geostrategic reality: the indivisibility of North American security. The whole of North America is deemed part of US homeland defence strategy, meaning that an attack on, or emanating from, Canada would invariably be perceived as an attack on the United States.

The validity of this norm remained unchanged following the attacks of 9/11. For Ottawa, it meant continuing to accept US ascendency over North American defence in exchange for Canadian assistance to American efforts to protect Canada's territorial integrity.[36] There are numerous examples,[37] including the Chrétien government's rejection of the idea of a formal North American "security perimeter" (due to concerns over sovereignty), even as it adopted a series of security measures aimed at reassuring Washington, including intensified screening processes in ports and airports, a new identification card for permanent residents, and new anti-terrorism and immigration bills; the creation of new security and defence institutions (Public Safety and Emergency Preparedness Canada [now Public Safety Canada] and Canada Command [now Canadian Joint Operations Command]); the expansion of NORAD's mandate to include maritime surveillance and missile detection; and the establishment of the Security and Prosperity Partnership of North America.

Despite these initiatives, the Chrétien government's response to 9/11 was criticized for its reactiveness, tardiness, and limited scope. The April 2006 State Department report on counterterrorism, for example, deplored Canada's "liberal immigration policies" for allowing continued terrorist activities in the country.[38] Despite a vast new legislative framework against terrorism, Canada was not able to satisfy US demands. Its counterterrorism strategy, which sought to avoid another 9/11 effect on the Canadian economy, was constrained by the enduring fear over Canadian sovereignty. Preferring soft to hard bandwagoning, the Canadian government rejected the idea of a comprehensive security and defence agreement with the United States. It opted to modestly support the United States in its new emphasis on anti-terrorism in order to optimize Canadian security. Focusing on sovereignty protection, it chose minimal and reactive compliance, thereby adapting its continental security policies to meet the hegemon's needs while retaining significant national control over its home territory.

Perhaps Ottawa shared Frank Harvey's assessment that fully meeting US demands would be an impossible task.[39] It sought to reassure Washington that it was doing "enough" by harmonizing many of its policies with those of the United States and by investing modestly in its security and defence apparatus, but refrained from proposing a comprehensive agreement for greater and deeper integration. In other words, the Canadian government preferred a defensive soft bandwagoning strategy to an opportunistic hard bandwagoning one.

Growing Hard Bandwagoning

A debate is emerging over the possible transition of Canada's security policy toward greater (or "heavier") bandwagoning with the United States. The shift could be attributable to the accession to power of Conservative (and reputedly continentalist) Stephen Harper, or to the growingly multipolar distribution of power due to the rise of China. Regarding the first, Kim Nossal argues that "Harper's hyperbolic rhetoric about Canada as America's 'most reliable ally' tends to gloss over the disconnects from both Canadian thought and Canadian practice than can be seen."[40] This rhetoric/policy gap, he claims, is apparent in both Harper's continental and forward security policies, including such issues as ballistic missile defence (BMD) and the wars in Iraq and Afghanistan. The gap can be explained by the fact that, unlike during the Cold War era, when Canadian territory had geostrategic importance for the United States, Canada has become "strategically irrelevant" for US defence today. This gives Canada greater leeway to disagree with the United States, for it is less pressured by Washington to shape its defence policy according to US needs. Canada could afford to decline to participate in BMD and in the war against Iraq, as well as to withdraw its combat troops from Afghanistan in 2011, without suffering any substantial retribution from the United States. If Nossal's assessment is correct, we should expect less bandwagoning as well as softer balancing in Canada's future foreign and defence policy.

Examining Canadian foreign policy in light of China's rise as a global power, Bruce Gilley comes to the opposite conclusion. He contends that the rise of China makes bandwagoning with the United States ever more appealing. Hence Canada might have to make a greater contribution to US foreign and defence policy, especially if China emerges as an illiberal, revisionist state.[41] Charles Doran makes a similar argument in Chapter 1. The structural change that is slowly occurring in world politics makes the rise of China a major challenge to North America. If, on the contrary, China rises as a responsible, status quo liberal power, it will significantly reduce its challenge to US hegemony. "In that scenario," claims Gilley, "Canada-US relations over Asia might drift apart, but only in a narrow, technocratic sense. In a bigger sense, liberal principles in Asia would have triumphed and with them the fundamental basis of Canada-US relations."[42] Therefore, whether or not US hegemony comes to an end, bandwagoning with the United States will remain Canada's preferred defence policy. Its hard variant is more likely in the context of an emerging revisionist China, whereas a softer variant is to be expected in the context of an emerging status quo China.

A third perspective is gaining strength among scholars. It focuses on Nossal's puzzle – the impact of the Conservative Party as a potentially new "natural governing party" – but reaches Gilley's conclusion with regard to Canada's security policy.[43] Since the attacks of 9/11, continentalism has become an increasingly dominant discourse in Canadian foreign policy. The thickening of the border since 9/11 has indeed led many to extend the continentalist logic to the realm of security. Michael Hart, for example, argues that given growing North American economic interdependence, new threats to international security (terrorism, rogue states, weapons of mass destruction), and US unipolarity, Canada must clearly and more vigorously bandwagon with the hegemon.[44]

This new form of continentalism – neocontinentalism, if you will – is illustrated by the debate surrounding the establishment of a security perimeter. Such a perimeter involves a standardization of Canadian and US procedures regarding the traffic coming from outside North America in order to reduce the controls between the two countries. After 9/11, despite repeated calls by US Ambassador Paul Cellucci, the expression "security perimeter" was officially banned by the Chrétien government because of its political implication – that any standardization process would end up being an Americanization of Canadian procedures. The idea nonetheless survived among Canadian commentators, especially among conservatives and within the business community.[45] More substantially, the Canada-US Beyond the Border proposal appears to represent a step in that direction. Its ultimate goal, according to one proponent, is to integrate Canadian and American procedures in order "to make the flow of traffic – people, goods and services – within the single biggest bilateral trading relationship in the world as easy as that enjoyed within the European Union."[46] The concept of a security perimeter thus accepts the indivisibility of North American security, and hence US dominance over it. As Prime Minister Harper has said: "There is no such thing as a threat to the national security of the United States which does not represent a direct threat to this country."[47] Canada's continental security policy should therefore seek to support (bandwagon with) the hegemon's national security policies.

The neocontinentalist prescription for hard bandwagoning is also illustrated with regard to North American ballistic missile defence. Paul Martin's notorious "no" to BMD is often portrayed as a failure to bandwagon with the United States. True, it does not constitute an instance of hard bandwagoning, but one could argue that it illustrates a softer variant, for Canada is in fact playing a de facto part in missile defence thanks to an August 2004 agreement permitting NORAD to continue transmitting missile warning and assessment data to BMD command and control. This represents a clear example of tacit support given to the US BMD system. Furthermore, during the 2006 federal election, Martin repeatedly claimed that a Conservative government would have Canada "join" BMD. Although Harper did not formally commit to reversing the Liberal's position, he did specify conditions under which Canada could formally "participate."[48] By opening the door to full support of BMD, he implicitly acknowledged that Canada would adapt its defence policy based on the threats posed to the United States.

The motivation for Harper's approach to continental defence tilts toward hard bandwagoning because it moves from an essentially defensive to a more opportunistic policy toward the United States. Officially it strives to enhance Canada's status as a strong, reliable, and credible military partner of the United States.[49] The enhanced credibility it seeks is less about mitigating US pressures on Canadian sovereignty than about gaining influence over it. As Harper explained: "Not only can we advance our own interests in concert with the United States, the opportunity exists to strengthen Canadian influence on the Americans, and thus enhance our sovereignty in ways that no encirclement strategy could plausibly do." He identified three means to achieve this goal: (1) deploy hard power alongside the US military, including BMD; (2) strengthen Canadian military capabilities; and (3) "ensure that Canada is never again perceived as a potential source of threats" by the United States.[50]

Hard bandwagoning, as exposed by Harper, rests upon an assumption that is far from guaranteed: that the Canadian government has the ability and will to influence US foreign and defence policy. This implies that Ottawa has an alternative grand strategy to that of the US, and that more military capabilities will lead to greater influence.[51] Whether or not this is true, Harper does believe that refraining from investing in military expenditures or from joining US-led military initiatives such as the invasion of Iraq will make Canada "irrelevant" and, more to the point, destroy its "ability to exert influence on the events and the allies that will shape our future."[52]

Harper's hard bandwagoning relates to Gilley's analysis of China's rise. Among the reasons that should motivate Canada to focus its foreign policy almost entirely on its southern neighbour is the latter's liberal, benevolent, and hyper-powerful character. This helps explain why, for neocontinentalists, it is unnecessary to seek to constrain US power within multilateral institutions, for American power is not a threat but an opportunity for Canada. Rather than conceiving of Canada as a dependent or secondary power, neocontinentalism rests upon the belief that Canada is a "foremost" rather than a mere "middle" power. It depicts Canada as a state having huge potential influence on the international stage if it plays its card well and accepts the (military) responsibilities that come with such rank. "Canada is back as a credible player on the international stage," proudly claimed Prime Minister Harper in his 2007 Speech from the Throne.[53] This, of course, is consistent with Harper's characterization of Canada as an "energy superpower"[54] as well as a strong and reliable partner of the United States. The debate surrounding Canadian participation in the Iraq War clearly illustrated that point. "Supporting our allies is the right thing to do," claimed Harper.[55] He was not referring, evidently, to France and Germany. Whereas for Atlanticists it is necessary to secure a consensus among key Western allies (most notably France)[56] and comply with international law before resorting to the use of force, neither of these criteria applies to the neocontinentalist approach. The United States and, to a lesser extent, the United Kingdom represent the only allies on which Canada should rely.

Conclusion

I have argued that hard bandwagoning has gained prominence under the Harper government, and that it holds the potential of supplanting the traditional twin pillars of Canada's security policy: continental soft bandwagoning and transatlantic soft balancing. This means that Canada is likely to pursue policies that seek to leverage its close relationship with the United States in order to gain greater influence in global affairs, rather than attempt to broker compromises among its closest allies and fear the erosion of its sovereignty vis-à-vis the United States. Unlike continentalism, whose focus was limited to North American defence, neocontinentalism, if it proves enduring, will apply to Canada's security policy both at home and abroad.

The realist concepts of soft and hard balancing and bandwagoning were used to support this assertion. For lack of space, I have only briefly discussed the motivations and dynamics of Canada's evolving behaviour toward the United States, but this analysis suggests that neorealist theory contributes to a better understanding of Canadian foreign policy. If my assessment proves to be accurate, we should expect much greater alignment of the Harper government with Washington, both overseas and in North America.

NOTES

1 Justin Massie, "Making Sense of Canada's 'Irrational' International Security Policy: A Tale of Three Strategic Cultures," *International Journal* 64, 3 (2009): 625-35; cf. Jonathan Paquin, "Canadian Foreign and Security Policy: Reaching a Balance between Autonomy and North American Harmony in the 21st Century," *Canadian Foreign Policy* 15, 2 (2009): 103-12.

2 While some believe that China is hard-balancing the United States, most realist analysts tend to argue that soft balancing, or simply bandwagoning, is the present trend. See G. John Ikenberry, Michael Mastanduno, and William C. Wohlforth, "Introduction: Unipolarity, State Behavior, and Systemic Consequences," *World Politics* 61, 1 (2009): 1-27.

3 See Gideon Rose, "Neoclassical Realism and Theories of Foreign Policy," *World Politics* 51, 1 (1998): 144-72; Randall L. Schweller, "Unanswered Threats: A Neoclassical Realist Theory of Underbalancing," *International Security* 29, 2 (2004): 159-201; Deborah Welch Larson and Alexei Shevchenko, "Status Seekers: Chinese and Russian Responses to US Primacy," *International Security* 34, 4 (2010): 63-95.

4 Robert A. Pape, "Soft Balancing against the United States," *International Security* 30, 1 (2005): 38. The first soft-balancing arguments were made by Stephen M. Walt, "Keeping the World 'Off-Balance': Self-Restraint and US Foreign Policy," in *America Unrivaled: The Future of the Balance of Power,* ed. G. John Ikenberry (Ithaca, NY: Cornell University Press, 2002), 121-54; and Josef Joffe, "Defying History and Theory: The United States as the 'Last Superpower,'" in *America Unrivaled: The Future of the Balance of Power,* ed. G. John Ikenberry (Ithaca, NY: Cornell University Press, 2002), 155-80.

5 Pape, ibid., 9-10 and 36; Stephen M. Walt, *Taming American Power: The Global Response to US Primacy* (New York: W.W. Norton, 2005), 126.

6 Ilai Z. Saltzman, "Soft Balancing as Foreign Policy: Assessing American Strategy toward Japan in the Interwar Period," *Foreign Policy Analysis* 7, 1 (2011): 4.

7 G. John Ikenberry, *After Victory: Institutions, Strategic Restraint, and the Rebuilding of World Order after Major Wars* (Princeton, NJ: Princeton University Press, 2001), 63; Kai He, "Institutional Balancing and International Relations Theory: Economic Interdependence and Balance of Power Strategies in Southeast Asia," *European Journal of International Relations* 14, 3 (2008): 493.

8 Robert Gilpin, *War and Change in World Politics* (Cambridge: Cambridge University Press, 1981), 144-45; Barry R. Posen, "Command of the Commons: The Military Foundation of American Hegemony," *International Security* 28, 1 (2003): 5-46; Walt, *Taming American Power,* 187-91; G. John Ikenberry, *Strategic Reactions to American Preeminence: Great Power Politics in the Age of Unipolarity* (Washington, DC: National Intelligence Council, 28 July 2003), 35; Walt, "Keeping the World 'Off-Balance,'" 139.

9 William C. Wohlforth, "The Stability of a Unipolar World," *International Security* 24, 1 (1999): 9.

10 Ibid., 18; Kenneth N. Waltz, "Structural Realism after the Cold War," *International Security* 25, 1 (2000): 38.

11 See Alexandru Grigorescu, "East and Central European Countries and the Iraq War: The Choice between 'Soft Balancing' and 'Soft Bandwagoning,'" *Communist and Post-Communist Studies* 41, 3 (2008): 281-99; Birthe Hansen, Peter Toft, and Anders Wivel, *Security Strategies and American World Order: Lost Power* (New York: Routledge, 2009), 11-12.

12 Randall L. Schweller, *Deadly Imbalances: Tripolarity and Hitler's Strategy of World Conquest* (New York: Columbia University Press, 1998), 67-69.

13 Stephen M. Walt, "Alliance Formation in Southwest Asia: Balancing and Bandwagoning in Cold War Competition," in *Dominoes and Bandwagons: Strategic Beliefs and Great Power Competition in the Eurasian Rimland,* ed. Robert Jervis and Jack Snyder (New York: Oxford University Press, 1991), 55.

14 Cf. Randall L. Schweller, "Bandwagoning for Profit: Bringing the Revisionist State Back In," *International Security* 19, 1 (1994): 72-107.

15 Thomas H. Mowle and David H. Sacko, "Global NATO: Bandwagoning in a Unipolar World," *Contemporary Security Policy* 28, 3 (2007): 606.

16 Walt, "Alliance Formation in Southwest Asia," 36.

17 Ibid. With regard to its contribution to NATO, see Galia Press-Barnathan, "Managing the Hegemon: NATO under Unipolarity," *Security Studies* 15, 2 (2006): 271-309; Mowle and Sacko, "Global NATO," 597-618.

18 As argued by David G. Haglund and Stéphane Roussel, "Escott Reid, the North Atlantic Treaty, and Canadian Strategic Culture," in *Escott Reid: Diplomat and Scholar,* ed. Greg Donaghy and Stéphane Roussel (Montreal and Kingston: McGill-Queen's University Press, 2004), 45.

19 Press-Barnathan, "Managing the Hegemon," 274.

20 See David Leyton-Brown, "Managing Canada? United States Relations in the Context of Multilateral Alliances," in *America's Alliances and Canadian-American Relations,* ed. Lauren McKinsey and Kim Richard Nossal (Toronto: Summerhill Press, 1988); Joel J. Sokolsky, "A Seat at the Table: Canada and Its Alliances," in *Canada's Defence: Perspectives on Policy in the Twentieth Century,* ed. B.D. Hunt and R.G. Haycock (Toronto: Copp Clark Pitman, 1993).

21 Michael Tucker, *Canadian Foreign Policy: Contemporary Issues and Themes* (Toronto: McGraw-Hill Ryerson, 1980), 4 and 117-18. See also Tom Keating, *Canada and World Order: The Multilateralist Tradition in Canadian Foreign Policy,* 2nd ed. (Don Mills, ON: Oxford University Press, 2002), 12-14.

22 James Eayrs, *In Defence of Canada: Growing Up Allied* (Toronto: University of Toronto Press, 1980), 67; Robert A. Spencer, *Canada in World Affairs: From UN to NATO (1946-1949)* (Toronto: University of Toronto Press, 1959), 265-69.

23 Lester B. Pearson, "The Development of Canadian Foreign Policy," *Foreign Affairs* 30, 1 (October 1951): 24-26.

24 Janice Gross Stein and Eugene Lang, *The Unexpected War: Canada in Kandahar* (Toronto: Viking Canada, 2007), 48-50.

25 Charles Létourneau, *L'influence canadienne à travers les opérations de paix, 1956 à 2005* (Montréal: CEPES/UQAM, 2006).

26 Quoted in Paquin, "Canadian Foreign and Security Policy," 104.

27 Eddie Goldenberg, *The Way It Works: Inside Ottawa* (Toronto: McClelland and Stewart, 2006), 296.

28 David G. Haglund, "Canada and the Sempiternal NATO Question," *McGill International Review* 5 (Spring 2005): 19.

29 Kim Richard Nossal, Stéphane Roussel, and Stéphane Paquin, *International Policy and Politics in Canada* (Toronto: Pearson Education, 2011), 273-86.

30 Allan Gotlieb, "The Paramountcy of Canada-US Relations," *National Post*, 22 May 2003, A20; Allan Gotlieb, "No Access, No influence," *National Post*, 3 December 2003, A18.

31 Michael Hart, "Lessons from Canada's History as a Trading Nation," *International Journal* 58, 1 (2002-03): 39.

32 See John Holmes, "Shadow and Substance: Diplomatic Relations between Britain and Canada," in *Britain and Canada: Survey of a Changing Relationship,* ed. Peter Lyon (London: Frank Cass, 1976), 107; Marie Bernard-Meunier, "The 'Inevitability' of North American Integration?" *International Journal* 60 (2005): 703-11.

33 Desmond Morton, "Defending the Indefensible: Some Historical Perspective on Canadian Defense," *International Journal* 42, 4 (1987): 639.

34 Eayrs, *In Defence of Canada,* 369.

35 Haglund and Roussel, "Escott Reid," 53.

36 David G. Haglund and Michel Fortmann, "Canada and the Issue of Homeland Security: Does the Kingston Dispensation Still Hold?" *Canadian Military Journal* 3, 1 (Spring 2002): 18.

37 For a review, see Justin Massie, "Canada's (In)dependence in the North American Security Community: The Asymmetrical Norm of Common Fate," *American Review of Canadian Studies* 37, 4 (2007): 493-516.

38 US, Department of State, "Country Reports: Western Hemisphere Overview," in *Country Reports on Terrorism, 2005* (Washington, DC: Office of the Coordinator for Counterterrorism, April 2006), 160-62.

39 Frank P. Harvey, "The Homeland Security Dilemma: Imagination, Failure and the Escalating Costs of Perfecting Security," *Canadian Journal of Political Science* 40, 2 (2007): 310.

40 Kim Richard Nossal, "America's 'Most Reliable Ally'? Canada and the Evanescence of the Culture of Partnership," in *Forgotten Partnership Redux: Canada-US Relations in the 21st Century,* ed. Greg Anderson and Christopher Sands (Amherst, NY: Cambria Press, 2011).

41 Bruce Gilley, "Middle Powers during Great Power Transitions: China's Rise and the Future of Canada-US Relations," *International Journal* 66, 2 (2011): 256.

42 Ibid., 257.

43 See Justin Massie and Stéphane Roussel, "The Twilight of Internationalism? Neocontinentalism as an Emerging Dominant Idea in Canadian Foreign Policy," in *Canada in the World: Internationalism in Canadian Foreign Policy*, ed. Heather A. Smith and Claire Turenne Sjolander (Don Mills, ON: Oxford University Press, 2013), 36-52.

44 Michael Hart, *From Pride to Influence: Towards a New Canadian Foreign Policy* (Vancouver: UBC Press, 2008).

45 See Stéphane Roussel, "Pearl Harbor et le World Trade Center: Le Canada face aux États-Unis en période de crise," *Études internationales* 33, 4 (2002): 667-95.

46 Colin Robertson, "Taking the Canada-US Partnership to the Next Level," *Policy Options* 32 (2011): 76.

47 Quoted in Jeff Davis, "Harper Hits Mark with Border Security Message," *The Embassy*, 25 February 2009, 3.

48 See Isabelle Rodrigue, "Bouclier antimissile," *Le Droit*, 13 January 2006, A6; John Ibbitson, "Shunning Missile Shield Could Be a Grave Error," *Globe and Mail*, 12 October 2006, A6.

49 Canada, Department of National Defence, *Canada First Defence Strategy* (Ottawa: Department of National Defence, 2008), 8.

50 Stephen Harper, "A Departure from Neutrality," *National Post*, 23 May 2003, A18.

51 Philippe Lagassé and Paul Robinson, "Reviving Realism in the Canadian Defence Debate," Martello Paper 34 (Kingston, ON: Queen's Centre for International Relations, 2008), 104.

52 Harper, "A Departure from Neutrality," A18. See also Colin Robertson, "Advancing Canadian Interests with the US," *The Embassy*, 4 May 2011.

53 Canada, Governor General, "Strong Leadership. A Better Canada," Speech from the Throne, 16 October 2007, http://dsp-psd.pwgsc.gc.ca/collection_2007/gg/ SO1-1-2007E.pdf.

54 See Annette Hester, *Canada as the "Emerging Energy Superpower": Testing the Case* (Calgary: Canadian Defence and Foreign Affairs Institute, 2007).

55 Stephen Harper, "Liberal Damage Control: A Litany of Flip-Flops on Canada-US Relations," *Policy Options* (June-July 2003): 7.

56 The war in Libya demonstrated that Germany's support was not a necessary condition for Canadian participation in a US-led "coalition of the willing."

Canada, the United States, and Continental Security after 9/11

An Assessment Based on Attribution Theory

MARK PARADIS AND PATRICK JAMES

Canada and the United States constitute a special case for the field of security policy. While these long-standing allies are vastly different in military power, their foreign relations seem to fall largely outside of any standard model based on power capabilities. For example, an account of Canada-US relations across decades reveals the absence of hard linkage on the part of Washington relative to Ottawa. The term "hard linkage" refers to coercion in one issue area as a form of retaliation for actions in another.[1] Even high-profile irritants for the United States, such as Canada's rejection of ballistic missile defence (BMD) in February 2005 or Canada's refusal to support the war in Iraq in 2003, were insufficient to induce hard linkage. Thus, the relationship of Canada with the United States contains at least some elements that transcend realpolitik and invite outlooks that go beyond the state-centric world of competition under conditions of anarchy.

This chapter introduces attribution theory to the analysis of continental security policy for Canada and the United States. Already well understood at a psychological level are some basic differences between Ottawa and Washington. As stated by others in this volume, for leaders inside the Beltway, the dimension of security is primary; along the Rideau, elites view it primarily in terms of trade and commerce.[2] These differences have persisted for a long time and reflect foreign policy roles related to super-power versus middle power status, among other things. This chapter seeks to add specificity to what is known about the political psychology of Canada and the United States as a highly unusual and in some ways unique pairing of states.[3]

Attribution theory is applied to explain the evolving Canadian sense of self, along with views of the United States and Canada-US security relations in the challenging era after 9/11. In order to provide theoretical space to use attribution theory for the study of foreign policy, we begin with a review of some of the literature in the field of psychology on attributions. We then derive a general proposition and assess it in a preliminary way within the Canada-US context after 9/11. Memoirs from the prime ministers in power at the time, Jean Chrétien and Paul Martin, confirm the components of the general proposition. For example, Canada supported the US-led war against Afghanistan, but Ottawa fiercely resisted Washington's efforts to obtain its stamp of approval for the invasion of Iraq. Through application of concepts from attribution theory – namely, effects from disposition versus situation – the shift in policy as well as the intensity exhibited can be explained. The conclusion summarizes the main points and suggests ideas for future research based on attribution theory.

Attribution Theory

An attribution "refers to the linking of an event to its causes. [They] enable us to understand and react to our surroundings."[4] Beginning in the 1970s, attribution theory became one of the most dominant frameworks in social psychology. To summarize the entirety of the literature is beyond the scope and purpose of this chapter. Instead, this section provides a synthesis position on how attributions are made for events involving ourselves and others.

Attributions for Events Involving Others

Well suited for explaining attributions for events and actions involving others is the synthesis position developed by Hamilton.[5] His position integrates evidence about both correspondent inferences and attributions, and appears consistent with the maximum amount of evidence.[6] Correspondent inferences comprise the information about someone (or a situation) gained from an event. Attributions refer to an observer's explanation of events.

Depending on expectations, both correspondent inferences and attributions occur as described above, but at different times.[7] This assertion rests on three important research findings.[8] First, individuals spend more time processing unexpected information. Second, when individuals encounter unanticipated information, they automatically retrieve previously processed data about the target. No further processing occurs when individuals encounter expected information. Third, when individuals encounter unexpected information about a target, they seek to understand the new data through attributional thinking.

From these findings, Hamilton concludes that we use correspondent inferences when the observed behaviour conforms to expectations.[9] This process is "more spontaneous and less analytic, more automatic and less controlled, [and] more heuristic and less systematic."[10] Consistent with correspondent inferences, the observer is not engaged in causal thinking. Since the behaviour is expected, there is no need to explain the event. It is only when the outcome is unexpected that individuals engage in attributional thinking.

Attributional thinking is "more likely to be systematic, analytic thinking about the likely explanations for an unexpected event."[11] This analytical thinking will often, but not always, produce situational attributions.[12] For the most part, therefore, we should expect *situational attributions* when behaviour is unexpected. However, when a behaviour is deemed to require high skill levels, the likelihood of *dispositional attributions* rises.[13] Although inferences can influence future attributions, situational attributions do not impact upon dispositional inferences.[14] For example, if I infer from an aggressive stance that an opponent is aggressive, this inference can bias my future attempts to explain this event. However, situational explanations of an aggressive stance rarely affect future inferences. It becomes increasingly clear that correspondent inferences and attributions are different types of judgments that rely on different neural pathways.[15]

Explaining Our Own Outcomes

Models of attributions for events involving others do not explain attributions for *one's own behaviour.* Research reveals an increased tendency to attribute personal behaviour to situational factors.[16] The availability heuristic suggests a possible reason for this difference.[17] The actor does not see himself acting. Instead, it is the situation that is the most perceptually available. Beyond the perceptual differences, motivational factors may also explain the actor/observer difference.[18] Of greatest interest and potential application in the realm of policy, an actor may want to attribute socially undesirable actions to the situation rather than take personal responsibility. In other words, we are inclined to "give ourselves a break" that we might not so readily give to others.

One review of the findings on the actor/observer difference concludes that it does exist, but not always in the direction that had been assumed.[19] The self-serving bias builds on the motivational reasoning presented above and helps to explain why actors' attributions for their own behaviours are not always in the same direction.[20] According to this bias, there is a "need to view oneself in a favourable way following a success or failure." We attribute successes to dispositional factors such as ability and experience, and failures to situational factors such as lack of support or simply insurmountable odds. Many researchers consider the self-serving bias to be a motivational technique used to protect our self-esteem. Other researchers interpret the self-serving bias using non-motivational factors. For example, given that many people expect to succeed, they attribute their successes to dispositions but their failures to situational factors.[21] Based on an appraisal of research findings, the evidence suggests that the self-serving bias occurs only when individuals expect success.[22] When individuals expect failure, they use dispositional inferences for failures and situational attributions for successes. This logic leads to an outcome similar to that suggested by attribution theory because, according to both theories, expected outcomes lead to *dispositional* inferences and unexpected outcomes lead to *situational* attributions.[23]

Theory and a General Proposition

When an individual or group moves from in-group to out-group within an issue domain or due to a shift in the most salient domain, the mechanism for making attributions about events involving that group changes.[24] Dispositional inferences are likely when a group no longer forms part of the in-group and its behaviour conforms to expectations. If the observer is later asked to explain an event, the inference is likely to bias thinking toward a dispositional attribution. This can be exacerbated within the foreign policy realm, where a leader is a readily available target for dispositional attributions and inferences.[25] When the group's behaviour or events involving that group do not conform to expectations, situational attributions are more likely.

Figure 4.1 summarizes these findings. When both disposition and outcome are positive or negative, inferences are dispositional. When outcomes are mismatched, attributions are often situational.

For behaviour of, or involving, members of the in-group, expectations of success and failure are important factors in determining what type of inference/attribution is made. If success is expected, then positive outcomes result in dispositional attributions and negative outcomes are likely to result in situational attributions. When failure is expected, positive outcomes are likely to result in situational attributions and negative results should lead to dispositional attributions. Figure 4.2 summarizes these expectations.

FIGURE 4.1

Attributions for events involving members of out-groups

	Positive outcome	*Negative outcome*
Positive disposition	Dispositional inference	Attribution – often situational
Negative disposition	Attribution – often situational	Dispositional inference

FIGURE 4.2

Attributions for events involving members of the in-group

	Positive outcome	*Negative outcome*
Expectations of success	Dispositional attribution	Situational attribution
Expectations of failure	Situational attribution	Dispositional attribution

While affect may be a factor in changes in group membership, it is not the primary cause. Instead, changes in group membership within a given issue domain are likely to occur due to a violation of category-based expectancies by the group in question.[26] For example, if an ally consistently acts contrary to expected behaviour, it may no longer be considered an ally. Changes in group membership within a given issue domain, as well as changes in the relevant issue domain, can also be caused by focusing events. For example, 9/11 produced changes in issue and alliance priorities for the US government.

From the preceding analysis emerges a general proposition, which contains interlocking hypotheses:

We propose that attributions depend on both group membership and expectations. In the case of out-groups, situational attributions are made when behaviour does not conform to expectations and dispositional inferences are made when behaviour conforms to expectations. In the case of in-groups, we expect that situational attributions are made when outcomes do not conform to expectations of success or failure, and dispositional attributions are made when outcomes conform to expectations about success.

The main contrast here is between basing an inference about choice on disposition versus situation. The former emphasizes the actor's free will, whereas the latter focuses upon constraints. In a hockey game, when a goal is scored one might hear a fan attribute this to a superbly aimed and executed shot if it is for his or her team. This is a dispositional attribute. The team giving up the goal might instead say something about the situation; perhaps the play should have been whistled offside and thus the goaltender had let down his guard. The difference here is obvious: a desire to give credit for success and avoid blame for failure.

Continental Security after 9/11

For many people in the United States, Canada, and elsewhere, the attacks on September 11, 2001, changed the world. A shift in Canada-US relations came about as a result of the global war against terrorism launched by the Bush administration. Ottawa faced a major decision from the outset regarding participation in a US-led war against the Taliban and al-Qaeda. Moreover, the security environment had changed. Canada, as a border state and long-standing ally over and beyond common membership in NATO, would find itself immersed in the controversial byproducts of 9/11, which most prominently included the US war against Iraq.

Efforts to explain Canadian attributions and inferences for American behaviour and events involving Americans within the security realm after 9/11 must fulfill several requirements. It is essential to identify (1) the dominant security identity and its membership; (2) whether success or failure is expected for events involving in-groups; and (3) dispositional and outcome expectations for out-groups.

Two complicating factors must be addressed. First, a single Canadian conception of the dominant security identity never exists, even briefly at the height of a crisis. High levels of agreement can develop, but total consensus is unlikely because of underlying diversity in values. Second, while shocks will tend to produce simultaneous mass changes in security identity, violations in category-based expectations that result in changes in group membership are unlikely to be so orderly.

For members of the in-group, unexpected outcomes are generally attributed to situational factors. Since attributional thinking is more analytical, situational attributions are not automatic. If the behaviour of an individual or group does not conform to expectations for a prolonged period of time, this should eventually lead to a change in group member- ship due to violations in category-based expectations.

After the events of 9/11, the shock of an attack on North America pro- duced a greater focus on continental security for many Canadians. For both instrumental and ideational reasons, Canada and the United States shared the goal of guaranteeing North American security. While Canadian nationalism and uniquely Canadian security goals did not disappear, the United States entered Canada's national security in-group. This, however, did not occur for all Canadians. With an emphasis on Canadian identity as coterminous with pursuit of human security and a military devoted to peacekeeping, critics mobilized quickly.

Moreover, the duration of the continental security identity varied. As the events faded from the mind, prior beliefs re-emerged. As the mission in Afghanistan progressed, the United States shifted its priorities toward an invasion of Iraq. President Bush, in the eyes of Canadian leaders and most of the general public, clearly had chosen this war of his own voli- tion.[27] His efforts to obtain support fell on deaf ears as Canadians, most notably Prime Minister Chrétien, found themselves troubled by the lack of a UN mandate for the invasion. Thus, national, as opposed to conti- nental, security became the primary focus for a growing number of Cana- dians. Debate over the invasion of Iraq in particular precipitated changes in group membership due to the perceived violation of category-based expectations.

Views of the president and ideology, as with Bush and a "hard right" foreign policy emphasizing military force, should not affect whether situ- ational or dispositional attributions are made.[28] However, they may affect which security identity is dominant at any one time. As we move from left to right on the Canadian political spectrum, the United States is general- ly expected to spend a greater amount of time within the national secu- rity in-group. This results from a greater similarity in national security priorities between Americans and conservative Canadians. For example, poll numbers in Alberta and Quebec consistently stood at the top and bot- tom end of approval for the duration of the Canadian forces' fighting in Afghanistan.

Furthermore, when a group or individual is switching from in-group to out-group, ideology and views about the president will affect the prior knowledge about the target that informs expectations. Individuals who share a similar ideology with the out-group should be more likely to expect positive behaviours from the out-group than individuals who hold an opposing ideology. Similarly, individuals who hold a positive view of the president should be more likely to expect positive behaviours from the president than those who hold a negative view.

When making dispositional inferences and attributions about members of the out-group, the salience criterion and group attribution error suggest different possible targets.[29] According to evidence for the group attribution error, acts by one person can be used to infer a disposition for all group members. Therefore, acts by the government can be used to infer an American character. Group acts can also be used to infer an individual's disposition. Government policy can be attributed to the disposition of one person, such as a president or prime minister. The salience criterion suggests that dispositions are most likely to be attributed to such highly visible figures. The news will be an important source of information about who is significant.

Considerable experimental evidence exists for all of these effects. The relative weight of each factor is likely to be context-dependent. For example, the structure of the US government suggests that the president, the secretary of state, and the secretary of defense are important figures during a foreign policy crisis. The president, relevant cabinet members, and Congress are likely targets for Canadians when it comes to assigning dispositions.

Evidence

Events ushered in by 9/11 coincided with three prime ministerships: Jean Chrétien, Paul Martin, and Stephen Harper. As a first approximation, the memoirs of these leaders will be used to locate evidence. While a great many other approaches might be adopted, it seems reasonable to start with the recollections of those who served as prime minister.[30] Both published in 2008, the memoirs of Chrétien and Martin used here have the advantage of being fairly recent. In addition, the events at issue are among the most important of their terms of office, so the risk of error through lack of interest or concern is minimal. These autobiographies, moreover, have the advantage of greater authenticity than speeches in the House of Commons or elsewhere; such material obviously would have been contaminated by the usual concerns about maintaining popularity in the face of whatever challenge might have existed. Bias would be particularly at risk for attributions made regarding the decision making of others.

To be sure, there are disadvantages to using memoirs. All recollections, whether intentionally or not, are self-serving to some degree. Consider Chrétien's painfully honest remarks on this subject toward the end of *My Years as Prime Minister*:

Your memory isn't always a reliable resource. It plays tricks on your mind, not just over the years, but within hours of what actually happened. The times you've been proven right come back with much more facility than the times you've been proven wrong. Your best lines and finest moments remain remarkably vivid, not the least because you've kept replaying them in your head or over a glass of wine with friends, while your inappropriate wisecracks and embarrassing faux pas gradually fade – if they haven't immediately been shoved – into oblivion.[31]

Chrétien makes the case, as well as any methods textbook could, for triangulation of sources for any study that relies initially upon memoirs, as this one does.

The immediate crisis faced by Canada on September 11 was the closure of US air space. What would happen to the airplanes bound for US destinations? "Some forty thousand American passengers," Chrétien observes, "were welcomed, fed, and comforted for several days by thousands of Canadians, mostly in Newfoundland and Nova Scotia, who did their country honour by opening their homes, their hearts, and their wallets to strangers in distress."[32] His view of what happened is all about disposition: "Too often we Canadians don't appreciate how special we are."[33]

While 9/11 surely pushed the United States into Canadian in-group status, underlying strains of anti-Americanism could still be elicited quite easily. On 20 September, President Bush gave a speech in which he did not include Canada among those countries thanked for what they had done on and around 9/11 to help the United States. Chrétien observes that "many Canadians were outraged, considering that we had done more for the United States in its hour of need than any of those named, and the opposition used this omission as evidence that I had somehow offended the Americans."[34] The prime minister himself did not react in such a negative way, however. His experience came into play here: "Every leader (or his speechwriter) makes that kind of accidental mistake once in a while, and I personally didn't read any bad faith into it."[35] While never known for being well disposed toward the United States, with its generally more conservative ideology and pro-military culture, Chrétien understood the vast range of responsibilities faced by a chief executive and knew better than to make too much of the omission. Unconstrained by such experience or attendant responsibilities, Canadians who tended to be critical of the United States could "go to town" on the slight they perceived in Bush's address to Congress. Years later, a reasonable observer could guess that offending Canada would be the last thing on the mind of a world leader faced with nearly three thousand casualties and an economic crisis. Thus, on all of this, the prime minister made a lot more sense than many of his fellow Canadians.

Different, however, is the reaction Chrétien reserves for elements in the United States defined as ideologically disposed against Canada when they made false accusations regarding security lapses: 9/11 created a "cottage industry" blaming Canada for security leaks, and the completely false accusation that the culprits had entered the United States through Canada would resurface for years on end. For the prime minister, such accusations reflected bias against Canadian values among those politically right of centre:

> The story that a few of them had come into the United States on a ferry from Nova Scotia to Maine, though absolutely untrue, was a convenient way for them to attack our social programs, our cultural differences, and our immigration policies. Blaming the "strangers in our midst" for every kind of social and economic problem has long been an excuse for those in Canada and the United States who dream of returning to an illusionary [sic] white, Anglo-Saxon, Protestant utopia of the past. Unable to say so directly, given the politics and sensitivities of pluralistic democracies, they have to resort to indirect arguments and blatant fabrications to advance their ideas. And so they used the terrorist attacks to promote their prejudices, their anti-immigration policies, and their self-serving mythology.[36]

The prime minister effectively designates his own conservative critics in Canada as an out-group in league with pernicious right-wing ideologues in the United States. Their disposition is ethnocentric and reactionary, so to them 9/11 represented an opportunity to "turn back the clock." Chrétien, by contrast, views his own reaction on the policy front as constrained, most notably, with regard to US calls for higher levels of security: "Canada did respond to the call for tighter security, but first we needed to put in place the proper legal instrument to do the job."[37] In particular, the prime minister insisted on a balance between civil liberty and public safety – drawing an implicit contrast with US preoccupation with border safety, noted later on the same page of his memoirs.[38]

Further to that point, the prime minister regarded pressure for defence spending from the Canadian Forces, American government, and lobbyists as something with more of a political than substantively justified character. With regard to pro-military advocacy, collectively speaking, he sums things up by saying, "I wasn't always sure that its self-interest was the same as the national interest."[39] Chrétien goes on to describe his own situation as quite constrained: "It was hard as a matter of principle, politics and the heart to buy new equipment for the military while reducing assistance to the poor, the ill, and the old."[40] He also enumerates a range of demands upon whatever resources could be allocated to the pursuit of security: UN and NATO peacekeeping, North American security, and fighting terrorism.[41] The imperatives of staying in office, along with finite resources and a commitment to human security at home and abroad, combined to limit what the Canadian Forces could expect to receive even as its government participated in the war against terrorism.

Interesting to ponder, regarding in-groups and out-groups, is Chrétien's idiosyncratic recollection of how the Canadian role in Afghanistan moved up from the twilight zone between peacekeeping and peacemaking all the way to a combat role: "When my successor took too long to make up his mind about whether Canada should extend our term with ISAF [International Security Assistance Force], our soldiers were moved out of Kabul and sent south again to battle the Taliban in the killing fields around Kandahar."[42] Anyone familiar with Canadian politics knows about the long-standing rivalry between Chrétien and Paul Martin, who in the quotation is designated as the reason why pro-military forces in the United States and Canada got their wish for combat operations. Martin, in the eyes of Chrétien, clearly ends up in an out-group that failed to protect the Canadian force from being placed in the line of fire. In reality, the prime minister might have gone much further: Martin did not, strictly speaking, procrastinate his way into a combat role for the Canadian military. Instead, he appointed Rick Hillier Chief of the Defence Staff and, in the International Policy Statement of 2005, pledged publicly to make a difference in the world. All of this combined to move Canada into an active combat role in Afghanistan that was more in line with the centre-right of the Liberal Party led by Martin, as opposed to the centre-left, which favoured Chrétien.

With the Afghan war already in progress, Ottawa faced a new challenge in its security relations with the United States: what should be done in response to Washington's request for Canadian participation in the awkwardly named "Coalition of the Willing," those who would fight alongside the United States when it invaded Iraq? Chrétien describes the situation as it emerged in the fall of 2002: "All that autumn I was under increasing pressure to back the United States all the way – from Washington, from the business community, from the right-wing press, even from those Liberals who were in favour of military action or who opposed everything I did because they were supporting Martin's leadership bid."[43]

When it came to the evidence put forward regarding weapons of mass destruction (WMD) supposedly in the possession of Saddam Hussein, with an accompanying risk of use against the United States and its allies, the prime minister had expressed ongoing skepticism. In a colourful aside regarding a secret US intelligence report, he writes: "All I knew for certain was that I wouldn't have been able to convince a judge of the municipal court in Shawinigan with the evidence I was given."[44] The contrast between his position and that of the US government, with its commitment to war against Saddam Hussein, comes through clearly. The prime minister viewed himself in no position to join the Coalition of the Willing even after the address by Secretary of State Colin Powell, summing up available evidence on WMD against the Iraqi dictator, at the UN in February 2003: "I knew he was on very thin ice indeed. From what I had read, I figured he had been sold a bill of goods."[45]

To the Canadian prime minister, values mattered here, as well as facts. In addition to the shaky evidence about WMD, Chrétien also cited the eventual lack of UN endorsement as a key reason for staying out of Bush's war against Iraq: "We didn't approve of his actions because he hadn't convinced the United Nations of the urgent need to invade Iraq."[46] The prime minister, in light of how he perceived the situation, should have written "couldn't" as opposed to "didn't," given the degree of constraint imposed on a centre-left government by the mainstream of Canadian opinion at both elite and general levels regarding compliance with the UN.

Chrétien thus decided to redouble his efforts toward preventing war by inserting Canada as an "honest broker" between and among the major powers, who found themselves at loggerheads over what to do about Saddam Hussein. Note that the prime minister describes Canada, regarding efforts toward a diplomatic solution, as "one of the few countries with the courage and credibility to try, but the clock was running too fast."[47] From Chrétien's point of view, war came in spite of maximum and admirable but also doomed efforts on the part of Canada to preserve peace. Canada stayed out of the Iraq War, at least at an official level.[48]

From Chrétien's point of view, what did the Iraq War say about Canada and the United States? "I believe that Canada's decision not to go to war in Iraq," he observes, "was one of the most important moments in our history. It proved to us and to the world that we are a proud, independent nation." The prime minister goes on to praise his government for not giving in to heavy pressure from "the United States, the corporate interests, and the ideological [i.e., right-wing] press."[49] In other words, led by his government, Canadians had made a *choice* against war, despite pressures from within and without.

And what of the Americans? Chrétien says: "I'm still puzzled why the Bush administration decided to invade Iraq."[50] The question is answered, at least implicitly, a few pages later. While the prime minister offers some positive observations about the United States, he adds that "everybody recognizes the brashness and insulation that are weaknesses in that superiority, and the poverty, racism, and inequality that are hidden beneath its enormous wealth."[51] Thus, a government and people such as the Americans might be disposed toward arrogance as exhibited by the case of Iraq – acting unilaterally, using military force when not justified, and so on. It is likely that Chrétien, after confrontation with Washington over Iraq, left office with a greater sense of the United States as an out-group that had too much in common dispositionally with his conservative and increasingly vocal critics from within the right wing of the Liberal Party.

Speaking of that faction, its leader, Paul Martin, served a relatively short term as prime minister. As Chrétien's successor, he inherited involvement in Afghanistan and the quite recent refusal of US overtures on Iraq. He also had to deal with on-again, off-again, pressure from the United States over participation in ballistic missile defence. This issue had been on Chrétien's desk when he left office; at that time, the prime minister claimed that he did not have enough evidence, either way, to make a decision.[52] In a chapter of his memoirs titled "Tough Calls," Martin traces the issue of BMD back to the Reagan-era Strategic Defense Initiative, or "Star Wars" project, and describes Canadian policy in the area as "a position of studied ambiguity."[53] Although President Bill Clinton had let BMD lapse, it came back to prominence under Bush, especially after the events of 9/11. Matters came to a head late in 2004 when Bush came to Canada and gave a speech in Halifax that criticized Canada for not supporting the United States in Iraq and for dragging out a response on BMD. Martin believed that he and Bush had agreed not to discuss BMD publicly during the trip; thus, the president's subsequent open reference to the matter, the prime minister recalls, "infuriated me."[54]

Despite the interest American officials had shown in Canadian acceptance of BMD, and even the aggressive reference to it by Bush in apparent contradiction to prior assurances about keeping things private, Martin did not see his government as highly constrained in responding to the proposed initiative. The prime minister recalls that, "while it was clear to me that President Bush would like us in, I never had the impression that it was crucial to our overall relationship – nor did my officials at the PMO and PCO."[55] Given significant opposition to BMD in both the mass public and the Liberal caucus, the Martin government said no to the program in February 2005.

Meanwhile, war raged on in Afghanistan and Iraq. While continuing to eschew involvement in Iraq, which both the government and public opinion generally saw as inadequately explained or justified, Martin felt a sense of urgency about Afghanistan. Canada, according to the prime minister, had been in Afghanistan "for the right reasons" and "continued to have a duty to help construct something sturdy to replace it."[56] These views explain Martin's appointment of the high-energy General Hillier as Chief of the Defence Staff, alluded to earlier. Deployment of the Canadian military to Kandahar came soon after and seems, upon reflection, to be overdetermined. Hillier made the case for a war-fighting role and, as Martin points out, by the time the Canadian force was ready for redeployment, Kandahar was the only available option within US and NATO operations in Afghanistan.[57] It is therefore interesting to note that Martin lists neither the decision against war in Iraq nor the refusal of BMD participation among the reasons for returning to Afghanistan in a fighting role. Instead, it looks like a genuine change in policy orientation, in at least the short term, from peacekeeping to war fighting.

Martin's memoir reflects on values, resulting dispositions, and choices made by Canada and the United States. Canadians, according to Martin, "see the issues of development in the poorer parts of the globe being intimately tied with those of security."[58] This contrasts with the security-seeking United States. With an overwhelming concern for border safety, Washington is prone to "more and more unilateral decision-making."[59] This creates an ongoing challenge for Canada, which must engage with the United States as it exists after 9/11, as opposed to some other version of its superpower neighbour that Canadians might prefer.

Although Martin offers criticism of the United States, he also reveals understanding of the situation faced by any president in the policy domain. Of particular concern are the limits of executive power: "It is extraordinarily difficult to move administration policy at the international level if there are significant domestic forces at play in Congress."[60] Given the separation of powers in the United States, a president faces qualitatively greater challenges than a prime minister when it comes to achieving a coherent policy. Thus, it can be unwise to impute too much responsibility to the president when a US policy seems, from Ottawa's point of view, to be parochial and even damaging to Canadian interests. Not only the Congress but also the massive bureaucracy of the US federal government can impact upon policy in significant ways. This is a point Martin makes in various parts of his narrative.[61]

Upon reviewing the evidence, we find support for a general proposition. In the aftermath of the attacks, the United States was within Chrétien's national security in-group. Consistent with our expectation that the form of attributions depends on group membership, Chrétien made dispositional attributions about Canadian hospitality on 9/11 and situational attributions for perceived slights by Bush in the immediate aftermath. Conservative opponents in Canada and right-wing attacks on Canada from the United States are met with dispositional attributions. In the Canadian case, they are outside the political in-group and their attacks are expected. Likewise, although the United States is in the Canadian security in-group, the attacks of conservative Americans form part of a different identity. Therefore, their predictable negative attacks are attributed to dispositions. Chrétien makes situational attributions for the limited support that he could provide to the Canadian forces, but critiques Martin's disposition on Afghan questions.

We see a real shift in group membership during the lead-up to the invasion of Iraq. In the prewar phase, Chrétien seems to want to help the United States as much as possible. He uses situational attributions to explain why he could not support the war and argues that Canada's diplomatic efforts failed due to lack of time. We also see, however, negative dispositional inferences being made about Americans. This demonstrates the shift from in-group to out-group.

For Martin, it is more difficult to ascertain when and whether the United States shifted from in-group to out-group. From the evidence, the most likely conclusion is that it shifted from in-group to out-group around the time of the Iraq invasion. However, Martin still views the United States as an ally and friend, and therefore provides situational attributions – such as institutional constraints and post-9/11 security concerns – for negative outcomes.

Conclusion

Tentatively speaking, Canada-US security relations in the years since 9/11 are consistent with a general proposition derived from attribution theory. Evidence from the memoirs of two Canadian prime ministers demonstrates attributions about Canadian actions and Canada-US relations that would be expected on the basis of the theory. An overall tendency exists, in particular, for the prime ministers to see their actions as highly constrained, whereas the conduct of their presidential counterpart stems more from disposition.

The analysis in this chapter is intended to advance the agenda of blending political psychology with foreign policy analysis in the context of North American relations. In pursuit of more rigorous testing, further research on Canada-US security relations should introduce additional primary sources. Noted already are the strengths and weaknesses of the memoirs produced by prime ministers. Opinion data should be a priority, in order to probe the views of the mass public in tandem with those of the prime ministers. It also would be valuable to engage in a parallel analysis of the American president and general public.

Appendix 1: Competing Attribution Theories

Attribution theory is one of the most dominant frameworks in social psychology.[62] Theoretical debates in this vast field are plentiful; these dialogues are referenced below when necessary.[63]

To understand Hamilton's framework, it is necessary to provide a brief overview of two competing theories: Jones and Davis's and Jones and McGillis's correspondent inference theory, and Ross's and Nisbett and Ross's formulation of attribution theory.[64] As an introduction, the most important contributions summarized in this appendix are identification of (1) correspondence bias as the tendency to infer dispositions from behaviour; and (2) the fundamental attribution error as the inclination to emphasize actor dispositions over situational determinants in accounting for choices made. In other words, people have a tendency to underestimate the degree to which decision making by others is constrained.

When an individual "infers another's personal dispositions directly from behaviour," a correspondent inference exists.[65] According to the original theory, unless highly normative or socially desirable, behaviour leads to dispositional inferences.[66] In those other cases, situational inferences are made. A later version of the theory replaced social desirability with expectations.[67] We only gain dispositional information from *unexpected* behaviours. Dispositional inferences are not causal.[68] However, if later asked to make a causal attribution about the act, the perceiver possesses an easily accessible explanation.[69] This leads us to the cornerstone of attribution theory: the fundamental attribution error.

While not within the original formulation of attribution theory, research on the fundamental attribution error has been some of the most dominant within the field.[70] The fundamental attribution error refers to the "tendency to attribute behavior exclusively to the actor's dispositions and to ignore powerful situational determinants of the behavior."[71] Since we are dealing with attributions, the perceiver is making a causal claim about the action. The resemblance criterion (or the representational heuristic) and the salience criterion (or the availability heuristic) are cognitive mechanisms that produce the fundamental attribution error.[72]

According to the resemblance criterion, when making causal judgments, people favour explanations that resemble the phenomenon to be explained.[73] Like all heuristics, such as the fundamental attribution error, the judgment may not be wrong in every case; however, we are predisposed toward certain judgments regardless of their validity. The representativeness heuristic can contribute to the fundamental attribution error in two ways. First, conceptually, since it is "the actor who does the acting," internal dispositions may seem more representative than situations.[74] Second, linguistically, words used to describe both actions and actors are often very similar.

People tend to explain events based largely on the most easily retrieved and salient explanations. This is identified by the salience criterion, or the availability heuristic.[75] In the case of the fundamental attribution error, this adds an important perceptual dynamic. The person doing the act is often the most available explanation due to the person's "perceptual proximity" to the action. However, the salience criterion is not purely perceptual. An explanation may be the most salient due to priming.

Appendix 2: Coalitions and the Minimal Group Paradigm

Coalitions are an ever-present aspect of human society. Whereas boundaries are largely culturally constructed, evolutionary psychologists argue that our encoding of group information is innate.[76] Beyond gender and age, which are automatic, our encoding of coalitional information is context-dependent. The ever-changing social context forces these systems to update appropriate coalitional cues. A person who may be part of our group in one context may be outside of it in another. This shift in membership may result from changes in the salience of issues within a given domain, or from changes in the salience of domains.

These findings raise two important questions: (1) How many different coalitions do we form? (2) What effect does the designation of coalitions have on behaviour? On the first point, the minimal group paradigm is instructive. Research shows that even arbitrary assignment to a group is sufficient to produce some degree of group identification.[77] Social identity theory developed from these findings.[78] Second, our designation of groups impacts upon our behaviour and our attributions. Findings on the minimal group paradigm show that individuals not only identify with their arbitrarily designated group but also confer preferential treatment on fellow members.[79] While most subjects in experimental studies allocate resources fairly among others when no group designation exists, these same participants discriminate in favour of members of their ingroup.[80] When given the choice between maximizing total allocations or maximizing allocations to members of their own group, individuals chose to favour their own groups.[81] The impact of coalitions on attributions is addressed after the basics of group attribution theory have been introduced.

Appendix 3: Group Attributions

People make correspondent inferences and attributions about the behaviours of (1) individuals *and* (2) groups and individuals within groups.[82] Allison and Messick propose that "just as people frequently use one group member's behavior to make generalizations about other members, they also tend to use a group decision or judgment as an indicator of members' attitudes."[83] Similar to the fundamental attribution error, individuals are predisposed toward making dispositional inferences or attributions when faced with the behaviour of out-group members, and toward making situational inferences and attributions about members of their in-group.

Paralleling the self-serving bias, researchers also have identified a group-serving bias.[84] According to these findings, failures are explained by situational factors and successes are accounted for using dispositional factors.

To return to the earlier question about the impact of the minimal group paradigm, identification with groups affects not only behaviour but also the manner in which inferences and attributions are made about members of the in-group and out-group.

NOTES

1 Brian Bow, *The Politics of Linkage: Power, Interdependence, and Ideas in Canada-US Relations* (Vancouver: UBC Press, 2009). On contemporary Canada-US relations, also consult John H. Thompson and Stephen J. Randall, *Canada and the United States: Ambivalent Allies,* 4th ed. (Athens: University of Georgia Press, 2008); and Patrick Lennox, *At Home and Abroad: The Canada-US Relationship and Canada's Place in the World* (Vancouver: UBC Press, 2009); recent works on various aspects of US foreign policy include Ralph G. Carter and James M. Scott, *Choosing to Lead: Understanding Congressional Foreign Policy Entrepreneurs* (Durham, NC: Duke University Press, 2009); and Stephen G. Walker and Akan Malici, *US Presidents and Foreign Policy Mistakes* (Stanford, CA: Stanford University Press, 2011).

2 See Chapters 1, 2, and 5 of this volume.

3 Political psychology is a vast and expanding field. Recent major surveys include Alex Mintz and Karl DeRouen Jr., *Understanding Foreign Policy Decision Making* (Cambridge: Cambridge University Press, 2010); and Stephen G. Walker, Akan Malici, and Mark Shafer, eds., *Rethinking Foreign Policy Analysis: States, Leaders, and the Microfoundations of*

Behavioral International Relations (New York and London: Routledge, 2011). For an example of the use of attribution theory in the field of international relations, see Jonathan Mercer, *Reputation and International Politics* (Ithaca, NY: Cornell University Press, 2006).

4   Michael Ross and Garth Fletcher, "Attribution and Social Perception," in *Handbook of Social Psychology*, vol. 2, ed. G. Lindzey and E. Aronson (New York: Random House, 1985), 73.

5   David L. Hamilton, "Dispositional and Attributional Inferences in Person Perception," in *Attribution and Social Interaction: The Legacy of Edward E. Jones*, ed. John M. Darley and Joel Cooper (Washington, DC: American Psychological Association, 1998).

6   An introduction to Jones and Davis's and Jones and McGillis's correspondent inference theory, and Nisbett and Ross's and Ross's formulation of attribution theory is provided in Appendix 1. Edward E. Jones and Keith E. Davis, "From Acts to Dispositions: The Attribution Process in Person Perception," in *Advances in Experimental Social Psychology*, vol. 2, ed. Leonard Berkowitz (New York: Academic Press, 1965); Edward E. Jones and Dan McGillis, "Correspondent Inference Theory and the Attribution Cube: A Comparative Reappraisal," in *New Directions in Attributional Research*, vol. 1, ed. John H. Harvey, William Ickes, and Robert Kidd (New York: Erlbaum, 1976); Richard Nisbett and Lee Ross, *Human Inference: Strategies and Shortcomings of Social Judgment* (Englewood Cliffs, NJ: Prentice Hall, 1980); and Lee Ross, "The Intuitive Psychologist and His Shortcomings: Distortions in the Attribution Process," in *Advances in Experimental Social Psychology*, vol. 10, ed. Leonard Berkowitz (New York: Academic Press, 1977).

7   Hamilton, "Dispositional and Attributional Inferences in Person Perception."

8   Ibid., 105.

9   Ibid., 106; David L. Hamilton, "Causal Attribution Viewed from an Information Processing Perspective," in *The Social Psychology of Knowledge*, ed. Daniel Bar-Tal and Arie W. Kruglanski (Cambridge: Cambridge University Press, 1988); Douglas S. Krull, "On Partitioning the Fundamental Attribution Error: Dispositionalism and the Correspondence Bias," in *Cognitive Social Psychology: The Princeton Symposium on the Legacy and Future of Social Cognition*, ed. Gordon B. Moscowitz (Mahwah, NJ: Lawrence Erlbaum Associates, 2001), 214.

10 Hamilton, "Dispositional and Attributional Inferences in Person Perception," 106.

11 Ibid., 109.

12 Considerable evidence also suggests that attributional thinking leads to dispositional attributions – ibid., 110; Edward E. Jones, *Interpersonal Perceptions* (New York: W.H. Freeman, 1990), and Ross, "The Intuitive Psychologist and His Shortcomings" – although many of these dispositional attributions will be the result of reflections upon the causes of expected events. The dispositional inference serves as a readily available explanation.

13 Roos Vonk, "Trait Inferences, Impression Formation, and Person Memory: Strategies in Processing Inconsistent Information about Persons," in *European Review of Social Psychology*, vol. 5, ed. Wolfgang Stroebe and Miles Hewstone (Chichester, UK: Wiley, 1994), 682.

14 Joel T. Johnson, John B. Jemmott III, and Thomas F. Pettigrew, "Causal Attribution and Dispositional Inference: Evidence of Inconsistent Judgments," *Journal of Experimental Social Psychology* 20, 6 (1984): 581.

15 Krull, "On Partitioning the Fundamental Attribution Error"; Hamilton, "Causal Attribution Viewed from an Information Processing Perspective"; Hamilton, "Dispositional and Attributional Inferences in Person Perception"; John N. Bassili, "Traits as Action Categories versus Traits as Person Attributes in Social Cognition," in *On-line Cognition in Person Perception*, ed. John N. Bassili (Hillsdale, NJ: Lawrence Erlbaum, 1989); and Johnson, Jemmott III, and Pettigrew, "Causal Attribution and Dispositional Inference."

16 Nisbett and Ross, *Human Inference*, 123.

17 Ibid.; Edward E. Jones and Richard Nisbett, "The Actor and the Observer: Divergent Perceptions of the Causes of Behavior," in *Attribution: Perceiving the Causes of Behavior*, ed. Edward E. Jones et al. (Morristown, NJ: General Learning Press, 1972).

18 Ross and Fletcher, "Attribution and Social Perception," 101.

19 Thomas C. Monson and Mark Snyder, "Actors, Observers, and the Attribution Process: Toward a Reconceptualization," *Journal of Experimental Social Psychology* 13 (1977): 89-111.

20 Results on the self-serving bias are some of the most replicated findings in social psychology; see Ross and Fletcher, "Attribution and Social Perception."

21 Ibid.; Dale T. Miller and Michael Ross, "Self-Serving Biases in the Attribution of Causality: Fact or Fiction?" *Psychological Bulletin* 82, 2 (1975): 213-25; and Ross, "The Intuitive Psychologist and His Shortcomings."

22 This leads to interesting questions about what to anticipate when an individual expects failure. The motivational explanations suggest that people will want to protect their self-esteem, but studies show that the self-serving bias only emerges when there is a threat to one's self-concept: Keith W. Campbell and Constantine Sedikides, "Self-Threat Magnifies the Self-Serving Bias: A Meta-Analytic Integration," *Review of General Psychology* 3, 1 (1999): 35. Expectations about outcome are one factor in threat to self (33-34). Moreover, the non-motivational explanation suggests that if people expect to fail, then they will blame their failure on dispositional factors. Yacoov Trope finds that people are interested in gaining as much information as possible about their abilities: "Uncertainty-Reducing Properties of Achievement Tasks," *Journal of Personality and Social Psychology* 37 (1979): 1505-18.

23 Hamilton, "Dispositional and Attributional Inferences in Person Perception."

24 See Appendix 2 for a discussion of in-groups and out-groups. Appendix 3 shows how correspondent inferences, attributions, and the self-serving bias operate at the group level.

25 The manner in which we make dispositional attributions makes it easy for individuals to be conflated with the state; see Philip E. Tetlock, "Social Psychology and World Politics," in *Handbook of Social Psychology*, ed. Daniel Gilbert, Susan Fiske, and Gardner Lindzey (New York: McGraw-Hill, 1998).

26 Two sources of expectations are identified in Jones and McGillis, "Correspondent Inference Theory and the Attribution Cube"; see also Ross and Fletcher, "Attribution and Social Perception," 76. Past behaviour by targets informs target-based expectancies, whereas knowledge about category or group membership informs category-based expectancies.

27 For a compelling study of US decision making in both Gulf wars, see Steve A. Yetiv, *Explaining Foreign Policy: US Decision-Making in the Gulf Wars*, 2nd ed. (Baltimore: Johns Hopkins University Press, 2011).

28 By holding affect as constant as possible, we can better evaluate the proposed theory in isolation.

29 See Appendix 1 for a brief discussion of the salience criterion.

30 Jean Chrétien, *My Years as Prime Minister* (Toronto: Vintage Books, 2008); Paul Martin, *Hell or High Water: My Life in and Out of Politics* (Toronto: McClelland and Stewart, 2008).

31 Chrétien, ibid., 409.

32 Ibid., 295.

33 Ibid. Later on the same page, interestingly enough, the prime minister recounts an exchange, reported to him in a letter, between a Canadian and an American houseguest in which the former assures the latter, "You would have done the same for us." According to the Canadian who sent in the letter, the American replied, "I only wish we would."

34 Ibid., 299.

35 Ibid., 299-300.

36 Ibid., 300-1.

37 For example, the new security-oriented legislation passed by the Chrétien government would be subject to review through a five-year sunset clause. Ibid., 301.

38 Ibid.

39 Ibid., 303.

40 Ibid.

41 Ibid., 304.

42 Ibid., 305.

43 Ibid., 310.

44 Ibid., 309.

45 Ibid.

46 Ibid., 314.

47 Ibid., 312-13.

48 Controversy emerged over modest but still visible forms of unofficial participation. Canada kept officers on exchange programs with participating states in place, so some Canadian Forces personnel did enter Iraq with US and British units. Canada also provided five ships, more than the three it contributed in the first Gulf War; this reflected the virtually inevitable blurring of the line between operations related to Afghanistan and Iraq more than anything else.

49 Chrétien, *My Years as Prime Minister,* 318.

50 Ibid., 317.

51 Ibid., 332.

52 Ibid., 302.

53 Martin, *Hell or High Water,* 384-85.

54 Ibid., 388.

55 Ibid., 389.

56 Ibid., 391-92.

57 Ibid., 394.

58 Ibid., 371.

59 Ibid., 374.

60 Ibid., 369, 374.

61 One example, regarding the border, is as follows: "No amount of infrastructure will compensate for a U.S. bureaucracy bent on protectionism under the guise of security." Ibid., 373.

62 Michael Ross and Garth Fletcher, "Attribution and Social Perception," in *Handbook of Social Psychology,* vol. 2, ed. G. Lindzey and E. Aronson (New York: Random House, 1985), 73. An attribution "refers to the linking of an event to its causes. [They] enable us to understand and react to our surroundings."

63 Some of the most important works and reviews in the field include: Fritz Heider, *The Psychology of Interpersonal Relations* (London: Lawrence Erlbaum Associates, 1958); Edward E. Jones and Keith E. Davis, "From Acts to Dispositions: The Attribution Process in Person Perception," in *Advances in Experimental Social Psychology,* vol. 2, ed. Leonard Berkowitz (New York: Academic Press, 1965); Edward E. Jones and Dan McGillis, "Correspondent Inference Theory and the Attribution Cube: A Comparative Reappraisal," in *New Directions in Attributional Research,* vol. 1, ed. John H. Harvey, William Ickes, and Robert Kidd (New York: Erlbaum, 1976); Harold H. Kelley, "Attribution Theory in Social Psychology," in *Nebraska Symposium on Motivation,* ed. David Levine (Lincoln: University of Nebraska Press, 1967); Harold H. Kelley, *Causal Schemata and the Attribution Process* (Morristown, NJ: General Learning Press, 1972); Harold H. Kelley, "The Processes of Causal Attribution," *American Psychologist* 28 (1973): 107-28; Richard Nisbett and Lee Ross, *Human Inference: Strategies and Shortcomings of Social Judgment* (Englewood Cliffs, NJ: Prentice Hall, 1980); and Lee Ross, "The

Intuitive Psychologist and His Shortcomings: Distortions in the Attribution Process," in *Advances in Experimental Social Psychology,* vol. 10, ed. Leonard Berkowitz (New York: Academic Press, 1977); Mervin Lerner, *The Belief in a Just World: A Fundamental Delusion* (New York: Plenum Press, 1980); Steven J. Heine and Darrin R. Lehman, "The Cultural Construction of Self-Enhancement: An Examination of Group-Serving Biases," *Journal of Personality and Social Psychology* 72, 6 (1997): 1268-83; Daniel T. Gilbert and Patrick S. Malone, "The Correspondence Bias," *Psychological Bulletin* 117 (1995): 21-38; David L. Hamilton, "Causal Attribution Viewed from an Information Processing Perspective," in *The Social Psychology of Knowledge,* ed. Daniel Bar-Tal and Arie W. Kruglanski (Cambridge: Cambridge University Press, 1988); David L. Hamilton, "Dispositional and Attributional Inferences in Person Perception," in *Attribution and Social Interaction: The Legacy of Edward E. Jones,* ed. John M. Darley and Joel Cooper (Washington, DC: American Psychological Association, 1998); Daniel T. Gilbert, "Thinking Lightly about Others: Automatic Components of the Social Inference Process," in *Unintended Thought,* ed. James S. Uleman and John A. Bargh (New York: Guilford Press, 1989); Daniel T. Gilbert, Brett W. Pelham, and Douglas S. Krull, "On Cognitive Busyness: When Person Perceivers Meet Persons Perceived," *Journal of Personality and Social Psychology* 54, 5 (May 1988): 733-40; and Yaacov Trope, "Identification and Inferential Processes in Dispositional Attribution," *Psychological Review* 93 (1986): 239-57. Within international relations, see Philip E. Tetlock, "Social Psychology and World Politics," in *Handbook of Social Psychology,* ed. Daniel Gilbert, Susan Fiske, and Gardner Lindzey (New York: McGraw-Hill, 1998); and Jonathan Mercer, *Reputation and International Politics* (Ithaca, NY: Cornell University Press, 2006).

64 Jones and Davis, "From Acts to Dispositions"; Jones and McGillis, "Correspondent Inference Theory"; Nisbett and Ross, *Human Inference;* Ross, "The Intuitive Psychologist and His Shortcomings."

65 Ross and Fletcher, "Attribution and Social Perception"; Jones and Davis, "From Acts to Dispositions."

66 Jones and Davis, ibid.

67 Jones and McGillis, "Correspondent Inference Theory"; Ross and Fletcher, "Attribution and Social Perception," 76.

68 Hamilton, "Dispositional and Attributional Inferences in Person Perception," 106-7; Douglas S. Krull, "On Partitioning the Fundamental Attribution Error: Dispositionalism and the Correspondence Bias," in *Cognitive Social Psychology: The Princeton Symposium on the Legacy and Future of Social Cognition,* ed. Gordon B. Moscowitz (Mahwah, NJ: Lawrence Erlbaum Associates, 2001), 213. As Krull notes, "this is not merely a semantic distinction. Both research and theory suggest that causal attributions and correspondent inferences are not the same type of judgment and are probably not drawn through the same mechanism."

69 Hamilton, "Dispositional and Attributional Inferences in Person Perception," 107.

70   In detailing the fundamental attribution error, Ross and Nisbett and Ross addressed
     what they felt to be weaknesses in Kelley's covariation model of attributions; see Ross,
     "The Intuitive Psychologist and His Shortcomings"; Nisbett and Ross, *Human Inference;*
     Kelley, "Attribution Theory in Social Psychology."

71   Nisbett and Ross, *Human Inference,* 31.

72   Ibid.; Ross and Fletcher, "Attribution and Social Perception," 82-83.

73   Nisbett and Ross, *Human Inference,* 115.

74   Ibid., 122.

75   Ibid.

76   Leda Cosmides, John Tooby, and Robert Kurzban, "Perceptions of Race," *Trends in
     Cognitive Sciences* 7, 4 (April 2003): 173-79.

77   Henri Tajfel, "Experiments in Intergroup Discrimination," *Scientific American* 223
     (1970): 96-102; Henri Tajfel, M.G. Billig, R.P. Bundy, and Claude Flament, "Social
     Categorization and Intergroup Behaviour," *European Journal of Social Psychology* 2 (1971):
     149-78; and Mark G. Frank and Thomas Gilovich, "The Dark Side of Self and Social
     Perception: Black Uniforms and Aggression in Professional Sports," *Journal of
     Personality and Social Psychology* 54 (1988): 74-83.

78   Henri Tajfel and John C. Turner, "An Integrative Theory of Intergroup Conflict," in
     The Social Psychology of Intergroup Relations, ed. W.G. Austin and S. Worchel (Monterey,
     CA: Brooks/Cole, 1979); and Henri Tajfel and John C. Turner, "The Social Identity
     Theory of Intergroup Behaviour," in *Psychology of Intergroup Relations,* ed. S. Worchel
     and W.G. Austin (Chicago: Nelson-Hall, 1986).

79   Tajfel, "Experiments in Intergroup Discrimination"; Tajfel, Billig, Bundy, and Flament,
     "Social Categorization and Intergroup Behaviour"; and Frank and Gilovich, "The Dark
     Side of Self and Social Perception."

80   Tajfel, "Experiments in Intergroup Discrimination," 101.

81   Ibid., 102.

82   Ruth Hamill, Timothy D. Wilson, and Robert E. Nisbett, "Insensitivity to Sample Bias:
     Generalizing from Atypical Cases," *Journal of Personality and Social Psychology* 39 (1980):
     578-89; Patricia W. Linville and Edward E. Jones, "Polarized Appraisals of Out-Group
     Members," *Journal of Personality and Social Psychology* 38 (1980): 689-703; Bernadette
     Park and Myron M. Rothbart, "Perception of Out-Group Homogeneity and Levels of
     Social Categorization: Memory for the Subordinate Attributes on In-Group and Out-
     Group Members," *Journal of Personality and Social Psychology* 42 (1982): 1051-68; Thomas
     F. Pettigrew, "The Ultimate Attribution Error: Extending Allport's Cognitive Analysis
     of Prejudice," *Personality and Social Psychology Bulletin* 5 (1979): 461-76; George A.
     Quattrone and Edward E. Jones, "The Perception of Variability within In-Groups and
     Out-Groups: Implications for the Law of Small Numbers," *Journal of Personality and
     Social Psychology* 38 (1980): 141-52; and Scott T. Allison and David M. Messick, "The
     Group Attribution Error," *Journal of Experimental Social Psychology* 21 (1985): 563-79.

83   Allison and Messick, "The Group Attribution Error," 564.

84   Donald M. Taylor and Janet R. Doria, "Self-Serving and Group-Serving Bias in Attribution," *Journal of Social Psychology* 113 (1981): 201-11; Donald M. Taylor and Vaishna Jaggi, "Ethnocentrism in a South Indian Context," *Journal of Cross-Cultural Psychology* 5, 2 (1974): 162-72.

5 Canada-US Security Cooperation under the Security and Prosperity Partnership

An Autopsy Report

JONATHAN PAQUIN AND LOUIS BÉLANGER

Launched with great fanfare by US President George Bush, Canadian Prime Minister Paul Martin, and Mexican President Vicente Fox in Waco, Texas, in 2005, the North American Security and Prosperity Partnership (SPP) faded away in 2008-09. The annual North American Leaders' Summit held in Guadalajara in August 2009 marked the end of this trilateral forum, although no official declarations to that effect were made by any of the leaders. The SPP simply ceased to exist. The question is why this regional cooperative mechanism, which gave political momentum to greater security and trade policy coordination among the three partners in the North American Free Trade Agreement (NAFTA), ended abruptly less than five years after its creation.

The objective of this chapter is to perform a political autopsy on the SPP by evaluating some theoretical arguments that could explain its demise. In accordance with this volume's theme, we focus our analysis on the SPP's performance as a tool for Canada-US cooperation in the security realm, and we only indirectly discuss trade issues and Mexico's involvement in the process.[1]

Hence, this chapter tackles some of the most important questions addressed in this book, such as how Canada and the United States can avoid irritants in their future relations, and how the tension between state autonomy and the desire for greater regional integration can be resolved. Before going further, we first set the political context in which the SPP came to existence and recall its key objectives.

An Agenda-Led Framework to Stimulate Policy Coordination

The SPP was a significant step forward in the regional dialogue on policy coordination following the terrorist attacks of September 11, 2001. Its objective was to keep North American borders closed to security threats while remaining open to the movement of legitimate people and goods. It merged initiatives taken under the 2001 Canada-US Smart Border Declaration and the 2002 US-Mexico Border Partnership Agreement, to which new initiatives were added resulting from two years of discussions leading up to its creation.

The SPP was essentially an agenda-led intergovernmental process. It was not a formal, legally binding agreement. The initial Waco joint declaration did not even mention the convening of regular summits in the future.[2] Decisions were subsequently made to convene in Cancún (2006), Montebello (2007), New Orleans (2008), and Guadalajara (2009). These agenda-setting summits at the presidential and prime ministerial level were supported by a loose structure of cabinet-level coordination, with one minister in each country responsible for each of two pillars, security and prosperity. The ministers initially came out with a report listing no less than three hundred security and trade elements that posed coordination problems. From that first "Report to Leaders," ten intergovernmental working groups for each of the security and the prosperity pillars of the SPP were established. In the words of Ackleson and Kastner, this overarching model of governmental negotiations was "a large politically-supported framework that (gave) structure and energy to smaller agency-to-agency projects, often in the regulatory realm, that (were) being undertaken by the three governments."[3] Security initiatives ranged from compatible screening of air travellers and the adoption of common visa standards to the establishment of data-sharing systems on high-risk travellers. During these years, Canada, the United States, and Mexico negotiated on a wide range of issues to establish a common security system to protect North America from external and internal threats. Table 5.1 presents the ten intergovernmental security committees with their respective initial regulatory initiatives. All these committees were placed under the authority of the Privy Council Office (PCO) in Canada, the Department of Homeland Security (DHS) in the United States, and the Presidencia de la Republica in Mexico. Because of space constraints, the table does not show the hundreds of security targets that stem from these initiatives.[4]

Coordination Failure and the Demise of the SPP: Three Explanations

What accounted for SPP coordination problems and for the partnership's demise in 2009? Are the factors leading to coordination failure the same as those responsible for the end of the SPP's administrative structure? Over the years, experts on North American politics have developed a series of arguments to capture the dynamic of Canada-US relations and to describe the evolution of intergovernmental relations within the SPP.

Forced Trilateralism

For many Canadian commentators, the trilateral nature of the SPP was an impediment, especially for the advancement of Canada-US cooperation. For former Canadian ambassador to the US Derek Burney, Mexican-American issues simply diverted the attention from Canadian-American ones during SPP meetings: "We are inevitably dragged into U.S.-Mexico issues as long as we pursue the trilateral approach. Whether immigration or drugs, their issues are quite different from our issues."[5] The core argument here, as synthesized by Jean Daudelin, is that there is simply no trilateral security agenda and that the management of the vital Canada-US relationship "should not be cluttered by the massive complexity of Mexico-U.S. affairs."[6] And without a clear common agenda, it is argued, the SPP could only break up into four overlapping processes – one for "Upper North America," one for "Lower North America," one for "Across North America," and eventually one for "Fly Over North America" – and become too heavy to manage.[7]

The fact that American and Canadian leaders have recently announced a plan to reignite much of the late SPP agenda under the now bilateral Shared Vision for Perimeter Security and Economic Competitiveness may well be interpreted as an acknowledgment on their part that trilateralism was not as productive as had been expected. On the other hand, one could argue that without Mexico on board, considering the growing political clout of the Mexican American community and the country's strategic geopolitical importance for the United States, the SPP would never have attracted the level of attention it received in Washington, from the White House down the ranks. It may be too early to compare the new bilateral initiative with the SPP on this account. So, one institutional feature of the SPP that may or may not explain its failure was its trilateral nature.

TABLE 5.1

The security pillar of the Security and Prosperity Partnership

Committee	Regulation initiatives
Traveller security	• Ensure equivalent biometric standards and systems (passports, visas, permanent resident cards) • Ensure compatible immigration security measures (visa decision-making standards) • Ensure compatibility of systems for sharing data on high-risk travellers
Cargo security	• Secure the supply chain of goods arriving in North America • Develop compatible standards, technologies, and processes for intermodal supply chain security • Ensure compatible national and international export control systems • Develop a plan to control the import and export of nuclear and radioactive materials
Bioprotection	• Engage in joint exercises within the public health and the food and agriculture systems • Ensure coordination in a cross-border emergency • Share strategies for the stockpiling and distribution of human and animal countermeasures • Implement a regime to identify, assess, and mitigate the risk of intentional threats to animals, plants, and food products • Develop information-sharing agreements on enforcement activities and emergencies • Enhance human, animal, and plant health surveillance to detect and monitor infectious diseases • Enhance public health surveillance research by linking public health laboratories with food and agriculture laboratory networks
Aviation security	• Establish comparable aviation passenger screening, and the screening of baggage and air cargo
Maritime security	• Secure ports and vessels through the conduct of equivalent threat, vulnerability, and risk assessments • Implement a compatible regulatory and operational maritime security regime

Law enforcement cooperation	• Improve information sharing and law enforcement cooperation among investigators and prosecutors to address illegal activities between ports of entry and cross-border organized crime, counterfeit goods, economic crimes, and trafficking of alcohol, firearms, illegal drugs and explosives • Review existing counterterrorism efforts and coordination to maximize effectiveness • Cooperate on issues of detention and removals to expedite the return of illegal migrants to their home countries
Intelligence cooperation	• Enhance capacity to combat terrorism through the appropriate sharing of terrorist watchlist data
Protection, prevention, and response	• Develop and implement compatible protective and response strategies and programs for shared critical infrastructure in mutually agreed priority areas (e.g., electricity generation and distribution, oil and gas pipelines, dams, telecommunications, transportation, nuclear, radiological, defence industrial base, and cyber systems) • Cooperate on incident response, and conduct joint training and exercises in emergency response
Border facilitation	• Improve the efficiency of existing border infrastructure and reduce transit times by expanding low-risk facilitation programs such as NEXUS, SENTRI, and FAST • Work with the private sector, states, and provinces, as well as local governments, to construct new border infrastructure to meet long-term demand, including building of a low-risk port of entry to expedite the secure movement of cargo across the border
Science and technology cooperation	• Continue incorporating hi-tech equipment along the US–Mexico border for the efficient and secure flow of people and goods, and continue identifying appropriate sites for its deployment • Establish a joint research and development program for security-related science and technology based on priorities established through a coordinated risk assessment

Source: Adapted from Government of Canada, "Security and Prosperity Partnership of North America: Secure North America from External Threats," http://www.spp-psp.gc.ca/.

Inadequate Institutional Design

An institutional feature of the SPP that commentators have considered problematic was its location within the executive branch of each state.[8] According to Anderson and Sands, this could only fuel the suspicion of the US Congress and constituted a "tragic flaw in the SPP," representing "the biggest threat to [its] continuation."[9] While these authors primarily insist on the fact that the absence of involvement on the part of the legislative branches posed a problem because "funding domestic and border security requires congressional appropriations, and falls under congressional oversight scrutiny,"[10] others suggest that it contributed to a lack of transparency and accountability that irrevocably corrupted the image of the SPP in public opinion.[11] With no support from Congress, concludes Alexander Moens, the SPP project was doomed to fail.[12] Conversely, Louis Bélanger argues that executive-level agency-to-agency cooperation is the dominant channel used by states to achieve efficient regulatory coordination in Europe and elsewhere. There is therefore nothing unique or exceptional in the SPP design.[13] But Bélanger has also found that successful regulatory cooperation ultimately depends on the amount of regulatory power vested in the involved agencies in each state, and that a lack of such authority, particularly on the security side of the SPP, may have impeded its capacity to meet the original objectives.

Even when states cooperate within the perimeter of their respective executive authorities, they can commit themselves through legally binding obligations. In the United States, the government routinely engages in "sole executive" international agreements that do not require congressional ratification.[14] The SPP was kept a "soft," non–legally binding cooperation mechanism. According to Debra P. Steger, since the working groups and the ministerial meetings had no legal authority to decide on joint regulations and to monitor their implementation, they could not ultimately achieve their mandate.[15] So, the basic question here remains: to what extent, considering the North American context, was the non-treaty, executive-to-executive cooperation scheme devised for the SPP adequate for the task?

Asymmetry and Distributional Conflicts

The kind of security coordination the SPP was designed to achieve – that is, at the regulatory standards level – typically involves distributive conflicts, which are particularly acute when power asymmetry enters into the mix. Adopting new security standards is generally costly for states to implement and for firms and individuals to comply with, and the benefits achieved by the new common standards can vary significantly between parties in a cooperative agreement. Each state will therefore attempt to minimize its adaptation costs by trying to negotiate international standards that closely resemble its own while forcing others to absorb most of the costs by making most of the adjustments.[16] In other words, every player in this game will want to play the role of norms exporter and leave the role of norms importer to the others. Asymmetry can make the conflict particularly difficult to resolve because the stronger state can legitimately expect that the attractiveness of its large economic market should naturally lead its partners to import its standards and adapt. If a political negotiation occurs, it is presumably because, for different reasons, this "natural" process of harmonious adjustments has not played out.[17] Negotiation is difficult because while the larger state can obtain some level of favourable regulatory convergence without coordination (it has "go-it-alone power"), the less powerful state usually cannot do so and thus finds itself vulnerable to making concessions, which may be difficult to sell to a domestic audience.[18]

Many of the Canadian critics of the SPP and of greater security cooperation with the United States have articulated arguments coherent with this view that may in retrospect explain its ultimate failure. Bruce Campbell, the director of the Canadian Centre for Policy Alternatives, stated before the House of Commons Standing Committee on International Trade: "Given the huge power imbalance between Canada and the U.S., I can't help but think that harmonization means, in most cases, that Canada will bend its regulations or simply adopt U.S. federal regulations."[19] Stephen Clarkson maintains that the terrorist attacks of 9/11 ultimately served Washington's desire to strengthen continental integration and to minimize Canada's ability to adopt distinctive security policies.[20] Janine Brodie makes a similar contention and claims that the Bush administration played the economic prosperity card to obtain a counterpart agreement that integrates US security norms.[21] These authors appear to assume that the Chrétien and the Martin government were ready to concede almost everything in order to keep the US border open to Canadian exports, but perhaps it was not. Perhaps the SPP experiment failed due to irreconcilable conflicts over the distribution of the costs and benefits of policy coordination.

Distributional conflicts can be exacerbated by nationalist sentiments among the domestic constituencies of the less powerful. According to Joseph Nye, the Canadian-American case could be the perfect illustration of how "under conditions of great asymmetry," nationalistic reactions seriously limit the capacity of states to negotiate "norms and institutions to cope with interdependence among advanced international societies."[22]

Charles Doran developed this argument at length in *Forgotten Partnership*: Canada suffers from sovereignty and identity insecurity vis-à-vis its superpower neighbour, and thus reacts autarkically when the United States proposes to negotiate common norms and policies.[23] Clearly, nationalism did not prevent the Canadian government from embarking on the SPP initiative. But what the literature suggests is that nationalism in Canada makes the government hypersensitive to distributive issues. If this is the case, then the SPP's chances of success may have been particularly dim; asymmetry would make the more powerful expect the less powerful to assume a larger share of the costs, and the less powerful to reject such an uneven outcome.

Gathering Information

From a methodological point of view, the fact that the SPP was limited in time and that it is no longer active provides an opportunity to take a step back to reflect on its dynamic, achievements, and failure. However, the main obstacle that we encountered in our investigation was the lack of transparency and detailed media coverage of SPP negotiations. The five annual SPP summits, held in Waco, Cancún, Montebello, New Orleans, and Guadalajara, were all covered and amply discussed by media and pundits, but very little is known about the actual discussions on the security and economic initiatives that took place under the SPP. A search by key words in the archives of the main Canadian and American newspaper websites shows that very few articles addressed the discussions and debates on the main security initiatives.

Despite this difficulty, we managed to conduct interviews with current and former US and Canadian officials who were involved in the creation and management of the SPP to assess the validity of the different arguments delineated above.[24] These officials worked for the DHS, Public Safety Canada, the Canada Border Services Agency (CBSA), and the PCO. The list of interviewees was generated in a two-step process. First, the compilation was based on information found in internal documents, disclosed following several Freedom of Information Act (FOIA) requests to the US federal government by Judicial Watch, and cross-checked against agency websites, organizational charts, and directories. We also relied on the so-called snowball sampling strategy to collect additional contact information. We created an initial sample of individuals and asked each of them to provide additional names of current and former officials who might be relevant for the subject. This sampling technique was useful since the population of cases (i.e., the population of US and Canadian officials involved in the creation and management of the SPP) was initially hidden from us. Second, the list was generated by the rate of positive responses (57 percent) that we received after sending interview requests.[25]

We conducted ten semi-structured phone interviews, all of which followed a protocol designed to facilitate respondents' assessment of the theoretical arguments and to allow for comparison of answers. Interviews lasted one hour on average and, with one exception,[26] were recorded and transcribed. Despite the fact that government officials are not objective actors, we found a high level of convergence in the assessment of several of the arguments presented in the previous section of this chapter. So, what did we learn from the analysis?

Assessing Theoretical Explanations

Before the different arguments are assessed, one general observation should be made. The information gathered during interviews clearly suggests that both the United States and Canada had common interests under the SPP, but that their preferences were differently ordered. The American government feared further terrorist attacks and was deeply concerned with security regulations. As for the Canadian government, it feared that a "thicker" border could seriously jeopardize the Canadian economy at a time when over 80 percent of Canada's exports were going to the United States. Our investigation revealed a consensus among interviewed officials that the United States and Canada had to strengthen security harmonization because their economy and security were interconnected. At the political level, however, tensions were sometimes perceptible because the "political space" for negotiations did not always match. The president of the United States and the prime minister of Canada had different political constraints and different constitutions, legal systems, identities, and policies to deal with. Thus, the level of security coordination fluctuated on a case-by-case basis, depending on the issues addressed and on whether their political spaces were aligned.

Was Trilateralism a Problem?

According to a Canadian official who was in charge of most of the border security initiatives from 2005 to 2008, no less than 95 percent of the SPP discussions were conducted in two bilateral forums.[27] The interviewees were unanimous that there was a lot of artificiality in the trilateral nature of the SPP. We were reminded that the initiative encouraged both bilateral and trilateral discussions, so that the SPP was not even conceived as a strictly trilateral mechanism. Trilateral talks were rare and usually occurred once Canada-US and Mexico-US security agreements had been settled. This was a logical way of proceeding since Canada, the United

States, and Mexico faced different security issues, had different perceptions of security threats, and therefore had different interests and needs.
This goes back to the idea that the political spaces of North American
leaders were not always aligned. The SPP was therefore a sort of double
competitive bilateral forum instead of a trilateral dialogue, since there
was no clear common agenda.[28] But was it a problem? For Canadians, of
course, a lot of time was wasted just being in the room while Mexico-US
issues were discussed. However, one key architect of the SPP on the Canadian side was of the opinion that there would have been no SPP without Mexico because Canada alone would not have been able to attract the
necessary level of political attention from the US side.[29] Our investigation therefore suggests that although the trilateral nature of the SPP was a
source of frustration, it was also a precondition for its mere existence.

Was the Institutional Design a Problem?

The fact that the SPP was an executive-to-executive type of agreement
was rejected as a factor responsible for the lack of interministerial coordination or for the demise of the trilateral forum. The objectives of the
SPP could all have been achieved through executive agreements, and its
field of action did not require congressional or legislative action. In fact,
the idea that the SPP was too limited in scope because its negotiating power was vested in the hands of the executive branches, and that it could
not achieve enough without the involvement of the US Congress and the
Canadian Parliament was seen as an insignificant factor at best, if not as
a false argument. Rather, interviewees indicated that the flexibility of this
non-legalistic forum stimulated ministerial-level coordination among the
working groups and did not impede the SPP's capability to meet its original objectives. As an American official pointed out, once you get a congressional legal agreement, "negotiations become cumbersome and not
particularly efficient."[30] Moreover, an executive mechanism appeared to
be the only option since a treaty-based accord would have required the
approval of the US Senate; thus the Bush administration did not have the
political appetite to turn the SPP into a treaty.

    As for the "soft," non–legally binding nature of the SPP, officials on
the US side considered it a significant factor explaining the SPP's demise.
First, they pointed out that legally binding agreements usually come with
more resources and with annual reporting requirements. Without these,
mere political agreements are no more than engagements between the
willing that are difficult to sustain over time.[31] Second, the officials com-
plained about the lack of clear authority for the agencies concerned to
approve and implement decisions taken at the working group level. As

a result, there was no hierarchical treatment and monitoring of the literally hundreds of security initiative targets, which made the intergovernmental dialogue cumbersome and complex.[32] As one American official pointed out, "I remember endless large reports on progress on SPP initiatives. Committee members tried to break them down so they would have numbers like 2.1.3.2, which meant goal 2, initiative 1, sub-initiative 3, and task 2. After a while, we just kind of lost it. When you're prioritizing everything, you're prioritizing nothing."[33] Moreover, neither the minister of public safety nor the DHS secretary had full authority to implement all of these initiatives of the security pillar. This led to interagency discussions and frictions that created a major challenge for the SPP.[34] As a result, the original SPP expectations expressed by the North American leaders in 2005 were quickly dashed by the ponderousness of the process and the paucity of concrete results.

A third problem can be linked to the non-binding nature of the SPP. All interviewed officials claimed that the change of government in Ottawa, Washington, and Mexico City ultimately explains why the SPP faded away. Yet this effect was precisely linked to the fact that the SPP was not a legally binding accord. When such an agreement is essentially dependent on the renewed commitment of the executive members of a government, it is regarded as the policy of a given leader, not as a legally embedded regime of cooperation that must be sustained. In the case of the SPP, its existence depended on the will of the North American leaders who were in power in 2005, and was therefore highly vulnerable to government change. Indeed, Canadian and American officials all mentioned that the change of governments in the three countries between January 2006 and January 2009 was a central cause of the SPP's demise. Although the new leaders recognized the importance of the SPP, it was not their own initiative and did not have their imprimatur. One American official stated: "These initiatives kind of get tagged against a particular government and then when someone new is elected, the new people want to make new announcements, new programs, and new initiatives."[35] The Obama administration, for instance, lost interest in the way the SPP conducted its dialogue, and the Harper government wanted to focus on a shorter list of priorities to achieve greater results.[36]

In sum, the executive nature of the SPP was not an obstacle to security coordination between Canada and the United States, and its design provided the necessary flexibility to respond to the security challenges of the post-9/11 era. The input and oversight of the US Congress and the Canadian Parliament would not have strengthened the negotiating process but would have made it more cumbersome. By limiting the SPP to a non-binding agreement, however, the Bush administration and the Martin government planted the seeds of its demise, since this trilateral forum was unable to sustain itself in its original form under new governments.

The Effect of Asymmetric Relations

The power asymmetry between Canada and the United States has always been a reality. The question for us here is whether this structural dynamic impacted the way the costs of new security standards were distributed between the two states. What should be evaluated is whether uneven distributions in the costs and benefits of adopting shared security standards gave rise to incompatible negotiating objectives between the two states.

The first point stressed during the interviews is that the Canadian government embarked fully on the SPP initiative, which shows that it accepted the underlying power structure. Ottawa could have rejected the adjustment costs of greater security harmonization, but instead chose the economic benefits of integration. Indeed, in the years following 9/11, the reality of economic survival has compelled Ottawa to harmonize its security norms with those of the United States as much as possible. But this does not mean that security measures were all decided in Washington and imported into Canada; in fact, some regulatory measures were developed in Canada and then adopted by Washington.[37] For instance, the NEXUS program was initiated by the Canada Border Services Agency to reduce border clearance time by preapproving low-risk travellers crossing the border via land, air, and marine ports. The Free and Secure Trade (FAST) program, which pre-clears commercial truck drivers crossing the border, is another Canada-initiated program. These security measures, which also include the preliminary analysis of air passengers, were developed by Canadians and became binational once adopted by the US government. These programs were eventually improved under the SPP and led to greater security and trade.[38] This finding reinforces the claim of André Donneur and Valentin Chirica that bilateral security measures adopted in the years following the 2001 terrorist attacks were not imposed by Washington but were often made in Canada.[39] It is also in accordance with Von Hlatky and Trisko's point that "the underlying distribution of capabilities cannot predict which partner will drive the agenda."[40] Moreover, according to one Canadian official who was directly involved in the creation of the SPP, security harmonization was not a top priority of the Bush administration. Once the initial shock of 9/11 passed, Canada had to take the initiative and design a harmonization process. "We wrote most of the SPP statement and then the White House touched it up at the end, to make it look very presidential. But we had to do most of the work because it was not urgent for the U.S."[41]

What this investigation suggests is that the SPP experiment did not fail as a result of irreconcilable conflicts over the distribution of the costs and benefits of policy coordination. Although important financial resources were used on the Canadian side, the costs of harmonization were ultimately higher for the United States in both absolute and relative terms. The US created the massive Department of Homeland Security with more than 200,000 employees, and spent hundreds of billions of dollars to protect its territory from terrorist attacks. These resources were expended to increase the level of security, whereas security investments in Canada were a prerequisite for greater and faster cross-border trade with the United States. Although Canada's security budget increased significantly under the SPP to enable Public Safety Canada, the CBSA, and the Canadian Security Intelligence Service (CSIS) to implement better security initiatives, this was compensated by greater fluidity at the border.[42] In the post-9/11 context, distributive issues did not lead to a one-way importation of norms from the United States to Canada. Rather, it forced Canadian agencies to use their imagination to promote new security norms to reassure American officials and prevent the border from becoming "thicker."

Interviews also suggest that Charles Doran's and Joseph Nye's arguments – according to which, under conditions of great asymmetry, the nationalist reaction of the weaker partner might seriously limit the capacity of states to negotiate and harmonize their policies – does have some validity in the context of the SPP. For instance, based on US accounts, Canadian national pride slowed down the adoption of common critical infrastructure protection measures at the border because they had been developed and paid for by the DHS.[43] Some Canadian officials make similar arguments. The Canadian government could have gone further if the nationalist dimension had been absent. Canada would have progressed more, for instance, if it had harmonized its visa and immigration policies with those of the Americans. This would have meant adopting the same visa restrictions for foreigners and the same security clearance for immigrants, but this is something that the Canadian government was not willing to do, for political reasons.[44]

Our investigation suggests, however, that it would be incorrect to conclude that national pride, as a reflection of Canadian political vulnerability, was the only cause of coordination problems. Although Canadian officials recognized that nationalism tainted political discussions in Ottawa and that Paul Martin's Liberal caucus was particularly driven by nationalist feelings, the deceleration of the security harmonization process was also caused by legal and constitutional issues. The Canadian Charter of Rights and Freedoms and the Office of the Privacy Commissioner of Canada created some of the obstacles to greater harmonization, over issues such as security pre-clearance, information sharing, and compatible immigration measures. Canadian legal and value systems probably accounted for more friction and irritants than blunt national insecurity on the part of the Canadian government. These issues will be discussed in more detail in the next section.

The last observation in connection with the asymmetric burden refers to the issue of linkage theory. Linkage is a bargaining situation where states make benefits in one area of bilateral cooperation dependent on negotiation results in another sector. It is a tool used by powerful states to influence the behaviour of other states in one political domain by threatening to change behaviour and preferences in another domain. Yet, as Keohane and Nye argued more than thirty years ago, in a world of complex interdependence in which free trade, multinational corporations, and international organizations define international relations, linkage politics is more difficult to carry out since states have a limited control over sectoral agendas. Canada-US relations have often been described as non-linkage relations that reflect a high level of complex interdependence.[45]

Yet, one of our findings is that linkage politics did come into play to a certain degree during the SPP negotiations, which goes against this conventional wisdom. Although Canada-US cooperation was relatively good overall, the Bush administration had reached a point where no risk was acceptable, and was therefore reluctant to address trade impediments without first settling border security issues. As an American official put it: "From my perspective at DHS, where we were focused on border principally, linkage was inextricable and inevitable and was quite right. Security and prosperity are deeply linked at the border."[46] Hence, the post-9/11 context naturally linked security and trade issues. Linkage was not politically expressed but the context compelled the Canadian government to align its security policies with those of the United States in order to maximize trade relations with that country.[47] The security and prosperity pillars of the SPP were communicating vessels, and Canada was willing to make investments in the security sector in exchange for payoffs in the economic realm.

As a Canadian official recalls:

The impact of the slowdown in commercial transaction at the border (following 9/11) was enormous for Canada. Each time the US adopted new security measures, they produced negative impacts on the fluidity at the border. We were "terrorized" and therefore we had to follow the US on security measures since 83% of our exports were going to the United States. So, we sought to develop ways to meet US objectives while facilitating trade.[48]

These security imperatives did not mean, however, that Washington was explicitly looking for trade-offs. Rather, the guiding principle was to promote and maximize both security and prosperity. Hence, linkage was not so much a negotiating strategy as a structural reality in the post-9/11 context. "I would not talk about linkage per se," indicated a Canadian official. "I would rather talk about building blocks. What can lead to greater economic facilitation? I would say that it is security prerequisites."[49]

Coordination and Irritants in the Security Working Groups

What was the level of coordination and norm production in the ten security working groups of the SPP? Without providing a definitive answer to this question, our investigation sheds light on the key committees.

Coordination within the *traveller security* committee was inconsistent and difficult at the political level. The main stumbling block was immigration standards. Issues concerning immigration illustrate why several Canada-US initiatives failed. The US government sought compatible immigration security measures with Canada, such as same security clearance standards for immigrants and common visa restrictions, but Ottawa was reluctant to agree to such harmonization as a matter of political values and national interests. For instance, negotiations on common visa regulations were a source of irritants. Washington wanted Ottawa to align the latter's visa waiver program with its own. However, there is a significant difference in how both programs operate. In the US, the program is statutory and there is little political discretion. In Canada, the visa waiver program is more administrative and gives the minister of immigration more discretion.[50] For instance, South Koreans need a visa to travel to the United States but not to Canada. Although South Koreans tried for a long time to avail of the US visa waiver program, Seoul could never meet its statutory requirements, whereas it was economically important for Canada to keep South Korea on *its* program. From the point of view of the US government, this gap between the two programs raises security issues. As a former DHS official pointed out: "Certain people will attempt to get into the country that does require a visa via the country that does not. And we had some evidence that South Koreans were being smuggled into the United States via Canada."[51] In addition, even if the US had wanted to

adjust its visa waiver program to Canadian standards, the executive officials at the SPP table could not take such a step since a change in the visa
waiver list of countries requires the approval of Congress. This highlights
the limit of executive-to-executive cooperation schemes when it involves
agencies that do not have sufficient autonomous regulatory power. Thus,
under the SPP, Ottawa and Washington worked hard to harmonize their
visa requirements but ultimately failed to achieve identical visa standards
because their interests did not match and because the US agencies participating in the working groups did not have the appropriate rule-making
authority.

Coordination of *aviation security* was also tough. Sharing lists of Canadian passengers travelling by air to the United States and of US passengers
going to Canada was not a problem, as sovereign states can require information on travellers landing in their territory. Aviation security became
a burning issue, however, when the DHS and the Transportation Security
Administration (TSA) asked Canadian airlines to hand over personal
information of passengers on flights crossing US airspace to southern destinations and on domestic flights going through US airspace from one
Canadian city to another without landing in the United States.[52] Since terrorists do not always intend to land, as 9/11 has shown, the US government wanted to have the full picture of all foreigners entering its airspace
to identify potential terrorist threats. According to Canadian officials, the
US government was determined to forbid access to US airspace to Canadian airlines that refused to comply. The Air Transport Association of
Canada (ATAC) opposed this measure because it would have had serious business consequences for the industry. The Canadian government,
specifically Public Safety Canada and the Office of the Privacy Commissioner of Canada, had strong concerns and found it unreasonable of the
United States to demand lists of Canadian citizens flying point-to-point in
Canada. The issue posed a real dilemma between risk assessment on the
one hand and Canadians' privacy rights on the other, and created frustration on both sides of the border.[53]

According to a DHS official, other issues unrelated to aviation, such
as the Maher Arar case and the Omar Khadr saga at the detention camp
in Guantánamo Bay, led the Canadian government to be more cautious
and reluctant to share information with the US government.[54] Another
interesting part of the puzzle was that, on the US side, the "secure flight"
program is a congressionally mandated one in which the DHS exerts limited discretionary regulatory authority.[55] Ultimately, the Canadian government yielded and Canadian airlines now share their passenger lists
with US agencies when flying over American airspace. Ottawa came to this

decision to limit the negative economic consequences for Canadian airlines, despite concerns over privacy issues.[56] There is now one integrated measure for Canadian passengers going to or flying over the United States. As this case shows, privacy issues, institutional differences, and a lack of trust over information sharing gave rise to several irritants over aviation security. Interestingly, the limited manoeuvre room of the relevant US agency appears to have convinced Canadians of the immutability of the American position.

One of the biggest challenges in security coordination arose in the *border facilitation* working group, which was negotiating a reciprocal agreement to exchange customs and immigration officers at the border to perform land pre-clearance. Under the SPP, both governments worked on a pilot project to transfer US border agents across the Peace Bridge that connects Buffalo, New York, to Fort Erie, Ontario. The DHS insisted, however, that armed US border patrols be permitted to perform their duties in the pre-clearance area on the Canadian side.[57] Ottawa was reluctant to have unarmed CBSA agents working with armed US border patrols in Canada, but agreed in 2006 to equip its 4,800 border officers at land and marine ports of entry with firearms.[58] Public Safety Canada continued to worry that the pre-clearance agreement would raise Charter issues in Canada, and indeed the establishment of a US pre-clearance zone in Fort Erie where armed US border patrols would perform their duties raised a series of legal questions in Ottawa. The main issue had to do with whether US agents would have the right to detain Canadian citizens in the pre-clearance zone, which was located on Canadian territory.[59] The DHS eventually withdrew from pre-clearance negotiations with Canada. Washington had asked for a "full force and effect clause" in the agreement, and unless it had all the powers and rights to perform its duties in the pre-clearance zone, the DHS was not willing to continue negotiations because of the potential risk to US homeland security. Despite these problems, the border facilitation working group was successful on other issues – for example, displaying great coordination in establishing a series of measures to reduce transit times at the border. Indeed, the NEXUS and FAST programs were developed and adopted by the border facilitation committee and significantly improved cross-border trade.

The committee on *law enforcement cooperation* faced issues similar to those faced by the aviation and traveller security committees. The main problem lay in the legal differences over information sharing. The sharing of private information on Canadian citizens remained a big issue and the Maher Arar case had a major impact, especially on the issue of extradition.[60]

The mission of the *protection, prevention, and response* committee was to develop shared critical infrastructure programs on energy and telecommunications, among other things, to effectively respond to emergency situations. However, this committee never really took shape. According to a former DHS official, it met only once, during its inauguration in 2005, and never again because Public Safety Canada did not want to engage in a formal discussion. The nominal reason was that "there was a political election at the horizon, the Canadian government was near term, Public Safety Canada could not commit to anything because the politics was nebulous. Or, there was a reorganization excuse, such as we just activated Public Safety Canada. So, there was always either a political election that caused the delay or there was a reorganizational issue."[61]

Coordination of *maritime security* issues was much more successful. The adoption of equivalent threat and security assessments in ports and ships as well as the implementation of a common maritime security regime were quickly achieved. The US coast guards took the lead on these issues since they had already adopted security norms prior to the SPP and had the resources to implement their programs. Throughout the negotiations, they worked with their Canadian counterparts and the Canadian government adopted US norms and adjusted its programs to them.[62] This coordination was not politically sensitive in Canada and did not necessitate major administrative changes. One program consisted of sending Canadian and American representatives to foreign ports to clear commercial goods before they entered North American ports.

From the SPP to the Beyond the Border Action Plan

What we have learned about the SPP from our interviews can inform an early prognosis of the chances of success of the more recent Canada-US Perimeter Security and Economic Competitiveness (PSEC) initiative announced in 2011. This new cooperative mechanism serves objectives similar to those of the SPP and shares many of its key features except for its membership (it is a bilateral process instead of a trilateral one) and its political boldness (it is managed by one committee at the assistant secretary/assistant deputy minister level instead of the SPP's hierarchy of cabinet-level coordination and bureaucratic working groups).

What does not seem to have impeded negotiation among SPP partners is the potentially conflictual distribution of adjustment costs that unequal powers must face when they want to harmonize their security standards and policies. Canadian negotiators were confident that these costs would be compensated by the economic benefits of a more fluid trade relationship. As for the PSEC, a look at its first action plan shows that the Canadian government has conceded up front that it would mainly align itself with US regulations. For example, it has already been determined that Canada will adopt an exit information system at its borders similar to the US one, something Ottawa had previously refused to do.[63] Canada will also implement an electronic system for travel authorization of visa-exempt nationals that will "mirror measures taken in the United States."[64] "Canada also will implement an enhanced, scenario-based passenger targeting methodology consistent with the U.S. methodology."[65] Canada will "align with U.S. existing investments" at border crossings.[66] Canada will align its value threshold for exemption from NAFTA's certificate of origin with the US one.[67] Canada will adopt the standards of the Council of Europe Convention on Cybercrime, to which the United States, but not Canada, is already a party.[68] On the other hand, nowhere in the action plan is it stated that the United States will adopt a Canadian standard.

Officials told us that the framing of the SPP as an executive-to-executive instrument of cooperation was not an impediment in itself as long as the participating agencies were vested with sufficient discretionary authority. The PSEC seems to confirm that a lot can be achieved at the executive level, as exemplified by the recent adoption of the Immigration Information Sharing Treaty, an executive-to-executive agreement that will soon govern the systematic exchange of information between the two administrations on third-country applicants for visa, travel permit, and in-land asylum.[69] However, we saw in cases such as the SPP discussions on the visa waiver programs and the no-fly lists that the US negotiators insisted that the two countries harmonize their practices but had been unable to make concessions because of inflexible statutes passed by Congress. There is a risk that the relatively low level of executive discretion vested in US agencies responsible for domestic security will remain a problem with the PSEC.[70] This gives the US side a typical "Putnamian" negotiation advantage that Canada may or may not find acceptable.[71]

The officials we interviewed were confident that the SPP could produce significant results despite its non–legally binding nature, but they conceded that it was extremely difficult to sustain the kind of cooperation they envisioned without legal commitments, especially when governments change. We were also told that legal terms of reference would have provided the SPP with clearer designation of authorities responsible for the implementation and monitoring of decisions reached at working group level, and may have prevented the SPP from developing an array of non-hierarchized initiatives. It is perfectly clear, however, that the two governments have no intention of seeing the PSEC evolve in a legally binding cooperative instrument. A preliminary comment, found in the first pages of the PSEC Action Plan, states unequivocally: "Nothing in this action plan is intended to give rise to rights or obligations under domestic or international law; this action plan is not intended to constitute an international treaty under international law."[72] Moreover, the political commitment undertaken by President Obama and Prime Minister Harper in February 2011 has a lifespan of only three years, "with the expectation of continuation."[73] There is a risk, therefore, that the PSEC will face the same sustainability issues that undermined the SPP.

Monitoring of the implementation of the PSEC Action Plan will be ensured by an executive steering committee formed at the assistant secretary/assistant deputy minister level, which will submit an annual public report.[74] This would be an improvement over the SPP process, which stopped issuing public implementation reports after the first year. It is also interesting to note that the steering committee will deal with security issues only. For its part, the economic pillar of the Beyond the Border initiative falls under the responsibility of a regulatory cooperation council, operating under distinct terms of reference that essentially defer to the judgment and expertise of regulatory authorities on both sides of the border.[75] Thus, there is a slight relaxation of the linkage found in the SPP, where the security and the economic working groups had to work and report almost synchronically. Practitioners told us that the linkage under the SPP made sense since prosperity and security issues are effectively meshed together at the border. The new initiative maintains the linkage, but adapts the process to the different regulatory environments.

The SPP Autopsy Report

Discussions on security regulation neither began nor ended with the SPP. This trilateral forum was, however, an important link in the long chain of security coordination that marked the last decade. As indicated at the outset of this chapter, the SPP was a strategy designed by North American leaders to generate political momentum for security and economic priorities. The momentum eventually faded, and the trilateral form was abandoned.

Several main irritants in Canada-US security relations will need to be resolved to improve the future of the bilateral relationship. A central issue faced by the Canadian government throughout all the SPP discussions and coordination work was the dilemma involving its economic calculation (prosperity) and its values, laws, and principles (sovereignty). The government's sensitivity to the potential erosion of Canada's sovereignty certainly hindered coordination under the SPP. More specifically, legal and constitutional issues, such as those concerning immigration policies and information sharing, were partly responsible for coordination failure and prevented greater harmonization between the two countries.

As for the demise of the SPP, the attractiveness of the large US economic market did lead the Canadian government to favour greater security harmonization, and the SPP did not fail because of irreconcilable conflicts over the costs of policy coordination. Rather, the SPP's institutional design itself was the biggest problem; indeed, the initiative's non-legal nature almost guaranteed that it would not survive the change of government on both sides of the border. Lack of focus, the overwhelming number of security initiatives and sub-initiatives, and the differing realities and needs of the three North American partners also contributed to its demise.

NOTES

1 The authors would like to thank Kim Fontaine-Skronski and David Lamontagne for their research assistance. One of us wrote a detailed account of the SPP's "prosperity pillar." See Louis Bélanger, "Governing the North American Free Trade Area: International Rule Making and Delegation in NAFTA, the SPP, and Beyond," *Latin American Policy* 1, 1 (2010): 22-51.

2 US, White House, "Joint Statement by President Bush, President Fox, and Prime Minister Martin: Security and Prosperity Partnership of North America" (Washington, DC: Office of the Press Secretary, 23 March 2005).

3 Jason Ackleson and Justin Kastner, "The Security and Prosperity Partnership of North America," *American Review of Canadian Studies* 36, 2 (2006): 217-18.

4 For a complete list of the 106 key milestones, see ibid.

5 Cited in Luiza Ch. Savage, "Ditch the Sombreros. Should Ottawa Quit a Continental Strategy and Go Back to One-on-One with the US?" *Maclean's*, 16 April 2008, 29. See also Derek H. Burney, "Our Free Trade Priorities Needn't Include Mexico – There's a Lot of Canada-US Issues Crying Out for Attention," *Globe and Mail*, 7 April 2008, A13.

6 Jean Daudelin, "The Trilateral Mirage: A Tale of Two North Americas," Paper prepared for the Canadian Defence and Foreign Affairs Institute (Ottawa: Carleton University, May 2003), 1.

7 Canada-US Project, *From Correct to Inspired: Blueprint for Canada-US Engagement* (Ottawa: Carleton University, 19 January 2009), v, 15.

8 Bélanger, "Governing the North American Free Trade Area."

9 Greg Anderson and Christopher Sands, *Negotiating North America: The Security and Prosperity Partnership* (Washington, DC: Hudson Institute, White Paper Series, 2007), 28.

10 Ibid., 5-6.

11 Jeffrey Ayres and Laura Macdonald, "Democratic Deficits and the Demise of the Security and Prosperity Partnership of North America: The Role of Civil Society," in *North America in Question: Regional Integration in an Era of Political Economic Turbulence*, ed. Jeffrey Ayres and Laura Macdonald (Toronto: University of Toronto Press, 2012).

12 Alexander Moens, "'Lessons Learned' from the Security and Prosperity Partnership for Canadian-American Relations," *American Review of Canadian Studies* 41, 1 (2011): 58.

13 Bélanger, "Governing the North American Free Trade Area."

14 Oona A. Hathaway, "Treaties' End: The Past, Present, and Future of International Lawmaking in the United States," *Yale Law Journal* 117, 7 (2008): 1236-72.

15 Debra P. Steger, "Institutions for Regulatory Cooperation in 'New Generation' Economic and Trade Agreements," *Legal Issues of Economic Integration* 39, 1 (2012): 109-26.

16 Daniel W. Drezner, *All Politics Is Global: Explaining International Regulatory Regimes* (Princeton, NJ: Princeton University Press, 2007).

17 Robert O. Keohane, *After Hegemony: Cooperation and Discord in the World Political Economy* (Princeton, NJ: Princeton University Press, 1984), 53.

18 Lloyd Gruber, *Ruling the World: Power Politics and the Rise of Supranational Institutions* (Princeton, NJ: Princeton University Press, 2000).

19 Bruce Campbell, "Standing Committee on International Trade," *House of Commons*, No. 058, 1st Session, 39th Parliament, 26 April 2007.

20 Stephen Clarkson, *Does North America Exist? Governing the Continent after NAFTA and 9/11* (Toronto: University of Toronto Press, 2008), 367. See also Stephen Clarkson, *Lockstep in the Continental Ranks: Redrawing the American Perimeter after September 11th* (2002), http://homes.chass.utoronto.ca/~clarkson/publications/Lockstep in the Continental Ranks - Redrawing the American Perimeter after September 11th.pdf.

21 Janine Brodie, "Mobility Regimes: Reflections on the Short Life and Times of the Security and Prosperity Partnership of North America," Paper presented at the Annual Meeting of the International Studies Association, 17-21 February 2010, New Orleans, Louisiana.

22 Joseph S. Nye, "Transnational Relations and Interstate Conflicts: An Empirical Analysis," *International Organization* 28, 4 (1974): 996.

23 Charles F. Doran, *Forgotten Partnership: US-Canada Relations Today* (Baltimore: Johns Hopkins University Press, 1984).

24 On the American side, we conducted interviews with Michael Chertoff, former US secretary of homeland security; Paul Rosenzweig, who served as deputy assistant secretary for policy in the DHS and as acting assistant secretary for international affairs in the DHS; Theresa Brown, who acted as DHS director for Canadian affairs and as DHS attaché to the American embassy in Ottawa; and Robert Stephan, former DHS assistant secretary for infrastructure protection. On the Canadian side, we interviewed Philip Ventura, who was the assistant secretary for US-Canada relations at

the Privy Council Office. The five other Canadian officials whom we interviewed required anonymity.

25 Of the 23 people surveyed, 13 agreed to be interviewed. Of these, 10 were interviewed; 3 could not be interviewed due to scheduling conflict.

26 One interviewee refused to grant permission to record the interview.

27 Interview with a Canadian official, 30 June 2011. This was confirmed by a former US official, 21 October 2011.

28 Interview with a Canadian official, 17 June 2011.

29 Interview with a former Canadian official, 10 November 2011.

30 Interview with a US official, 1 July 2011.

31 Interview with a US official, 8 June 2011.

32 Interview with a former US official, 21 October 2011.

33 Interview with a US official, 10 June 2011. A similar assessment was also made by Canadian officials: interview with a Canadian official, 9 June 2011; interview with a Canadian official, 7 July 2011.

34 Interview with a former US official, 21 October 2011.

35 Interview with a US official, 8 June 2011. See also interview with a former Canadian official, 10 November 2011.

36 Interview with a Canadian official, 17 June 2011.

37 Interview with a Canadian official, 30 June 2011.

38 Ibid.

39 André Donneur and Valentin Chirica, "Immigration et sécurité frontalière: Les politiques canadienne et américaine et la coopération bilatérale," in *Le Canada dans l'orbite américain: La mort des théories intégrationnistes?* ed. Albert Legault (Quebec City: Les Presses de l'Université Laval, 2004), 15-40.

40 Stéfanie von Hlatky and Jessica N. Trisko, "Sharing the Burden of the Border: Layered Security Cooperation and the Canada-US Frontier," *Canadian Journal of Political Science* 45, 1 (2012): 64.

41 Interview with a former Canadian official, 10 November 2011.

42 In the federal budget of 2008, Canadian Finance Minister James Flaherty invested greatly in border security. His budget included million over two years to improve the CBSA's efficiency; million to expand the NEXUS program; million to incorporate biometric data into Canadian visas issued to foreigners; million to improve the security of the Great Lakes and the St. Lawrence Seaway; and million to meet the general goals of the SPP. The Honourable James Flaherty, *The Budget in Brief 2008*, 16 February 2008, http://www.budget.gc.ca/2008/pdf/brief-bref-eng.pdf .

43 Interview with a US official, 8 June 2011; interview with a US official, 10 June 2011.

44 Interview with a Canadian official, 30 June 2011.

45 Robert O. Keohane and Joseph S. Nye Jr., *Power and Interdependence*, 4th ed. (Toronto: Pearson, 2012).

46 Interview with a US official, 10 June 2011.

47   Interview with a Canadian official, 30 June 2011.

48   Ibid.

49   Interview with a Canadian official, 20 July 2011.

50   Interview with a former US official, 21 October 2011.

51   Ibid.

52   Brent Jang, "US Wants Passenger Data for All Sun-Seeker Flights," *Globe and Mail*, 11 October 2007.

53   Interview with a Canadian official, 7 July 2011; interview with a US official, 10 June 2011; interview with a Canadian official, 30 June 2011.

54   Interview with a US official, 10 June 2011. This point was also made by a Canadian official, interview on 17 June 2011. Maher Arar, who has dual Canadian and Syrian citizenship, was arrested at a New York City airport in 2002 and detained without being charged. The Bush administration suspected him of belonging to al-Qaeda and decided to deport him to Syria, where he was eventually tortured by the regime. Arar had been living in Canada for several years when he was arrested. He was later cleared of suspicion by the US government and was financially compensated by the federal government of Canada. Omar Khadr is a Canadian citizen who was captured by the Americans in Afghanistan at age fifteen and sent to the Guantánamo Bay detention camps in 2002 for the murder of a US soldier. Khadr was imprisoned at Guantánamo for ten years and was eventually repatriated to Canada in late 2012. Khadr's conviction was widely denounced by civil rights activists and by Canadian commentators who referred to him as a child soldier.

55   Interview with a former US official, 21 October 2011.

56   Interview with a Canadian official, 17 June 2011.

57   Interview with a US official, 10 June 2011; interview with a Canadian official, 7 July 2011.

58   Canada Border Services Agency, "The Canada Border Services Agency's Arming Initiative," March 2011, http://www.cbsa-asfc.gc.ca/.

59   US, Government Accountability Office, *Various Issues Led to the Termination of the United States–Canada Shared Border Management Pilot Project*, Report to the Congress, GAO-08-1038R (Washington, DC: Government Accountability Office, 2008).

60   Interview with a US official, 10 June 2011.

61   Interview with a former US official, 8 June 2011.

62   Interview with a Canadian official, 30 June 2011; interview with a US official, 10 June 2011.

63   Government of Canada, *Beyond the Border: A Shared Vision for Perimeter Security and Economic Competitiveness. Action Plan* (Ottawa: Public Works and Government Services Canada, 2001), 11.

64   Ibid., 10.

65   Ibid.

66   Ibid., 16 and 21.

67 Ibid., 19.
68 Ibid., 28. Canada signed the convention in 2001 but has never ratified it.
69 Citizenship and Immigration Canada, "Backgrounder – Immigration Information Sharing Treaty," 12 December 2012, http://www.cic.gc.ca/.
70 Bélanger, "Governing the North American Free Trade Area."
71 Robert D. Putnam, "Diplomacy and Domestic Politics: The Logic of Two-Level Games," *International Organization* 42, 3 (Summer 1988): 427-60.
72 Government of Canada, *Beyond the Border,* iv.
73 Ibid., 32.
74 Ibid. The bilateral working group that came out with the action plan was similarly formed. "Simon Kennedy, the Senior Associate Deputy Minister of Industry Canada, (was) Canada's lead on the bilateral discussions. Mr. Kennedy's counterpart in the U.S. (was) Dan Restrepo, a special advisor to the President with regard to Western Hemisphere, and a member of the National Security Council staff." Public Safety Canada, "Seminar Proceedings: Perimeter Security and the Beyond the Border Dialogue: Perspectives from the PNW-Western Canada Region," Summary of remarks made by Chris Gregory, Border Policy Research Institute, Western Washington University, Bellingham, 20 June 2011.
75 Government of Canada, "Terms of Reference for the United States–Canada Regulatory Cooperation Council," 3 June 2011, http://canada.usembassy.gov/.

PART II

SIGNIFICANT DEVELOPMENTS IN NORTH AMERICAN SECURITY AND DEFENCE

6 The Disintegrative Effects of North America's Securitization on the Canada-Mexico Relationship

STEPHEN CLARKSON

This book on security relations in North America takes 9/11 as its point of departure. The calamity of 9/11 marked a turning point in the United States' trajectory that transformed both its internal politics and its then-dominant global position. Washington's shift from a globally expansive, neoconservative, border-shrinking paradigm to a fixation on anti-terrorist security then proceeded to deeply affect the interdependent relations of the North American continent's three countries. This chapter addresses a relatively specific aspect of the weightier issues that ensued: namely, whether Canada and Mexico's relationship has become closer following this historical moment.

At first glance, the Canada-Mexico relationship should have become both closer and warmer. After all, the two national governments faced one common, double problem. From overseas, terrorist organizations' dramatically demonstrated capacities represented a new and real threat to all countries. More significant for the two countries occupying the northern and southern ends of the North American continent, having the United States as their shared neighbour presented them with similar challenges with respect to how they should respond to Washington's quickly declared war on terrorism. While there was some basis for this expectation, digging deeper reveals that, even though they may have begun to grow closer in some respects, Canada and Mexico ended up further apart in other ways.

To judge whether a relationship has grown closer over time, we need a baseline. Accordingly, our first task is to review the nature of the Canada-Mexico relationship on the eve of 9/11. We then examine its evolution during the next decade's three main phases: US ascendancy (2001-04), US reversal (2005-08), and the economic crisis and further decline under the administration of President Barack Obama (2009 to the present). This three-part analysis will give rise to a brief concluding reflection on the nature of regional security cooperation in North America.

The Relationship on the Eve of 9/11

A remarkable feature of the old North America was Canada's manifest disinclination – whether in terms of political ambition, economic self-interest, or even cultural affinity – to connect with Mexico.[1] The opposite was equally true: even though Mexico's economic ties with Canada in terms of exports were considerable, its political and cultural ties were minimal. Canada and Mexico gradually developed a bilateral relationship of their own once the process of negotiating trade liberalization that began in the early 1990s linked them within a formal trilateral economic arrangement driven by the United States, a new situation for both countries that helped stimulate not just increased commercial relations but also new political understandings.

It was far from a matter of love at first sight when senior trade officials were introduced to one another during the North American Free Trade Agreement (NAFTA) negotiations. On the contrary, although Prime Minister Brian Mulroney had pleaded with President George H.W. Bush and President Carlos Salinas de Gortari in 1991 to let him intrude on their impending bilateral integration talks, Ottawa was at first wary of becoming involved with Mexico City lest it somehow contaminate its long-standing cozy relationship with Washington. Besides, the Canadian government feared that its southern might obtain competitive advantages that would make it more attractive to foreign investment or would give it superior access to the US market, thereby jeopardizing something for which Canada had paid a very high price in signing the Canada–United States Free Trade Agreement (CUFTA), which had come into effect just two years earlier.

NAFTA was a watershed from which the new bilateral relationship flowed, tentatively at first when negative factors predominated, then with greater assurance as more positive forces began to prevail. Heretofore always marginal to Canada, Mexico suddenly impinged directly on Ottawa's vital US relationship.

Inklings of future collaboration were present from the beginning. Mexican trade officials sought their Canadian counterparts' institutional advice about how best to involve the business community in the negotiating process. Civil society connections blossomed briefly as Mexican labour and environmental leaders, along with some academics and policy experts, tapped their Canadian counterparts for lessons learned from Canada's experience with CUFTA.

During the negotiations, Canadian officials came to know their Mexican interlocutors. On issues such as energy, the Canadians abstained: CUFTA's energy provisions were retained whereas Washington went toe-to-toe with Mexico City, unsuccessfully trying to crack open the Mexican petroleum market for US corporations. Canada was fully engaged in reworking CUFTA's dispute settlement mechanism. Although the Canadian team resisted Washington's attempt to introduce investor-state arbitration, Mexico declared it a deal breaker since it wanted to assure foreign investors that they would be fully protected – and Canada gave way.[2] The ensuing years of NAFTA implementation saw a gradual increase in the interactions and mutual knowledge among the two governments' senior officials as they participated in such mandated committees as the trilateral working group to negotiate accelerated tariff reductions.

In the marketplace, economic relations strengthened. Mexico's exports to Canada rose 240 percent from 1990 to 2000 and a further 70 percent from 2000 to 2006, with Canada remaining Mexico's second-largest market. Although exports to Mexico grew 73 percent from 1990 to 2000, they remained a minuscule 0.5 percent of Canada's international market, and from 2000 to 2006, they grew a paltry 54 percent more. Mexican investment in Canada was negligible, growing by one-third, from a tiny $161 million in 1995 to only $215 million in 2000 and $277 million in 2006; on the other hand, Canadian direct investment in Mexico multiplied thirteen times in five years, from $294 million in 1995 to $3.9 billion in 2000 and a not insignificant $4.4 billion in 2006.[3]

As the two countries' bilateral corporate relations developed, particularly through transborder production chains in the auto sector, their respective embassy officials had more work to do. Several related multilateral issues also reinforced the growing relationship. In the ultimately unsuccessful project to negotiate a "Free Trade Area of the Americas," Canada and Mexico shared a common fear of diluting what they felt was their NAFTA-negotiated advantage in the US market. Nationally, they also had a common interest in sustaining (on Mexico's part) or forging (on Canada's part) relationships with the rest of Latin America that could help offset their hyperdependence on the US market, but there is no evidence that they developed a concerted plan of action.

Other multilateral endeavours were sources of tension between the two states. Ottawa's efforts in the late 1990s to deepen international human-rights norms were threatening to a Mexico City that, still under the authoritarian, one-party rule of the Institutional Revolutionary Party (Partido Revolucionario Institucional, or PRI), resisted expanded notions of human security that might legitimize the right of other countries to raise questions about its democratic deficits. Some economic issues also proved contentious. A serious direct dispute erupted over the bid of the Quebec company Bombardier for a contract to renew the Mexico City subway system's rolling stock.

The United States remained the elephant in the room. Nothing that the Canadian and Mexican governments contemplated doing with each other would be allowed to compromise each country's relationship with its main export market, its main supplier of imports, its main source of foreign investment, and its main locus of technology. Washington remained contested territory. Nostalgic for the special relationship Canada had enjoyed in earlier times – when it had been an indispensable military ally in the Second World War and played a valuable Cold War role in the North Atlantic alliance – Canadian diplomats resisted being associated in the minds of US politicians with a Mexico that translated politically into issues of illegal immigration and narco-trafficking. At the same time, Ottawa and Mexico City were attracted to each other as partners who might gain increased leverage in Washington by lobbying together against unfair US agricultural subsidies.

Meanwhile, other types of bilateral collaboration developed in domestic affairs. Following a memorandum of understanding signed in 1996, Elections Canada enthusiastically assisted in the establishment of the Instituto Federal Electoral (IFE) in Mexico, which became one of the world's best-rated electoral institutions.[4] On the economic front, considerable promotional efforts climaxed in 1996 with a blitz visit to Mexico City by the Chrétien government's Team Canada to woo and sign contracts. Results were not spectacular, however.

While the economic links were growing, the political relationship became more noteworthy. The two foreign services recognized each other's importance. The Department of Foreign Affairs and International Trade Canada (DFAIT) established a special division dealing with Mexico and beefed up its embassy in Mexico City. The Mexican foreign office created an under-secretariat for North American affairs and expanded its embassy in Ottawa. Visits back and forth between senior officials in various departments and secretariats multiplied. Summit meetings between the two heads of government increased in frequency and substance. President Ernesto Zedillo's visit to Ottawa in 1996 led to the signing of a Declaration of Objectives for the Mexico-Canada Relationship, the Action Plan of which was extended at the 13th Joint Ministerial Committee meeting in February 1999.[5] In short, by the end of the millennium the two governments had developed a vibrant working relationship.

Distrust and disconnect lingered, however. When the former governor of the state of Chihuahua was triumphantly elected president of Mexico in July 2000 and the former governor of Texas was declared president of the United States five months later, Canadian diplomats in Washington were far from delighted. Since Vicente Fox and George W. Bush had been territorial neighbours, fellow conservatives, wear-it-on-their-sleeve Christians, and political friends, Canadian Embassy staff worried that they would not be able to get attention for Canadian issues from a White House that more naturally looked south than north. When Fox reiterated his election campaign proposal to refashion NAFTA with more effective institutions that could transfer funding from the two rich partners to help develop desperately needed infrastructure in Mexico, Prime Minister Jean Chrétien was markedly cool. The government of Canada had nourished amicable diplomatic relations with Mexico, but it was not about to endorse European-style practices of economic equalization and social solidarity in order to promote an economic competitor.

Despite this Canadian resistance to a committed relationship, Mexico had become Canada's main partner in Latin America by the time the Summit of the Americas convened in Quebec City in April 2001. The focal point of the gathering – the Free Trade Area of the Americas – turned out to be doomed, but by this point Canada and Mexico had at least become familiar, though not intimate, associates in the new North America. This cautiously warming relationship was not exactly close, but it helped ease both countries through the crisis in continental governance that stemmed from the United States' extreme reaction to the terrorist attacks of September 11, 2001.

Post 9/11, Phase 1: US Ascendancy under George W. Bush, 2001-04

As the Bush administration reviewed its strategic and tactical options while debris was still floating around lower Manhattan, it felt close to omnipotent as the world's only superpower, which had not only won the Cold War ten years earlier but had asserted its economic hegemony by exporting many of its economic norms into the powerful new World Trade Organization in 1995. The United States' quick declaration of war on Afghanistan put pressure on Canada and Mexico to respond. In this military crisis, they reverted to their Cold War scripts, confirming how alien the Canadian and Mexican military cultures were to each other as they reacted first to the United States' offensive intervention in Central Asia and the Middle East and then to its defensive shoring up of the homeland.

Pushing Apart Overseas Militarily: Afghanistan

Mexico's constitution forbade the sending of troops abroad except for humanitarian relief in emergencies, and Mexican public opinion constrained President Fox from expressing even moral support for the US intervention to oust the Taliban government. Mexico's cool official response to the al-Qaeda attack, which instantly chilled the once-effusive Fox-Bush friendship, also highlighted its deep difference with Canada, both immediately after 9/11 (a Canadian was acting commander of the North American Aerospace Defence Command (NORAD) that day, directing air force surveillance and diverting 1,500 aircraft to safe landings, including hundreds to Canadian airports[6]) and in its aftermath. The US invasion of Afghanistan had international legitimacy because of the immediate global outburst of sympathy for New York's Ground Zero calamity and because the United States had managed to get NATO to invoke Article V, declaring the al-Qaeda coup to be an attack on the whole alliance. This consensus helped legitimize Ottawa's commitment of troops, with 750 soldiers eventually being sent to fight under American command. On this overseas military issue, the chasm between Canada and Mexico was deep.

Coming Together Overseas Diplomatically: Iraq

Washington's subsequent determination to invade Iraq showed how Canada and Mexico could bridge their differences and cooperate in the multilateral arena. Seventeen months after 9/11, Prime Minister Chrétien visited President Fox in Mexico City to support the coalition of unwilling states that were trying to block or at least delay the impending US invasion of Iraq. Although the Liberal prime minister had refused to consider deepening NAFTA's trilateral governance, he enthusiastically supported Mexico and Chile, two non-permanent members of the UN Security Council, in their opposition to the US position. Ottawa and Mexico had chosen to bowl separately in Afghanistan, but they bowled together when the international community strongly questioned the United States' dubious rationale for pre-emptive war.

Pushing Apart on the Continent: "Smart Borders"
Systemically more transformative than the United States' offensive on terror abroad was its revolution in homeland defence, an issue to which it had not given supreme priority since the Royal Navy burned down the White House in the War of 1812. The hijacked airliners' graphically destructive capacity caused a psychic shock, which caused within the Beltway a prioritizing of domestic anti-terrorism policies. This sea change in turn focused the United States' attention on the possible threat coming from its two neighbours. Bipartisan unanimity led to the creation of a vast bureaucracy, the Department of Homeland Security, dedicated to the anti-terrorism mandate. Suddenly the United States' northern border with Canada and its southern border with Mexico took on renewed significance, appearing even more threatening than during the Second World War or the Cold War. Even if all air and sea traffic heading for the United States could be purged of terrorists and weapons of mass destruction (WMD), the long frontiers of its two geographically contiguous neighbours might still offer a terrorist the opportunity to enter the US homeland.

There were two variations in Washington's approach to these land boundaries. The more obvious was to make them impregnable militarily. Conceptually more appealing but practically less achievable was to erect a security perimeter around the whole continent so that the external boundaries of Canada and Mexico became as secure as the United States wanted its own to be.

Washington's negotiation of "Smart Border" agreements with Canada and Mexico showed how inconsequential the continent's third bilateral relationship was with regard to issues of concern to the United States. When Canada and Mexico found themselves under American pressure for drastically increased security along their borders with the United States, they responded alone. At Canada's insistence, Washington negotiated first and separately with Ottawa, and only later with Mexico City. Although it had tried to dissuade Washington from a hub-and-spokes approach to negotiating economic liberalization with its northern and southern neighbours, Ottawa ended up helping to fashion separate security spokes emanating from the US control hub.

When Bush-administration security officials began talks in the autumn of 2001, Ottawa was delighted that Washington was finally paying attention to proposals that had been agreed to by the two governments in the late 1990s but had not been implemented. Desperate to restore border trade flows to the status quo ante, the Canadian business community participated actively in the security consultations that resulted in the Canada-US thirty-point Smart Border Declaration of December 2001. In this process, no direct consideration was given to Mexico's stance on security issues. Instead of working out a trilateral agreement entrenching security norms for both borders, the Bush administration used the Canadian deal as a template for the twenty-two-point border agreement with Mexico City that was more imposed than negotiated the following February.

That the common driver (the US imperative to achieve total security along its land borders) could have such an alienating effect on the Canada-Mexico relationship reflected, and then reinforced, their distinct continental cultures. Canada placed far lower priority on its autonomy than Mexico. Unlike the Mexicans' historical distrust and fear of the "Gringo," Canada's economic and political elites embraced a deeply integrative continentalism and were desperately anxious to maintain their close, junior-partner relationship with Washington, whether by enhancing the interoperability of their armed forces, sharing intelligence, integrating data systems, or cooperating on the "rendition" of suspected terrorists to be tortured in Syria or Egypt.

Mexico had a less apocalyptic assessment of the terrorist threat, but this difference did not distinguish it from Canada as much as did its institutional weakness. Whereas Canada could reorganize its home-based military into a Canada Command that expressly mirrored the United States' new Northern Command, Mexico could not even integrate its own armed forces since its navy had an institutional structure and budget within the Mexican government that was separate from that of its army and air force. Whereas Canada could budget significant funds to implement its smart border commitments, Mexico required financial help (which came from Washington, not Ottawa) just to begin delivering on its own smart border undertakings to integrate data systems and install new WMD detection technology at crossing points.

Faced with the common problem posed by Washington's abrupt shift toward seeking maximum security against non-state actors – a paradigm change that turned its land borders into one of its prime concerns – Canada and Mexico were pushed further apart, a development that had a good deal to do with two additional factors. On the one hand, Canada's multicultural society and extremely high rate of annual immigration caused DHS to consider it the more dangerous of the two neighbouring countries. On the other hand, Canadian elites wholeheartedly believed that their country was also threatened by Islamic terrorism since it had sent troops to fight the Taliban and had, in practice even if not rhetorically, supported the invasion of Iraq with naval assets and military personnel. For its part, Mexico's racial heterogeneity had to do with the admixture of indigenous and Spanish blood since the Spanish conquest, not with large waves of recent migration from countries overseas. Indeed, Mexican immigration policy was as restrictive as Canada's was welcoming. Given its profound commitment to the principle of non-intervention, the Mexican government had little reason to fear Islamic terrorism as a direct threat, and thus responded to US pressure to upgrade its border security in order to please the Americans enough to keep the maquiladoras' and other integrated transnational production chains' cross-border commerce flowing.

In short, Canada and Mexico were pushed further apart despite being confronted by their huge common neighbour's same security imperatives. It was only when a trinational framework was established for managing North American security issues that Canada and Mexico drew closer once more.

Post 9/11, Phase 2: US Reversal under George W. Bush, 2005-08

Although the United States' global military predominance was grievously weakened by its perceived failure to destroy al-Qaeda, to eliminate the Taliban as a security threat in Afghanistan, or to establish order in Iraq, and although the legitimacy of its War on Terror was undermined by the abuses revealed in its prisons in Iraq (Abu Ghraib) and Cuba (Guantánamo), the second Bush administration continued to drive the agenda of its homeland security relations, which took on a new trilateral form of governance for the continent.

Because security measures had thickened the US borders with Canada and Mexico, they had at the same time stalled the forces of economic integration. Conscious that excessive efforts at anti-terrorist security could increase the United States' economic insecurity along with that of Canada and Mexico, the Bush administration undertook a trilateral initiative to rebalance the three governments' differing security and economic priorities. Ironically, this began at the very moment – March 2003 – when the White House's public anger with its neighbours over their resistance to giving United Nations support to a US invasion of Iraq was at its hottest.

The March meeting at 1600 Pennsylvania Avenue between American officials and senior officials from the Fox and Chrétien governments concluded that border bottlenecks caused by US security measures should no longer be allowed to jeopardize the transboundary flows of goods and people that were essential to the three economies and their hopes of future global competitiveness.[7] Security might trump trade in theory but should not jeopardize prosperity in practice.

The gestation of this executive consensus took two years, largely because the 2004 US presidential election campaign distracted the administration's attention for months. At length, the three heads of government met in Waco, Texas, for the first time in over a decade and formally proposed the launch of a new North American governance agenda. There, on 23 March 2005, Presidents Bush and Fox and Prime Minister Paul Martin signed a document of uncertain legal status called the Security and Prosperity Partnership of North America (SPP).[8]

Galvanized by their leaders' commitment and by a tight, three-month deadline to produce an action plan, officials in the three governments dealing with border security, transportation, agriculture, energy, and economic policy began a trilateral consultation process in order to insert policy content into the SPP. Content did not necessarily mean coherence. The measures proposed for the transportation sector were cobbled together on the telephone and by email without their authors in the three capitals ever getting together for a meeting. When ministers from the three countries met in Ottawa in June 2005 to announce the SPP's work plan, their trilingual document detailed some three hundred proposals for regulatory changes that were intended to square the familiar post-9/11 circle: achieve the highest possible level of border security for North America while facilitating the smoothest possible transboundary flows of people and commerce.[9] (See Chapter 5 for an extensive discussion of SPP security coordination.)

There was little public discussion of these proposals, and even less general comprehension of their significance. For one thing, outsiders had no way of telling the difference between meaningless measures (initiate dialogue to identify issues in moving toward a trilateral agreement on expanding air transportation), trivial projects (improve transparency and coordination in energy information, statistics, and projections), and powerful proposals (greater economic production from oil sands). For another, there were no obvious institutional means through which each federal government could credibly administer the SPP's targets, let alone a trinational authority to monitor progress on a continental basis. Nor was there any indication where money to pay for these initiatives would come from. Disinterested observers were not the only ones to voice their doubts. Highly interested businesses whose production chains traversed the Canada-US and/or Mexico-US border were happier that action was being promised than with the actual program or the bureaucratic process through which it had been drafted.

When newly elected Canadian Prime Minister Stephen Harper managed to get himself invited to what had been scheduled as a Mexico-US summit in Cancún in March 2006, the now trilateral conclave was able to mark the SPP's first anniversary by announcing three further decisions. The leaders accepted one of the recommendations of a 2005 Council of

Foreign Relations task force, agreeing to meet on an annual basis. Next, they simplified the previous June's action plan into five more manageable priorities: strengthening competitiveness, emergency management, avian and human pandemic influenza, energy security, and smart, secure borders. Then, with a handful of big businessmen whom they had brought along for the event, they announced the creation of a North American Competitiveness Council (NACC) that would insert the three national corporate communities directly into their governments' decision-making processes.

Beyond its institutional novelty, the SPP's impact in creating new norms and rules for each country's legal order was modest. Since its programmatic thrust focused on measures that could be implemented quickly and without legislative involvement – preparation for handling medical emergencies and natural disasters; harmonization of certain minor peripheral standards with those of the United States – immediate changes in each country's rules were limited.

Within each federal government, the fit between security and economic agencies remained awkward. Mexico's Centro de Investigación y Seguridad Nacional (Centre for National Security and Intelligence) was a young institution with little power to do much more than try to get the federal government's various agencies with security and intelligence operations to pull together. The prosperity dossier was better rooted in Mexico's governmental structure, since the same generation of technocrats that had negotiated NAFTA was still staffing its working groups and driving the process of economic policy development.

In Ottawa, the shift from the narrow focus of the original smart border agreement to the multi-dimensional Security and Prosperity Partnership was accompanied by a parallel bureaucratization. The former had been negotiated and implemented on the Canadian side by John Manley when he was deputy prime minister operating in the Privy Council Office, where he was able to interact personally and continually with his American alter ego, Tom Ridge, then in the White House. Political and administrative control of the SPP then moved down the bureaucratic ladder to associate deputy ministers in the Department of Public Safety and the Department of Industry, with DFAIT having an overall coordinating function – hardly a structure to guarantee dynamic and effective interaction with the Canadians' American and Mexican interlocutors.

Much worse, in Washington the nightmare known as the Department of Homeland Security remained in control of security issues. Unlike Ottawa, where the centralization characteristic of parliamentary government ensured close collaboration between the assistant deputy ministers responsible for the prosperity and security portfolios, little could be done to force the DHS to compromise its goal of making the United States' land borders impermeable by accepting concessions that might improve US economic competitiveness.

This tension broke into the open in May 2007, when DHS secretary Michael Chertoff cut off talks on establishing a pilot project on land pre-clearance at the Fort Erie–Buffalo crossing. Although the two-year-long negotiations had been premised on the principle that the agreement would respect the laws of the country hosting the pre-clearance area, and although fingerprinting is mandatory in Canada only for those charged with a crime, Chertoff insisted that American officials in Fort Erie be able to fingerprint even those US-bound travellers who got cold feet and decided at the last minute not to cross the border. Despite tremendous political and corporate support for a land pre-clearance system similar to the long-established pre-clearance facilities in major Canadian airports, Chertoff's unilateral decision showed how difficult it was to bridge the gap between the SPP's prosperity rhetoric and the practical problem of getting Homeland Security to modify its security obsession. The failure of the pilot pre-clearance project despite endorsement by the Council on Foreign Relations task force and enthusiastic support in the NACC's February 2007 report called into question the ability of the White House and the SPP to prevail over the DHS.

The pre-clearance debacle illustrated how different the issues on each of the United States' borders were. The Canada-Mexico relationship remained constrained by Ottawa's reluctance to invest significant sums in solidarity with its much poorer and frailer partner. In May 2007, Minister of Foreign Affairs Peter MacKay met his Mexican counterpart, Patricia Espinosa, to discuss a "full bilateral agenda" and "opportunities for hemispheric collaboration" leading up to a visit to Canada by President Felipe Calderón – potentially a sign of growth in the third bilateral relationship.[10] For the prime concern of both Mexico City and Ottawa – their relationship with Washington – the SPP had introduced an important consultative process that they hoped would transcend the institutionally moribund NAFTA on which both capitals had pinned so many of their economic dreams a decade earlier.

Mexico and Canada operate simultaneously in two interacting worlds. In their multilateral sphere, they are located in the mid to higher ranks of the global hierarchy – neither so weak that they can exert no influence abroad nor so strong as to operate without regard for international pressures.[11] As middle powers with a strong interest in a well-functioning liberal multilateral order, they take their participation in international institutions very seriously, not least because this multilateralism may offer each government some room for manoeuvre outside the direct control of its dominant patron.

In their continental sphere, Mexico and Canada have to confront the reality of their location in both the United States' backyard and its defence perimeter. Given that the major constraints in Mexico City's and Ottawa's operating systems are the multifarious interests of their generally over-bearing, sometimes imperialistic, often isolationist neighbour, the Security and Prosperity Partnership can best be understood in the context of two long-standing relationships that had altered significantly over the decades, sometimes in harmony, other times in conflict.

In this way, the SPP created a double-edged operating framework. On the one hand, it gave official recognition to the continent's basic political reality: nothing could proceed that the United States did not want to see happen, and Mexico City and Ottawa pursue their own economic objectives only by first meeting US security requirements. Accepting the United States' security fixation as its point of departure, the SPP provided a framework within which US pressure could be managed and perhaps mitigated. On the other hand, the SPP's annual heads-of-government summits created new capacity for the Canadian and Mexican governments acting in concert by legitimizing their voices in a number of key Washington agencies whose policies affected the periphery's interests.

Trilateralizing formerly bilateral issues affected the continent's power dynamic. Mexico has historically preferred a more formalized relationship with Washington than Canada's more informal approach. For its part, Ottawa has long resisted being identified with the United States' other territorial neighbour, lest its US relationship be jeopardized by congressional fears of illegal immigrants and drug dealers. The SPP and the NACC seriously challenged North America's transborder governance through two disconnected dyadic relationships that required bringing Canada and Mexico closer. The Western Hemisphere Travel Initiative (WHTI), obliging American travellers to have secure identity documents when returning to the United States, had caused Mexico and Canada to lobby together and with their American business allies. To the extent that US policies designed to counteract the problems of illegal immigration at the Mexican border were applied to Canada, Canadians would be affected. To the extent that US policies designed to counteract the infiltration of terrorists across the Canadian border were applied to Mexico, Mexicans would be affected. To the extent that Canada and Mexico together exerted some power vis-à-vis their continental giant, their capacity was increased, the power asymmetry was offset, and the skewed quality of the continent's two US-centred bilateral relationships was reduced.

More than the SPP brought Canada and Mexico closer each other in this second post-9/11 phase. In addition to their federal governments, other players in Mexico and Canada had become more assertive. The government of Quebec had operated an autonomous delegation in Mexico City for two decades, which paved the way for Ontario and then Alberta to send representatives who were housed in the Canadian Embassy. Canadian and Mexican activists in environmental, labour, educational, and religious organizations had maintained some communications (albeit more distant) in the decade following their intense cooperation in opposition to the NAFTA negotiations. Some cities twinned with each other. Some Canadian provinces connected with counterpart Mexican states.

During these ten years, as the relationship between Canada and Mexico slowly became more complex, the two economies also grew closer. By 2004, bilateral trade had tripled – admittedly from a small base – reaching US$12 billion.[12] Mexico had become Canada's fourth-largest export market globally, but its largest in Latin America. Encouraged by the sense that NAFTA had made business possibilities more secure in this foreign setting, some 1,400 Canadian companies, many of them small- and medium-sized, had invested $3.2 billion there. For Mexico, Canada had advanced to become its third foreign investor and its fourth trading partner after the United States, Japan, and the entire European Union.[13]

With the war in Iraq distracting the Bush administration's attention from its continental relations and with congressional and DHS initiatives causing continued tension along the borders, the two peripheral states began to reframe their relationship. Once again, the initiative came from the south and was initially resisted in the north. President Fox called for a new strategic partnership with Canada, but Paul Martin, who became Canada's prime minister in December 2003, evinced the same lack of interest as had his predecessor in deepening NAFTA's institutions, repeatedly emphasizing his commitment to a reactivated US relationship. By setting up and chairing a special cabinet committee to handle US relations, Martin reaffirmed Ottawa's historical concentration on achieving – and nostalgia for nurturing – intimate relations with Washington.

Never shy about embracing contradictory positions, Martin nevertheless committed himself to enhancing Ottawa's connection with Mexico City. And, as a second-best position when actual relations with Washington deteriorated – which they quickly did when the prime minister resisted President Bush's pressure to support the ballistic missile defence program – it did make sense to coordinate positions with Mexico. There was a natural convergence of interests when both governments differed from Washington (on NAFTA dispute settlement), when they defended common positions (opposing US proposals requiring American citizens to have passports at the border), or when they wanted to avoid being isolated and played off against each other by the United States. It also made sense to raise the third bilateral relationship to a higher level for its own sake.

Modelled on the quadripartite Partnership for Prosperity, which the United States and Mexico signed in 2003 to bring business into closer coordination with government on specific bilateral issues, the Canada-Mexico Partnership (CMP) was announced with considerable fanfare in October 2004. The CMP consisted of five working groups: urban housing, sustainable cities, human capital, competitiveness, and agribusiness. Also quadripartite in its leadership, each working group was to be chaired by representatives from each government and a representative from civil society or the private sector in each country.

Even several years after their establishment, it was difficult to believe that these working groups had achieved much. Their meetings were closed to observers, and they published no reports of their activities or recommendations. Interviews suggested that the structure was stumbling under its own weight, with the chief players spending inordinate amounts of time attending meetings of committees with overlapping mandates. The diplomats in charge were driven by the process, spending their time getting meetings organized. Excessively bureaucratic and largely dependent on Canadian government funding, the groups appeared oriented toward doing little more than helping the Canadian private sector drum up some business in Mexico.

Modest though it may have been in policy production, the CMP's value appeared to lie in its contribution to sustaining a high level of interaction between the two countries' federal governments and selected members of their civil societies. Ottawa felt supported when Vicente Fox, attending a bilateral summit meeting in Vancouver in October 2005, endorsed the Canadian position on NAFTA's dispute-settlement processes, even though the ongoing softwood lumber case was an entirely Canada-US issue. For its part, the Mexican government appreciated Prime Minister Stephen Harper's attendance at Felipe Calderón's controversial inauguration.

By 2007, George W. Bush was worse than a lame duck. His foreign policy had made collaboration on multilateral issues impossible. As far as his domestic agenda affected Mexico, he had failed to improve the treatment of immigrants at the border, where vigilantism and wall building prevailed. With no hope for serious relations being re-established with Washington until the White House changed hands in January 2009, the new Canadian prime minister and the even newer Mexican president realized that they could best push ahead on some common continental issues by having their two governments work more seriously with each other.

There was much to work on. President Calderón was recalibrating Mexico's relationship with Latin America in general and Cuba in particular, trying to fix the damage done by his predecessor. For his part, Harper had signalled his lack of interest in Africa and affirmed that Latin America was to have special priority. With Mexico as its prime Latin American relationship, this implied that Canada was interested in further developing that relationship, as was also suggested by Calderón's spending family time at the prime minister's summer residence before the SPP's 2007 Montebello meeting.

However, what seemed at the end of George W. Bush's second term to be a healthy institutional trend toward the development of both North America's third bilateral relationship and a reinforced trilateralism turned out to have a very short lifespan. After growing quite close through their collaboration on many dossiers, Canada and Mexico have appeared to be seeking their fortunes along separate paths in the next phase.

Post 9/11, Phase 3: Further Decline under Barack Obama, 2009 to the Present

The SPP and NACC enjoyed scant democratic legitimacy but gave the periphery's political and business elites much coveted "face time" with their US counterparts, including with the president himself. The next three years saw this phenomenon reversed. That newly elected President Obama could mothball the SPP showed that Washington needed no institutions at all to get what it wanted from its periphery. That he could unilaterally abolish a cooperative mechanism that the three countries had spent two years negotiating before its launch in 2005 showed how the power asymmetry inherent in North America's informal governance had only deepened during its latest phase of security continentalization. As these new North American institutions flamed out, old ones also fizzled. In 2010, one of NAFTA's vaunted innovations, its Commission for Labor Cooperation, quietly closed its doors.

In this third phase, Canada has played a leading role in breaking down whatever trilateral solidarity NAFTA had originally generated. Fearful that its influence in Washington was being compromised by its association with Mexico, Ottawa took pains to turn its back on that country. Quietly, it helped discontinue the annual trilateral Leaders' Summit by not arranging the meeting in 2010 for which it was responsible. Openly, it instituted visa requirements that offended Mexican travellers to Canada. Privately, it expressed reluctance to support a trilateralism that would link it with Mexico in Washington's eyes. Although the political, economic, and military conditions that had sustained Canada's cordial transnational political culture with the United States[14] had long since eroded, the Harper government was bent on resurrecting the two countries' special relationship.

By 2012, humiliated by Canada and walled off by the United States, the Mexican government found itself politically isolated from – even if economically integrated in – the two developed systems to the north with which it had implemented NAFTA sixteen years earlier. Battered by destructive storms, shaken by an influenza panic, displaced by China as the United States' prime source of low-cost products, destabilized by ever more violent drug cartels, and symbolically ostracized by the US security barrier along its northern border, Mexico has been left to cope on its own with the disastrous consequences of having deliberately hitched its productive forces to the hegemon's now falling star. Whereas other economies in the hemisphere stagnated during the 2008-09 economic crisis, Mexico's was the only one to suffer a 7.5 percent decrease in its GDP. It suffered unassisted.

In response to this predicament, the Mexican government made a show of founding a new hemispheric entity that included all the Latin American and Caribbean states but excluded the United States and Canada. It also made an effort to diversify its economic relationships by strengthening the trade and investment agreements it had already signed with other countries. However, gestures of solidarity toward its Latin American counterparts and aspirations for economic diversification cannot reverse Mexico's integration with the United States, although it can disengage from Canada. Managing its northern border remains a central preoccupation, although the issues remain too inflamed – whether from public outcries over American agents killing unarmed migrants or US drones violating Mexico's airspace – for the border's administration to be jointly bureaucratized.

Meanwhile, Canada negotiated with the White House a Beyond the Border Action Plan, announced in December 2011, which picked up the traces of the 2001 Smart Border Declaration. Exactly one decade after this declaration was signed, the United States prevailed on Canada to deliver more information on cross-border travellers.[15] Canada hoped thereby to persuade the United States that, if its security policies were so tough that its external borders could constitute a continental defence perimeter for the United States, then the Department of Homeland Security would soften its restrictions on goods and people crossing the Canada-US border.

Although Canada's rejection of trilateralism might suggest that North America has returned to its pre–free trade hub-and-spokes profile, the continent's two-speed bilateralism is nevertheless different from the cross-border governance of three decades ago, before Mexico's relationship with Canada has developed economically. In matters of homeland security, however, these US neighbours' swings between greater cooperation and further alienation after 9/11 have left them almost as far apart as they were before.

It would be excessive to claim that 9/11 changed the world forever, but it certainly changed North America. Part of this change was the ultimate alienation of Canada and Mexico from each other.

Conclusion

The key policy development that has negatively affected the capacity of both Mexico and Canada to cooperate on North American security has comprised US policy responses against non-state actors. Beltway politics have increasingly driven Canada and Mexico to "parallel" US policies,[16] with the contradictory result of preserving American autonomy while diminishing that of Canada and Mexico. Greater regulatory cooperation with Washington takes place as a result of the two countries' choice to conform to the United States' unilateral definition of its security threat. If Ottawa and Mexico City continue to avoid irritants with Washington in order to achieve better security relations, they will lock themselves into further, societally disruptive securitization. One can only hope that the United States will awaken from its nightmare of self- and neighbour-wounding behaviour in time to address the world's real security threats, from global crime cartels more immediately and catastrophic environmental degradation more irreversibly. It would be helped along this path if Canada and Mexico could establish a cohesive bilateralism dedicated to achieving a sensible degree of security for the whole continent.

NOTES

1 This section is based on several dozen off-the-record interviews with government officials in Mexico City, Washington, and Ottawa in the winters of 2006 and 2007.

2 See Stephen Clarkson, *Does North America Exist? Governing the Continent after NAFTA and 9/11* (Toronto: University of Toronto Press, 2008), ch. 3.

3 Mexico, The NAFTA Office of Mexico in Canada, "Trade Intelligence: Statistics," Mexican Ministry of Economy, Underministry of International Trade Negotiations, http://www.nafta-mexico.org/; Canada, Department of Foreign Affairs and International Trade Canada (DFAIT), "Foreign Direct Investment Statistics," http://www.international.gc.ca/.

4 Olga Abizaid Bucio, *The Canada-Mexico Relationship: The Unfinished Highway* (Ottawa: FOCAL Policy Paper, October 2004), 5.

5 Ibid., 6.

6 NAV CANADA, "NAV CANADA and the 9/11 Crisis," Newsroom – Backgrounder, http://www.navcanada.ca/.

7 This analysis is based on confidential interviews carried out in Mexico City in 2006 and 2007 (primarily in the secretariats of External Relations, Agriculture, Transport, and the Economy) and in Washington, DC, in 2006 and 2007 (in the Mexican and Canadian embassies, the National Security Council, and the Department of Commerce, as well as with officers in the US Chamber of Commerce, the Council of the Americas, and the Canadian American Business Council).

8 US, White House, "Joint Statement by President Bush, President Fox, and Prime Minister Martin: Security and Prosperity Partnership of North America" (Washington, DC: Office of the Press Secretary, 23 March 2005).

9 Government of Canada, "Security and Prosperity Partnership of North America – Report to Leaders," June 2005, http://www.spp-psp.gc.ca/.

10 Foreign Affairs and International Trade Canada, "Minister MacKay Meets with Mexican Secretary of External Affairs in Halifax, Nova Scotia" (Ottawa: Foreign Affairs and International Trade Canada, 23 May 2007).

11 Stephen Clarkson and Marjorie Griffin Cohen, "Introduction: States under Siege," in *Governing under Stress: Middle Powers and the Challenge of Globalization,* ed. Stephen Clarkson and Marjorie Griffin Cohen (London: Zed Books, 2004), 1–11.

12 Abizaid Bucio, *The Canada-Mexico Relationship,* 5.

13 Noemi Gal-Or, "The Future of Canada-Mexico Relations according to Canada's International Policy Statement," *Nueva época* 11 (Summer 2006): 2.

14 Brian Bow, *The Politics of Linkage: Power, Interdependence, and Ideas in Canada-US Relations* (Vancouver: UBC Press, 2009), 2-3.

15 US, White House, *United States–Canada Beyond the Border: A Shared Vision for Perimeter Security and Economic Competitiveness. Action Plan,* December 2011, http://www.whitehouse.gov/sites/default/files/us-canada_btb_action_plan3.pdf.

16 Geoffrey E. Hale, "'In the Pipeline' or 'Over a Barrel'? Assessing Canadian Efforts to Manage US-Canadian Energy Interdependence," *Canadian-American Public Policy* 76 (February 2011): 25.

Mexico's Ambiguous Foreign Policy toward North America

ATHANASIOS HRISTOULAS

Mexican foreign policy, at least in rhetoric, has gone through dramatic changes in the last few decades. Historically emphasizing its independence and autonomy in foreign and security policy, Mexico is beginning to show signs of a greater willingness to collaborate with its neighbours to achieve regional security and stability. This evolution is the result mainly of the recognition on the part of decision makers that the country can no longer realize its short- and long-term interests by pursuing an autonomous and independent foreign policy.

Yet this shift in foreign policy has had setbacks. Particularly since 9/11, Mexico's attempts to integrate more closely with its North American partners have started and stalled on repeated occasions. Partly for domestic reasons, but also because of international events, this has led to criticisms that Mexican foreign policy, particularly with respect to Canada and the United States, is ambiguous at best. This chapter will outline the evolution of Mexican foreign policy vis-à-vis the country's North American partners. First, it presents Mexico's classic definition of national security and its historical, cultural, and political origins. Next, it examines the reasons for a shift in foreign policy, at least rhetorically. It then focuses on the Fox and Calderón administrations and their policies vis-à-vis North America, and concludes that, given the country's current domestic situation, a more coherent North American foreign policy is unlikely.

Ideological Underpinnings

Legally speaking, Mexico's foreign policy is based on the principles of self-determination, non-intervention, and the peaceful resolution of conflict.[1] These legal requirements are the result of Mexico's 180-year history of independence, and have manifested themselves in a foreign policy that emphasizes independence, autonomy, respect for sovereignty, and ultimately non-intervention in the domestic affairs of other states.

The historical and cultural roots of this foreign policy can be traced to the Mexican-American war of 1846-48, in which Mexico lost half its territory; the French intervention of 1861; and the various attempts by Great Powers during the nineteenth and early twentieth centuries to use Mexico as a geopolitical pawn. These experiences caused Mexican policy makers and public opinion to elevate the twin issues of respect for sovereignty and non-intervention as priorities in foreign policy. In practical terms, this meant that Mexico's foreign policy had to avoid entangling alliances of any kind, either bilateral or multilateral.

Of particular importance for this chapter has been the specific impact of Mexico-US relations. A long-standing suspicion of US motives dating back to the war of 1846-48 further solidified Mexico's Cold War foreign-policy orientations of autonomy, independence, and non-intervention. Indeed, argues one Mexican scholar, "the direct vicinity with such a colossus has cost Mexico ... the loss of more than half of its original territory, several military interventions, constant interference in internal political affairs and economic penetration at all levels ... In few countries, as is the case in Mexico, has the phenomenon of geographical situation operated as a major factor in foreign policy."[2]

Post-Nationalist Foreign Policy

In the post–Cold War era, Mexican decision makers appear to have abandoned strict definitions of defence of sovereignty and nationalism in favour a policy that emphasizes "pragmatism" and recognizes the limits of Mexican foreign policy.[3]

This new foreign policy pragmatism is essentially the result of domestic developments. First, Mexico suffered dramatic economic crises in 1982, 1988, and 1994 that resulted in a slow but definite evolution in the manner in which Mexican foreign policy decision makers perceived the United States. These events highlighted the fact that a nationalist foreign policy may not necessarily be compatible with other goals.[4] In practical terms, this meant that, given the size of the US economy and its capacity to absorb Mexican exports, the neighbour to the north should no longer be considered a threat to Mexican national interests. The culmination of this radical reorientation occurred in the early 1990s when Mexico, Canada, and the United States entered into negotiations toward the North American Free Trade Agreement (NAFTA). Heredia argues that NAFTA signalled three fundamental changes in Mexican foreign policy: a new openness toward the United States, a dominance of economic themes in foreign policy, and a strategic reorientation toward participation in multilateral institutions.[5]

Second, a strengthened opposition emerged and contributed to the decision to open the political system. Beginning in the late 1980s, civil organizations within Mexico began linking up with international and non-governmental organizations (NGOs). The immediate effect was a move toward transparency in the formulation of both domestic and foreign policy. For example, the issue of human rights practices within Mexico gained importance throughout the 1990s precisely because of the aforementioned linkages between domestic and international actors. In order to legitimize the government's handling of human rights issues domestically, the Ernesto Zedillo administration began to emphasize the theme in foreign policy as well. Similarly, the Vicente Fox administration, which took office in December 2000, strongly signalled that respect for human rights would be a guiding principle in Mexican foreign policy in the coming years.

In sum, successive economic crises (managed with the help of the United States), coupled with the signing of NAFTA, resulted in a more pragmatic foreign policy orientation, which served to change Mexican policy makers' perception of the United States. The United States was no longer seen as threat to Mexico, a view that had dominated Mexican diplomatic discourse for many decades. Although relations were not perfect, policy makers in Mexico began to recognize that through careful and consistent diplomacy, a partnership between the two countries could slowly emerge. Consequently, the Mexico-US relationship began to change from confrontation to cooperation.

Vicente Fox and 9/11

The victory of Vicente Fox in 2000 was an important turning point in Mexican foreign policy in general and with the United States in particular. Fox and George W. Bush maintained a close personal relationship, announcing on a number of occasions that they were the "best of friends." President Bush went as far as to say that Mexico was the United States' most important bilateral relationship.

This dramatic warming of relations was highlighted by the terrorist attacks of 9/11. Mexico took steps to politically demonstrate its solidarity with the United States. For example, in October 2001, President Fox stated that Mexico "considers the struggle against terrorism to be part of the commitment of Mexico with Canada and the United States to build within the framework of the North American free trade agreement a shared space of development, well-being and integral security."[6] Later that year, Foreign Minister Jorge Castañeda said that "Mexico would favour a continental approach to border security issues, extending a North American partnership that already operates at a trade level."[7] In the same speech, he signalled that the Mexican government would prefer to take perimeter security "as far as possible, but that depends on the Canadians and the Americans."

The Mexican government saw continental and border security as offering multiple opportunities in the areas of trade, security, migration, and even social development. Similar to Canada, Mexico worried that enhanced security at the border would hurt trade between it and the United States. However, Mexico's interests went beyond simply trade. Mexico's strategy had been one of issue linkage, or the attempt to trade security for other types of benefits. A first issue linkage related directly to the expansion of NAFTA to include non-trade-related issues. When Carlos Salinas signed NAFTA in the early 1990s, his administration argued that the trilateral trade agreement would improve the standard of living of all Mexicans. Two administrations later, Fox was under tremendous domestic pressure to deliver on those promises. In the months following 9/11, he argued repeatedly that as long as Mexico was a place where 40 percent of the population made less than $2 a day, US borders would never be secure. The solution was either a migration agreement under which the United States would legally absorb a substantial number of Mexican migrant workers, a North American social cohesion program similar to that found in the European Union, or preferably both. Pushing this linkage idea even further, Mexican officials even went as far as to argue that it was in the national security interests of the United States to legalize the 10 to 12 million undocumented Mexican workers because, in the context of homeland defence, it is better to know who they actually are.

Thus, migration was the key to understanding Mexico's strong support for continental security, the perimeter agenda, and the strengthening of relations with the United States and Canada. Mexican decision makers hoped that if they gave the United States what it wanted in security terms, there would be positive spillover effects in areas of greater concern to Mexico. A sign of the shift in the strategic relationship between Mexico and the United States came in early 2002, when the two countries signed the twenty-two point Smart Border agreement.

The next step was the signing of the now-defunct Security and Prosperity Partnership in 2005 in Waco, Texas.[8] The leaders of Canada, Mexico, and the United States declared their desire to develop new avenues of cooperation. The partnership was a trilateral effort to increase security and enhance prosperity among the three countries through greater cooperation and information sharing. Through the formation of trilateral cabinet-level working groups, the three countries undertook to develop concrete work plans for securing North America. The terrorist attacks served as the trigger for this move toward continental security integration, but the end result was the binding together of the three countries not only because of economic necessity but also by a desire to coordinate security, political, and even social policy.

Fox's Fly in the Ointment

However, even though politically Mexico's leaders pursued closer relations with both Canada and the United States, Mexico could not keep up, either politically or operationally, with the changes occurring in North America. Consider, for example, the border agreements signed late in 2001 between Canada and the United States and early in 2002 between Mexico and the United States: it almost goes without saying that the Canada-US version is much more comprehensive in nature. Those areas of the Canada-US border agreement that focus on harmonization and cooperation – such as pre-clearance, joint training and exercises, integrated intelligence, and Integrated Border Enforcement Teams (IBETS) – simply do not appear in the Mexico-US version.

Three other interrelated factors combined to limit Mexico's ability to fulfill the promises made by President Fox immediately after 9/11. The first was the capacity of the Mexican government to respond to the perceived threat. Besides the fact that Mexico is a developing nation and by definition has less capacity than its two North American partners, the US-driven criminalization of certain transactions (narcotics and labour markets) has radically altered the nature of corruption in Mexico and also magnified the size of this problem, weakening, in turn, the institutional capacity of the state. The criminalization of these transactions rests at the heart of the problem of corruption and ultimately explains the recurring difficulties experienced by Mexican-American efforts at law enforcement cooperation.

Second, the six years of President Fox's administration were characterized by intense political infighting between different ministries. There was intense interagency competition at the crucial moment when Mexico was deciding how it would pursue North American security cooperation.

Combined with the fact that the Mexican Congress was (and still is) deeply divided, this led to a situation where the country's leaders simply could not make any decisions of a substantive nature. The implications of this problem were fairly obvious: much of the decision-making structure of the state was heavily permeated by this personal and institutional competition, and for all intents and purposes, President Fox essentially muddled through his presidency.

The case of Mexico's national security strategy after the 2000 general election is a classic example. When Fox came to office, he tried to formalize the national security agenda by creating the nation's first National Security Presidential Advisor. The move was an attempt to develop a coherent national security doctrine by rationalizing the different agencies in charge of intelligence: the Center for Research and National Security (Centro de Investigación y Seguridad Nacional, or CISEN), Naval Intelligence, Army Intelligence, the Attorney General's Office (Procuraduria General de la Republica, or PGR), the Federal Preventive Police (Policia Federal Preventiva, or PFP), and the Federal Investigation Agency (Agencia Federal de Investigación, or AFI).

The president's policy failed because the national security advisor he chose, Adolfo Aguilar Zínser, was extremely unpopular with those agencies (he had previously been a senator from a left-leaning party). Indeed, Zínser's access to the intelligence community was deliberately limited not only by CISEN (which saw him as a direct threat) but also by other intelligence agencies. In the end, he left for a diplomatic post in New York and, more significantly, Fox decided that no replacement was needed. In an ironic yet telling decision, he decided to formally name himself his own national security advisor, as he did not want to appoint another individual who might create further problems. Thus, political infighting between the agencies as well as Fox's lack of interest in the subject precluded a real restructuring of national security doctrine and intelligence services, and left Mexico's intelligence agencies without a clear mandate.

If Mexican officials have a hard time dealing with one another, the situation along the northern border is even worse. There are few, if any, mechanisms for cooperation and communication between the authorities of both countries, and Mexican and American officials have deeply entrenched trust issues. There is little communication and information sharing between the two sides. "U.S. law enforcement officials often find themselves in frustrating situations, unable to deal with the inefficiency that often characterizes Mexican officials, while Mexican authorities are overly sensitive to U.S. unilateralism, and lack the technical expertise to foment the kinds of cooperative mechanisms that exist along the Canada-

U.S. border."[9] Thus, no "security confidence" exists along the US-Mexican border, and as argued by David Shirk, "bi-national cooperation is typically focused on reducing cross border interagency irritants and misunderstandings rather than on coordinated operations, and while occasionally stronger at the local level of inter-agency cooperation – tends to vary from place to place and time to time."[10]

The third and final obstacle is the use of nationalism and sovereignty by Mexican political actors in order to pursue their own personal agendas. For example, the bilateral Mérida Initiative (see below) provided for US assistance to Mexico to fight drug cartels, but opposition leaders argued that the plan would violate Mexico's sovereignty.

Thus, although rhetorically there was a significant shift in Mexican foreign policy toward closer relations with the United States and Canada under Fox, significant obstacles prevented a fully articulated North American security policy. This is particularly important given the context of the first few years immediately after 9/11. Mexican decision making essentially broke down at probably the most crucial moment in the evolution of the country's foreign policy. Whereas Canada was arguably much more consistent in its behaviour toward the United States, Mexican foreign policy was disjointed and ill-conceived. This led to the perception in Washington that Mexico was less than an ideal ally in the "war against terrorism."

Felipe Calderón and the "War" against Drugs

Felipe Calderón (2006-12) did not tolerate cabinet dissension the way Vicente Fox did, and some of these problems were resolved during his presidency. This had more to do with the governing style of Calderón himself, however, rather than any kind of structural reform within government. Peña Nieto has continued Calderón's approach and has even taken steps to formally centralize decision making with respect to security agencies by endowing the interior ministry's "super" status, meaning that from now on it will coordinate the security agenda for the entire federal government. This, too, however, is merely a policy change: future presidents are free to revert to other models.

Priorities also shifted under Calderón. Migration lost its lustre principally because the level of Mexican migration to the United States had slowed, as reported by the New York Times on 23 April 2012.[11] The article also argues that many Mexicans are actually returning to Mexico. There are two main reasons for these developments. First, the weak US economy has made migration northward less appealing, and has even caused Mexicans to return home. Second, new, more effective border enforcement measures implemented by US authorities have made crossing the border illegally more difficult.

Calderón's focus was on defeating the drug cartels, and this required a domestic and foreign policy shift. Domestically, as argued by Bailey, he made the restoration of public security and legality one of the main priorities of his presidency.[12] The first priority consisted of joint military and police operations to regain territory controlled by the cartels, mainly in northern Mexico, along the border with the United States. The second priority was reform of the judicial system, which was incapable of dealing with organized crime. Finally, a new federal police force, free of corruption, was established.

According to Bailey, Mexico's new drug strategy emphasized policies designed to promote public security and justice reform. Indeed, "similar to U.S. military surges in Iraq and Afghanistan, the Mexican government sought to implement a reaction-suppression model driven by the army while its prevention-justice administration model was constructed ... The theory was that the Mexican armed forces would stand down when the justice system was ready to stand up."[13]

To support this strategy, Calderón made a significant shift in Mexican foreign policy by specifically asking the United States for help in the campaign against organized crime. In October 2007, he and President Bush announced a major new initiative to combat the threats of drug trafficking and organized crime. Known as the Mérida Initiative, the plan called for the United States to provide Mexico with $1.4 billion in equipment, training, and technical cooperation over a three-year period (2008-11). About 40 percent of the money will be used to purchase fixed- and rotary-wing aircraft designed to facilitate interdiction and rapid response. The rest is for inspection equipment.

In signing the Mérida Initiative, Mexico wholeheartedly placed its security emphasis on the United States. The initiative is considered a turning point in Mexico-US relations. It is the first time the United States has provided such a substantial amount of military and police assistance to Mexico (prior to the Mérida Initiative, Mexico received an average of $30 million annually in assistance from the United States through the Bureau of International Narcotics and Law Enforcement Affairs). Moreover, the level of cooperation between Mexican and US authorities, specifically in the area of training, is unprecedented. Indeed, more than an assistance package, "the Merida Initiative should be seen as a central element in a broader strategy of growing cooperation between the United States and Mexico to address a shared threat presented by organized crime."[14] Along similar lines, others have argued that the initiative "can serve as an important element in building confidence and cooperation between the two countries."[15]

Calderón's Fly in the Ointment

Compared with a decade ago, Mexico has made significant efforts to break out of its nationalist shell. Indeed, there has been a noteworthy increase in intelligence sharing and cooperation along the border, particularly since the signing of the Smart Border agreement in 2002. Moreover, Mexican authorities have been willing to overlook the stricter definitions of sovereignty and to permit FBI and Drug Enforcement Agency (DEA) agents to operate in Mexican territory. A significant number of Mexican public security officials and army/navy personnel are receiving training from not only US but also Canadian authorities. Finally, as discussed above, the Mérida Initiative is the first real framework for cooperation between Mexico and the United States. All of this has occurred after a twenty-year deep freeze between US and Mexican authorities with respect to security issues.

Problems still exist, however, and are important impediments to further bilateral and trilateral cooperation. First, the United States was slow to dispense Mérida funding, which was criticized by Mexican officials and pundits alike. By the end of 2011, for example, close to the end date of the program, only about $500 million of the $1.4 billion had been allocated. There are several possible explanations for this: (1) US staff was simply not available, meaning that although the money was there, the United States had not committed enough personnel to the project; (2) filling out contracts takes time, more time than the initially anticipated three years; (3) Mexico had requested custom-made equipment, which by its very nature is not an overnight endeavour; (4) the projects that could be implemented quickly, such as the training of public security forces, did not cost that much; and finally and perhaps most importantly, (5) Mexican officials did not realize that although Mexico is important, the United States has other priorities as well, such as the continuing conflict in Afghanistan and the stability of the Middle East.

Some have argued that money from the initiative was misdirected and that it was not working to reduce violence.[16] There needs to be a greater focus on institution building or security sector reform before any progress is made on dealing with the cartels. Three areas stand out: reform of the judicial system, reform of the public security forces, and reform of the armed services. Future collaborative efforts should also take into account socioeconomic issues. This suggests that a holistic approach to the "war against drugs" is lacking. Decision makers on both sides of the border need to recognize that the drug trade involves production (cocaine from Colombia, marijuana from Mexico), distribution (now mainly through Mexico, but also through the Caribbean) and consumption (principally in the United States and Europe). The Mérida Initiative dealt with distribution almost exclusively.

Moreover, what Mexican officials worry about, such as the movement of weapons from the United States into Mexico, will not be managed in the context of a Republican Congress. Talk in Congress of deficit and foreign aid reduction, as well as an increasingly unilateral focus on the part of American officials, has caused frustration with the United States. It is important to note that in asking for money from the Americans to help Mexico deal with the cartels, President Calderón violated a sacred tenet of Mexican foreign policy, namely, that Mexico would use its own resources to defend its own sovereignty. Mexican decision makers worry that by asking for money, they have shown their vulnerability to the United States. Having US politicians and policy makers respond with unilateralist policies only causes further anxiety for Mexicans.

Another source of frustration for Mexican decision makers is that, even taking into account the Mérida Initiative, US drug policy remains essentially the same, meaning that it is still focused on supply. On the other hand, Mexico views the drug problem from both a supply and a demand perspective, but its policy makers have been unable to convince successive US administrations to view the issue in a similar manner. This is nothing new in bilateral relations. The Fox administration (2000-06) tried unsuccessfully to convince the Bush administration and the Republican congress that migration was a bilateral problem. The problem in both cases, of course, is US domestic politics, about which Mexican policy makers have a profound lack of understanding. This only causes further problems in the bilateral relationship.

What Mexican policy makers also do not understand is that effective drug policy is simply not a priority in Washington. Mexico does not understand that US decision makers are also tackling other problems, which include, but are not limited to, deficit reduction and debt, the possibility of a new recession, the war in Afghanistan, and instability in the Middle East following the so-called Arab Spring.

Mexican policy makers also have a hard time defining what they want from an assistance package. There is a debate among officials over whether the money should be spent on social programs or equipment, or even on security sector reform. The problem is exacerbated by the fact that different agencies in Mexico are fighting over access to new equipment and funding for institutional reform and modernization.

As though all of these were not enough, the WikiLeaks scandal has made matters worse. A number of criticisms of Mexico's handling of the "war on drugs" were sent by cable to Washington by the American ambassador, Carlos Pascual, and later made public on the WikiLeaks website. Specifically, the documents criticized the Mexican army's handling of the crisis in Mexico, arguing that they were ill-prepared and risk-averse. The leaked cables went on to argue that there was significant infighting between Mexico's different security institutions over how to deal with the cartels. The leaks resulted Pascual's recall and the appointment of Earl Anthony Wayne as US ambassador to Mexico.

Relations with Canada

Before NAFTA came into effect in 1994, relations between Canada and Mexico were marginal at best, and important differences existed with respect to defence and security policies. Central to the Canadian conception of security is international cooperation, specifically with the United States and Great Britain (previously), as well as the United Nations and, more recently, the Organization of American States. On the other hand, the epicentre of Mexican security and defence doctrine is found internally.[17] Prior to the Fox administration (2000-06), Mexico, unlike Canada, did not have an active international security policy.

As NAFTA was being implemented between 1994 and 2000, the Zapatista uprising occurred in Mexico and the country's security policies turned inward. Many Canadian NGOs supported the Zapatista Army of National Liberation (Ejército Zapatista de Liberación Nacional, or EZLN) and the indigenous cause, and the Canadian government repeatedly mentioned that human rights needed to be respected. This did not please Mexican policy makers.

With the wave of democratization in 2000, it was assumed that Mexico would change its autarkic and nationalistic foreign policy. This did not happen. Canada offered assistance in the area of peacekeeping operations, making the Pearson Peacekeeping Centre available to Mexican military students. Members of the Mexican military took courses there, but the Mexican government declined to commit troops to the United Nations Stabilization Mission in Haiti (MINUSTAH) in 2004 when it could have been done so, despite a specific request from the UN.

A number of bilateral cooperation and assistance programs exist, the most significant of which is the Canada-Mexico Partnership (CMP, 2004). The CMP meets once a year, with meetings alternating between Canada and Mexico. It is coordinated by senior public servants from Canada's Department of Foreign Affairs, Trade and Development and from Mexico's Ministry of Foreign Affairs. This partnership does not have a set membership. Rather, participation is determined by membership in one of the seven working groups. As of 2010-11, the working groups included:

- Trade, Investment and Innovation
- Housing and Sustainable Communities
- Human Capital
- Agro-business
- Energy
- Labour Mobility
- Environment and Forestry.

In March 2009 a number of priority areas were identified for enhanced security cooperation between Canada and Mexico, principally police and justice system reform.

Through the Department of Justice Canada, the National Judicial Institute, Federal Judicial Affairs Canada, and the Quebec Bar Association are coordinating with the Secretaría Tecnica para la Implementación de la Reforma Judicial (SETEC) to assist Mexico in implementing its judicial reform. And with respect to law enforcement training, Canada, through the Royal Canadian Mounted Police and the Canadian Police College, is contributing to the development of a well-trained and professional police force in Mexico by offering various managerial and specialized courses to working-, middle-, and senior-level law enforcement officials.

Canada-Mexico bilateral relations have been hurt, however, by a persistent fear on the part of Canadian decision makers that inclusion of Mexico in the "North American agenda" is not in their country's best interests. This is not a new phenomenon in Canadian foreign policy: during the negotiations leading up to the signing of NAFTA, Canada repeatedly tried to torpedo Mexico's inclusion in the discussions.

After 9/11, Canadian policy makers tried to distinguish their country from Mexico, arguing that the kinds of security threats present at the Canada-US border were different from those at the Mexico-US border and should therefore be treated separately. While Canada emphasized bilateral Canada-US responses to the 9/11 terrorist attacks, Mexico pursued a trilateral approach, ironically trying to convince US policy makers to treat the country more like Canada. A further area of contention between Canadian and Mexican decision makers was the pace of change in response to 9/11.[18] While Canada preferred an incremental, piecemeal approach to dealing with security threats, Mexico wanted what its foreign minister at the time, Jorge Castañeda, called the "whole enchilada," or a comprehensive renegotiation of NAFTA to include areas such as security and migration.

In response, Canadian policy makers argued that the issues facing Canada and the United States were (and still are) the efficient flow of legitimate goods and travellers within the context of heightened US security concerns. On the other hand, the Mexico-US border was depicted as far more complex, characterized not only by a high level of trade but also by the existence of illegal migration, drug trafficking, and corruption. The negotiation of a trilateral security mechanism would require much more time and the introduction of a third actor – from a Canadian perspective – would unnecessarily delay the entire process or possibly stall it completely. Moreover, "smart border" technology at the Canada-US border had been in place for a while, predating the terrorist attacks by a number of years. The same was not the case along the Mexico-US border. By design, therefore, Canada chose to differentiate itself (in terms of both issues and solutions) from Mexico. While this stance could be justified on technical grounds, it also underscored important symbolic/political factors, depicting Mexico not so much as a partner but as a complicating ingredient in the neighbourhood.

This stands in sharp contrast to Mexico's position vis-à-vis Canada. Mexican officials want to encourage closer relations between the two countries because of perceived domestic political benefits. For reasons discussed at the outset of this chapter, Mexican public opinion is weary of close relations with the United States. To manage this anxiety, the Calderón, and especially the Fox, administration pushed for a trilateralization of security relations. By including Canada in the process, Mexican officials believe that closer relations with the United States will be more tolerable. "Canada needs to be part of integration process," argued Under-Secretary of State for North American Affairs Gerónimo Gutierrez in an informal discussion with this author, "for purely political reasons: it will be easier to sell it to Mexican public opinion."[19]

Conclusion

Recurrent economic crises, the signing of NAFTA, the events of 9/11, and the war on drugs are the key policy events that explain Mexico's reinterpretation of its role in North America. With these events, Mexican policy makers slowly came to realize that it was in the country's best interests to work more closely with Canada and the United States. The economic crises and NAFTA injected an element of pragmatism into Mexican foreign policy, and pushed economic issues to the forefront of a foreign policy agenda that had previously been guided by ideological imperatives.

Given geographic limitations, policy makers came to realize that closer economic relations with Canada and the United States were critical to Mexico's national interest.

From the perspective of its policy makers, 9/11 placed Mexico in an awkward but enviable position. On the one hand, given its geographic proximity to the United States, Mexico experienced extreme pressure from US policy makers to act as a good ally in the war against terrorism, resulting in the signing of the Smart Border agreement between the two countries in March 2002. On the other hand, Mexican policy makers saw 9/11 as offering opportunities, especially with respect to a possible migration agreement with the United States. They attempted to link migration to US national security, arguing that, in light of the heightened terrorist threat, it would be better for the United States to legalize undocumented migrants.

Lastly, the "war against drugs" has firmly conditioned Mexican national security on closer cooperation with its northern neighbour. Not only does Mexico need funding and technology from the United States in order to fight the cartels, it also needs that country to (1) manage internal demand, (2) control arms sales, (3) combat money laundering, and (4) coordinate with other regional actors. Indeed, never before has Mexican national interest been more closely intertwined with that of the United States.

In sum, Mexican foreign policy has come a long way in the last twenty years. Previously focused on nationalism, many of its decision makers now believe that it is in the country's best interests to work more closely with its North American partners, particularly the United States. However, this shift in foreign policy will continue to be met with resistance from domestic actors, ranging from public opinion and opinion makers to the Mexican Congress and even the president's cabinet. Calderón's strong-arm tactics, particularly with respect to his cabinet, muted some of the resistance to closer ties with the United States, but other nationalist actors still resist opening up Mexican foreign policy.

This tension in Mexico between state autonomy and the greater need for regional cooperation will take some time to resolve, but there are strategies that both Canada and the United States can pursue to facilitate Mexico's transition from a traditional state-sovereignty perspective to a more open regionalist perspective. As noted earlier, problems with the Mérida Initiative disbursements as well as with the WikiLeaks scandal have damaged relations with the United States and were important irritants in the bilateral relationship. The United States can therefore be more consistent in its behaviour toward Mexico.

As for Canada, the ongoing conflict with the drug cartels has dramatically de-prioritized closer relations with that country, but problems in Canada-Mexico bilateral relations had already emerged earlier. As discussed, Canadian policy makers repeatedly tried to prevent Mexico's inclusion in North America. Mexico used to consider Canada a strategic partner; it no longer does. The imposition of a visa requirement for Mexican travellers to Canada has only served to exacerbate relations between the two countries.

President Calderón has departed the scene and the country is at a crossroads. The new president, Enrique Peña Nieto, will need to decide whether the costly war on drugs is really worth continuing. This decision will have a direct impact on the extent to which Mexico continues its shift away from a traditionalist and toward a more regional and pragmatic foreign policy. Without support from Canada and the United States, Mexican decision makers will experience increasing pressure to come to some kind of arrangement with the cartels as in the days prior to the Calderón administration. If that happens, it is likely that Mexico will revert to a pseudo-isolationist foreign policy. To keep Mexico in North America, therefore, Canada and the United States will have to engage with it in a more consistent and coherent manner.

NOTES

1 Jorge G. Castañeda, "El principio de No Intervención," in *Obras Completas,* vol. 1, *Naciones Unidas,* ed. Jorge G. Castañeda (Mexico: IMRED-El Colegio de Mexico, 1995), 529; Raul Benítez-Manaut, "Sovereignty, Foreign Policy, and National Security in Mexico, 1821-1989," in *Natural Allies? Canadian and Mexican Perspectives on International Security,* ed. Hal Klepak (Ottawa: Carleton University Press; FOCAL, 1996).

2 Mario Ojeda, "La realidad geopolítica de México," *Foro Internacional* 17, 1 (July-September 1976): 1.

3 Ana Covarrubias, "No intervención versus promoción de la democracia representativa en el sistema interamericano," in *Sistema interamericano y democracia: Antecedentes históricos y tendencias futuras,* ed. Arlene B. Tickner (Bogotá: CEI-Ediciones Uniandes-OEA, 2000), 49.

4 Blanca Heredia, "La política y reforma económica: Mexico, 1985-2000," in *Chile-Mexico: Dos transiciones frente a frente,* ed. Carlos Elizondo (Mexico: Fonda de Cultura Economica, 2002).

5 Ibid., 130.

6 Ibid.

7 "Mexico Would Support Shift to Security Perimeter with US and Canada," Canadian Press, 2 February 2002.

8   For a more detailed discussion of the Security and Prosperity Partnership, see Chapter 5.

9   David Shirk, "Law Enforcement and Security Challenges in the US-Mexican Border Region," *Journal of Borderlands Studies* 18, 1 (Fall 2003): 7.

10 Ibid.

11 Julia Preston, "Mexican Immigration to US Slowed Significantly, Report Says," *New York Times*, 23 April 2012, http://www.nytimes.com/.

12 John Bailey, "Combating Organized Crime and Drug Trafficking in Mexico: What Are Mexican and US Strategies? Are They Working?" in *Shared Responsibility*, ed. Eric Olson, David A. Shirk, and Andrew D. Selee (Washington, DC: Woodrow Wilson International Center for Scholars, 2010).

13 Ibid., 332.

14 Andrew Selee, "Overview of the Merida Initiative" (Washington, DC: Woodrow Wilson International Center for Scholars, May 2008), 2, http://www.wilsoncenter.org/sites/default/files/overview_merida_initiative.pdf.

15 Eric Olson, "Six Key Issues in United States–Mexico Security Cooperation" (Washington, DC: Woodrow Wilson International Center for Scholars, July 2008), http://www.wilsoncenter.org/sites/default/files/six_issues_usmex_security_coop.pdf.

16 Athanasios Hristoulas, "Algo Nuevo, Algo Viejo," *Foreign Affairs Latinoamerica* 10, 1 (2010): 34-42.

17 Raul Benítez-Manaut, "Mexican Security and Defense Doctrines: From the 19th to the 21st Centuries," *Creating Community in the Americas*, no. 9 (November 2002): 1-4, http://www.wilsoncenter.org/sites/default/files/CreatingCommunity9-Benitez.pdf.

18 Loretta Bondi, *Beyond the Border and across the Atlantic: Mexico's Foreign and Security Policy Post-September 11th* (Washington, DC: Center for Transatlantic Relations, 2004).

19 Interview with Gerónimo Gutierrez, Under-Secretary of State for North American Affairs, 14 October 2003, Mexico City.

8

From the Border Partnership Agreement to the Twenty-First-Century Border

Enforcing Security on the US-Mexico Border

ISABELLE VAGNOUX

I reiterated that the United States accepts our shared responsibility for the drug violence. So to combat the southbound flow of guns and money, we are screening all southbound rail cargo, seizing many more guns bound for Mexico, and we are putting more gunrunners behind bars. And as part of our new drug control strategy, we are focused on reducing the demand for drugs through education, prevention and treatment ... We are very mindful that the battle President Calderón is fighting inside of Mexico is not just his battle; it's also ours. We have to take responsibility just as he's taking responsibility.

–PRESIDENT BARACK OBAMA, 3 MARCH 2011

Everything that is constantly on the diplomatic agenda goes through the US-Mexico border: people (legal or unauthorized entrants), trade, drugs, arms, electricity, water, pollution, as well as oil and gas in the near future. "A border is not only a line which separates, it is also a line which unites,"[1] and in the case of the United States and Mexico, their border – the most trafficked in the world[2] – tightly unites their two peoples and two economies, and is also the theatre of their diplomatic bones of contention. Although attempts to control "evil" flows from the south began as early as 1924 with the creation of the Border Patrol, the longest border in the world between a wealthy nation and a developing country has never been fully monitored. The southwest border has ever since been seen as a line continuously trespassed by illegal immigrants and traffickers of all sorts: liquor during Prohibition, drugs, weapons. The outcry "We've lost control of our borders" is thus purely rhetorical as they have never been fully controlled, and cannot possibly be in a democratic and open society. The fear of violence from the south spilling over north and endangering US security also finds its roots in history, in the revolutionary acts of several "heroes" of the Mexican Revolution, notably Pancho Villa. Thriving in fertile ground, the attacks of September 11, 2001, revived these deeply entrenched fears. The southwest border came to be viewed as a potential backdoor for terrorists entering the country, and triggered vivid debates that pitted continental integration against homeland security. Nowhere have domestic constraints combined so intimately with foreign affairs.

Since the 1990s and increasingly so since 9/11, the semantic field of *security* has been used repeatedly when talking about the US border with Mexico. Not that Mexico has ever been a *security* threat to the United States and its sovereignty in the traditional meaning of the word. In the context of this bilateral relationship, only terrorist acts – passage of terrorists to the United States, smuggling of biochemical or nuclear components through lawful cargoes heading north, biochemical attacks or attacks against critical infrastructure targets – belong to the category of threats to the nation-state and to the traditional scope of security. Increasingly, however, the word "security" has been stretched to include issues that do not pose an existential threat to the nation per se but rather, directly or indirectly, represent a safety threat to its *citizens* and society: illegal immigration, violence, drugs, and transnational organized crime.[3] There has been a similar shift in official speeches in the US: border security was closely associated with terrorism right after 9/11, then with illegal immigrants, and now with transnational organized crime. The same word thus encompasses a wide range of different issues.

Security appears to be a formidable rhetorical tool indeed. Not only is "security" part of the very name of the most recently created cabinet department (Homeland Security) but it also appears in a remarkable number of bills, laws, programs, policies, and speeches. In George W. Bush's Arizona speech of November 2005, the words "secure" and "security" recurred thirteen times, about the same number as "strengthen" and "enforcement," making Mexico central to the rhetoric of security. Most of the rhetoric consisted in associating the immigration issue with security, targeting illegal immigrants rather than potential terrorists.[4] Today, US Representative Michael McCaul (R-TX), now chairman of the Committee on Homeland Security, is leading the "secure border" movement in Congress:

> We indeed have a war on our southern border. Cartels are controlling the flow of illegal drugs into the U.S., and weapons and cash into Mexico. They kill anyone that gets in their way – including police officers and elected officials. It is a multi-billion dollar business. As the violence increasingly spills onto U.S. soil, it is imperative that we substantially increase the resources of our Border Patrol and Border Sheriffs.
>
> America's borders are also our nation's last line of defense in the War on Terror and they must be secured. Evidence in our 2006 report that terrorists want to exploit our porous borders to gain entry into the United States still exists today. It is for that reason alone America must make securing our borders the top priority. America has a right and, more importantly, a responsibility to determine who enters our nation and for what reasons. While reform of our legal immigration system is needed, I believe we must first secure our borders to stem the flow of illegal traffic before we begin debate on a temporary guest worker program.[5]

Border security also became a catchword and a key issue for the Republican contenders for the 2012 presidential nomination. All of them vowed to "secure the border," with promises ranging from the deployment of troops, to a drastic increase in the number of National Guard and Border Patrol agents, to the building of a fence where it does not yet exist.[6] Border issues being intermestic issues[7] par excellence, border security appears as a multi-dimensional catch-all concept to which other loosely related issues can be easily attached for purely political purposes, a word whose litany-style repetition appears to be itself part of the solution and reassuring to a portion of the US electorate.[8]

This chapter has two main objectives: (1) to analyze the security-related developments on the US-Mexico border over the past decade, and (2) to assess how Presidents Bush and Obama have addressed this issue.

Border Security in the Bush Administrations

The Aftermath of 9/11 and the Smart Border Agreement

Although "securing that border" did not start with 9/11, the attacks crystallized old fears and old clichés about the Mexico border, and allowed "low-intensity conflict"[9] methods and means, already in use in the southwest border area, to increase to unprecedented levels. The 9/11 attacks did not create the fear of threats to national security; it only magnified elements, measures, and behaviours that were already in existence. The ever-increasing presence of the Border Patrol – which increased from 4,200 agents in fiscal year 1994 to 9,200 in fiscal year 2000 – the use of high technology to monitor the border, including military equipment such as drones, as well as the construction of the fence as early as 1994 in the El Paso (Operation Hold the Line) and San Diego (Operation Gatekeeper) areas, all predated 9/11 and the War on Terror.[10]

The 9/11 attacks did not directly strike the border but they had huge ripple effects that affected the binational lifestyle in many ways and disrupted much of the trade under the North American Free Trade Agreement (NAFTA). In the days following the attacks, the southwest border was blocked: only a trickle of the tens of thousands of passages that normally occurred daily was allowed. The wait swelled up to four hours, and even pedestrian-only lines stretched a mile at the San Ysidro checkpoint, disrupting trade – 80 percent of Mexican exports to the US go through this border – and daily activities for all those with a binational lifestyle for work, study, or leisure. In the words of Peter Andreas, there began the "rebordering"[11] of North America, paradoxically at a time when free trade was in full swing and precisely when Mexican Secretary of Foreign Relations Jorge G. Castañeda was calling for and seeking to negotiate a border modelled on the European Union, open to people as well as goods. *La gran enchilada,* or a historic comprehensive immigration reform that was expected by the Mexicans earlier in 2001, simply became anathema after the attacks.[12] A decade later, a European Union–style open border is simply not on the table and will not be any time soon. Fear returned to the border when the United States waged war against Iraq: officials and residents feared terrorist attacks in retaliation, a paralyzing fear that reduced economic activity and increased controls at the border and near the strategic and military installations in the borderlands.

Although Mexico maintained a distinct voice on the international stage, as exemplified in 2003 by its opposition to the intervention in Iraq, it willingly complied with US demands in the new War on Terror, reiterated its total solidarity, and proved its good neighbourliness in anti-terrorism throughout its territory and along the common border: entry visas were refused to travellers from countries hostile to the United States, cooperation with US military forces (Northern Command) and intelligence reached unprecedented levels, and information was increasingly shared. For Mexico, it was at the same time quid pro quo and self-interest: any use of Mexican territory by terrorists against the United States or against US interests and citizens in Mexico would be disastrous and would ruin for a long time the recent progress achieved under NAFTA, the recent status of "partner," and any hope of reaching a migration agreement, still the ultimate aim of Vicente Fox's administration. One fundamental divergence has remained, however: whereas Washington focuses exclusively on security, Mexico wants to incorporate the safety dimension, which is directly related to the migration issue.

Following a similar agreement between the United States and Canada, the Border Partnership ("Smart Border") Agreement was announced in March 2002, listing twenty-two points that fell into three categories: secure infrastructure, secure flow of people (leading to the expansion of the Secure Electronic Network for Travelers Rapid Inspection – SENTRI – lanes for border residents), and secure flow of goods (with the creation of the first Free and Secure Trade – FAST – lanes),[13] to enhance border security by utilizing technology to strengthen infrastructure while facilitating the transit of people and goods across the border in order to keep NAFTA running.[14] Efforts also focused on "de-bordering" controls, such as pre-clearing frequent travellers or checking truck cargoes at the place of shipment anywhere in Mexico rather than at the border. Such operations had already begun in the late 1990s in order to relieve congestion at the ports of entry, but they were significantly increased after 2003 in order to integrate security *and* trade. Such efforts complemented those already on the way within NAFTA, and they also meant new institutional cooperation. On the Mexican side, the efforts were coordinated through the Ministry of Interior through the Centre for National Security and Intelligence (Centro de Investigación y Seguridad Nacional, or CISEN), while on the US side the White House Office of Homeland Security was in charge before the newly formed Department of Homeland Security took over in 2003. Observers and experts pointed out some organizational problems on the US side, with the DHS now gathering several agencies as well as some prerogatives heretofore held by the State Department. It took some time before everything was fully coordinated and, at least in the initial phase of the agreement, there was a slowing down of the high-level cooperation with Mexico, which had to develop new channels of interaction with the new bureaucracy.[15] Working groups on each of the twenty-two points as well as intergovernmental groups met regularly, however, and these efforts were furthered with the 2004 Plan of Action for Cooperation on Border Safety.

The tight cooperation it imposed certainly represented one of the main successes of the Border Partnership Agreement. It contributed toward reinforcing NAFTA and the interdependence of both countries. In other words, 9/11 forced the partners to agree to large-scale cooperation in areas such as information and intelligence where tight cooperation would have been difficult otherwise. At the same time, it was plagued by organizational and funding problems. Mexico was not in a position to meet all the costs entailed by US security expectations, and although the US Congress approved a supplemental appropriation in late 2002 to help Mexico implement the agreement, the funding granted in 2002 and subsequent years was generally insufficient and was often delayed due to the usual US administrative labyrinth between Congress and the executive branch. By contrast, the two countries were able to make significant progress on all actions that did not entail supplemental funding. Information sharing, consulting, coordination on visa policies, bilateral improvement of ports-of-entry management and customs agencies, and technological progress all proved quite successful. In spite of the SENTRI program, however, wait times for passenger and commercial vehicles increased, along with pollution. Above all, the migration agreement was put on the back burner of US priorities, while enhanced border security made things more difficult for those trying to migrate north and led to the criminalization of migration. According to Castañeda, "Mexico essentially gave up on linking the [security and migration] issues"[16] ... or at least became less vocal about it.

The Security and Prosperity Partnership of North America and the Secure Border Initiative

The second important step came in George W. Bush's second term, in the wake of a new trilateral agreement, the Security and Prosperity Partnership (SPP) of North America, launched on 23 March 2005 to advance the common security and common prosperity of the three North American countries through expanded cooperation and harmonization of immigration, border, and security policies.[17] Proposed initiatives for future cooperation included common methods for screening individuals and cargo, expansion of the SENTRI and FAST programs, common principles for electronic commerce, and harmonization of regulatory processes. In November of the same year, the DHS launched the Secure Border Initiative (SBI), "a comprehensive multi-year plan to secure America's borders," reach "operational control" of them, and reduce illegal migration. It included an additional 1,000 Border Patrol agents (an increase of nearly 3,000 agents since 9/11), highly sophisticated military technology transferred to a civilian implementation to control the border (SBInet; Boeing was later contracted to implement this huge task), the construction of 670 miles of pedestrian and vehicular fencing, as well as better enforcement of US immigration laws. Total funding of over $7 billion was provided. An additional $3.9 billion was provided for US Immigration and Customs Enforcement (ICE), a 9 percent increase over the previous year.[18]

The year 2006 witnessed a presidential will to augment the border buildup with Operation Jump Start (2006-08), involving the deployment of six thousand National Guardsmen to support the Border Patrol,[19] as well as implementation of the Secure Border Initiative when President Bush signed the Secure Fence Act on 26 October. The legislation provided for the construction of a double-layered fence in the main corridors used to cross the border illegally,[20] in addition to the largest points of entry already "secured" in the mid-1990s. Again, the politically correct link between "securing" the border and immigration reform was established: "This bill will help protect the American people. This bill will make our borders more secure. It is an important step toward immigration reform," said Bush upon signing the bill into law.[21] From the time it was passed by the House of Representatives in December 2005 to its signature by the President, this "hateful" plan, in Castañeda's words,[22] drew intense criticism – including from US editorialists, experts, chambers of commerce, and many borderlands local officials. Stigmatized as the new Berlin Wall, the fence marred the end of the Fox administration (President Fox called it "the wall of ignominy") and the early relationship with the newly elected Mexican president, Felipe Calderón, who had called the proposal "historically inacceptable," "deplorable," and a "grave mistake." Coming after the Iraq War, the fence increased Mexican distrust of the Bush administration. Worse, most of the Secure Border elements were deemed impracticable by the experts, due to difficult terrain and a cost that was largely underestimated. The comprehensive immigration reform that was supposed to counterbalance the act was defeated in Congress. Only the most punitive aspects – raids on employment sites and deportations of illegals – were actually implemented.

SBInet raised even more doubts, including those from the congressional investigative arm, the Government Accountability Office (GAO). As early as February 2007, the program was found to lack sufficient management controls and to be marred by cost overruns and performance problems.[23] Although the DHS and Boeing took action to address the weaknesses identified by the agency, the results were hardly satisfactory. Until the virtual border was halted in 2010, the GAO released fourteen critical reports on a system that was "overpromised and underdelivered," paving the way for Janet Napolitano's conclusion in March 2010 that it was "plagued with cost overruns and missed deadlines" and ultimately for its demise one year later.

In 2007, the Mérida Initiative, inspired by the Plan Colombia, was launched to address the drug-related violence that was flaring up in northern Mexico, adjacent to the United States. The US military diagnosed that this violence "could represent a homeland security problem of immense proportions to the United States."[24] With a $1.8 billion assistance package to Mexico and Central America, Mérida contributed significantly toward increasing US-Mexican security and law enforcement cooperation, while NAFTA contributed toward easing it. Although not focusing on the border, the Mérida Initiative adopted the "holistic approach" later championed by the Obama administration. To improve the police, the rule of law, and the judicial system, and to disrupt transnational organized crime, are all long-range objectives that are bound to "secure the border" along with the rest of Mexico.[25] Although Mérida did in fact launch the "shared" concept, the Obama administration developed the rhetoric attached to it.

Shared Problems and Shared Responsibility

The Obama administration has largely built upon its predecessor's border policies. The number of Border Patrol agents has continued to soar, as planned by the Bush administration, reaching 18,546 for the southwest border alone in fiscal year 2012, or 86.7 percent of the total number.[26] Deportations of unauthorized immigrants have not abated (approximately 400,000 a year). More and more drones are used to monitor the border. The number of intelligence analysts working on the border has tripled. The fence is now nearly complete. The Mérida Initiative still gets US funding, although at slightly lower levels than in the early years. More SENTRI/FAST lanes have been opened and 100 percent of southbound shipments are screened. Only the SBInet program was ended. The state of the US economy, the administration's ideology, and public opinion all account for this reorientation of the management of border security.[27]

   Although it continues to strengthen border enforcement, the Obama administration has chosen to address the narcoviolence issue by emphasizing the responsibility of the United States in the development of this curse and sharing the load with Mexico.[28]

> The violence in Mexico is not only an international threat. It is a homeland security issue in which all Americans have a stake. America has a significant security stake in the success of Mexico's efforts against drug cartels ... The dynamic of the border region makes violence on one side of the border a pressing concern on both sides. The transnational nature of this threat clearly makes addressing the violence in Mexico a top priority in securing the United States.[29]

In an interview at the Migration Policy Institute in Washington, DC, in October 2010, Customs and Border Protection Commissioner Alan Bersin emphasized that underlying the new twenty-first-century border vision is a "paradigm shift," "a change in how people view the border."[30] This paradigm shift is at the core of President Obama's declarations. The terms "shared" as well as "lawful" recur in the 19 May 2010 Joint Declaration concerning twenty-first-century Border Management (Pillar 3 of the Beyond Mérida Initiative, officially launched in March 2010 by Presidents Obama and Calderón). Rather than the blame game or scare tactics, the new paradigm consists in strengthened cooperation on preventing illegal flows in which both governments recognize their responsibilities, and in managing the border in a holistic fashion, together. Whether Mexican or American, the diplomats interviewed for this chapter all agreed that cooperation was more intimate now than under the previous administration.

Evaluating the Terrorist Threat along the Mexican Border

Obviously, the initial raison d'être of the huge border enforcement, terrorism, is passé and was already so in the second Bush administration. The Obama administration has never linked terrorism with border security. Border Patrol and Department of Justice data show that over the past six years an annual average of 339 people from "special interest countries" (i.e., with links to terrorism) have been apprehended at the southwest border, which amounts to less than 1 percent of the total number of apprehensions along the border. In addition, these people presented no credible terrorist threat. In only a handful of cases did suspected terrorists cross the border illegally, but they were not involved in any terrorist act. Actually, of the thirty-six people convicted by US federal courts of charges relating to international terrorism in 2010, none came into the United States from Mexico and none was an illegal immigrant: all were US citizens, legal residents, or people entering the country on legal visas. In other words, in the ten years since 9/11, the southwest border has never been used as a passage for terrorists.[31] The State Department further confirmed the absence of significant terrorist threat in Latin America, particularly in Mexico:

> The threat of a transnational terrorist attack remained low for most countries in the Western Hemisphere ... No known international terrorist organization had an operational presence in Mexico and no terrorist group targeted U.S. interests and personnel in or from Mexican territory. There was no evidence of ties between Mexican criminal organizations and terrorist groups, nor that the criminal organizations had aims of political or territorial control, aside from seeking to protect and expand the impunity with which they conduct their criminal activity.[32]

Yet, whether in the US Congress, at the state level, or at the local law enforcement level, many fear collusion between terrorist groups and drug cartels with the latter letting the former use their routes to the US side of the border. Although such an alliance is theoretically possible – and the improbable October 2011 plot to kill the Saudi ambassador to the United States, allegedly involving contacts with a Mexican drug cartel, has increased this fear – it has not materialized so far.[33] Drug traffickers are money-driven, not ideology-driven. A terrorist attack would lead to full militarization and sealing of the border, seriously disrupting their routine business.

The "Spillover" Effect

A "security threat" to the United States, Mexican drug trafficking organizations (DTOs) are accused of "spilling violence over the border," which would justify the need to "secure the border" and to devote more human and financial resources to that end. It was precisely in order to elevate drug trafficking to a full security threat and increase the judicial, financial, and personnel resources to fight it that Representative Michael McCaul (R, Texas) introduced legislation in March 2011 (HR 1270) to direct the secretary of state to designate as "foreign terrorist organizations" the most dangerous Mexican drug cartels, thus exposing Mexican drug traffickers and US gunrunners to charges of supporting terrorism. Representative Connie Mack (Florida) introduced similar legislation (HR 3401) the following November, but neither bill became law. Ten years after 9/11, terrorism was again part of border security rhetoric.

Although the extreme violence wrought by DTOs throughout Mexico cannot be denied, the spillover argument is the object of a statistics battle waged largely along partisan lines. McCaul's subcommittee is particularly active in advancing this argument.[34] On the other hand, State Department and DHS officials, chambers of commerce, and an array of local officials deny the existence of any such spillover, depict the US side of the border as safe and thriving,[35] and urge Republicans to stop hurting the image of US border cities. Such scare tactics, they argue, are bound to have adverse effects on the socioeconomic fabric of the US side of the border, which in turn will aggravate poverty and increase the risk of collusion with cartels. One side emphasizes the increase in apprehensions of criminal aliens in Texas; the other uses FBI statistics to point out that Detroit, St. Louis, Baltimore, or even Washington, DC, all have much higher violent crime and murder rates than any town along the southwest border.[36]

In a report issued early in 2011, the Congressional Research Service, drawing on maps and figures from the US Department of Justice, emphasized that Mexican DTOs were present in virtually every single state and in some 230 cities, and that the phenomenon went far beyond the border region.[37] It concluded:

> The data, however, do not allow analysts to determine what proportion of the violent crime rate is related to drug trafficking or, even more specifically, what proportion of drug trafficking-related violent crimes can be attributed to spillover violence. In conclusion, because the trends in the overall violent crime rate may not be indicative of trends in drug trafficking-related violent crimes, CRS is unable to draw definitive claims about trends in drug trafficking-related violence spilling over from Mexico into the United States.[38]

In other words, the influence of DTOs should be monitored throughout the nation, and not exclusively along the border. The threats related to drug trafficking go way beyond the border. The consumption issue and its corollary, the debate on the legalization of marijuana, involve the whole fabric of US society and the Obama administration has hardly addressed the issue so far.

The Holistic, Start-at-Home Approach

"Shared problems" entail "shared responsibilities." Launched in March 2009, the Southwest Border Initiative emphasized the need to address US responsibility for what makes drug-related violence possible: the illegal flow of money and the smuggling of illegal weapons into Mexico, two movements whose scope is extremely difficult to measure accurately. On the US side, the initiative also took into account the federative fabric of the nation and called for coordinating the federal response with state and local stakeholders. It also recognized the Mérida Initiative as the cornerstone of the partnership with Mexican law enforcement, a partnership that should be expanded. Finally, the initiative included planning for "worst case scenarios – even if they are unlikely," such as "increased spillover violence into the U.S."[39]

Whereas the first National Southwest Border Counternarcotics Strategy, released in 2007, focused primarily on what the US government could do to prevent the illegal trafficking of drugs across the border with Mexico, the 2009 version called for more dialogue among the various actors, expanding "its focus beyond stemming the inbound flow of illegal drugs from Mexico." It recognized "the role that the outbound flow of illegal cash and weapons plays in sustaining the cartels," and concluded that "the strategy also is the result of an expanded consultation process, including more thorough coordination with Congress, State and local authorities, and the Government of Mexico."[40] In keeping with the 21st-Century Border spirit and the "shared responsibility"/"start at home" mantra, the 2011 version added expansion of access to drug treatment and support for programs that break the cycle of drug use, violence, and crime – in other words, it directly addresses the consumption side of the narcotics equation.

As for illegal weapons, at least 70 percent of those recovered reportedly come from the United States. From the early days of his administration, President Obama showed his will to address the arms issue in the United States and to have the Senate ratify the Inter-American Arms Treaty (unsuccessfully so far).[41] In July 2011, a federal regulation addressed the issue by requiring gun dealers in the US border states to report to the Bureau of Alcohol, Tobacco, Firearms and Explosives (ATF) whenever they sell to the same buyer within a five-day period two or more semi-automatic rifles of at least .22 caliber with ability to accept a detachable magazine. Dealers nationwide are already required to report bulk sales of handguns. It is much too early to determine whether this rule will be successful or even whether it will be implemented at all, as the National Rifle Association has filed a suit against it, arguing that it had been issued without congressional permission. As of July 2013, the 2011 federal regulation had been upheld by the US Court of Appeals for the District of Columbia Circuit, but two other cases were still on appeal. It was also the determination to be proactive on the issue that prompted the ATF to launch Operation Fast and Furious from 2009 to 2011, which derailed disastrously.[42]

As for money laundering, experts point to the great number of bank branches along the border, a number that does not correspond to local living standards. The proportion of money laundering in total banking operations remains difficult to evaluate; consequently, the struggle is based on a case-by-case approach.[43]

The "holistic approach" also includes improving Mexico's civilian environment by institutionalizing the rule of law (Pillar 2 of the Beyond Mérida Initiative) and "building strong and resilient communities" (Pillar 4) by expanding already existing programs. Under the aegis of the United States Agency for International Development (USAID), the objective of Pillar 4 is to support projects that reduce border communities' risk of and vulnerability to violence by funding crime prevention programs or helping civic organizations influence local politics. Pillar 4 aims to strengthen the social fabric of border communities, which often consist of an unstable migrating population, in between two worlds, who live close to the border until they can cross over to the US side. Hardly committed to community life, this population tends to be more vulnerable to organized crime. The holistic and shared-responsibility approach definitely takes a long-term view, and it will be a long time, perhaps up to a generation or more, before significant results are seen.

Conclusion: Of Measures and Results

In a recent *Foreign Affairs* article, Edward Alden and Bryan Roberts argue that both the lack of definition of expectations and the lack of effective ways to measure progress prevent the US government from knowing whether or not the border is secured and proving it.[44] Consequently, the message to the public is blurred. "Security" is never adequately defined, and neither is what exactly the Department of Homeland Security seeks to achieve. Over the past decade, the total number of Border Patrol agents has more than doubled – up to some 21,444 in fiscal year 2011 – and billions of dollars have been spent on border security, yet the challenges remain very much the same as when Timothy J. Dunn published his *Militarization of the US-Mexico Border* in 1996.[45] Illegal immigration and drug trafficking have not subsided, and the politicians' rhetoric is strikingly similar. The "secure our borders" mantra was already being heard during the Nixon administration.

As far as unauthorized immigration is concerned, contradictory figures for apprehension of illegals (the peak of a decade ago as well as the recent drop[46]) have been presented to the public as a victory for better border enforcement, which blurs the government's message and confuses Congress. Some members of the Republican Party refuse to discuss immigration reform until "the border is secured." But with neither a clear definition of what exactly security means nor effective ways of measuring progress, when will we know that the border is secured? When no unauthorized immigrants cross it? This is an unattainable goal in a democratic society, and especially when the US economy depends partly on illegal labour.[47] Moreover, numerous unauthorized migrants have never tried to cross the border illegally; rather, they entered the United States legally and outstayed their visas. Whether the border is fully secured or porous has no impact on this portion of the illegal population. In addition, how do we know that potential illegal immigrants have been deterred because of stepped-up border enforcement and not for other reasons? Recent studies have emphasized the role of the economic downturn in the United States as one such deterrent, as well as the greater number of visas granted to Mexicans. Using Mexican government data, the Pew Hispanic Center also showed that better job opportunities and a thriving economy in Mexico were significant disincentives to illegal immigration, along with increasing violence accompanying the journey to the US side. Significant demographic changes in Mexico have led to new parameters: population growth has slowed considerably and the Mexican population is aging, leading to fewer people competing for more jobs. In other words, while both the Bush and the Obama administrations have consistently empha- sized the role of border enforcement in the decline of illegal crossings, it appears that a whole array of factors are actually involved, whether or not the US government pours millions of dollars into southwest border enforcement.[48]

The US government data provide only the *number* of seizures (for drugs) and apprehensions (for immigrants), but not the *proportion* of these arrests and seizures. What does an increase in the number of drug seizures mean? That customs agents are more efficient (which is positive in terms of securing the border) or that more drugs are entering the country (which is negative in that respect)? What does a decrease mean? That cus- toms agents have been less efficient or that fewer drugs are entering the United States? To be sure, drugs and unauthorized immigrants are by def- inition impossible to measure accurately, but as long as objectives are not clearly defined and proportions, rather than absolute numbers, are not published, it will be impossible to evaluate the success of the various bor- der policies implemented over the last decade and the rhetoric of an inse- cure border will continue to thrive.

In both cases, the answers are mainly to be found on the domestic front, in terms of demand reduction in the United States and more effec- tive judicial procedures in Mexico, regardless of increases in the number of Border Patrol agents, high-tech surveillance equipment, and miles of fencing, although the latter may still be necessary before the former are achieved. Although there is still room for improvement, bilateral cooper- ation has reached unprecedented levels. At the same time, the two coun- tries face domestic hurdles and challenges that, in spite of the concept of shared responsibility, cause them to focus on their national interests to the detriment of the twenty-first-century border and NAFTA paradigms.

NOTES

1   Wendell Gordon, "A Case for a Less Restrictive Policy," *Social Science Quarterly* 56, 3 (December 1975): 490.

2   In 2010, the southwest border was crossed by 64 million personal vehicles, 218,754 buses, 7,667 trains, 39 million pedestrians, and 4.7 million trucks. US, Department of Transportation, Research and Innovative Technology Administration, "Border Crossing/Entry Data: Quick Search by Rankings," http://www.bts.gov/.

3   US, White House, *Strategy to Combat Transnational Organized Crime*, 25 July 2011, http://www.whitehouse.gov/sites/default/files/Strategy_to_Combat_Transnational_Organized_Crime_July_2011.pdf.

4   US, White House, "President Discusses Border Security and Immigration Reform in Arizona," Office of Press Secretary, 28 November 2005, http://georgewbush-whitehouse.archives.gov/.

5   Michael McCaul, "Border Security," Congressman Michael McCaul's Official Website, http://mccaul.house.gov/border-security/. The first report drafted in 2006 by the House Committee on Homeland Security, Subcommittee on Oversight, Investigations and Management, was updated in November 2012: *A Line in the Sand: Countering Crime, Violence and Terror at the Southwest Border*, http://homeland.house.gov/sites/homeland.house.gov/files/11-15-12-Line-in-the-Sand.pdf.

6   Comments by Michele Bachmann are available in "Bachmann: US-Mexico Border Wall OK," *Austin Daily Herald*, 16 August 2011, http://www.austindailyherald.com/; quotations from Governor Perry in 2010 can be retrieved from Dan Hirshhorn, "Perry: May Need Troops in Mexico," *Politico*, 18 November 2010, http://www.politico.com/; as for Mitt Romney, his plan for Latin America included the fact that he "will use the full powers of the presidency to complete an impermeable border fence protecting our southern frontier from infiltration by illegal migrants, trans-national criminal networks, and terrorists": "The US Presidential and Vice Presidential Candidates' Views on US-Mexico Border Security," Washington Office on Latin America, http://www.wola.org/.

7   The term was initially coined by Bayless Manning, "The Congress, the Executive and Intermestic Affairs: Three Proposals," *Foreign Affairs* 55 (January 1977): 306-24, and subsequently elaborated upon by Robert D. Putnam, "Diplomacy and Domestic Politics: The Logic of the Two-Level Game," *International Organization* 42, 3 (Summer 1988): 427-60.

8   See Chapter 2.

9   For a definition of low-intensity conflict and its application to the US-Mexico border, see Timothy J. Dunn, *The Militarization of the US-Mexico Border, 1978-1992* (Austin: CMAS Books, University of Texas, 1996), 20-23.

10 As early as 1999, Peter Andreas wrote the aptly titled "Borderless Economy, Barricaded Border," *NACLA Report on the Americas* 33, 3 (November-December 1999): 14-21.

11 Peter Andreas and Thomas J. Biersteker, *The Rebordering of North America: Integration and Exclusion in a New Security Context* (New York: Routledge, 2003).

12 Jorge G. Castañeda recognizes in his book-memoir that the failure of the reform cannot be attributed to the terrorist attacks but to other purely political and domestic factors in the United States. *Ex Mex: From Migrants to Immigrants* (New York: New Press, 2007), 78-81.

13   US, White House, "Smart Border: 22 Point Agreement. US-Mexico Border Partnership
     Action Plan," http://georgewbush-whitehouse.archives.gov/.

14   For the chronology of the bilateral steps over the period 2001-05, see K. Larry Storrs,
     Mexico–United States Dialogue on Migration and Border Issues, 2001-2005, CRS Report for
     Congress RL32735, 2 June 2005, http://www.fas.org/sgp/crs/row/RL32735.pdf.

15   Deborah Waller Meyers, "Does 'Smarter' Lead to Safer? An Assessment of the Border
     Accords with Canada and Mexico," *International Migration* 41, 4 (December 2003): 7-12;
     US-Mexico Binational Council, *US-Mexico Border Security and the Evolving Security
     Relationship: Recommendations for Policymakers* (Washington, DC: Center for Strategic
     and International Studies, April 2004), 29, http://csis.org/files/media/csis/pubs/
     0404_bordersecurity.pdf.

16   Castañeda, *Ex Mex,* 98-99.

17   See Chapter 5.

18   Dozens of towers equipped with thermal-imaging cameras would be placed along the
     border. Using Global Positioning System (GPS), operators would watch monitors in a
     control room and transmit information to Border Patrol agents.

19   The National Guardsmen were commissioned to relieve Border Patrol agents of
     administrative and logistical duties and to improve and construct roads necessary to
     efficient border enforcement. Six thousand "citizen soldiers" were sent down to the
     border during the first year. Only three thousand remained in the second year of the
     operation. Today smaller numbers of National Guardsmen help the Border Patrol in
     their counter-narcotics activities. An official summary of Operation Jump Start is
     available in Michael D. Doubler, *Operation Jump Start: The National Guard on the
     Southwest Border, 2006-2008* (Arlington, VA: National Guard Bureau, Office of Public
     Affairs, Historical Services Division, 24 October 2008), http://www.ng.mil/features/
     Border/factsheets/NGB_JumpStart.pdf.

20   Tecate, California; between Calexico, California, and Douglas, Arizona; between
     Columbus, New Mexico, and El Paso; between Del Rio and Eagle Pass; and between
     Laredo and Brownsville, the latter all in Texas.

21   US, White House, "Fact Sheet: The Secure Fence Act of 2006," Office of the Press
     Secretary, 26 October 2006, http://georgewbush-whitehouse.archives.gov/. The text of
     the act is available at Govtrack, "H.R. 6061 (109th): Secure Fence Act of 2006,"
     http://www.govtrack.us/.

22   Castañeda, *Ex Mex,* 165.

23   US, Government Accountability Office, *Secure Border Initiative: SBInet Planning and
     Management Improvements Needed to Control Risks,* Report to the Congress GAO-07-504T
     (Washington, DC: United States Government Accountability Office, 2 February 2007).

24   US, Joint Forces Command, *The Joint Operating Environment 2008: Challenges and
     Implications for the Future Joint Force* (Suffolk, VA: United States Joint Forces Command,
     2008), 34, http://www.jfcom.mil/newslink/storyarchive/2008/JOE2008.pdf.

25   See Chapter 7.

26　The annual evolution of Border Patrol staffing as well as maps and other Border Patrol statistics are available at http://www.cbp.gov/xp/cgov/border_security/border_patrol/usbp_statistics/.

27　A Sky Island Alliance, YouGov, and Sierra Club poll taken in May 2011 showed that a majority of Americans supported border security measures, but that after being informed of the financial and environmental costs of additional border fence construction, 92 percent preferred beefing up ports of entry to building more fences. The detailed poll results are available at Sky Island Alliance, "New Poll: Americans Support Greater Investment in Ports of Entry – Not Border Walls," 14 July 2011, http://www.skyislandalliance.org/misc/SIA Border Poll Press Release.pdf; Brady McCombs, "Border Boletín: Poll Shows Lukewarm Support for More Border Walls," *Arizona Daily Star,* 14 July 2011, http://azstarnet.com/news/.

28　President Clinton had already hinted at this co-responsibility during his second term. The Mexican officials interviewed for this chapter argued that the drug-related violence in Mexico may indirectly result from the increased border security enforcement on the US side. Finding it more difficult to transport drugs across the border, drug cartels were led to redefine their systems of alliances and to compete more fiercely.

29　US, Department of Homeland Security, "Testimony of Secretary of Homeland Security Janet Napolitano before the Senate Homeland Security Committee, Southern Border Violence: Homeland Security, Threats, Vulnerabilities and Responsibilities," 25 March 2009, http://www.dhs.gov/.

30　Migration Policy Institute, "Customs and Border Protection Commissioner Alan Bersin Addresses MPI," 14 October 2010, http://migrationpolicy.podbean.com/.

31　Brady McCombs and Tim Steller, "Border Seen as Unlikely Terrorist Crossing Point," *Arizona Daily Star,* 7 June 2011.

32　US, Department of State, Office of the Coordinator for Counterterrorism, "Country Reports: Western Hemisphere Overview," in *Country Reports on Terrorism 2010* (Washington, DC: Department of State, 18 August 2011), http://www.state.gov/documents/organization/170479.pdf.

33　US, House of Representatives, "Joint Subcommittee Hearing: Mérida Part Two: Insurgency and Terrorism in Mexico" (Washington, DC: Committee on Homeland Security – Subcommittee on Oversight, Investigations and Management, 4 October 2011); US, House of Representatives, "Subcommittee Hearing: A Call to Action: Narcoterrorism's Threat to the Southern U.S. Border" (Washington, DC: Committee on Homeland Security – Subcommittee on Oversight, Investigations and Management, 14 October 2011), http://homeland.house.gov/.

34　Barry McCaffrey and Robert Scales, *Texas Border Security: A Strategic Military Assessment,* Texas Department of Agriculture, September 2011, http://mccaul.house.gov/uploads/Final Report-Texas Border Security.pdf.

35 Author's interviews with Department of State officials and various Texas officials, April 2011. See also Veronica Escobar, "All Quiet on the Southern Front," *New York Times,* 5 October 2011.

36 The FBI cautions against ranking that leads to "simplistic and/or incomplete analyses that often create misleading perceptions adversely affecting communities and their residents." Federal Bureau of Investigation, "Crime in the United States," Table 8, "Offenses Known to Law Enforcement by State by City, 2010," http://www.fbi.gov/.

37 The maps showing the presence of Mexican DTOs in US cities as of 2008 are available at National Drug Intelligence Center, "Situation Report: Cities in Which Mexican DTOs Operate within the United States," 11 April 2008, http://www.justice.gov/archive/ndic/pubs27/27986/27986p.pdf.

38 Kristin M. Finklea, William J. Krouse, and Mark A. Randol, *Southwest Border Violence: Issues in Identifying and Measuring Spillover Violence,* CRS Report for Congress R41075, 25 January 2011, summary.

39 Ibid.

40 US, Office of National Drug Control Policy, "Message from the Director," in *National Southwest Border Counternarcotics Strategy* (Washington, DC: Office of National Drug Control Policy, June 2009), http://www.whitehouse.gov/sites/default/files/ondcp/policy-and-research/swb_counternarcotics_strategy09.pdf.

41 Organization of American States, "Inter-American Convention against the Illicit Manufacturing of and Trafficking in Firearms, Ammunition, Explosives, and Other Related Materials," OAS Department of International Law, 14 November 1997, http://www.oas.org/.

42 Agents monitored straw buyers who bought two thousand guns but did not arrest them because the agents were trying to identify higher-ups in the network. The operation derailed when the ATF lost track of many of the guns, some of which were smuggled into Mexico and used in a shootout in Arizona where an American Border Patrol agent was killed.

43 Interview with Mexican official, June 2011.

44 Edward Alden and Bryan Roberts, "Are US Borders Secure? Why We Don't Know, and How to Find Out." *Foreign Affairs* 90, 4 (July/August 2011): 19-26.

45 Dunn, *The Militarization of the US-Mexico Border.*

46 Ninety-seven percent of Border Patrol apprehensions occur on the Mexico-US border. As many as 1.7 million in fiscal year 2000, they reached a low of 356,873 in fiscal year 20120. Over three-quarters of those apprehended are Mexicans: US, Department of Homeland Security, "U.S. Border Patrol Nationwide Apprehensions by Sector, Fiscal Year, 1992-2012," http://cbp.gov/xp/cgov/border_security/border_patrol/usbp_statistics/usbp_fy12_stats/.

47 According to the Pew Hispanic Center, in 2008 unauthorized immigrants nationwide represented 25 percent of workers in the farming sector, 19 percent in the building/groundskeeping and maintenance sector, and 17 percent in construction. Such

percentages might be higher in border states. Jeffrey Passel and D'Vera Cohn, *A Portrait of Unauthorized Immigrants in the United States* (Washington, DC: Pew Hispanic Center, 14 April 2009), http://pewhispanic.org. Two years later, despite a decrease in the unauthorized population, they still represented 5.2 percent of the labour force, compared with 5.4 percent in 2008.

48 Damien Cave, "Better Lives for Mexicans Cut Allure of Going North," *New York Times*, 6 July 2011; Pew Hispanic Center, "The Mexican-American Boom: Births Overtake Immigration," 14 July 2011, http://www.pewhispanic.org. World Bank data show that Mexico is faring much better than the United States in terms of GDP growth (5.5 percent in 2010, 3.9 percent in 2011). Its fertility rate (2.2 per woman in 2012) is now very similar to that of the United States (2.1), unlike in the 1960s, when the average was seven children. Only 28 percent of the population was under fifteen in 2012, compared with 45 percent in the 1960s. See http://data.worldbank.org/indicator.

9 National Interest or Self-Interest?

Advocacy Think Tanks, 9/11, and the Future of North American Security

DONALD E. ABELSON

The purpose of this chapter is not to chronicle the events of 9/11 or to retrace the steps taken by the Bush White House in the ensuing weeks and months to combat terrorism.[1] These avenues of inquiry have been pursued elsewhere.[2] Rather, we will broaden our discussion by considering how various non-governmental organizations (NGOs) with expertise in foreign and defence policy have helped shape the political discourse around American national security policy in the post-9/11 era. More specifically, we will highlight how a select group of advocacy think tanks have developed a narrative, rooted in the tragedy of 9/11, to enhance their power and influence in the political arena. As Frank Harvey reminds us in Chapter 2, policy makers, government departments and agencies, NGOs, and the media often have a vested interest in exaggerating the nature of security threats confronting the United States. Indeed, convincing the public that the United States has no option but to wage a global war against terror can pay handsome dividends to these and other stakeholders that are committed to shaping the political climate in the United States.

Several advocacy think tanks have joined the chorus of voices calling for the United States to take a hard-line position against terrorists and the states that harbour them. In the process, some advocacy think tanks have willingly abandoned their commitment to policy research, a hallmark of think tanks created during the Progressive era of the early 1900s. Instead, they have elected to embrace the role of policy advocates by becoming vocal combatants in the war of ideas. Although think tanks may claim to be non-partisan research institutions committed to serving the national interest, their primary goal is not necessarily to improve governmental decision making. At times, they are more committed to influencing the policy preferences and choices of decision makers in ways that advance their own institutional goals and objectives.

A handful of former policy makers, including anti-terrorism czar Richard Clarke, have written bestselling tomes about why the Clinton and Bush administrations did not take sufficient precautions to prevent acts of terrorism.[3] Even more has been penned about why successive governments have committed the United States to fighting unwinnable wars. Yet few scholars have paid close attention to how various think tanks with close ties to policy makers on Capitol Hill, in the White House, and throughout the bureaucracy have helped the Bush and Obama administrations justify and promote the war on terror. From celebrating the invasions of Afghanistan and Iraq to endorsing a host of domestic security measures to protect the American homeland, think tanks have made their presence felt in key policy debates.

This chapter begins by providing an overview of the rise of advocacy think tanks in the United States, and the various channels on which they rely to communicate their ideas to policy makers and other stakeholders. Once we have laid the foundation for a more detailed discussion of the role of think tanks, we will turn our attention to the efforts of a handful of think tanks to shape North American security relations in the post-9/11 era. Among other things, we will briefly discuss why few think tanks have assessed the impact of Washington's security posture on its continental neighbours. Much of the discussion in the think tank community since 9/11 has revolved around conceptions of American security and global security, but relatively little attention has been given to the issue of North American security and prosperity. For instance, the security perimeter that was adopted by President Barack Obama and Prime Minister Stephen Harper in 2011 was advocated by some policy makers as a way to supplement border security, but little consideration was given to how tighter border restrictions have impeded the United States' trade relation with Canada and Mexico. The priority for many think tanks continues to be how best to defend the US homeland from enemies at home and abroad rather than how to manage North American relations. This will be illustrated by revealing how a handful of think tanks made their presence felt immediately after the 9/11 attacks. We will reveal how and to what extent scholars from the American Enterprise Institute (AEI) and the now defunct Project for the New American Century (PNAC) attempted to make the war on terror more palatable to the American public.

The Rise of Advocacy Think Tanks

Until the early 1980s, political scientists and historians paid little attention to think tanks and their efforts to convey ideas to policy makers.[4] Indeed, think tanks were barely mentioned in most textbooks on American government and US foreign and defence policy. To those familiar with the evolution of think tanks in the United States, however, this is not entirely surprising. Unlike interest groups, political action committees, and foreign lobbies, whose express purpose is to influence legislation on Capitol Hill, think tanks were, for much of the twentieth century, perceived as institutions that made a concerted effort to insulate themselves from partisan politics. This is not to suggest that think tanks necessarily avoided participating in policy debates that had obvious political overtones. Rather, I am suggesting that engaging in politics with the public and with policy makers was simply not considered their raison d'être. To work at the Brookings Institution, the Carnegie Endowment for International Peace, the National Bureau of Economic Research, or the RAND Corporation, scholars armed with PhDs were expected to engage in research that adhered to rigorous scientific standards. In this respect, as Kent Weaver points out, these organizations resembled "universities without students."[5] The primary goal of these institutions and the scholars who laboured there was to help government think its way through complex policy problems. Robert Brookings, Andrew Carnegie, and other leading philanthropists of the Progressive era believed that by engaging in long-term strategic thinking, a luxury rarely afforded to policy experts in government, think tanks could make a significant contribution to the well-being of the nation.[6]

There is little doubt that several of these institutions made their presence felt in the first half of the twentieth century. In the late 1970s and early 1980s, however, a new breed of think tank began to capture the attention of policy makers and the public. Rather than adhering to a traditional think tank model that emphasized the virtues of policy research, two former congressional aides, Paul Weyrich and Edwin Feulner, recognized the value of creating a think tank capable of combining policy research with political advocacy. With $250,000 in seed money from

Joseph Coors, Weyrich and Feulner established the Washington-based Heritage Foundation in 1973. Their vision of creating an institution that could successfully compete in the marketplace of ideas would have a profound impact on shaping an entire generation of think tanks.[7]

Advocacy think tanks, described as such because of the importance they assign to aggressively marketing and promoting ideas, now constitute the majority of the more than 2,500 think tanks headquartered in the United States. What distinguishes advocacy think tanks from other institutions that comprise the think tank community in the United States is their emphasis on what is commonly referred to as quick-response policy research. Instead of encouraging resident scholars or fellows to devote years to writing academic books on esoteric topics, advocacy think tanks instruct them to generate timely and policy-relevant briefs and analyses that address a wide range of domestic and foreign policy issues. These briefs are posted on institute websites and are sent electronically to thousands of policy makers, journalists, academics, and business leaders on a regular basis. Besides writing concise reports that provide policy recommendations, scholars at advocacy think tanks are expected to prepare op-ed pieces for national and international newspapers, appear as guests on radio and television news programs and political talk shows, testify before congressional committees, and maintain blogs. The more prestigious advocacy think tanks, such as Heritage, have large media relations teams with multi-million-dollar budgets who are dedicated to enhancing their employer's public profile.[8]

Another common characteristic of advocacy think tanks is their willingness to showcase the ideological underpinnings of their research. As 501(c)(3) tax-exempt organizations under the Internal Revenue Code, think tanks are prohibited from engaging in partisan activities such as donating money to political campaigns or publicly endorsing candidates for office. Remaining non-partisan is a legal requirement, but this does not in any way prevent think tanks from publicly embracing an ideology. In their annual reports and research publications, advocacy think tanks proudly proclaim their ideological principles.

By combining policy research with – or, more accurately, subsuming it under – political advocacy, the Heritage Foundation and its many disciples have forever changed the complexion of the think tank community. To suggest that think tanks have willingly abandoned their commitment to academic research in favour of political advocacy is no longer considered heresy. For most observers of American think tanks, this is axiomatic. Furthermore, there is little expectation among scholars and policy makers that advocacy think tanks will generate cutting-edge research. On the contrary, the expectation is that think tanks will continue to contribute personnel to new administrations – the revolving-door phenomenon – and will stake out and defend positions on a host of controversial policy issues. There is a further expectation that think tanks will provide a steady stream of information and ideas to satisfy the 24-7 news media.

Is There a "North American Security Policy"?

It bears repeating that, unlike the first generation of think tanks that graced America's political landscape in the early 1900s, the ultimate goal of advocacy think tanks is not to think in terms of the national interest. If it were, many of these institutions would have assigned a much higher priority to considering the myriad complex security issues confronting the United States in the twenty-first century and the impact that stronger domestic security measures would have both at home and abroad. To the dismay of some observers of American politics, however, few advocacy think tanks have been prepared to think outside the box. Rather than engaging in a thoughtful and provocative discussion about why America's obsession with its security after 9/11 may in the long run lead to future terrorist attacks, advocacy think tanks have, for the most part, embraced the narrative cultivated by President Bush and preserved by President Obama. In many respects, conservative advocacy think tanks have become cheerleaders for America's war on terror. But have they done this out of a sense of patriotism, or simply to advance their own self-interest?

As noted, in the immediate aftermath of 9/11, several Washington-based think tanks devoted considerable resources to sharing their insights with policy makers, academics, journalists, and other stakeholders about the war on terror and its implications for America. The Brookings Institution, AEI, the Center for Strategic and International Studies, the Heritage Foundation, and several other institutes hosted dozens of conferences, workshops, and seminars about various aspects of terrorism and future threats to the United States. Scholars from think tanks also published a steady stream of articles, newsletters, policy briefs, and books about protecting the United States. When scholars were not sitting in front of their computers, they were testifying before congressional committees or answering countless questions from the print and broadcast media.[9]

There is little doubt that on issues of American and global security, several think tanks, including RAND, the Brookings Institution, the Center for Strategic and International Studies, the Hoover Institution, and the Center for Security Policy, can speak with authority. Many of their scholars were trained during the Cold War and understand America's role as the world's remaining superpower. Indeed, there is a long and distinguished history of the many contributions American think tanks have made to enhance the security of the United States. But when it comes to North American or continental security, the majority of foreign and defence policy think tanks in the United States have far less expertise. Even more troubling is their apparent lack of interest in better understanding the impact of America's post-9/11 security posture on its continental neighbours. While think tanks that specialize in defence and security studies are familiar with the history of the North American Aerospace Defence Command (NORAD) and the strategic importance of the Arctic, few think tanks have, for instance, paid close attention to how America's preoccupation with security has affected its trade relationship with Canada and Mexico. One of the exceptions is Washington's Hudson Institute, which has produced some interesting research on the now defunct Security and Prosperity Partnership (SPP) between Canada and the United States.[10] Christopher Sands, a senior fellow at Hudson and a respected authority on Canada-US relations, has also written a recent account of an initiative signed by President Obama and Prime Minister Harper in February 2011 to address the challenges of facilitating cross-border trade without comprising national security.[11]

A handful of scholars such as Sands are aware of the importance of balancing the interests of security with trade, but their voices are often muffled by others in the think tank community who are not prepared to advocate compromise when it comes to America's security. It is also important to note that there are only a small number of scholars in the United States who are familiar with the complex relationship between that country and Canada. As both scholars in this field and Canadian policy makers and lobbyists trying to establish stronger presences inside the Beltway have acknowledged for years, Canada is a tough sell on Capitol Hill. As important as the trade relationship between the United States and its continental neighbours is, in the post-9/11 era Canada and Mexico generally garner attention only when they are portrayed as weak links in America's security chain.

In the immediate aftermath of 9/11, Canada was chastised by many policy makers in the United States who claimed that several of the hijackers took advantage of the porous Canadian border. Although these accusations were completely unfounded, US policy makers did little to change this perception. Indeed, it took months before they acknowledged that Canada was not at fault. In the end, sparing Canada's feelings was not high on America's list of priorities. Protecting the United States from another terrorist attack was what mattered most. Despite Washington's concerns about terrorists penetrating its northern border, few American think tanks seem interested in broadening their understanding of the politics, history, and culture of Canada. There are several academic programs and centres in universities throughout the United States devoted to the study of Canada, but this interest has not spilled over into the think tank community. Think tanks in Canada have demonstrated even less interest in studying the United States. As a result, much of the research emanating from the think tank community about North American security relations has been spotty. When it comes to Mexico, policy makers on Capitol Hill have expressed more concern about drugs, guns, and illegal immigration than about terrorism.[12]

Little has changed in US security policy since President Obama assumed office in 2009. If anything, Obama has reinforced President Bush's commitment to fighting the war on terror. Whether it has meant sending more troops to Afghanistan or imposing tighter security measures at the border, he has not softened the government's position. Moreover, until recently, he has paid little attention to critics throughout North America who fear that the thickening of America's borders will continue to have a detrimental impact on cross-border trade and on border communities.

In a political environment where security ranks above virtually everything else, advocacy think tanks need to pick their battles. Insisting that policy makers on Capitol Hill and in the executive branch pay more attention to managing "North American security" is simply not a battle that most of them are prepared to wage. Recommending measures to better secure the border may gain traction for some think tanks, but highlighting the negative impact of those measures on Canada and Mexico is unlikely to pay handsome dividends. In the end, what advocacy think tanks covet most are attention, recognition, and political influence. For these institutes, the best way to attain these is by supporting and promoting a stronger and more effective security policy for the United States. Furthermore, since most advocacy think tanks specializing in foreign and defence policy tend to have a conservative orientation, it stands to reason that they have found themselves advocating tighter security measures both at home and abroad. Although several think tanks have criticized America's handling of its wars in Afghanistan and Iraq and the manner in which domestic security legislation has been implemented, few have questioned the need to respond to the threat of global terrorism.

In the following section, we will examine the reaction of a select group of advocacy think tanks to the events of 9/11. As noted, in the hours and days following the attacks, scholars at several of these institutes made a concerted effort to influence the debates over America's response. They did this by producing policy briefs, writing op-ed pieces, and sharing their ideas with the print and broadcast media. The extent to which think tanks were able to gain media exposure has been documented in other studies. Here we highlight the main contributions made by a small group of think tanks to the war on terror.

The War of Words over the War on Terror

Despite the increase in terrorist activity during the 1980s and 1990s, little was done in the intelligence community to protect the United States against future attacks, a concern expressed by Stephen Flynn of the Council on Foreign Relations. In an article in his think tank's flagship journal, *Foreign Affairs,* before the terrorist attacks of September 11, 2001, Flynn outlined a scenario whereby Osama bin Laden "might exploit our perilously exposed transportation system to smuggle and detonate a weapon of mass destruction on our soil."[13] To his delight, the article sparked interest in the policy-making community and eventually led to his giving briefings about the vulnerability of America's transportation system. Unfortunately, Flynn's fears about terrorism and the unwillingness of policy makers to take necessary precautions to protect the American homeland were not widely shared. As he points out, "The common refrain I heard was, 'Americans need a crisis to act. Nothing will change until we have a serious act of terrorism on U.S. soil.'"[14]

When terrorists did strike the United States, policy makers had no alternative – at least no viable alternative – but to react. As the initial shock and horror of 9/11 began to wear off, scholars in the nation's think tanks and universities took time to reflect on why the attacks took place and what the United States had to do to protect its citizens. For policy experts on the left, the story line was clear: Islamic extremists had made their way to the United States to punish America's leaders for their foreign policy in the Middle East, particularly their steadfast support for Israel. Once the United States adopted a more even-handed approach to resolving the Israeli-Palestinian conflict and abandoned its imperialist goals, the threat of terrorism would be significantly reduced.[15] If the United States did this, it would no longer have to worry about the bin Ladens of the world. Order, rather than chaos and fear, would come to reflect the state of the international community. As a bonus, America's strained relations with the United Nations and with much of Western Europe would improve dramatically and the rising tide of anti-Americanism sweeping across the globe would gradually subside.

But for those on the right who believed that this solution could work only in fairy tales, America's response to dealing with terrorism had to convey a very different message. Rather than coddling terrorists and the states that either directly or indirectly supported them, what was needed, according to many conservative policy experts, was a clear and forceful demonstration of American resolve. As David Frum, formerly an AEI scholar, and Richard Perle, one of AEI's resident fellows, state in their book *An End to Evil:*

> The war on terror is not over. In many ways, it has barely begun. Al-Qaeda, Hezbollah, and Hamas still plot murder, and money still flows from donors worldwide to finance them. Mullahs preach jihad from the pulpits of mosques from Bengal to Brooklyn. Iran and North Korea are working frantically to develop nuclear weapons. While our enemies plot, our allies dither and carp and much of our own government remains ominously unready for the fight. We have much to do and scant time in which to do it.[16]

For Frum and Perle, the invasion of Afghanistan in October 2001 was a good start. Among other things, it enabled the United States and its coalition partners to topple the Taliban regime and to destroy bin Laden's terrorist training camps. An even better idea, according to the two authors, was invading Iraq in 2003, a much overdue intervention that enabled the United States to remove another dictator from its roster of enemies. However, they insist that for America to win the war on terror much more has to be done, including removing terrorist mullahs in Iran and ending the terrorist regime in Syria, recommendations that, if adopted, would no doubt lead to new and more virulent waves of anti-Americanism.

Frum and Perle's recipe for defeating terrorism has found strong support among several conservative members of Congress and think tank scholars, including the Brookings Institution's Ken Pollack, whose book *The Threatening Storm* made a strong case for the invasion of Iraq.[17] Not surprisingly, however, their recommendations for future interventions have generated considerable controversy in more liberal policy-making circles. The absence of an exit strategy in Iraq,[18] combined with an escalating body count, has produced little tolerance for additional conflicts. Regardless of how well or poorly Frum and Perle's grand plan for winning the war on terror has been received, their insights help shed light on the complexity of waging a war that, according to several critics of the Bush and Obama administrations, must be fought but may never be won. Their well-publicized views also help to explain why many advocacy think tanks should assume some responsibility for creating a political climate that fosters anti-American sentiments.

In their ongoing efforts to dissect the US government's handling of the war on terror, journalists and scholars will continue to offer different explanations for what motivates American foreign policy. They may also comment on the think tanks that are best positioned and equipped to influence the policies of future administrations, and may again succumb to the temptation to assume that proximity to those in power guarantees policy influence. This was the mistake that several journalists, scholars, and pundits made in claiming that the blueprint for the Bush adminis-tration's foreign policy was drawn entirely by the now-defunct Project for the New American Century.

By the time George W. Bush entered the Oval Office in 2001, it had become Washington's worst-kept secret: a small think tank with modest resources but powerful connections to key members of the Bush team was rumoured to have developed a comprehensive foreign policy for the incoming administration. The think tank that had become a favourite topic of discussion for journalists covering Washington politics and for pundits searching for any clues that would help them predict Bush's behaviour in his first one hundred days in office was not the Heritage Foundation or AEI, the darlings of the conservative movement. The heir apparent was the Project for the New American Century (PNAC), a neo-conservative think tank whose foray into the policy-making community in 1997 had sparked considerable interest among, and support from, sev-eral high-level policy makers, including Dick Cheney, Donald Rumsfeld, Paul Wolfowitz, Scooter Libby, and Jeb Bush, the former governor of Florida and the president's younger brother.

If there were any doubts about which sources of information would help the president manage American foreign policy after 9/11, they were put to rest when the decision was made to invade Iraq. When journalists and scholars skimmed through PNAC's open letter to President Clinton of 26 January 1998, which called for toppling Saddam Hussein, and its Sep-tember 2000 study *Rebuilding America's Defenses,*[19] which justified a new and more aggressive foreign policy around the globe, they thought they had found the Holy Grail. In both its letter and study, PNAC made several policy recommendations that closely resembled initiatives being pursued by the Bush administration. In fact, the recommendations they had made four months before President Bush assumed power, such as "defending the homeland and fight[ing] and win[ning] multiple, simultaneous major theater wars," may as well have been taken directly from his playbook.

Could this have been just a coincidence? Not according to several jour-nalists and scholars who made the connection between PNAC, mem-bers of Bush's inner circle, and the foreign policy the United States had embraced. Writing in the *Guardian* in the fall of 2003, Michael Meacher, a British Labour member of Parliament, stated:

> We now know that a blueprint for the creation of a global Pax Americana was drawn up for Dick Cheney, Donald Rumsfeld, Paul Wolfowitz, Jeb Bush, and Lewis Libby. The document, entitled *Rebuilding America's Defences*, was written in September 2000 by the neoconservative think tank, Project for the New American Century (PNAC). The plan shows that Bush's cabinet intended to take military control of the Gulf region whether or not Saddam Hussein was in power. It says, "While the unresolved conflict with Iraq provides the imme- diate justification, the need for a substantial American force presence in the Gulf transcends the issue of the regime of Saddam Hussein." The PNAC blue- print supports an earlier document attributed to Wolfowitz and Libby which said the U.S. must "discourage advanced industrial nations from challenging our leadership or even aspiring to a larger regional or global role."[20]

Meacher's assessment of PNAC is similar in tone to that of Andrew Austin, who writes: "Not content with waiting for the next Republican administra- tion, Wolfowitz and several other intellectuals formed PNAC, a think tank 'to make the case and rally support for American global leadership.' Top corporate, military, and political figures aligned themselves with PNAC ... Powerful economic interests [also] threw their support behind PNAC."[21] Similar comments about PNAC's origins and its strong ties to the policy- making establishment and the business community continue to make their way into the academic literature on the neoconservative network in the United States.[22] As discussed below, however, evaluating the extent of PNAC's influence is not as straightforward as Meacher and others main- tain.

"If It Looks Like a Duck and Swims Like a Duck ...": PNAC's Influence in Perspective

Gary Schmitt, the former president of PNAC and a senior adviser to Republican presidential nominee Senator John McCain, spent years in the academic community and in government before running a think tank. He understood the world of Washington politics and how decisions were made in Congress, in the White House, and in the bureaucracy. And he understood and appreciated that the right ideas presented at the right time could make a profound difference. Founded in 1997 to pro- mote American global leadership, PNAC spent its early years developing a new conservative approach to foreign policy. This approach or strategy was based on the belief that the United States could and should become a "benevolent global hegemon." William Kristol and Robert Kagan's approach struck a responsive chord with several conservative policy makers and policy experts, who encouraged the authors to create an organization that would promote their vision of American foreign policy. As Schmitt points out, "we got approached by a lot of people saying why don't you try to institutionalize this?"[23] After Kristol and Kagan convinced Schmitt to become PNAC's president, they secured sufficient funding to launch the new institute.

Building on the success of their 1996 article, Kristol and Kagan, both project directors at PNAC, published an edited collection in 2000 titled *Present Dangers*,[24] which further explored the options and opportunities available to the United States as it set out to redefine its role in the international community. Among the many topics addressed by the long and impressive list of contributors were regime change in Iraq, Israel and the peace process, and missile defence, all of which became hot-button issues for President Bush. But it was the September 2000 release of *Rebuilding America's Defenses*, a seventy-six-page document endorsed by several people who would come to occupy senior positions in the Bush administration, that turned the national spotlight on PNAC.

Written by Thomas Donnelly, Donald Kagan, and Gary Schmitt, the report was intended to encourage debate among policy makers and the public about America's military strength and how it could be harnessed to achieve the country's foreign policy goals. Based on a series of seminars in which participants with specialized areas of expertise were encouraged to exchange ideas about a wide range of defence and foreign policy issues, the document left few stones unturned. But did this document – or blueprint, as it is often described – amount to an "extreme makeover" of US foreign policy, or did it simply propose some minor modifications? Moreover, were PNAC's plans for advancing American national security interests in a world in which the United States could market itself as a "benevolent global hegemon" the product of original thinking or were these ideas recycled from other sources?

The PNAC document, as Schmitt acknowledged, was intended to provide a more coherent conservative vision of American foreign policy. "We weren't satisfied with what the isolationists and realists were saying about foreign policy [and felt] that they were very much drawing the United States back from the world at large ... We thought that even though the cold war had ended, the principles of conservative foreign policy enunciated during the Reagan years, were still applicable to the world today." In this sense, the PNAC study offered new and innovative ways of promoting American interests in the post–Cold

War era. Ironically, when the study came out, "its real impact was on the Clinton folks, not on the Bush people."[25]

When it comes to evaluating the work of his institute, however, Schmitt, like any responsible policy entrepreneur, can ill afford to be modest. "I think we do a good job of getting our vision on the table because I think we're very good at what we do ... We get a lot of feedback from editorialists and you can tell they read the stuff. If you make a poignant argument and present a case that's well reasoned and brief, you have a lot of impact, or you can at least have some impact."[26]

Scholars studying PNAC's ascendancy in the political arena cannot possibly overlook the fact that several of the original signatories to its statement of principles received high-level positions in the Bush administration. As Ted Koppel, formerly of ABC News, pointed out, you do not have to be a conspiracy theorist to acknowledge the intimate ties between some of Bush's closest advisers and PNAC.[27] Still, acknowledging these important connections is a far cry from making the claim that PNAC was the architect of Bush's foreign policy. The president appointed Rumsfeld, Wolfowitz, and other foreign policy experts to serve in his administration not because they were card-carrying members of PNAC or of any other think tank but because they were people Bush could trust.

PNAC may have been considered the architect of President Bush's foreign policy but several other think tanks in and around the nation's capital had also become preoccupied with assessing the domestic and global implications of the war on terror. The Brookings Institution, RAND, the Heritage Foundation, the Center for Strategic and International Studies, the Council on Foreign Relations, and a number of other institutes specializing in defence and foreign policy had produced dozens of studies, held workshops, seminars, and conferences, and testified before congressional committees and subcommittees about various aspects of US foreign policy. Indeed, in the immediate aftermath of 9/11, it was difficult to pick up a newspaper, listen to the news, or watch one of the many political talk shows without hearing the views of policy experts from various think tanks. Interestingly enough, while several think tanks struggled for airtime, others were being secretly courted by senior officials in the Bush administration.

President Bush and his small circle of advisers known as "the vulcans" were well aware of PNAC's recommendations for revamping the US military.[28] Since several of the key advisers had lent their name to PNAC's recently released study, it is likely they would have raised any pertinent ideas contained in the report with the president. It appears, however, that PNAC did not have all the answers the president and his advisers were looking for. Shortly after the terrorist attacks, Paul Wolfowitz, deputy secretary of defence, contacted his old friend Christopher DeMuth, who until recently had been the long-time president of AEI. His reason for contacting DeMuth, according to veteran journalist Bob Woodward, was to ask him to form a working group of the nation's top Middle East experts to provide the Bush administration with guidance on how to address the political and military problems associated with waging war in this historically troubled region.[29]

DeMuth agreed to assemble the working group on short notice, and on 29 November 2001 the group met "at a secure conference center in Virginia for a weekend of discussion."[30] After hours of talks, DeMuth produced "a seven-page, single-spaced document entitled 'Delta of Terrorism' which included several policy recommendations." Although DeMuth was not prepared to provide Woodward with a copy of the document, he stated: "We concluded that a confrontation with Saddam was inevitable. He was a gathering threat – the most menacing, active and unavoidable threat. We agreed that Saddam would have to leave the scene before the problem would be addressed."[31]

The conclusions reached by the group did not take long to make their way to the president's top advisers. According to Woodward, Vice President Cheney noted that the report helped the president focus "on the malignancy" of the Middle East, and National Security Advisor Condoleezza Rice found the report to be "very, very persuasive."[32] Although several members of the group DeMuth assembled were not affiliated with AEI, it is difficult to ignore the important role the think tank president played in generating ideas and disseminating them to the Bush White House. This would not be the last time AEI had a profound impact on helping the Bush administration manage the war on terror.

In December 2006, two AEI scholars, retired general Jack Keane, a former Army vice chief of staff and a member of the advisory Defense Policy Review Board, and Fred Kagan, a military historian, met with Cheney to discuss their plans for a "surge" in Iraq. Based on months of work at AEI, Keane and Kagan found an ally in Cheney and in Senator McCain, who played a key role in selling the idea to President Bush.[33] Although AEI's involvement in promoting the surge warrants a detailed case study, for now it is useful in illustrating an earlier point: that scholars must be careful in making claims about the nature and extent of think tank influence. As noted earlier, although PNAC should be credited with bringing scholars and policy makers together to reconsider how to pursue US foreign and defence policy interests in the twenty-first century, it would be an exaggeration to suggest that this organization was solely responsible for laying the foundation for US foreign policy during the Bush years. Several other think tanks, including AEI, played a key role in disseminating ideas to senior officials in the Bush administration.

In a recent interview with Peter Feaver, former special adviser for strategic planning and institutional reform on the National Security Council, more information about the relationship between think tanks and the foreign policy-making establishment under President Bush has come to light.[34] Recognizing the growing frustration among policy experts in the think tank community over their lack of access to the Bush White House, National Security Advisor Stephen Hadley instructed his staff in 2005 to begin coordinating several meetings with a select group of Washington-based think tanks. The purpose of the meetings was to solicit input from leading experts on a range of foreign and defence policy issues. According to Feaver, however, this initiative had little success, in part because Bush had lost the confidence of the think tank community. To put it bluntly, "it was too little, too late."

Bush may have lost the confidence of the think tank community because of the intensely insular foreign policy–making environment he and his advisers cultivated. Even so, limited access to the White House did not discourage scholars at several of these institutions from communicating their ideas on a wide range of security-related policies to members of Congress and their staff, to policy experts throughout the bureaucracy, and to journalists, academics, and business leaders. Below, we will highlight some of the contributions advocacy think tanks have made to discussions about national security policy in the post-9/11 era. A new administration may be in office but the motivation behind the involvement of these organizations remains the same: to establish a strong and dominant voice in the increasingly crowded marketplace of ideas.

Conclusion

The decisions made by the Bush administration in the days and weeks following 9/11 serve as a reminder of how critical it is for the American public to consider what is truly in the national interest. It also serves as a reminder that the United States can benefit by listening to the concerns of its closest allies and continental neighbours. While there is little doubt that America needed to respond to the terrorist attacks, the nature and duration of its response continues to generate considerable debate both in the United States and around the globe. Thousands of lives have been lost and trillions of dollars have been spent on two wars that, in all likelihood, may never be won. In the meantime, several policy experts at some of Washington's most prestigious advocacy think tanks continue to advocate stronger security measures to protect the American homeland, despite the impact of these measures on cross-border trade. Policy briefs praising the virtues of missile defence and highlighting the benefits of introducing more effective biometric technologies to screen the millions of people who enter the United States each year continue to appear on institute websites. However, little attention is being devoted to explaining how America's behaviour in the post-9/11 era is damaging its relationship with its continental neighbours.

Although policy makers bear ultimate responsibility for the policies they have introduced since 9/11, the think tank community should also reflect on what it has or has not contributed to discussions about national security. A dozen years after this historic event, it is incumbent upon scholars, many of whom work in think tanks, to share their thoughts about how America can move forward. If anything, the recent debt crisis in the United States revealed what can happen when partisan bickering gets in the way of the national interest. Think tanks would be well advised to take note. At the very least, they need to understand how much damage they can cause when the interests of the nation take a back seat to their own narrowly defined goals.

Robert Brookings and Andrew Carnegie believed that think tanks could play an important role in helping to cure the nation's social, political, and economic problems. Unfortunately, as think tanks have transformed themselves from institutions engaged in rigorous policy research to organizations immersed in political advocacy, their ability to offer pragmatic solutions to the many challenges confronting the United States has been called into question. Since 9/11, a select group of advocacy think tanks have indeed waged an intense and well-rehearsed battle in the war of ideas. The wars that they advocated are being fought and the thicker borders they envisioned are in place. But at what cost to the national interest, and at what cost to the security relationship the United States maintains with Canada and Mexico? This is a question that needs to be addressed as scholars continue to make sense of how the war on terror has been marketed to the United States and its neighbours.

NOTES

1 For a recent overview of the events of 9/11, see Jason Burke, *The 9-11 Wars* (London: Allen Lane, 2011).

2 Dozens of books have been written about the events of 9/11. For a comprehensive account, see Bob Woodward, *Bush at War* (New York: Simon and Schuster, 2002); David Frum and Richard Perle, *An End to Evil: How to Win the War on Terror* (New York:

Random House, 2004); Daniel Pipes, *Militant Islam Reaches America* (New York: W.W. Norton, 2002); and Frances Fox Piven, *The War at Home: The Domestic Costs of Bush's Militarism* (New York: New Press, 2004).

3   Richard A. Clarke, *Against All Enemies: Inside America's War on Terror* (New York: Free Press, 2004); and Richard A. Clarke, *Your Government Failed You: Breaking the Cycle of National Security Disasters* (New York: Harper Perennial, 2009).

4   See Donald E. Abelson, *American Think Tanks and their Role in US Foreign Policy* (London and New York: Macmillan and St. Martin's Press, 1996).

5   R. Kent Weaver, "The Changing World of Think Tanks," *PS: Political Science and Politics* 22, 2 (September 1989): 563-78.

6   For more on the early history of American think tanks, see James A. Smith, *The Idea Brokers: Think Tanks and the Rise of the New Policy Elite* (New York: Free Press, 1991), and Donald T. Critchlow, *The Brookings Institution, 1916-1952: Expertise and the Public Interest* (Dekalb: Northern Illinois University Press, 1985).

7   For a comprehensive history of the early years of the Heritage Foundation, see Lee Edwards, *The Power of Ideas: The Heritage Foundation at 25 Years* (Ottawa, IL: Jameson Books, 1997).

8   The rise of advocacy think tanks in the United States is discussed by Donald E. Abelson in "From Policy Research to Political Advocacy: The Changing Role of Think Tanks in American Politics," *Canadian Review of American Studies* 25, 1 (1995): 93-126; and in R. Kent Weaver, "The Changing World of Think Tanks."

9   See Donald E. Abelson, *A Capitol Idea: Think Tanks and US Foreign Policy* (Kingston and Montreal: McGill-Queen's University Press, 2006), appendices 3-5.

10 Greg Anderson and Christopher Sands, *Negotiating North America: The Security and Prosperity Partnership* (Washington, DC: Hudson Institute, White Paper Series, 2007).

11 Christopher Sands, *The Canadian Gambit: Will It Revive North America?* Security and Foreign Affairs Briefing Paper (Washington, DC: Hudson Institute, 2011). Also see Donald E. Abelson and Duncan Wood, *People, Security and Borders: The Impact of the WHTI on North America* (Ottawa: Fulbright Foundation, 2007).

12 For more on this, see Chapter 7.

13 Referred to in Stephen E. Flynn, *America the Vulnerable: How Our Government Is Failing to Protect Us from Terrorism* (New York: HarperCollins, 2004), xi.

14 Ibid., xii.

15 See Alex Callinicos, *The New Mandarins of American Power: The Bush Administration's Plans for the World* (Cambridge: Polity, 2003); and Andrew Ross and Kristin Ross, eds., *Anti-Americanism* (New York: New York University Press, 2004).

16 Frum and Perle, *An End to Evil*, 4.

17 Kenneth M. Pollack, *The Threatening Storm: The Case for Invading Iraq* (New York: Random House, 2002).

18 See Christopher Preble, *Exiting Iraq: Why the US Must End the Military Occupation and Renew the War against al Qaeda* (Washington, DC: Cato Institute, 2004); and Thomas Ricks, *Fiasco: The American Military Adventure in Iraq* (New York: Penguin, 2006).

19 See Project for the New American Century, "Letter from the Project for the New American Century to the Honorable William J. Clinton, President of the United States," 26 January 1998, http://www.newamericancentury.org/; and Project for the New American Century, *Rebuilding America's Defenses: Strategy, Forces and Resources for a New Century* (Washington, DC: Project for the New American Century, September 2000).

20 Michael Meacher, "The War on Terrorism Is Bogus," *Guardian*, 6 September 2003.

21 Quoted in Bernd Hamm, ed., *Devastating Society: The Neo-Conservative Assault on Democracy and Justice* (London: Pluto Press, 2005), 55.

22 See Stefan A. Halper and Jonathan Clarke, *America Alone: The Neo-Conservatives and the Global Order* (New York: Cambridge University Press, 2004); and John Micklethwait and Adrian Wooldridge, *The Right Nation: Conservative Power in America* (New York: Penguin Books, 2004).

23 Quoted in Abelson, *A Capitol Idea*, 214.

24 Robert Kagan and William Kristol, *Present Dangers: Crisis and Opportunity in American Foreign and Defense Policy* (San Francisco: Encounter Books, 2000).

25 Abelson, *A Capitol Idea*, 215-16.

26 Ibid., 217.

27 Ibid.

28 James Mann, *Rise of the Vulcans: The History of Bush's War Cabinet* (New York: Viking, 2004).

29 Bob Woodward, *State of Denial: Bush at War, Part II* (New York: Simon and Schuster, 2006), 83-85.

30 Ibid., 84.

31 Ibid., 84-85.

32 Ibid., 85.

33 See Fred Barnes, "How Bush Decided on the Surge," *Weekly Standard* 13, 20 (4 February 2008); and Christopher DeMuth, "Think-Tank Confidential: What I Learned during Two Decades as Head of America's Most Influential Policy Shop," *Wall Street Journal*, 11 October 2007.

34 Telephone interview with Peter Feaver, 17 January 2011.

10

A Common "Bilateral" Vision

North American Defence Cooperation, 2001-12

PHILIPPE LAGASSÉ

Canada–United States continental defence cooperation has plateaued. A topic of considerable debate in the immediate aftermath of the September 11, 2001, terrorist attacks against the United States, a strengthening of the binational defence of North America has gradually become a secondary consideration in Ottawa and Washington. Although a number of bilateral military agreements were signed the past decade, talk of a more comprehensive, binational approach quietly dissipated as the two neighbours focused on their respective homeland defences. Indeed, even as security cooperation between Canada and the United States expanded in other areas, such as law enforcement and border controls,[1] efforts to meaningfully expand the North American Aerospace Defence Command (NORAD), address the still awkward interaction between and among NORAD, Canada Command, and US Northern Command, or revive the idea of an official Canadian role in missile defence have failed to gain traction or capture the attention of policy makers. Although the February 2011 announcement of a yet-to-be-defined continental "security perimeter" by Prime Minister Stephen Harper and President Barak Obama could reverse this trend and lead to an expanded binational defence of North America, the fact that it took ten years since 9/11 for this to take place is remarkable. Contrary to what might have been expected at the time, the events of September 2001 did not encourage the development of a truly binational approach to the defence of the continent. Instead, the defence of North America has become an increasingly bilateral affair.

This chapter explores the evolution of the Canada-US continental defence relationship in three phases: (1) initial reaction to the September 11 attacks in 2001-02; (2) the ambivalent period of binational cooperation between 2003 and 2006; and (3) the marginalization of the binational approach to North American defence from 2007 to 2010. It concludes with a discussion of prospects for a renewed focus on binational continental defence cooperation as part of a possible North American security perimeter.

Canada and US Northern Command, 2001-02

In the weeks that followed the 9/11 attacks against New York and Washington, the US Secretary of Defense Donald Rumsfeld, asked planners at the decades-old NORAD to outline ways to improve the defence of the American homeland and the North American continent. By mid-October, NORAD planners had prepared a list of options for Rumsfeld to consider. Chief among these was a proposal to expand NORAD to include a comprehensive, binational defence of the continent's land mass and maritime approaches. Rumsfeld was favourable to the idea. At the end of October 2001, he wrote a confidential letter to his Canadian counterpart, Minister of National Defence Art Eggleton, recommending that the two countries expand NORAD's mandate to include an integrated defence of North America on land and at sea.[2] This would, in effect, have made the defence of the continent a truly binational affair in the aerospace, land, and maritime domains.

For reasons that became clearer as time went on, the Canadian government quietly declined Rumsfeld's overture. In a December 2001 letter, Eggleton explained that Canada was not yet prepared to expand NORAD.[3] As a result, the United States opted to move ahead with a uniquely American approach to improving the defence of its homeland and the North American continent. Up to that point, the defence of the US homeland had been assigned to US Joint Forces Command, a functional command under the Pentagon's Unified Command Plan (UCP), the structure that the Department of Defense has used to divide the American military's geographic and functional responsibilities since 1946. In April 2002, the Pentagon announced that the homeland defence mission would be transferred to US Northern Command (NorthCom), the UCP's newest command. In keeping with the UCP's other geographic commands, NorthCom was also assigned a specific geographic area of responsibility: the

North American continent. All non–NORAD-related American military efforts to defend the continent would therefore be part of North-Com's purview.

Word of NorthCom's creation prompted questions about how it would affect NORAD and the larger Canada-US continental defence relationship.[4] When it was announced that the commander of NORAD would be "dual-hatted" as the commander of NorthCom and that the two commands would operate alongside each another at Peterson Air Force Base in Colorado Springs, observers, including this author, speculated that NORAD's mission might still be expanded beyond aerospace defence to include a binational maritime and land defence of the continent, as Rumsfeld had confidentially sought in October 2001.[5] A number of interrelated factors suggested that this would eventually occur, despite the Canadian government's initial refusal. Among these were geography, historical precedent, comparable threat perceptions, and the asymmetrical power dynamic between Canada and the United States.

Geography has profoundly shaped the Canada-US continental defence alliance since its inception. Canada's size, vulnerability, and proximity to the United States led the American government to take an initial interest in Canada's defence in the 1930s, and drove the two countries to arrive at a series of defence arrangements during the Second World War and in the late 1940s.[6] The importance of Canada's geography truly came to the fore, however, when the Soviet Union acquired long-range bombers and the hydrogen bomb in the early 1950s. An effective defence of the US nuclear deterrent against this threat required the stationing of radars on Canadian soil and, equally important, the establishment of a binational air defence command, NORAD, in the late 1950s – a development that the Canadian government had dismissed a decade earlier.

The importance of Canadian geography to the security of the United States and its nuclear deterrent waxed and waned in subsequent decades, as novel technologies and concerns either enhanced or diminished its value.[7] After 9/11, Canadian geography still did not matter as much as in the 1950s, but its relative importance did increase, as Rumsfeld's October 2001 proposal and NorthCom's continent-wide area of responsibility highlighted. Fears that transnational terrorists could exploit the maritime approaches to North America or cross land borders to carry out further attacks against the United States were palpable at the time. And although protecting the United States against these possibilities fell largely under the mandates of civilian agencies on both sides of the border, there was no question that armed forces were expected to play a vital supporting role. Here again, the very idea of an expanded NORAD and the creation of a dedicated homeland defence command was a testament to this thinking. Above all, however, the possibility that American forces might need to enter Canadian waters or territory to address a threat or manage the consequences of an attack, or vice versa, rekindled the notion that an effective homeland defence rested on strong continental defence cooperation.

What stronger continental defence cooperation might mean was shaped by historical precedent. Between the late 1940s and the late 1950s, the Canada-US continental air defence relationship gradually evolved from bilateral cooperation to binational integration under NORAD. The nature of the Soviet threat, American and Canadian military planners surmised in the mid-1950s, necessitated a fully coordinated binational response, one that brought the air defence of the continent under a single commander who controlled the air defence forces of both nations and answered to the Canadian prime minister and American president equally. This arrangement satisfied both the United States' security concerns and Canada's desire to be recognized as a formally equal, sovereign continental defence partner.[8] When the question of improving continental defence cooperation arose in the fall of 2001, these same rationales likely informed the recommendation of NORAD planners that the command should be expanded to provide for the binational control of North America's land and maritime defences. A binational effort would provide the greatest degree of coordination and ensure that Canada was, at least in principle, a full partner in an expanded defence of the continent.

Furthermore, comparable threat perceptions guaranteed that the necessity of strengthening the continent's defences was appreciated in both countries. Although the United States' sense of vulnerability was no doubt higher than Canada's in the aftermath of the 9/11 attacks, the Canadian government realized that there were gaps in North America's security and defences.[9] Indeed, since Canada stood to lose economically by not following the United States in re-evaluating its homeland and continental security efforts, due to tightening of border controls and Canada's higher dependence on cross-border trade, any significant divergence in terms of the threat perceptions of the two governments was offset by Ottawa's acute sensitivity to trade disruptions. The United States' vastly superior power also meant that Canada would be compelled to respond more or less positively to American security initiatives. Had the US government pressured Canada to contribute to a larger continental defence regime, if the American government had insisted that NORAD should be expanded, it is not unlikely that the Canadian government would have eventually acquiesced. These factors further contributed to the possibility of an expanded NORAD.

As strong as these influences were, however, they failed to produce an expanded NORAD mandate in the year that followed the 9/11 attacks. To understand why this did not happen, the impact of several countervailing factors must be appreciated. Foremost among these were the primacy of homeland and border security cooperation, the standard practices of the US military, and the continued lack of interest of Canadian political leaders.

Improving homeland security, primarily a concern of law enforcement and civilian security agencies, was the pre-eminent concern of the United States and Canada in the aftermath of 9/11.[10] Although important to the two governments, homeland and continental defence cooperation paled in comparison. As a result, improving their homeland security and working to strengthen ties and information sharing between their respective law enforcement and border enforcement teams and civilian security agencies dominated continental security discussions between Canada and the United States. Although it was evidently on the agenda, as the Rumsfeld-Eggleton correspondence highlights, the defence relationship was a lower priority in both countries. It simply was not as important as homeland security was for the United States or as guaranteeing an open border was for Canada.[11] Instead of being assigned to leading ministers and advisers, as in the case of border and homeland security cooperation, after the exchange of letters between Rumsfeld and Eggleton continental defence discussions were left with the defence departments and militaries of the two countries. Thus, the discussions that followed were largely shaped by the organizational cultures and standard procedures of these bureaucracies.

When setting up NorthCom in 2002, the US Department of Defense followed the UCP's geographic command template. The new command was given an area of geographic responsibility, and it was assumed that defence relations with countries included in that area would be conducted along bilateral lines. Hence, the US military's default position was to establish a uniquely American homeland defence command that would work to defend North America through bilateral cooperation efforts with Canada. Although the possibility of expanding NORAD to work alongside NorthCom was still being discussed in US defence circles at the time,[12] it was not important enough to slow the establishment of the new US homeland defence command. Indeed, even if the idea of expanding NORAD had been revived in 2002, US military planners would have first ensured that NorthCom was properly set up. Because of Canada's unwillingness to immediately work toward expanding NORAD, building the United States' homeland defences necessarily overshadowed efforts to improve

the binational defence of the continent. The Canadian defence department and military, meanwhile, were left in a reactive position. It was
understood that they were to work with their American counterparts to
re-evaluate North America's defence requirements, build ties with North-
Com, and reassess NORAD's air defence mission in light of the 9/11
attacks. However, the Canadian defence minister had explicitly ruled out
an expansion of NORAD, which meant that Canadian defence officials
could not promote the idea.

Lastly, it is now obvious that Canadian political leaders were still not
interested in expanding NORAD in 2002. The idea did not become more
attractive in the months and year that followed the Rumsfeld-Eggleton
correspondence, despite the creation of NorthCom and the United States'
clear intent to improve the continent's defences along bilateral lines. The
only tangible expression of interest in perhaps moving toward a binational model of cooperation was the creation of a Canada-US Bi-National
Planning Group (BPG) in late 2002. The BPG, however, was mandated
only to study various continental defence challenges and propose options
for deeper cooperation.

The continued lack of interest of Jean Chrétien's Liberal government
appears to have been informed by two considerations. During this period, the
Canadian government was preoccupied with improving homeland security,
border security, and the counterterrorism capabilities of law enforcement.[13]
Ottawa invested significantly in these initiatives, in terms of both time and
money. The prospect of having to do the same to improve the continental
defence relationship was unattractive.[14] Canadian leaders, moreover, were hes-
itant to involve Canada in security or defence arrangements that might be seen
to undermine Canadian sovereignty and independence.[15] Although NORAD's
binational command structure had previously protected Canada's status as an
equal continental defence partner, critics were warning that the situation
would be different in a post-9/11 environment.[16] Accordingly, because the
United States was not insisting on anything more than better bilateral cooperation, the Chrétien government seems to have determined that it would be
better to first assess how the continental defence relationship would evolve
with the arrival of NorthCom and see whether growing NORAD was actually
required to improve the defence of North America. Simply put, expanding
NORAD was not a pressing concern for the Chrétien government, especially
when the United States was focused on establishing NorthCom; Canada's primary interests lay with keeping trade flowing across the border; and countering terrorism in North America was largely a law enforcement and civilian
security agency mission.

Hence, although a number of factors were impelling Canada and the United States to pursue a broader binational defence of the continent in 2001-02, these were outweighed by a second set of factors that kept them apart. This pattern continued throughout the rest of the decade.

Binational Ambivalence, Bilateral Achievements, 2003-06

Canada-US relations weathered a difficult period between 2003-06. Although counterterrorism and border security cooperation continued apace because both countries considered it part of their vital interests, the larger relationship ran into trouble when the United States decided to invade Iraq in 2003. Specifically, the Canadian government's decision to oppose the Iraq War briefly chilled Canada-US relations. Whereas American politicians and officials became frustrated with the undiplomatic manner in which the Ottawa opposed the war, Canada's political leaders and the Canadian public demonstrated a greater degree of discomfort with Canada's ties to the United States. These developments dampened the already fading interest in greater binational continental defence cooperation.

The question of a possible Canadian and NORAD role in the latest US ballistic missile defence (BMD) system was immediately affected by the souring of relations that followed the beginning of the Iraq War. In other, less controversial areas, continental defence cooperation progressed steadily despite continuing tension between the two governments at the political level, but the possibility of expanding NORAD lost ground as North American defence cooperation increasingly focused on bilateral arrangements. By 2006, in fact, the very relevance of NORAD was being called into question.

In June 2002, the United States withdrew from the US-USSR Anti-Ballistic Missile Treaty of 1972, signalling that it was determined to move ahead with the deployment of a BMD system. The first stage would protect the American homeland, and potentially the entire North American continent, with interceptor sights located in California and Alaska. NORAD was the natural place to house missile defence command and control. Since the early 1960s, NORAD had provided warning and assessment of ballistic missile launches and attacks. Known as integrated tactical warning attack assessment (ITWAA), this mission ranked alongside conventional air defence as NORAD's main contributions to the defence of the continent. It also meant that NORAD would be involved in the operations of the new American BMD system. In effect, as long as it kept the ITWAA function, NORAD would be assessing whether a ballistic missile launch represented a threat to the continent and how the missile defence system should go about engaging an incoming warhead. Assuming it did retain ITWAA, it seemed logical to also assign the operation of BMD to NORAD.[17] Simply put, it made sense to give control of the missile defence system to the command that was responsible for identifying ballistic missile launches and trajectories. To give this role to NORAD, however, the United States would need to offer Canada a part in the missile defence system and the Canadian government would need to accept it.

American officials were not keen on including Canada in missile defence.[18] Given the Canadian government's long-standing aversion to missile defence, the importance of prioritizing the defence of the United States, and Canada's opposition to the Iraq War, certain American officials thought it unwise to include NORAD in BMD. At the political level, however, President George W. Bush was open to the idea. For him, it simply made sense that Canada would take part in a system that could defend Canadians from a growing, and potentially devastating, threat. In the last years of his premiership, it appeared that Jean Chrétien was not opposed to the possibility either. His government began talking to the United States about Canada's role in missile defence shortly after the Bush administration announced the new system, and his ministers of foreign affairs and national defence stated that the Canadian government was inquiring about BMD in 2003. When Paul Martin succeeded Chrétien, moreover, it seemed that the new prime minister was equally interested in negotiating a Canadian role in missile defence. Martin's first defence minister, David Pratt, discussed formal Canadian participation in BMD with Secretary Rumsfeld in a public exchange of letters in January 2004. This correspondence further stated that NORAD would formally contribute to missile defence in the future, perhaps as the official BMD command-and-control centre.[19]

The Martin government's interest in missile defence rapidly dissipated, however. Anti-BMD activists had mobilized when the United States announced the deployment of the system. By the time Martin took office, the activists were poised to dominate the public debate.[20] With Canadian views of the United States and the Bush administration soured by the Iraq War, they chose to cast the issue in terms of the dangers that deeper defence integration posed to Canada's sovereignty and global stability. They also kindled fears that the missile defence program would eventually lead to the weaponization of space, something that the Canadian government had long fought to prevent. These warnings resonated with a large number of Canadians. For Martin, whose electoral support was already falling because of a domestic party financing scandal, this growing aversion to missile defence was a worrisome trend: the government's apparent backing of a Canadian role in BMD could drive the Liberal base to left-leaning parties, such as the New Democratic Party and Bloc Québécois. These concerns were amplified following the 2004 election, in which the Liberals lost their majority in the House of Commons and returned to power as a minority government. The party's weakened position proved to be a strong deterrent to negotiation of a formal Canadian role in missile defence.

A few months after the 2004 election, Canada and the United States amended the NORAD agreement to allow the command's ITWAA data to be transmitted to missile defence command and control. Although this amendment could be interpreted as a sign that the Martin government favoured a part for NORAD in BMD, the opposite was true. In reality, the amendment served to protect NORAD's ITWAA function if Canada declined to take part in missile defence; it ensured that ITWAA would not be taken away from NORAD if missile defence command and control were assigned to NorthCom or another American command. As Canada's foreign minister Pierre Pettigrew stated: "This amendment safeguards and sustains NORAD regardless of what decision the government of Canada eventually takes on ballistic missile defence."[21] The stage was thus set for the Canadian government to back away from BMD altogether, as Canada's anti–missile defence activists and parties were demanding.

During a November 2004 visit to Canada, President Bush called on the Canadian government to join BMD. In so doing, the president lent credence to the view that the United States was pressuring Canada to take part in the system. Coming from such a polarizing and unpopular figure among Canadians, his statement further reduced any lingering interest the Martin government might have had in agreeing to a formal role in missile defence. In the months that followed the president's visit, the prime minister became increasingly critical of BMD, taking up the critics' concerns that BMD would lead to weaponization of space and launchers on Canadian soil. When the American government chose not to publicly assure Martin that missile defence would not lead to interceptors on Canadian soil or weapons in space, the prime minister and his advisers finally decided that the issue should be settled. On 24 February 2005, the Martin government announced that Canada would not formally take part in BMD. In line with the August 2004 amendment, NORAD retained its ITWAA role, but Canada would not be involved in the command and control of the continent's latest defence system. BMD command and control was assigned to NorthCom, giving the uniquely American command a key role in the aerospace defence of the continent. Whatever the merits of

Martin's decision, it represented a post-9/11 low point for binational continental defence cooperation.

Despite the missile defence kerfuffle, Canada and the United States continued to work toward improving their conventional continental defence cooperation, under both the Martin Liberals and their successors, Stephen Harper's Conservatives.[22] Geography and a mutual appreciation of the threats to the continent prevented the disagreement over BMD from stalling the North American defence relationship altogether, although continental defence talks continued to be a largely bureaucratic affair, which discouraged novelty and policy innovation. Nevertheless, the two countries were able to make progress in a few areas. Two long-standing pillars of the Canada-US defence relationship, the Permanent Joint Board on Defence (PJBD) and the Military Cooperation Committee (MCC), re-examined the foundational agreements of the North American continental defence alliance. Canadian and American officers also strove to facilitate interactions between NorthCom and NORAD at Peterson Air Force Base, and to recommend ways to further binational defence cooperation under the aegis of the BPG. These efforts produced notable results, including the negotiation of homeland and continental defence–related memorandums of understanding, the release of the BPG's final report on enhancing continental defence cooperation in 2006,[23] and the signing of a new Canada-US Basic Defence Document (BDD) that same year.[24]

Behind these bilateral achievements, however, lay continued uncertainty about the value of NORAD and of a binational approach to North America's defence. As part of its 2005 Defence Policy Statement, the Canadian government announced that it would establish Canada Command (CanadaCom), a new Canadian homeland defence command.[25] Doubtless inspired by the American decision to establish NorthCom, the creation of CanadaCom added another degree of complexity to the North American defence relationship. With both the United States and Canada sporting dedicated homeland defence commands, NORAD's continuing relevance came under scrutiny. In principle, of course, NORAD remained the pre-eminent command among the three. As the binational command, it continued to serve as the key link between the two neighbours in matters of continental defence. As well, NORAD's air defence mission was still relevant in a post-9/11 environment, and the creation of CanadaCom could be seen as a preparatory step toward expanding NORAD's mandate to include a binational defence of the continent's land and maritime domains. In reality, the establishment of CanadaCom implied the opposite. It highlighted the fact that North American defence cooperation was becoming an increasingly bilateral affair, with NorthCom and Canada-Com as the central commands and NORAD as a vestigial entity. Indeed, when the NORAD agreement was renewed in perpetuity in 2006, ostensibly in an effort to demonstrate that the command was still at the forefront of North American defence affairs, the two foremost scholars of the continental defence relationship, Joseph Jockel and Joel Sokolsky, speculated that this might signal its approaching descent into a mere political instrument.[26] Their assessment was informed by the sense that officers at NorthCom were no longer satisfied with NORAD's monopoly over the air defence of the United States, the sense that the air defence of the continent no longer needed to be organized in a binational manner, and the possible end of NORAD's ITWAA function.

The 2006 NORAD agreement renewal, however, included one innovation that seemed to indicate that an expansion of the command was on the horizon: the addition of maritime warning to NORAD's mandate. On the surface, this new mission appeared to answer calls for the establishment of a "maritime NORAD."[27] Advocates had argued that North America's coasts represented a vulnerable point of entry into the continent.[28] Ships carrying extremists, weapons of mass destruction, or even rudimentary cruise missiles represented a danger that merited a properly coordinated, binational response from Canada and the United States. Similarly, environmental disasters at sea could best be handled in a binational fashion, with vessels from both countries being allowed to navigate one another's waters, under the operational control of a single commander and headquarters. NORAD's maritime warning function fell far short of this model. Instead of establishing a binational continental maritime defence headquarters, NORAD's maritime warning function simply transferred national maritime domain information from national sources to Peterson Air Force Base. What NORAD would do with the data was unclear. Although it could be shared and jointly analyzed by American and Canadian officers, NORAD could not act on the information. Both the collection of maritime domain data and the determination of appropriate responses were left with national marine security agencies and forces, who cooperated in a bilateral fashion to guard the continent's maritime approaches. At best, NORAD's new function was meant to improve the assessment of threats to North America by adding an extra level of maritime domain data analysis. At worst, the new role was an example of tokenism, giving a semblance of renewal and expansion to an outdated arrangement.

Indeed, notwithstanding the bilateral progress and the NORAD renewal, it is evident that continental defence cooperation was not a priority for

the newly elected Conservative government in 2006. Their election platform stressed the need to put "Canada First" and did not even mention
the defence of North America. "Canada First" meant paying a great deal of
rhetorical attention to homeland defence and the protection of the Arctic from various hypothetical dangers. The language used to promote this
approach to national defence, in fact, implied that the Conservative government was determined to face any challenge to Canada's sovereignty in
the Arctic, including those that might emanate from the United States.[29]
The reality was much different, of course; the Conservatives' actual investment in Arctic defence was far from grandiose, and northern nations
worked quietly to improve their cooperation in the North.[30] Nonetheless, the tone they employed demonstrated the Conservatives' belief that
electoral advantage lay in emphasizing the protection of Canada, not re-
engaging with the idea of a deeper binational defence of the continent
alongside the United States.

Marginalized Binational Defence Cooperation, 2007-10

Continental defence cooperation was a marginal concern in the latter part
of the 2000s as well. With the United States struggling to bring order and
stability to Iraq, and in the absence of new attacks on American soil, interest in homeland and continental defence plateaued. By 2007, NorthCom
was well established and its roles and duties were understood and appreciated within the US defence community. While the defence of homeland
and continent still needed refinement and improvement, the issue was not
especially pressing in Washington. The situation was similar in Canada.
As the insurgent threat grew in Afghanistan and Canadian casualties from
the Canadian Forces' deployment in Kandahar mounted, decision makers
in Ottawa were preoccupied with Canada's involvement in that country.
As a result, the defence of the Canadian homeland and the North American continent received scant attention from political leaders. Although
the defence department worked to build up CanadaCom and prepare it
for various missions, the defence of Canada was not seen to require much
more, with the possible exception of a larger military presence in the Arctic. CanadaCom entrenched itself with little fanfare or controversy, save
for questions about the resources it and the three other new operational commands were absorbing.[31] From a Canadian standpoint, moreover,
improving the defence of North America meant ensuring that Canada-
Com and NorthCom developed a strong, collaborative bilateral relationship. Further expanding NORAD was not a viable or desirable option.

The continued bilateral focus was evident in how the continental
defence relationship developed toward the end of the decade. The 2006

Canada-US Basic Defence Document, which was signed by the Canadian Chief of the Defence Staff and the American Chairman of the Joint Chiefs of Staff, instructed the commanders of NorthCom, NORAD, and Canada-Com to strengthen the ties between and among their three commands. Given their overlapping roles and areas of responsibility, the commanders were directed to properly define their respective responsibilities, and the so-called Tri-Commands were ordered to find ways to function more efficiently together, in spite of any organizational aversion they might have to doing so. Over the next few years, the Tri-Commands did just that. They examined ways to coordinate their crisis planning, support each other's operations, and share information and intelligence. They also conducted a number of joint exercises.

In spite of these achievements, however, cooperation between and among the three commands still faced barriers and obstacles. In their 2009 Tri-Command Framework, the commanders noted that sharing classified information was a "cumbersome and time consuming process."[32] Information systems lacked true interoperability and the three commands required a greater degree of interaction. In addition, the Tri-Command Framework noted that "command authorities, capabilities, and responsibilities were not sufficiently clear," despite ongoing efforts to delimit them. Indeed, it argued that this lack of clarity exacerbated the information-sharing problem. Simply put, the commanders observed that those working within the commands were still unsure about who did what, and who could see what. The problem was especially evident in the area of maritime intelligence. "The nature of maritime intelligence," the Framework lamented, "creates significant legal and organizational culture considerations."[33] With both countries filtering their maritime intelligence, the Tri-commands were left with a "limited picture" of the continent's maritime domain. To address these lingering deficiencies, the three commanders agreed to develop a Tri-Command Common Vision and Strategy, improve officer liaisons between the commands, better educate officers about the three commands, enhance information and intelligence sharing, and develop "a compatible and practical process for tri-command coordination and synchronization during planning and execution of bi-national and bilateral operations."[34]

On 12 March 2010, the three commands released a command vision statement. The document highlighted the advances made in bringing about a closer degree of cooperation and collaboration between and among NorthCom, CanadaCom, and NORAD. However, the language employed by the commanders also hinted at the difficulties that continued to nag at them: "As we look to the future, it is imperative that our role and responsibilities remain clearly defined and understood," which suggested that they were not. Indeed, developing "a culture of continuous collaboration and cooperation in planning, execution, training, information management, and innovation" remained a goal for the commanders, rather than an accomplishment they could highlight.[35] Although there was no question that the three commands had improved their working relations and built practical principles of collaboration, tensions persisted. Arguably, the preference for bilateral collaboration aggravated these tensions, as the two newer homeland defence commands struggled to define their roles and missions, forge a cooperative relationship with each other, and understand how NORAD fit within the bilateral continental defence framework they were constructing.

The commanders of NorthCom and CanadaCom also negotiated two significant bilateral contingency plans between 2007 and 2010. As instructed by the BDD, the commanders sought to develop a classified Canada-US Combined Defence Plan (CDP). The CDP's stated purpose was to provide "a framework for the combined defence of Canada and the United States during peace, contingencies, and war."[36] In other words, the plan would outline how the Canadian and US militaries would collaborate to jointly defend North America from a conventional or high-intensity asymmetrical attack. Although the CDP had yet to be finalized in 2009, it appears that the plan has now been completed.[37]

The second contingency plan, the Canada-US Civil Assistance Plan (CAP), was completed in February 2008. Subject to the approval of civilian authorities in either country, this plan allows for NorthCom and Canada-Com to "provide support to the military of the other nation in the performance of civil support operations (e.g., floods, forest fires, hurricanes, earthquakes, and effects of a terrorist attack)."[38] It outlines how the Canadian and US militaries will go about assisting each other during operations of this type. In addition, the CAP explains how requests for assistance are to be made, ways in which the sovereignty of both nations will be guarded and respected, and the respective roles and responsibilities of North-Com and CanadaCom. Given that civil support operations address likely threats to Canadians and Americans alike, the negotiation of CAP represented a notable, if largely unrecognized, bilateral continental defence achievement.

By the end of the decade, then, North American defence relations had reached an acceptable but still incomplete level of bilateral cooperation between NorthCom and CanadaCom. The possibility of expanding NORAD's binational aerospace defence of the continent had been wholly discarded, however. NORAD itself was no longer the locus of Canada-US continental defence cooperation.[39] The NorthCom-CanadaCom relationship was now of equal, and growing, importance.

Conclusion: Continental Defence Cooperation after 2012

During the May 2011 election, the Stephen Harper's Conservatives won a majority of the seats in the House of Commons. With years of largely unchecked governing power ahead of them, the Conservative government is ideally placed to re-examine the state of the Canada-US continental defence relationship with an aim toward solidifying bilateral continental cooperation between the two countries' militaries. Alternatively, the Conservatives could propose a truly binational approach to the defence of North America on land and at sea as part of an expanded NORAD. Regardless of whether they consider either of these options, the Conservative government could potentially reconsider Canada's involvement in the missile defence system. Each of these opportunities could be seized in the coming years, since (at the time of this writing) the countries are in the midst of negotiating a new continental security perimeter accord. Yet there are also reasons to think that none of these options will be pursued. I conclude my analysis with a brief discussion of these different possibilities.

The negotiation of a so-called North American security perimeter offers an opportunity for Canadian and American political leaders to elevate continental defence planning above the bureaucratic level, where it has been stuck since the early part of the decade. Were Prime Minister Harper and President Obama to take a personal interest in the state of the continental defence relationship, unresolved issues surrounding the respective roles and responsibilities of the three commands, as well as the obstacles that continue to impede a greater degree of collaboration, could be overcome more easily. Absent the direct intervention of these leaders,[40] it is unlikely that these challenges will be eliminated or prevented from re-emerging over time. The Canadian and US militaries may have compelled their political masters to accept the necessity of stronger defence cooperation in the past, but the last decade suggests that this is unlikely to happen again without presidential and prime ministerial leadership. An accord signed by the two leaders outlining how NorthCom, NORAD, and the Canadian Joint Operations Command (CJOC), which absorbed Canada Command in 2012, should interact and cooperate would provide an authoritative blueprint for the future of North American defence relations.

Given recent trends, it is probable that such an accord would focus on bilateral relations between NorthCom and the continental operations branch of CJOC. Although the concept of a continental perimeter might seem to accord with an expanded NORAD, it is hard to identify any movement in that direction in recent years. The last official report to recommend this course of action was the 2006 final report of the Bi-National Planning Group.[41] After 2006, the emphasis was on strengthening the bilateral ties between NorthCom and CanadaCom, the Tri-Command Study and Command Vision being cases in point. Unless Canadian and American officials have been quietly working on a plan to expand NORAD in the meantime, or Harper and Obama impose a change in emphasis, it is likely that any effort to enhance the continental defence relationship will reflect this preference for bilateral arrangements, with the NorthCom-CJOC relationship at the centre of this activity.

Of course, there is no guarantee that the continental perimeter will involve any alteration of the existing NorthCom/CJOC/NORAD dynamic. Assuming that it can overcome the hurdles it still faces, the perimeter will likely be restricted to improving trade flows and homeland and border security cooperation. Should this be the case, continental defence affairs will remain a largely bureaucratic concern, devoid of any significant policy shifts or innovations. Under this scenario, the three commands will still seek ways to improve their collaborative efforts and remove the barriers that prevent them from operating together as effectively as they should, yet the motivation to address their unresolved problems will be weakened.

The absorption of CanadaCom into CJOC, however, may have created an opportunity to re-emphasize NORAD's continuing relevance, since Canada no longer has a command dedicated to continental and domestic operations. This returns NORAD to a place of symbolic prominence in the Canada-US continental defence relationship. The question is whether this prominence can lead to the actual revitalization of NORAD's role.

One way to reaffirm NORAD's continuing importance would be for Canada to request a role in the US ballistic missile defence system.[42] As part of such a request, Canada could ask the US government to transfer the BMD command-and-control centre from NorthCom to NORAD. This would not be particularly complicated, since NORAD shares a headquarters with NorthCom and the United States has already agreed to give NORAD ITWAA data from its newest radars, satellites, and sensors.[43] True, it would not solve other questions concerning NORAD's relationship with

NorthCom and CJOC, but assigning the missile defence mission to NORAD would cement its standing as North America's unique aerospace defence command and could reinvigorate the idea of a binational approach to the defence of North America and reopen the debate over NORAD expansion.

Thus far, however, the Harper government has shown no interest in missile defence. In fact, when NATO endorsed missile defence in 2010, Canada was the only country that withheld its support for the system. Although NATO-wide support might have provided the Canadian government with the ideal cover for an unpopular position,[44] the Conservatives did not exploit it. This suggests that the Harper government is unwilling to expend any political capital, no matter how minor, on missile defence. What this means for the survival of NORAD is unclear.

At this juncture, then, it appears that the Canada-US continental defence relationship will continue to develop incrementally in bilateral fashion, with NorthCom and CJOC as the loci of future cooperation. Binational continental defence, like NORAD, the command that exemplifies it, will remain as a model of collaboration that cannot be easily replicated.

NOTES

1 For an overview of these developments, see Chapter 5.

2 The author gratefully acknowledges confidential sources who brought these facts to his attention. Parts of the correspondence between Eggleton and Rumsfeld have been released by Library and Archives Canada. See Library and Archives Canada, Access to Information Request A-2001-00360, February 2012.

3 Information provided by confidential sources.

4 Joseph T. Jockel, "Five Lessons from the History of North American Aerospace Defence," *International Journal* 65, 4 (Autumn 2010): 1021.

5 Philippe Lagassé, "Northern Command and the Evolution of Canada-US Defence Relations," *Canadian Military Journal* 4, 1 (Spring 2003): 15-22.

6 Michel Fortmann and David G. Haglund, "Canada and the Issue of Homeland Security: Does the 'Kingston Dispensation' Still Hold?" *Canadian Military Journal* 3, 1 (Spring 2002): 17-22.

7 Jockel, "Five Lessons," 1014-16.

8 Joseph T. Jockel, *Canada in NORAD 1957-2007: A History* (Montreal and Kingston: McGill-Queen's University Press, 2007), chs. 1-5.

9 Canada, Privy Council Office, *Securing an Open Society: Canada's National Security Policy* (Ottawa: Privy Council Office, April 2004).

10 Joel J. Sokolsky and Philippe Lagassé, "Suspenders and a Belt: Perimeter and Border Security in Canada-US Relations," *Canadian Foreign Policy* 12, 3 (2005/2006): 15-30.

11   Ibid.

12   Jockel, "Five Lessons," 1021.

13   Sokolsky and Lagassé, "Suspenders and a Belt."

14   Joseph T. Jockel and Joel J. Sokolsky, "Renewing NORAD – Not if Not Forever," *Policy Options* (July-August 2006): 56.

15   Dwight Mason, "The Canadian-American North American Defence Alliance in 2005," *International Journal* 60, 2 (2005): 385-96.

16   Michael Byers, "Canadian Armed Forces under United States Command," *International Journal* 58, 1 (Winter 2002-03): 89-114.

17   James G. Fergusson, *Canada and Ballistic Missile Defence 1954-2009: Déjà Vu All Over Again* (Vancouver: UBC Press, 2010), 221-27.

18   Ibid., 230-31.

19   David Pratt, Minister of National Defence, Letter to Secretary of Defense Rumsfeld, January 2004. For Rumsfeld's reply, see http://www.dod.mil/pubs/foi/ International_security_affairs/other/07-F-2630 Letter from Secretary Donald Rumsfeld to The Honorable David Pratt 15 January 2004.pdf.

20   For details of the anti-BMD campaign, see Steven Staples, *Missile Defence: Round One* (Toronto: Lorimer, 2006).

21   Canada, Department of National Defence, "Canada and United States Amend NORAD Agreement," news release, 5 August 2004.

22   For details, see Brad W. Gladman, "Strengthening the Relationship: NORAD Expansion and Canada Command," *Journal of Military and Strategic Studies* 9, 2 (Winter 2006/07).

23   Bi-National Planning Group, *The Final Report on Canada and the United States (CANUS) Enhanced Military Cooperation* (Colorado Springs: Peterson Air Force Base, 13 March 2006), 37-38.

24   Canada, Department of National Defence, *Framework for Enhanced Military Cooperation among North American Aerospace Defense Command, United States Northern Command, and Canada Command*, September 2009, http://www.cpcml.ca/publications2012/ 091002-EnhancedFrameworkNAMilitaryCooperation.pdf.

25   Canada, Department of National Defence, *Canada's International Policy Statement: A Role of Pride and Influence in the World* (Ottawa: Department of National Defence, 2005).

26   Jockel and Sokolsky, "Renewing NORAD," 56.

27   Eric Lerhe, "Will We See a Maritime NORAD?" *Journal of Military and Strategic Studies* 9, 2 (2006/07).

28   Philippe Lagassé, "A Maritime NORAD?" *SITREP: Journal of the Royal Canadian Military Institute* 64, 5 (November-December 2004): 10-12.

29   Conservative Party of Canada, *Stand Up for Canada: Conservative Party of Canada Federal Election Platform 2006* (Ottawa: Conservative Party of Canada, 2006), 45.

30   Michael Byers, "Cold Peace: Arctic Cooperation and Canadian Foreign Policy," *International Journal* 65, 4 (Autumn 2010): 899-912.

31 Philippe Lagassé, "A Mixed Legacy: General Hillier and Canadian Defence, 2005-2008," *International Journal* 64, 3 (Summer 2009): 614-16.

32 Canada, Department of National Defence, *Framework for Enhanced Military Cooperation,* para. 14.

33 Ibid., para. 16.

34 Ibid., para. 25.

35 NORAD, NorthCom, and CanadaCom, *Tri Command Vision,* 12 March 2010, http://www.northcom.mil/News/Signed Vision in English 12 Mar 10.pdf.

36 Canada, Department of National Defence, *Framework for Enhanced Military Cooperation,* para. 12.

37 "Allies in Defence," *Maple Leaf* 15, 3 (March 2012).

38 Canada Command and United States Northern Command, *Canada-US Civil Assistance Plan (CAP),* 14 February 2008, para. 1, http://www.northcom.mil/News/2008/CAP - For Public Posting - 28 May 08.pdf.

39 For an alternative reading of the current state of affairs surrounding NORAD and the continental defence relationship, see Alan Stephenson, "Securing the Continent: Where Is NORAD Today," Strategic Studies Working Group Papers (Ottawa: Canadian International Council and Canadian Foreign Affairs and Defence Institute, November 2011).

40 This point draws on the findings of Donald Savoie, *Power: Where Is It?* (Montreal and Kingston: McGill-Queen's University Press, 2010).

41 Bi-National Planning Group, *Final Report on Canada and the United States,* 37-38.

42 For a discussion of this possibility, see Philippe Lagassé, "Canada, Strategic Defence, and Strategic Stability," *International Journal* 63, 4 (Autumn 2008): 935-37.

43 Information provided by confidential sources.

44 On this point, see David S. McDonough, "Canada, NORAD, and the Evolution of Strategic Defence," *International Journal* 68, 3 (Summer 2012): 768; James Fergusson, "The Return of Ballistic Missile Defence," *On Track* (Autumn 2010): 36.

11

Defence Policy and the Aerospace and Defence Industry in North America

The Changing Contours of the Post-9/11 Era

YAN CIMON

Much has been said about the fallout from September 11, 2001, on many aspects of everyday life beyond its purely financial aspects, especially given the great human cost of the terrorist attacks on New York and Washington, DC.[1] Its aftershocks reverberated globally, causing a seismic shift that affected the strategic and military environment and the policy-making context. The aerospace and defence industry was not immune, and underwent significant transformation as it tried to adapt to the new reality. The purpose of this chapter is to examine the impact of 9/11 on this industry in the context of successive, and concurrent, iterations of defence policy and force employment philosophies.

We begin by examining the changing context from the Cold War to the post-9/11 era and its impact on defence policy, doctrinal issues, and, by extension, the aerospace and defence industry. We look at the industry's adaptation to this dynamic environment, in the way programs are developed and confirmed by selected economic indicators. The North American industry has experienced heavy pressure resulting from successive policy shifts or from the growing realization that the industry is an important element of defence policy making. We discuss such changes in the policy environment and their impact on the industrial base in light of their influence on force structure and industrial regional benefits, and conclude by outlining some implications for both academics and policy makers.

A Rapidly Changing World: The Cold War and Beyond

The Cold War, characterized by a bipolar world, was geared toward a large classical conflict in Europe between NATO and the Warsaw Pact.[2] One type of conflict likely to break out would have been a war of attrition along the lines of a "super Second World War" type of engagement. During this period, the tactical picture was greatly influenced by the lessons learned by the United States and NATO in various engagements, such as the Korean War (1950-53), the Suez Crisis (1956), the Cuban Missile Crisis (1962), and the Vietnam War (mid-1950s to 1975). Similarly, numerous interventions in Soviet republics and satellites, the Soviet war in Afghanistan (1979-88), and various guerrilla engagements contributed to shaping the structure and tactics of the Soviet Union and Warsaw Pact forces. Full-spectrum warfare was the outcome that cold warriors actively sought to avoid, but limited engagements occurred. Canada and the United States cooperated actively on the cruise missile testing program, among others.[3]

The fall of Soviet communism produced a very different, multipolar security environment, although many observers have, in retrospect, described this period as "America's unipolar moment," since the "hyperpower" was unrivalled and remained the only one left standing. The post–Cold War period was a tumultuous one. Indeed, the wave of newly independent countries accompanied by regional and national rivalries that were no longer tempered by the interests of opposing superpowers created strategic challenges of their own. NATO members began to be more selective in their defence investments and budgets were drastically reduced, resulting in program cancellations and force reduction. On the other hand, successes in Operation Just Cause (Panama, 1989), in Operation Desert Storm (Iraq, 1991), and in the Balkans (Bosnia, 1995-96; and Kosovo, 1999) underscored the importance of air power, overwhelming force, and targeted action. High-precision weapons and related ordnance became a well-known feature of this operational environment. There was evidence of capability or doctrinal shortcomings when Western forces operated in certain types of asymmetric environments, as in the failure of Operation Restore Hope (Somalia, 1993), but the "own the night" approach became a cornerstone of ground operations. This success in dominating night operations was made possible by the proper combination of doctrinal adjustments, training, and the wide distribution of night vision equipment.

In the post-9/11 era, non-state actors have become common adversaries or actors in the operational environment. The US military has undergone significant changes since 9/11,[4] but emerging economies such as China, Brazil, and Turkey are fast closing the military and economic gaps with the West. In this changing environment, military engagements now focus more on counterinsurgency (COIN) environments such as Operation Enduring Freedom (Afghanistan, since 2001) and Operation Iraqi Freedom (2003-11), and other operational environments such as Operation Odyssey Dawn (Libya, 2011).[5] These operations have dramatically altered how force projection efforts are led by modern armed forces. They typically imply smaller military deployments coupled with a focus on increased agility and better information-related capabilities, as well as increased reliance on technology and a recognition of the need for "jointness."[6] Other core ideas, such as increased mobility, flexibility, and higher levels of readiness, are now at the heart of swift deployments for maximum effect.[7]

The net effect of these new doctrinal and operational developments has been a slow transition from war as part of an alliance (e.g., through NATO) or multinational environment (e.g., the UN) to coalition warfare where interfacing is done primarily with US forces as coalition leaders.[8] Thus, the evolution of the operational environment has led to a renewed focus on interoperability as exemplified by the ABCA environment.[9] Special attention is given to the interoperability of communication systems because of the importance of command and control in contemporary warfare.[10]

The changing environment and ensuing doctrinal and operational imperatives have had an important influence on the evolution of the North American aerospace and defence industry.

The Aerospace and Defence Industry: An Adaptive Player

The North American aerospace and defence industry, sometimes referred to as the "military-industrial complex," has undergone major changes in recent years. Once perceived as a relatively stable industry, it has consistently demonstrated an ability to adapt to an increasingly dynamic conditions, as exemplified by new trends in program development and the evolution of a small set of economic indicators.

Program Development

During the Cold War, the industry was characterized by a focus on a variety of large weapons development programs. These programs would often compete until a final decision by national authorities on which platform or weapon system would be chosen. Thus, the industrial base was diversified and the development of many competing versions of a given big-ticket item or system (fighter planes, armoured vehicles, and so on) was the often the norm. Although some multi-role equipment was developed, many systems were very specialized.[11]

The fall of Soviet communism and the end of bipolarity ushered in a period of decreasing defence budgets that put more pressure on national acquisitions processes to be streamlined and efficient. Between 1990 and 1998, a wave of consolidation of defence contractors – whether original equipment manufacturers (OEMs) or integrators – took place.[12] An underlying assumption was that the new firms would be more viable and would provide more cost-effective solutions as a result of economies of scale and scope. Furthermore, this would be done with a focus on safeguarding a healthy competitive dynamic in the consolidated industry.[13] During the same period, many European countries began initiating multi-country and multi-firm efforts to develop new weapon systems, such as the Eurofighter.[14]

Economic Indicators

Three sets of indicators may facilitate an appreciation of the health of the aerospace and defence industry: (1) the level of industry concentration, (2) the level of employment in the industry, and (3) the evolution of US imports, especially those from Canada.

Examining the concentration of the industry tells us about its competitive dynamics. As concentration increases, competition decreases and industry margins tend to increase. Throughout the Cold War and since the fall of communism, industry concentration has been increasing, and the one hundred leading companies globally have become more and more important, accounting for an ever-growing proportion of total industry revenue (see Table 11.1).[15] These companies have exerted more and more influence over the industry as their market power increased. Although industry concentration has been increasing steadily since 1990, the rate of growth of this concentration has slowed in the 2000-05 period, suggesting that the post-9/11 era made for larger opportunities and more fragmentation. This can be interpreted as a positive sign – of rapid growth and more comfortable margins – for an industry that suffered through the major restructuring effort following the end of the Cold War.

The Stockholm International Peace Research Institute (SIPRI) data for the largest companies in the industry show that most of them are prime contractors, that is, large-scale integrators that put systems or entire platforms together. Some have a wide range of products and services, whereas others are niche players that are very focused on limited market seg-

TABLE 11.1

Growth of concentration in the global aerospace and defence industry

Company size	Average growth in arms sales (%)			Average growth in total sales (%)		
	1990-95	*1995-2000*	*2000-05*	*1990-95*	*1995-2000*	*2000-05*
Largest 5	27.27	46.43	4.88	3.03	26.47	4.65
Largest 10	13.51	35.71	8.77	1.96	17.31	1.64
Largest 15	10.42	22.64	6.15	4.92	10.94	2.82
Largest 20	7.02	14.75	5.71	4.35	9.72	2.53

Source: Stockholm International Peace Research Institute, "The Arms Industry," http://www.sipri.org/ (raw data); calculations by author.

ments. In fact, in 2009 only twelve of the one hundred largest companies in the world were component providers, also called top-tier suppliers, compared with only eight in 2000. This is an indication that supplier markets are growing, and provides further evidence of a change in value-creation patterns, as some highly specialized proprietary technologies, components, and subsystems generate interesting margins.

The picture is different when considering the Canadian industry, however: in 2009 only one of those companies was Canadian,[16] whereas three Canadian companies were among the top one hundred in 2000. The Canadian industry consists of Canadian branches of global (mostly American) players. It is highly integrated with the American industry. It provides subsystems, training, and niche equipment and services. Some Canadian firms have opened American subsidiaries to facilitate the provision of goods and services to the US government.[17]

The level of employment in the industry is another indicator of its overall health. After a decline following the fall of communism, the number of Canadians employed by the aerospace and defence industry has grown steadily in the post-9/11 period. It grew by 11.3 percent between 1998 and 2002, reaching almost the same level as in 1995 (Figure 11.1). In the United States, employment increased more sharply, by 22.8 percent over the same period (Figure 11.2).

The evolution of imports provides a third indicator of the state of the industry. Given the nationalistic outlook in defence procurement matters,

FIGURE 11.1

Employment in the Canadian aerospace and defence industry

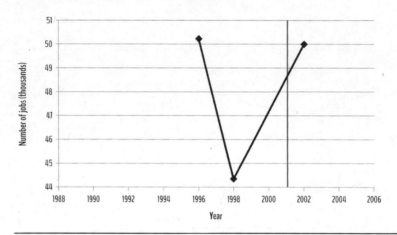

Source: Stockholm International Peace Research Institute, "The Arms Industry,"
http://www.sipri.org (raw data); calculations by author.

and the usual concern of states for industrial regional benefits (IRBs), a significant level of imports may signify a healthy industry. Imports often rise when national contractors and suppliers experience significant backlogs or do not possess the capabilities associated with some defence acquisitions. In the case of the North American industry, one indicator is the level of US arms imports. The Canadian industry is significantly smaller than the American, and the latter is a driver for the former because of the high level of cross-border integration in their value chains as a result of NAFTA. Thus, the level of globally sourced American imports helps us gauge the health of the US industry, while the level of American arms imports from Canada helps in assessing the health of the Canadian industry.

In the decade prior to 9/11, US defence imports were decreasing globally, as were those specifically from Canadian sources (Figure 11.3). This is especially meaningful because of the complicated process of importing defence materiel from foreign countries, even NATO partners, over the last thirty years creates a potential disincentive.[18] This decrease in imports prior to 9/11 is therefore consistent with the consolidation of the industry following the end of the Cold War. After 9/11, however, there was a sharp rise in defence imports from global sources, fuelled by massive increases in US defence needs and budgets. Imports from Canada have also grown, but at a much slower pace.[19]

FIGURE 11.2

Employment in the US aerospace and defence industry

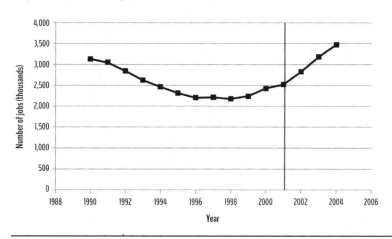

Source: Stockholm International Peace Research Institute, "The Arms Industry," http://www.sipri.org (raw data); calculations by author.

In summary, the North American aerospace and defence industry underwent significant changes but remained healthy overall. No matter which economic indicator we look at, however, it is necessary to consider the policy dynamics that are involved, as they often have an important impact beyond policy-making circles.

Policy Shifts

The major qualitative shift in the defence-related policy environment since 9/11 was the result of a series of policy shocks, dramatic and sudden policy changes with long-term effects. In the case of Canada, there has also been a recognition that industry should be factored into the development of defence policy.

Policy Shocks

There were two major policy shocks: (1) the loss (and recovery) of Canada's International Traffic in Arms Regulations (ITAR) exemption and (2) the security measures put in place after 9/11.

The first policy shock occurred prior to 9/11. The environment had begun to change as American threat assessment evolved from a focus on large-scale conflict avoidance to renewed interest in mitigating threats from terrorism, especially in light of the 1993 World Trade Center bomb-

FIGURE 11.3

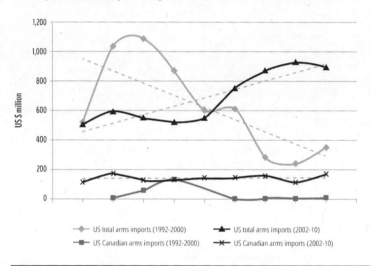

US aerospace and defence imports from global and Canadian sources before and after 9/11

Source: Stockholm International Peace Research Institute, "The Arms Industry," http://www.sipri.org (raw data in 1990 US dollars); calculations by author.

ing and the 1998 bombings of American embassies in Tanzania and Kenya, and from economic espionage, which had increased after the fall of communism. The US security establishment felt that security in Canada in relation to terrorism and espionage was too lax.[20] Canada's exemption under ITAR – the American International Traffic in Arms Regulation – was therefore suspended from 1998 to 2000,[21] a development that shocked the country's defence industry and caused a sharp drop in Canadian employment levels and exports to the US before the exemption was reinstated in 2000.[22]

The second major policy shock took the form of various security measures in the aftermath of 9/11 that led to the emergence of a new institutional environment and a focus on border management issues. In Canada, there is a need to continually find a sustainable alignment between defence policy and the national interest.[23] The problem was not so much that Canadian and American defence-related agreements changed – NATO's Article 5 and other continental agreements, such as NORAD, continued to apply – but that as new organizations were created, defence and security-related issues have expanded beyond their traditional spheres. First, the Americans created a Northern Command (North-

Com) as an operational command with an area of responsibility spanning Canada and Mexico and a mission related to homeland security and civil defence matters.[24] Canada reciprocated with the creation of Canada Command to coordinate the "domestic and continental" operations of the three services and interface with civilian authorities and with NorthCom. Second, the non-military security sphere has expanded greatly in scope. In the United States, the creation of Department of Homeland Security and the Office of the Director of National Intelligence reflect the need for coordinated responses. The net result has been an emphasis on border security at all ports of entry, including some pre-clearance zones in select non-US airports. Better monitoring and new intelligence capabilities were developed and deployed.

Another element of the policy shock that characterized the decade following 9/11 has to do with Canada-US border management. A lot has been said in the media about the need to better secure the border.[25] On the political front, many agreements have been negotiated to mitigate the negative effects of increased security on Canada-US trade. The Smart Border Declaration (SBD, December 2001) had the objective of reinforcing collaboration and trust at the border in order to increase the level of security while facilitating flows of travellers and goods. Another initiative, the Security and Prosperity Partnership of North America (SPP), which was active between 2005 and 2009, had a deeper objective – namely, that Canada, the United States, and Mexico would attempt to harmonize some security-related practices with the concurrent objective of facilitating their mutual trade through a trilateral forum. More recently, Beyond the Border declaration, a "shared vision for perimeter security and economic competitiveness" announced by President Barack Obama and Prime Minister Stephen Harper in February 2011, promised better cross-border coordination of law enforcement agencies while facilitating trade and protecting infrastructure.[26]

Over the years, these initiatives have resulted in the expansion of defence and security issues outside the traditional defence policy circles. They have also given rise to an impression that the United States was arrogating to itself extended extraterritorial powers and authority. For lack of better options,[27] the net result has been an uneasy voluntary quasi-alignment by Canada with US policies, although Canada is in a position to help shape the changes coming its way, as it did with the Smart Border Declaration.

Industry and Canadian Defence Policy
Historically, Canada's defence policy did not include much consideration for the aerospace and defence industry, except perhaps through

procurement policies.[28] It was generally assumed that the industry would, as a default position, adapt to the needs outlined for defence procurement. Recently, however, there has been a realization in Canadian policy circles that the industry needs to be involved in order for the country to face threats from the future security environment.[29] Nowadays, there is more recourse to industry to fill capability gaps and deliver services such as logistics, food services, and so on in a timely manner.[30] This trend began after the fall of communism with an emphasis on alternate service delivery in order to reduce costs by outsourcing functions that, it was thought, could be handled more efficiently by the private sector.

The Canada First Defence Strategy (CFDS), unveiled in 2008, is a break from earlier White Papers in that it more closely involves the industry in defence policy. It recognizes and aims to leverage Canada's industrial base and capabilities in that industry.[31] Furthermore, the CFDS tends to present industry as a partner in defence policy implementation, especially on the procurement and industrial development side.[32] This had been deemed a primordial strategic imperative[33] especially since the Department of National Defence's Strategy 2020 – a core document projecting Canadian defence policy in, and outlining possible capability requirements for, the twenty-first century – was elaborated prior to 9/11. Yet, one year after its implementation, the results of the CFDS appear to be mixed. On the one hand, funding increases stabilize the situation for the Canadian Forces as well as for Canadian industry. On the other hand, much still remains to be done to implement the many programs that were announced.[34] The defence industry went on the record as supporting Canada's new defence strategy and is eagerly awaiting more information and resources.[35] There is now a greater possibility of improving coordination between the industry and the military,[36] which would simply be an acknowledgment of the link between force structure and the industrial base. However, the CFDS depends as much on political will as on the state of the economy, not just in Canada but also in the United States and globally.[37] This affects the benefits that can be expected from a better alignment between industrial and defence policy, as these two have a mutually reinforcing relationship.

A Renewed Perspective on the Industrial Base?

This newfound interest of defence policy in industrial issues has implications for three realities: (1) unrealized large-scale projects have an economic cost; (2) policy and force structure have repercussions on the shape of the industrial base; and (3) the way industrial regional benefits are distributed matters from an economic perspective.

The Cost of Unrealized Projects

Defence policy and the aerospace and defence industrial base are linked. Investment in military projects and their spillover effects have geopolitical impacts of their own. A look at large multinational military exercises during the Cold War supports the conclusion that although Canada is a minor player on the world stage, it has maintained a certain level of relevance by selectively collaborating with a select group of armed forces, mostly from NATO.[38] From the mid-1990s to the early 2000s, the Canadian Forces experienced a surge in deployments and operational tempo,[39] but the absence of guidance led to management challenges. For example, aligning information technology systems and objectives in the Canadian Forces is a challenge, in part because of the nature of the organization's budget cycle.[40]

Defence-related commitment changes – whether national or international – impact policy and attitudes and imply more uncertainty for the industry. After 9/11, in the Martin era, Canada was often pressured by its neighbour to the south to increase military spending.[41] In response, it sent mixed messages to its American ally, participating in the war in Afghanistan but rejecting involvement in ballistic missile defence, a program that would have been a boon to military contractors but that was not considered a priority by the Canadian government.

Policy, Force Structure, and the Industry

Policy and its influence on industry have had an effect on shaping the industrial base. The Canadian military was always prepared to fight a war throughout the Cold War, but the myth of its being solely a peacekeeping force continues to endure in the general population. This led to its being underequipped and underfunded from the end of the Cold War all the way to 9/11, to the point that renowned historian Jack Granatstein publicly expressed doubts that the Canadian Forces were a fighting force.[42] In the United States, 9/11, the subsequent wars in Afghanistan and Iraq, and a renewed focus on homeland security have contributed to the current shape of the North American defence industry.

Furthermore, future force structures entailed by policy-driven organizational transformation often require substantial financial investment from both the military and industry.[43] Transformation implies new military capabilities[44] and therefore a renewed mix of capabilities from contractors. The American industry is one of the few that offers militaries the full spectrum of capabilities. The Canadian defence industry is positioning itself as a champion of the national interest, with regard to both security and the economy.[45] The Canadian government's efforts to promote the industry emphasize Canada's role as an effective supplier.[46] This will help move the industry beyond its self-perception as having a competitive advantage when it comes to supporting legacy systems, as in the case of airframes, and push it toward other types of complex systems in high value-added segments of the defence industry's value chain, for instance.[47] In fact, as discussed earlier, Canada's defence industry is growing.[48] This growth comes from top-tier suppliers, OEMs, and integrators in specific niches that are able to capitalize on incremental investments and leading-edge simulation systems.[49] These are in part attributable to the impact of industrial regional benefits (or IRBs), the nature of which may be changing dramatically, as prime contractors are no longer content with the political process that surrounds them.

The Shape of Industrial Regional Benefits to Come

Reflecting the usual practice in large government systems acquisitions, a defence purchase consists of the acquisition price of an item plus offsets (ancillary products and services such as maintenance and training, etc.). Governments have traditionally wanted to minimize the former; the latter, being more complex to evaluate, would be dealt with at later stages in the process or while the contract was ongoing or had been awarded.[50]

Furthermore, a contract award would have to provide and guarantee a certain set of industrial regional benefits. This was often done by governments to build or sustain specific types of industrial activities or to develop specific industrial capabilities, more often on the manufacturing side but also on the service- and maintenance-provision side. These benefits are factored into the contract's total cost.

In recent years, IRBs have been a contentious subject as they were deemed to create inefficiency and raise costs because prime contractors faced limitations on supplier selection. This meant delays because of engineering and manufacturing challenges. They have also been the bone of contention in political battles in the United States and Canada, pitting regions against each other. In Canada, Industry Canada oversees IRBs. A rule of thumb has been that the business generated in Canada should equate to the amount of a given contract that would be awarded.

This policy is slowly changing. Indeed, the Canadian position on IRBs may have been relaxed de facto on two occasions. The first involved the C-17 acquisition contract awarded in 2007, when it was publicly announced that a market-based approach was preferred to traditional IRB determination.[51] Further loosening is seen in the case of the F-35 program, in which Canada has been a participant since 1997, especially since this fighter plane acquisition, announced in 2010, is controversial but deemed essential.[52] The prime contractor is refusing to give any guarantee of IRBs as it wishes to have more freedom of action in selecting its suppliers.[53] An advantage to the prime contractor could be the extraction of important cost reductions from a small set of highly efficient suppliers, reductions that could potentially be passed on to customers, although this remains to be seen. This may yet redefine the shape of the industry in years to come.

Conclusion

In conclusion, the North American aerospace and defence industry appears to have changed a lot since 9/11 – but then again perhaps not so much. In a more fluid and uncertain environment, the industry became more adaptable, although it is still dependent on the policy-making process and the strategic context.

After the end of the Cold War, the transition from a bipolar to a unipolar environment brought with it a series of changes. The strength of armed forces decreased, as did acquisition budgets, prompting a paradigm shift in the North American aerospace and defence industry. Firms have moved beyond go-it-alone approaches and – although the industry as a whole gradually became more consolidated – they have moved toward greater collaboration in the development and production of complex platforms and weapon systems.

This trend was accentuated in the post-9/11 era, with the added constraint of interoperability and new capability requirements that came from armed forces. The industry now shows signs of health: the rate of concentration has slowed, employment has gone up, and the national industry has so many opportunities that imports have been rising to fill the gap.

At the same time, the policy environment has been very dynamic. A first policy shock occurred when Canada lost its ITAR exemption at the end of the 1990s and regained it in 2000.[54] A second policy shock has been the advent of a new institutional environment and a more restrictive approach to the management of the Canada-US border. Nevertheless, Canadian defence policy, with the Canada First Defence Strategy, began taking the importance of the industry into account.

The industrial base still suffers from unrealized projects, especially in the context of mixed policy signals. As well, policy has an impact on force structure and thus on the capabilities that the aerospace and defence industry may leverage to develop the required products and services. Enormous pressures on the industry's cost structure are pushing it – and governments – to find innovative ways to provide industrial regional benefits.

The coming years will see new sets of challenges for academics and policy makers concerned with the state of the aerospace and defence industry. With the twenty-first century likely to be Asia's, transformations in the security environment will continue to shape the architecture of the industry. China's new capabilities, such as the ability to shoot down satellites, to put men in space, and to develop stealth fighters and a blue-water navy, will no doubt have tremendous implications and will exert dramatic pressure on the rest of the world to innovate. Regimes in Iran and North Korea will continue to create uncertainty, and an effective way to contain them will need to be devised, with the help of the North American defence industry.

In the post-9/11 world, contemporary militaries need to master classical ways of war. They will also need to be efficient in both localized and wide-scale asymmetric conflicts characterized by technological disparities. These will constitute a powerful force for change and provide opportunities for the industry, along with the increase in border and airport security and the advent of ever-smarter borders. An integrated, adaptable, and competitive North American aerospace and defence industry will enhance Canadian and American security. It could also be the cornerstone of a coherent North American approach to solving our common security dilemmas.

NOTES

1 Joseph Stiglitz, "The True Cost of 9/11," *Slate,* 1 September 2011. The author would like to thank the Fonds québécois de la recherche sur la société et la culture (FQRSC) and the research start-up fund of Université Laval for providing financial support for portions of this research. Reviewers provided feedback that greatly enhanced an earlier version of this paper. The usual caveats apply.

2 In the sense of attrition warfare characterized by an intensive use of conventional weapons where nuclear means are used as a deterrent.

3 See John Barrett and Douglas Ross, "The Air-Launched Cruise Missile and Canadian Arms Control Policy," *Canadian Public Policy* 11, 4 (1985): 711-30.

4 Fred Kaplan, "The Post-9/11 Military," *Slate,* 2 September 2011.

5 Called Operation Mobile by Canada.

6 Operations that combine army, navy and air force assets. This may be at a national or multinational level.

7 David Hughes, "Nato Transformation US, Canadian, French Military Officials Agree Nato Must Change, but Funding Is Limited," *Aviation Week and Space Technology* 159, 16 (2003): 78-79.

8   An example is the US-led "coalition of the willing" that invaded Iraq in 2003, although
    Defense Secretary Robert Gates has expressed the Obama administration's desire to
    see Europe take a more proactive role in such coalitions. The 2011 intervention in
    Libya may be an example of seeing the United States "leading from behind."

9   Dean C. Bell, *Canadian–United States Army Interoperability in the Age of Modularity* (Fort
    Leavenworth, KS: School of Advanced Military Studies, United States Army
    Command and General Staff College, 2005). "ABCA" stands for the American, British,
    Canadian, Australian, and New Zealand program that aims to increase interoperability
    among these five armies. See Richard A. Cody and Robert L. Maginnis, "Note to File –
    Coalition Interoperability: Abca's New Focus," *Canadian Army Journal* 10, 1 (2007):
    86-90.

10 P.C. Cooper, K. McKay, and S.J. Murray, "Digital Interoperability," *Army Doctrine and
    Training Bulletin* 6, 1 (2003): 40-45.

11 Classic examples are seen in fighter aircraft: the F-15 was developed as a high-altitude
    long-range interceptor, while the F-16 is especially adept at air-to-air close combat
    and is designed for increased manoeuvrability. At the time of their development,
    having a single fighter fill both of these roles was not considered a priority.

12 See US, General Accounting Office, *Defense Industry: Consolidation and Options for
    Preserving Competition,* Report to Congressional Committees GAO/NSIAD-98-141
    (Washington, DC: United States General Accounting Office, 1 April 1998).

13 A great case is made here: William E. Kovacic and Dennis E. Smallwood, "Competition
    Policy, Rivalries, and Defense Industry Consolidation," *Journal of Economic Perspectives*
    8, 4 (1994): 91-110.

14 This trend toward internationalization is not as strong in shipbuilding. Contracts in
    North America are mostly awarded along national lines, although lower-tier suppliers
    are often international.

15 See Stockholm International Peace Research Institute (SIPRI), "The Arms Industry,"
    http://www.sipri.org/.

16 Simulation systems provider CAE.

17 For example, CGI has an American subsidiary.

18 See John S.W. Fargher Jr., "Defense Contract Management in Multinational Programs,"
    National Contract Management Journal 15, 2 (1982): 1-14.

19 This may be a sign that the competitiveness of the Canadian industry is decreasing.
    The high degree of cross-border integration would have led to an assumption that
    imports from Canada should have grown faster than those from the rest of the world.

20 The 1999 arrest of Ahmed Ressam through joint Canada-US efforts proved the
    terrorism concerns to have been inflated. With regard to the risks associated with
    espionage, some perspective may be gained from documents archived by the
    Canadian Security Intelligence Service (CSIS). For interesting insights, see Canadian
    Security Intelligence Service, "Economic Espionage: Conducting Business in the
    International Marketplace" (Ottawa: Canadian Security Intelligence Service, 1999).

21 The ITAR is a trade control regulation that has an impact on Canadian and American
    contractors and customers for defence and defence-related articles. We thank an
    anonymous reviewer for prompting the clarification.

22 See Alexander Moens and Rafal Domisiewicz, *European and North American Trends in
    Defence Industry: Problems and Prospects of a Cross-Atlantic Defence Market* (Ottawa:
    Department of Foreign Affairs and International Trade, April 2001),
    http://www.international.gc.ca/arms-armes/assets/pdfs/moens_domisiewicz2001.pdf.

23 David J. Bercuson, "A Defence Policy to Serve Canadian Interests," *Fraser Forum* (May
    2004): 4-5.

24 See Chapter 10 for issues related to NorthCom.

25 Andrea Mandel-Campbell and Ken Warn, "Security Puts Strain on Nafta Partners:
    Border Controls," *Financial Times*, 16 October 2001.

26 Prime Minister Harper and President Obama have agreed in principle. See
    Theophilos Argitis and Andrew Mayeda, "Obama Agrees to Perimeter Security with
    Canada to Bolster Trade," *Bloomberg Business Week*, 12 December 2011.

27 Mary Janigan, "An Open Border?" *Maclean's*, 24 September 2001, 42-43.

28 For a discussion of procurement, see Jeff Tasseron, "Facts and Invariants: The
    Changing Context of Canadian Defence Policy," *Canadian Military Journal* 4, 2
    (Summer 2003): 19-30.

29 Shaye K. Friesen and Andrew N. Gale, "Slaying the Dragon: The Future Security
    Environment and Limitations of Industrial Age Security," *Canadian Military Journal* 11,
    1 (2010): 32-37.

30 For example, private military companies in Iraq and Afghanistan are providing
    training and protection services.

31 Canada, Department of National Defence, *Canada First Defence Strategy* (Ottawa:
    Department of National Defence, 2008).

32 Daniel J.L. Lachance, Joe T. Fernandes, Tim R. Gushue, Andrew B. Godefroy, and Lisa
    Moulton, *Projecting Power: Trends Shaping Canada's Air Force in the Year 2019* (Trenton,
    ON: Canadian Forces Aerospace Warfare Centre, 2009).

33 Maurice Baril, "Canadian Defence Force: This Institution's Future," *Vital Speeches of the
    Day* 66, 12 (1 April 2000): 357-60.

34 See George McDonald, *The Canada First Defence Strategy – One Year Later* (Calgary:
    Canadian Defence and Foreign Affairs Institute, 2009).

35 Carl Meyer, "Promised Strategy to Bolster Defence Industry Cautiously Welcome,"
    Embassy, 8 June 2011.

36 For example, ADM (Mat) – the assistant deputy minister (materiel) and his group –
    may be viewed as a link between the Department of National Defence and industry. It
    serves as such through many channels, one of them being the North American
    Technology and Industrial Base Organization (NATIBO). See Douglas L. Bland,
    "Institutionalizing Ambiguity: The Management Review Group and the Reshaping of

the Defence Policy Process in Canada," *Canadian Public Administration* 30, 4 (1987): 527-49.

37   Martin Shadwick, "Darkness Revisited?" *Canadian Military Journal* 9, 3 (2009): 95-97.

38   See Yan Cimon and Louis Hébert, *How Networks Matter: Insights from Armed Forces Collaborative Activity* (Quebec City: Faculté des sciences de l'administration, Université Laval, 2009); and Yan Cimon, *Capacités et collaboration* (Montreal: École des Hautes Études Commerciales, 2006).

39   Robert Michael Hartfiel, "Planning without Guidance: Canadian Defence Policy and Planning, 1993-2004," *Canadian Public Administration* 53, 3 (2010): 323-49.

40   Sharon Hartung, Blaize Homer Reich, and Izak Benbasat, "Information Technology Alignment in the Canadian Forces," *Canadian Journal of Administrative Sciences* 17, 4 (2000): 285-302.

41   Joel Baglole, "Washington Is Urging Canada to Increase Military Spending," *Wall Street Journal*, 17 October 2002, A16.

42   Jonathon Gatehouse, "Why the Canadian Military Isn't Ready for a War," *Maclean's*, 30 September 2002.

43   James C. Stone, "Doubling the Size of the Defence Budget: The Economic Realities of Strategy 2020" (PhD dissertation, Royal Military College of Canada, 2004).

44   Paul T. Mitchell, "A Transformation Agenda for the Canadian Forces: Full Spectrum Influence," *Canadian Military Journal* 4, 4 (2003): 55-62.

45   Canadian Association of Defence and Security Industries, *Canada's Defence Industry: A Vital Partner Supporting Canada's Economic and National Interests* (Ottawa: Canadian Association of Defence and Security Industries, 2009); Baril, "Canadian Defence Force."

46   Canadian Trade Commissioner Service, *Canada's Defence Industries* (Ottawa: Government of Canada, 2005).

47   Lachance et al., *Projecting Power.*

48   Sharon Hobson, "Risk-Bound Rewards: Canada's Defence Industry," *Jane's Information Group*, 20 October 2008.

49   Lachance et al., *Projecting Power.*

50   This strategy has obvious political benefits. It makes it easier to manage the wide range of stakeholders in the defence acquisition process.

51   Daniel Leblanc, "Market Forces Will Determine Distribution of Boeing Benefits, PM Says; Ottawa's Decision Not to Interfere Thwarts Fortier's Efforts to Boost Share for Quebec," *Globe and Mail*, 27 January 2007.

52   See Industry Canada, "Industrial Regional Benefits." http://www.ic.gc.ca. See also Julian Fantino, "Le F-35 Essentiel," *Cyberpresse*, 15 August 2011, http://www.lapresse.ca/.

53   Daniel Bordeleau, "Ottawa Commande des F-35," Radio-Canada, 29 March 2011, http://www.radio-canada.ca/.

54   Moens and Domisiewicz, *European and North American Trends in Defence Industry.*

12 The Canada-US Alliance in the Post-9/11 Context

Any Room for Mexico?

DAVID G. HAGLUND

Nearly two decades ago, one of Canada's leading students of Latin American security, Professor Hal Klepak of the Royal Military College of Canada, published a book whose title surprisingly implied that Canada and Mexico might be considered "natural allies."[1] This inference was far from a "natural" one for anyone to be drawing, not only because Canada and Mexico appear to reside on different planets when it comes to their publics' and elites' respective valuations of alliances in general but also because, to the extent that Canada could be said to have any "natural" ally, it would have to be the country with which it has been so closely linked militarily (to say nothing of economically) for more than six decades – and that, of course, is the United States. As for Mexico, although it is true that at one time it *was* an ally of the United States – indeed, it even sent a few combat units to the Pacific theatre during the Second World War – it severed its bonds of alliance with its northern neighbour in September 2002, when it withdrew from the Inter-American Treaty of Reciprocal Assistance (the Rio Pact). Mexico, therefore, is no one's ally, meaning that it is enmeshed with no partners in a formal or informal arrangement for "collective defence," whereas Canada is arguably America's most "special" ally.[2] Thus, it might seem, at first glance, that my task in this chapter – to address the question of Mexico's somehow being fitted into the Canada-

US alliance – can only lead to one easy, and negative, conclusion. It cannot be so fitted, for if it were inclined to ally itself with its two North American neighbours, why has it been moving in the opposite direction from alliance over the past decade? This is not the conclusion I will reach in this chapter, however, because I happen to believe that a case can be made for Mexico's becoming part of the "Canada-US alliance."

That case will unfold in three stages. To begin with, it is necessary to consider, since alliances must be about threat before they can be about anything else, how Mexico relates to the purpose of this book, which is of course to explore the altered threat environment facing North America as a result of the terrorist attacks of September 11, 2001, on New York and Washington. As Jonathan Paquin and Patrick James indicate in their introduction to this volume, the three North American states currently operate in a security environment that is far different from the one prevailing before 9/11. Each of the three has placed security at the top of its policy agenda, presumably for reasons eminently traceable back to the events of a dozen years ago. As a result, the new security environment on the continent is characterized by "rigorous border management." In the next section, I am going to probe closely this assumption that it has been terrorism that has been the single most important transformative aspect of North American security, writ large. I think it can be said to have been transformative directly in the case of Canada and the US, but only indirectly at best in the case of Mexico. The difference, I will argue, is important.

The second substantive section of this chapter will address more closely the precise meaning of the term "Canada-US alliance," for it is not self-evident whether in using this term we have in mind the myriad *bilateral* politico-military arrangements that have regulated cooperation between Canada and the United States since August 1940,[3] or the subsequent *multilateral* alliance (NATO) to which the two North American countries adhered in 1949, nearly a full decade after they had forged their own alliance. Again, it makes a difference.

The third section will be a deliberately controversial (some might say, bizarre) one, for in it I will suggest reasons why room should be made for Mexico in the Canada-US *multilateral* alliance – that is, NATO. It is far from commonplace to encounter arguments along the lines I will follow in that section, but if the history of NATO has revealed anything, it is that initiatives once thought to be simply out of the question can become, with the benefit of hindsight, so obvious and logical as to raise doubt about why anyone should ever have considered them controversial in the first place.

One thinks, in this regard, of the breathtaking addition to the allies' ranks in 1955 of the transatlantic allies' recent foe, Germany. Then there is, closer to our own day, the spectacle so many former Soviet allies (including three former Soviet *republics*) joining NATO, beginning in 1999.

I conclude by drawing together the various threads of the analysis, and end with the suggestion that, even if related only indirectly to the terrorism issue, the potential adhesion of Mexico to the Canada-US alliance might help ease some of the terrorism-related strains that have become a feature of North American security since 9/11, by rendering the question of border management more tractable.

What's Mexico Got to Do with It?

I do not mean to be facetious in titling this section thus. Given that this book has been organized around the theme of the terrorist attacks of September 11, 2001, it might seem logical, indeed necessary, to begin any discussion of Mexico's part in this collective endeavour by establishing some direct connection between al-Qaeda and Mexico, or at least between the general phenomenon of Islamic discontent with the West and Mexico. Perhaps such connections can be found, but I think most people who ponder the current security challenges facing Mexico, as well as the manner in which Mexican realities impinge upon Canadian and American interests, would find themselves scratching their heads to come up with a compelling linkage between Islamist terrorism and Mexico.

A few years ago, the director of the US Department of Homeland Security at the time, Michael Chertoff, told Fox News that he did not know of a *single* instance in which a terrorist had tried to enter the United States from Mexico. Nevertheless, Chertoff was supporting a more stringent border management regime with respect not only to America's southern frontier but to its northern one as well. Clearly, whatever else accounted for what one author has styled the "closing of the American border,"[4] it could not – at least not to the south – have been chiefly motivated by the terrorist threat associated with radical Islam. While there have been some reports of the Somali-based terrorist group al-Shabaab being present in Mexico,[5] it is emphatically not Islamist terrorism that accounts for the current security anxieties swirling around Mexico.

Instead, it is drug-related criminal violence, associated with the political corruption that runs rampant through the organs of the Mexican state, especially below the level of the federal government; these are the problems that are currently afflicting the country and that to date have cost some 45,000 lives. In 2010 alone, nearly 11,000 deaths were attributed to drug-related violence, counting both the tally of the Mexican government's offensive against drug gangs and the latter's own warfare against their fellow *narcotraficantes*.[6] By early 2011, the violence was clearly spreading to states in central Mexico that had hitherto been regarded as more or less removed from the ambit of the chaos, so that by mid-February, the US State Department felt the need to add a further four Mexican states to its blacklist of trouble spots, bringing the total number of danger zones to eighteen out of thirty-one of the country's states. This advisory followed on the heels of a gang-related shooting of two US immigration officials as they travelled in broad daylight on a highway in the state of San Luis Potosí; one of them, Jaime J. Zapata, died in the ambush.[7]

Some Mexicans, embroiled as they had been in the chaos engulfing their country, hoped that the attack on the American officials would be taken as a wake-up call in Washington, reminding the United States of what they in Mexico have had to endure for the past several years.[8] One American who did not need the reminder was Admiral James A. (Sandy) Winnefeld, at the time commander of both the US Northern Command (NorthCom) and the North American Aerospace Defence Command (NORAD) and now vice chairman of the Joint Chiefs of Staff in Washington. In the wake of the Zapata killing, Winnefeld noted that while the United States had just lost an agent to the drug traffickers, the Mexican authorities had seen two thousand of their own agents perish in the drug-related violence. Mexico, commented Winnefeld, was fighting not only for its own future security but for the security of *all* of North America.[9]

For some time, American military officials have been thinking hard about the consequences, for the United States, at least, of the ongoing violence in Mexico. In early 2009, a bit of a stir was caused when a study was released by the US Joint Forces Command, outlining two plausible, albeit worst-case, scenarios that bid fair to requiring urgent policy consideration from Washington, each concerning an important American partner. One was Pakistan, the other Mexico, and the risk was said to be that one or the other (or both) might turn into a "failed" state. In the case of Mexico, the study's authors foresaw that "any descent ... into chaos would demand an American response based on the serious implications for homeland security alone."[10] Almost as soon as the ink had dried on this report came official disclaimers that Washington was not – repeat, *not* – suggesting the impending collapse of the Mexican state. Still, the worries lingered. And, truth to tell, such dire forecasts are hardly unknown even in Mexico, where in early 2011 the president of a leading Monterrey-based multinational, Cemex, warned bluntly that unless the local authorities could get control over the *narcotraficantes* in this important northern industrial city, the future of the entire country was in peril.[11]

One consequence of this heightened concern in the American military about the situation in Mexico has been an augmentation of military and other security cooperation between the two countries.[12] This observation might seem to fly in the face of my earlier comment about Mexico's being "nobody's ally," but it need not, because military cooperation alone does not an alliance make, and certainly (as I will argue below) it does not make an "alliance" along the lines of the one that is such a central institution in the case of Canada and the United States – NATO.

Prior to getting to that alliance, however, a few more words are in order regarding how one might actually link the Mexican security mess with this book's explicit post-9/11 theme. We have already seen that attempting to connect Mexican reality *directly* with the Islamist challenge is a non-starter, or at the very least misses the point. The irony is that if one wanted to link post-9/11 worries to North American security, then it would be Canada more than Mexico that would stand out, and indeed during the first several years after the terrorist attacks, it was not uncommon for American officials, when the subject of "homeland security" came up, to rivet their attention almost exclusively upon Canada, whose own officials faced a difficult task, in the early post-9/11 period, convincing their American counterparts that the northern border was secure.

Americans were not so sure. Partly the inability to take solace from Canadian assurances was due to their realization of how incapable their *own* border authorities had been of preventing terrorists from entering the United States directly from overseas – the implication being that if the sprawling US Immigration and Naturalization Service (INS), coupled with the vaunted and well-funded American intelligence services, could not have prevented the establishment of al-Qaeda sleeper cells in America, then it was at least as likely, and probably much more likely, that relatively laid-back Canada, with its propensity to chronically underspend on defence as well as to minimize the gravity of threats, would be a place terrorists would find to their liking, perhaps not as a target but certainly as a staging area and support base for operations directed against American targets.

Added to the hypothetico-deductive case for anxiety was a widely publicized empirical reality, the saga of the so-called Millennium Bomber, Ahmed Ressam, whose own New Year's eve plans for 2000 called for the detonation of a powerful explosive at the Los Angeles airport. He never did get to set off his fireworks display, as he was apprehended by the INS on 14 December 1999 trying to enter the state of Washington from the province of British Columbia, by ferry from Vancouver Island, with bomb-making materials hidden in the trunk of his rented car. The

Ressam affair, near-miss that it was, suggested a shockingly easy manner in which American security could be breached from a base in Canada.

But a great deal has changed in the decade since Ressam was tried and convicted, and today a different aspect of the Islamist threat has been occupying minds on both sides of the Canada-US border, the phenomenon of "home-grown" terrorism. It is not that the older fear of terrorists slipping into North America via Canada and then crossing the border to strike at the United States has disappeared; it is rather that the older fear has been eclipsed by the prospect that Islamists born and raised in North America might choose to perpetrate terrorist attacks on their native soil.

Canada has had its own experience with homegrowns, albeit not on the same bloody scale as the United States, where in the autumn of 2009 a US Army psychiatrist, Major Nidal Malik Hasan, a Virginia-born Muslim, went on a murderous shooting spree at Fort Hood, Texas, killing a dozen of his army comrades and wounding another thirty.[13] In Canada, by contrast, the most notorious such episode was the foiled bid, during the summer of 2006, to detonate bombs in the downtown core of the country's largest city, Toronto, as well as at an undisclosed Canadian Forces base located along the Highway 401 corridor, the major east-west axis in the southern part of Ontario.[14] How the home-grown phenomenon will play out has to be anyone's guess at this stage.[15] On the one hand, America's own homegrowns should, ironically perhaps, lead to a further *reduction* in anxiety about the northern border, because who needs a Canadian gateway to the United States if the problem stems from *within* America itself? On the other hand, home-growns anywhere in North America serve to remind security analysts that vigilance must remain the order of the day.

But let us get back to how Mexico can be said to figure in this. It seems obvious that, compared with the situation a decade ago, in the United States today there is much more anxiety about the country's *southern* border than about its northern one, as evidenced by the frequency and tone with which Republican aspirants for their party's 2012 presidential nomination invoked the "crisis" of Mexican immigration to the United States. Illustratively, it was not too long ago that border management expert Edward Alden wrote a book lamenting the increased "hardening" of America's border with Canada, yet at the same time emphasizing that "there was a real terrorist threat from Canada."[16] This same expert, in a co-authored article in a recent issue of *Foreign Affairs*, has managed to cover his topic without a *single* reference to America's northern border, validating the impression that, these days, when American security anxieties focus upon border management, they do so primarily with respect to the Mexico-US border.[17]

This does not mean that there are no implications for the Canada-US border in what is happening, and why, along the Mexico-US border. The challenge for Canadian policy making is to differentiate between the two borders, whereas for some in the United States it seems incumbent to eliminate such differentiation. Consider what it was that, early in the Obama administration, so troubled Canadian officials about statements made by the new homeland security secretary, Janet Napolitano, who in a speech in Washington on 25 March 2009 called for a "real" border to be constructed between the United States and its two continental neighbours, Canada and Mexico. Interestingly, although she was in some apparent confusion regarding whether some of the 9/11 attackers had slipped into the United States from Canada (she thought they had), it was not so much security as *political* logic that drove this former Arizona governor's thinking. As she explained to her audience at the Brookings Institution, an important reason why there needed to be a "real" border was *equity*, in the sense that "we need to be sensitive to ... the very real feelings among southern border states and in Mexico that if things are being done on the Mexican border, they should also be done on the Canadian border."[18]

At the very least, if the Canada-US border, no matter how safe it might otherwise be, is going to be implicated – on grounds of political correctness if nothing else – in the fate of the Mexico-US border, then it follows that resolving the problems with the northern border will in some way need to be tied up with resolving the problems of the southern one. And if this is so, then whether or not it makes more sense to build "North America" on the basis of a bilateral, not a trilateral, partnership,[19] excluding Mexico from the picture will be easier said than done. If this is so, what might it imply for the "Canada-US alliance" as well?

What "Canada-US Alliance"?

There are two paths we might follow in our bid to comprehend what it means to discuss the "alliance" between Canada and the United States, an alliance whose potential for expansion so as to include Mexico provides this chapter's subject matter. The easiest path, one that *mutatis mutandis* I will end up following, is simply to regard that bilateral alliance as being part and parcel of the North Atlantic Treaty Organization. If alliances, after all, are reciprocal obligations to safeguard partners from attack, then what better testimony to those obligations than pledges enshrined in treaties, such as the Washington treaty of 1949? But as Stephen Walt reminds us, alliances can and do take shape independently of the formal trappings associated with treaty making. They can exist "informally," even while being in reality every bit as meaningful as, if not more meaningful than, formal collective defence pacts: the operative notion is that alliances be effective instances of *reciprocated* defence collaboration.[20]

The problem with equating the Canada-US alliance with NATO is evident: the former predates the latter, and there is absolutely no reason to expect that in the absence of the formation of NATO, Canada and the United States would have ceased being the allies they very much became in August 1940, with the agreement struck by President Franklin D. Roosevelt and Prime Minister Mackenzie King in the upstate New York town of Ogdensburg, in mid-August 1940.[21] This accord led directly to the creation of the first of what would be a long line of binational defence arrangements, the Permanent Joint Board on Defence (PJBD), which set to work planning a series of measures to enhance continental security at a time when Britain's fate hung in the balance, after the fall of France in June 1940.[22]

Subsequently, the PJBD would be supplemented with, and to an extent very much eclipsed by, newer institutional means of strengthening North American defence cooperation, among the most important of these being the Military Cooperation Committee (MCC) of 1946, the North American Air (now Aerospace) Defense Command (NORAD) of 1958, and more recently the Bi-National Planning Group (BPG) of 2003 to 2006.[23] To these must be added a thick network of other accords, committees, and arrangements pertaining to North American defence, whose numbers are no easy matter to keep count of, but which run into the several hundreds.[24] Thus, in a manner distinctly different from most of America's transatlantic relations, the United States and Canada were solidly allied (if not always in total agreement in perceiving and responding to threats) well before the formation of NATO, and would almost certainly still be allied had the latter organization never come into existence. Moreover, I think it can be taken as given that the strength of their commitment to the "common defence" of North America far exceeds the strength of the commitment of most NATO allies to the defence of the transatlantic area. This is another way of saying the obvious: the "burden-sharing" dilemma is more keenly felt within NATO than it is within North America.

Any discussion of burden sharing leads easily to a discussion of NATO. Since it is this latter organization that I am taking to be the "Canada-US alliance" within which "room" might be found for Mexico, let us look, in the first instance, at what that alliance does. Even better, let us turn things around and ask what it does *not* do. Here the answer is obvious: it does not satisfy the two North American member-states that it is being taken seriously enough by the Europeans. To be sure, the latter seem to treasure it, for notwithstanding the existence of an "escape hatch" that was built into the Washington treaty back in 1949 (Article 13, specifying the manner in which a member-state might leave the alliance[25]), no ally, not even Charles de Gaulle when he hauled France out of NATO's integrated military command back in 1966, has ever availed itself of that escape mechanism. Just the opposite has transpired, the alliance has continued to expand from its original dozen members in 1949 to twenty-eight today. Not only that, but France itself has recently rejoined the integrated military command, so that one could say that NATO has been going from strength to strength.[26]

One could say as much, however, only if one wanted to be dismissed as a crank, for the reality is that, once again, as it has so many times over the course of its six decades in existence, NATO finds itself under scrutiny because of its shortcomings, and for the moment it is the two North American member-states who are drawing the most attention to those defects. One of Canada's best-known commentators on security and defence issues, the historian Jack Granatstein, published, ironically just a few weeks prior to the fall of Muammar Gaddafi, a scathing denunciation of an alliance staggering into irrelevance because of its "bumbling incompetence." Granatstein drew an analogy with baseball, and noted that "in diplomacy as in baseball, it's three strikes and you're out. Afghanistan was strike one; Libya was strike two. And strike three? No one yet knows where the next call for action might be – Syria? – but if NATO funks it again, then the pressure from Ottawa and, possibly, Washington may be irresistible."[27]

Nor is his a lonely perspective, certainly not on the North American side of the alliance, with both North American member-states becoming grumpily used to thinking of themselves as the "producers" of transatlantic security, a commodity getting disproportionately "consumed" on the other side of the ocean, in their view. Prime Minister Stephen Harper has been known, at a time when Canada was engaging in combat in Afghanistan and therefore in a position to wag the burden-sharing finger at Germans and others, to muse that NATO's future was in some jeopardy due to too much undercommitment on the part of too many allies. But if the message from Ottawa has lately softened for obvious reasons (to wit, the ending of Canada's combat mission), the same cannot be said of the message from an increasingly cash-strapped and impatient Washington. Consider the blunt remarks issued in Brussels in June 2011 by US Secretary of Defense Robert Gates, to the effect that if the allies did not get more serious about making the alliance "work," they ran the risk of seeing it disappear. And for Gates, their getting more serious entailed spending more money on the common defence, otherwise, as he said in Brussels, NATO faced "a dim if not dismal future."[28]

In light of the above, and particularly in view of the never-ending sense of foreboding surrounding the future of the alliance, why would I bother to suggest that to the extent there is going to be some "room" for Mexico in the Canada-US alliance, it should be found within the confines of NATO? To answer this requires a bit of inquiry into just what it is that NATO *does*.

As everyone knows, NATO is a "collective defence" organization, and the proof of that pudding is found in the most important of the Washington treaty's articles, Article 5, which states that the signatories "agree that an armed attack against one or more of them in Europe or North America shall be considered an attack against them all, and consequently they agree that ... each of them ... will assist the Party or Parties so attacked."[29] Some people will actually recall that NATO even did, *once* in the past sixty-two years, invoke Article 5, and that was a dozen years ago in response to the attacks of 9/11.

Significantly, the United States chose at the time not to avail itself of the assistance the allies as a group were apparently pledged to offer, although it certainly did work with Canada, the United Kingdom, and selected other allies in the initial campaign to unseat the Taliban government in Afghanistan. Just as significantly, however, is the reality that NATO has functioned far less as a collective defence entity and far more as some other kind of security organization. If the only thing NATO did was organize the collective defence of its membership against external aggression, that kind of alliance would continue to have zero appeal to Mexico, because whatever else may be the security challenges currently confronting it, Mexico has as little need of NATO as a collective defence organization as the NATO members appear to have of Mexico. So what exactly shall we call what the alliance has primarily been doing? There have been two chief arenas of activity for the alliance, one primarily military, the other largely political. The military arena has featured "conflict management" (some say "stability operations") in places such as the Balkans, Afghanistan, and most recently Libya.

The political dimension is seen in the part played by the alliance in spreading the "democratic zone of peace," by socializing former adversaries and others into Western security practices. In a word, NATO has very much become an instrument for what has come to be called "security sector reform" (SSR), and has done so primarily through its expansion of membership since the late 1990s. NATO's predicament in the immediate aftermath of the end of the Cold War was to find some new purpose, at a time when many pundits were expecting that the Western alliance could simply not long survive the demise of the Soviet adversary that had been responsible for its coming into existence in the first place. NATO need-ed a new vocation, and this it managed to find in SSR, which enabled it to play a role in helping spread democratic norms and practices through-out a part of Europe that had heretofore been considered outside its area of interest and operations. Admittedly, it would take until 1998 for the emerging concept to finally be christened "security sector reform," in a policy address given by Clare Short, a member of Tony Blair's cabinet.[30] Nevertheless, the deeds that the name depicted had been becoming ever more widespread during the first few years of the post–Cold War decade, a time when NATO was acting more and more as a promoter of SSR, albeit in the manner of Molière's Monsieur Jourdain – doing something without being able to name exactly what it was doing.

As things developed, SSR would evolve through two "generations."[31] The first had the primary objective of ensuring civilian control over the military in a variety of recent Soviet allies in Central and Eastern Europe (CEE), countries that would somehow need to be embraced by the West-ern democracies; at this time, SSR was virtually synonymous with "civil-military relations," and CEE countries such as Romania were among the earliest testing grounds for the concept.[32] The second generation wit-nessed a conceptual evolution, with SSR moving out of the "civ/mil" orbit and increasingly concerning itself with assuring effectiveness in "gover-nance" across a wide variety of sectors that might bear little relation to the military but assuredly could and did have a link with security broadly understood (especially the judiciary and other organs of justice adminis-tration).

It is in this connection that SSR would find applicability to Mexico, although one must be careful of expecting it to be, in and of itself, a *deus ex machina* for the Mexican dilemma, namely, too much corruption in too many parts of its system for administering justice, especially but not only the police. Let us turn, then, to whether and why a case might be made for NATO to provide the room for Mexico to become part of the Canada-US alliance.

Mexico in NATO?
Mexico does not need to be brought into the "Canada-US alliance" because of any compelling need for collective defence as properly understood (i.e., defence against another state that intends military aggression).[33] Nor does it need to be incorporated into an alliance for reasons related to military cooperation with the United States, because the latter is already furnishing that independently of the Canada-US alliance, and there is still much scope for further, *bilateral*

security and defence cooperation between the United States and Mexico. No, to the extent a case can be made for making an ally of Mexico, it is best done in the multilateral NATO context, more precisely in the specific SSR one. Why, though, should any "real-world" policy figures bother to make such a case, given the obstacles that would face a Mexican adhesion to NATO, assuming of course that the Mexicans would want such a thing to come to pass? The obstacles do not include just the familiar category (one might even call it a cliché) of "political will," about which I will have more to say later in this section; they also include what at first glance seems to be a formidable "constitutional" barrier to Mexico's entering the alliance.

NATO is considered to be a "regional" security organization, with much room for dispute as to where its region begins and ends. Often, and especially in Europe, it is styled as an organization first and foremost consecrated to enhancing *European* security. Thus, it might be said that Mexican membership has to be the ultimate non-starter, because whatever else Mexico is, it is not European, and therefore is a priori restricted from membership in the club, and this because of an apparent prohibition on NATO's part that effectively bars from new membership any countries that do not happen to be physically located in Europe (with the stress being on *new* members, for the non-European signatories of the Washington treaty that established NATO in 1949 – namely, the United States, Canada, and Iceland – are all "grandfathered").

This barrier is the treaty's Article 10, which states: "The Parties may, by unanimous agreement, invite any other European state in a position to further the principles of this Treaty and to contribute to the security of the North Atlantic area to accede to this Treaty."[34] This restriction alone would seem to close the book on any further discussion of Mexico as a future NATO member, were it not for one recent trend within the alliance – a trend toward creatively interpreting the meaning of the geographical entity known as "Europe." In particular, the development has been associated with controversial discussions as to whether Ukraine and Georgia might be added to the ranks, now that the last two on the list of easily suitable invitees (Albania and Croatia) have joined. The controversy has swirled largely if not exclusively around the issue of Russian opposition to Ukrainian and Georgian membership, but in the case of Ukraine, at least it can be maintained that it fulfills the geographical criterion.

Things look otherwise when it comes to Georgia, however. The geographical limits of Europe to the east are the Urals; to the southeast, they are the waters separating European Turkey from Asia Minor (i.e., the Bosporus, the Sea of Marmara, and the Dardanelles), as well as the line formed by the highest summits of the Caucasus mountains (with lands to the north of that line being in Europe, and those to the south being in Asia). Save for a very small and sparsely populated sliver of territory, Georgia lies entirely to the south of the geographical boundary separating Europe from Asia – that is, its population resides, as do those of its fellow Caucasian republics of Armenia and Azerbaijan, on *Asian* soil. In one respect, and one respect only, it might be said to be like Turkey, in being "transcontinental." But Turkey's membership in NATO "Europe" has much less to do with its tiny land mass outside of Asia Minor and much more to do with the fact that *Europe's* largest city, Istanbul, also happens to be in Turkey. Things are different with Georgia, meaning that if Georgia were ever to be admitted to NATO, Article 10 would have to be interpreted in a very flexible manner, so that European "culture" and not territory would become a guiding criterion (which would presumably also render Armenia eligible to join, given that this republic's inhabitants do consider themselves Europeans).

Realistically, the entry of Georgia into NATO any time soon must be regarded as a long shot, but at least the discussion of Georgia highlights the interpretive leeway that exists with respect to Article 10. Yet there are further words in that same article that can help us to understand whether Mexico might, after all, really be in NATO's geographic area, and they are contained in the article's stipulation of this prerequisite, namely, that aspirants for membership must be in a "position ... to contribute to the security of the *North Atlantic* area."[35] This wording testifies to one undeniable geographical reality: that more than many current NATO allies, Mexico qualifies as being a decidedly *North Atlantic* country. This is because the waters of NATO's "ocean" (i.e., the northern half of the Atlantic) abundantly wash Mexico's entire eastern shoreline, from Tamaulipas in the north to Quintana Roo in the south, which is more than can be said for perhaps a dozen of the so-called North Atlantic allies, whose relationship to the alliance's geographic epicentre is tenuous at best and in some cases utterly non-existent. Now, although most NATO members can be said to have a connection (direct or indirect) with the ocean that is so closely associated with both the alliance's area *and* its purposes (the latter in the context of the value system called Atlanticism), there are several for whom establishing a strong linkage with the North Atlantic really does require imaginative leaps. Add to this the recent debate pitting "globalists" against "Europeanists," with the former (mainly US-based) arguing for a radical expansion of membership toward states (such as Australia) that are neither European nor North Atlantic, and you quickly get the impression that

Article 10 might not prove to be very much of a barrier at all, assuming that anyone wanted Mexico to become a new member.

This, then, takes us back to the elusive category known as "political will." Why should anyone, whether Mexican, German, French, American, or Canadian, want Mexico in NATO? Let us start by postulating a Mexican interest in joining, even if in doing so we recognize that few in Mexico have ever given much, or any, thought to this question. Still, that need not deter objective analysis, and in the case of Mexico we can identify three categories of advantage that NATO membership might bring. First would be the democracy-enhancing credentials of an alliance that, as I have argued above, had become increasingly associated with the rubric of security sector reform in the aftermath of the Cold War. And though no one should be so deluded as to imagine that NATO's SSR capabilities are such as to solve the chronic corruption problem in Mexico, membership in the alliance would at least be a step in the direction of solving it.

Second, among the "interests" that can and do motivate states, whether members of NATO or not, is the enhancement of their prestige, or what Charles de Gaulle liked to regard as *rang* (status). I bring the French case into the discussion advisedly because we often associate de Gaulle with having taken France "out of" NATO, which of course he did not; he merely wanted to utilize the alliance in such a way as to cut for the French a special – you could even say, "exceptional" – figure therein, and he thought he accomplished this by his 1966 decision to take France out of NATO's integrated military structure, a decision that has recently been reversed by France's former president, Nicolas Sarkozy.[36] No matter how one might employ NATO in a bid to enhance status, it seems indisputable that in the society of equal sovereign states, NATO allies are usually regarded as being "more equal" than others, and part of that status flows simply from the fact of their membership in the world's most prestigious security club. If this is so, then Mexican prestige on the world stage could only be expected to increase pursuant to NATO membership.

Third and most important, there is the matter of where Mexico chooses to locate its geopolitical "identity": is it primarily a North American country, or is it a Latin American one?[37] If Mexican elites should somehow eventually decide that the country is more North American than anything else, and if there is to be some potential for converting what has been an apparent "regionalization" into something stronger, namely, a regional identity, then it can be argued that being a member of the most important security organization, to which its other two North American partners belong, would constitute a means of helping to "complete" Mexico as a North American country.[38]

So much for what might be regarded as an induced set of Mexican interests in NATO membership; what can we say of the *allies'* interests in having Mexico as a member? At the very least, they would find the idea more than a bit odd. Still, for the Europeans, there might be some solace to be derived from the knowledge that, to the extent they believe that NATO will have to continue enlarging, expanding the alliance southward in the Western hemisphere would be guaranteed not to generate the kind of controversy that expanding it eastward in Europe can be counted upon to stir up. Whatever else Moscow might think about NATO's addition of Mexico to its ranks (and its thoughts would probably feature a hefty dose of bemusement), it certainly could not claim that its security was being put at risk by such an expansion, or that it was somehow being "encircled." This alone would allay the anxieties of the Germans and other European allies who are always so eager never to upset Russia, and should enable them to regard with equanimity, even if not with enthusiasm, NATO's hopping across the Río Grande. And though the Europeans tend to contemplate the alliance in a geographically egocentric way as being primarily about Europe, the reality is that since its very inception, NATO's area of coverage has embraced more territory on the North American continent than on the European one. So adding Mexico would not upset a geographical balance that has been a constant feature of the alliance, but rather reconfirm the original balance as between North America and Europe.

There are, of course, the questions of cost and political risks associated with bringing Mexico into the fold. Since the entire point of the exercise would be to tap whatever SSR assets NATO (and perhaps, the European Union) might possess, the addition of Mexico would entail no major military commitments and would therefore be very unlikely to strain anyone's defence budget in an increasingly cash-strapped alliance. Moreover, since France and some other European allies do stress that NATO and the ESDP (or, as it has become known since the treaty of Lisbon came into effect, CSDP)[39] should no longer be regarded as competing but rather as complementary organizations, Mexico could provide an interesting arena for the two Brussels-based institutions to demonstrate collaboration, for SSR is all about "soft power," which is the currency in which the EU prefers to trade when it deals with security matters. And by trading in that currency and helping, however modestly, address a serious security problem in the New World, Europe would go a long way toward mitigating some of the current burden-sharing angst so recently on display among the North American allies.

As for those North American allies, Canada and the United States, what has been said about a North American regional identity for Mexico might also be said for them: to wit, should they increasingly interpret their geopolitical identity in terms of regional North American considerations (hardly a foregone conclusion for either country), then it would follow that a Mexico in NATO would be, for them, a better *North American* partner, one with whom it might become easier, not more difficult, to resolve a variety of collective problems of both an economic and political nature. Most importantly for the two North American NATO members, when they assess the implications of Mexico for their own security – an assessment that obviously occupies American attention more than it does Canadian – they tend to put a premium upon potential reforms that could enable Mexico to overcome its chronic difficulties with state corruption, especially in the security area, including the law enforcement and judicial systems. As one analyst recently put it, apropos security sector reform: "For the safety and prosperity of Mexico and the United States, Washington must go beyond its current focus on border control to a more ambitious goal: supporting Mexico's democracy."[40]

Conclusion

So, is there room for Mexico in the Canada-US alliance? I have argued that there is, but only on the condition that the alliance into which Mexico would be incorporated is NATO. I have stated, and will restate here, that this idea is at best idiosyncratic and at worst verging on the deranged. Nevertheless, strange things have happened with respect to NATO in the past, and there is simply no reason to rule out the possibility of strange things continuing to happen.

What, though, might the subject of my chapter have to contribute to some of the more theoretical issues adumbrated in this volume? In particular, how might international relations theorists account for the post-9/11 pattern of state behaviour I have addressed? Realists, of course, would have no difficulty grasping that security challenges, unless met in a constructive and coordinated fashion, can easily be more a disintegrative force than an integrative one, and there is no shortage of evidence to corroborate such pessimistic expectations, given that all who study the issue of North American borders do sense that these borders have become sites of contestation more than of cooperation over the past decade. But to halt the theoretical exploration on this pessimistic note seems a bit too extreme, even for some otherwise self-identifying realists, such as myself. This is because it is also accepted, and certainly not only by realists, that great problems can and do elicit innovative solutions. They do not always, or perhaps even typically, do so, else the world would be a happier place than it seems to be. Nevertheless, it is obvious that regional security challenges can set in motion processes of regional security cooperation that, in the absence of the challenges, would appear to be as impossible as they are strange.

I have argued in these pages that Canada, the United States, and Mexico might be able to reduce irritants in their future relations by taking a large step toward institutionalizing their regional security complex, paradoxically by embedding it within an extra-regional, transatlantic, setting. It is sometimes asserted, usually with respect to a China widely held these days to be "rising," that embracing a country thought to be problematical by bringing it into Western institutions constitutes a big step toward achieving fruitful cooperation, and thus eliminating, or at least minimizing the frequency of, future problems.

This is not a particularly novel idea (think of the original purpose of European integration, namely, to "lock in" Germany to a new institutional order and thereby render it less of a challenge to continental and global stability), and there is considerable merit in what one scholar argues to be the "binding" properties of Western institutions: "Today's Western order, in short, is hard to overturn and easy to join."[41] It is ironic, though, that the logic can be said to apply in the case of a country like China but not one like Mexico. Neither China nor Mexico can be considered "Western" countries if that implies being developed liberal democracies, but Mexico has to be regarded at least as more of a democracy than China. Moreover, Mexico is unambiguously a North Atlantic country, one whose integration into that region's leading security organization would promise to bring in its train considerable advantages – to Mexico itself, to the North Americans, and to Europeans.

NOTES

1 Harold P. Klepak, *Natural Allies? Canadian and Mexican Perspectives on International Security* (Ottawa: Carleton University Press, 1996).
2 Or so I have argued in "The US-Canada Relationship: How 'Special' Is America's Oldest Unbroken Alliance?" in *America's "Special Relationships": Foreign and Domestic Aspects of the Politics of Alliance,* ed. John Dumbrell and Axel R. Schäfer (London: Routledge, 2009), 60-75.
3 Arrangements are described and analyzed in Chapter 11.
4 Chertoff made his comments in June 2007; see Edward Alden, *The Closing of the American Border: Terrorism, Immigration, and Security since 9/11* (New York: HarperCollins, 2008), 270-74.

5　Colin Freeze, "Man Who Forced Grounding of Aeromexico Flight Sent to US," *Globe and Mail*, 1 June 2010.

6　Martin Edwin Andersen, "Beating Latin America's International Criminal Organizations," *Joint Forces Quarterly* 62 (3rd Quarter 2011): 81-88, citation at 83.

7　Silvia Otero, "Crecen las 'Zonas de Riesgo' para EU," *El Universal* (Mexico City), 19 February 2011, A2.

8　Eduardo Valle, "¿Arde México?" *El Universal* (Mexico City), 19 February 2011, A9.

9　J. Jaime Hernández and Silvia Otero, "Lucha anticrimen es por Norteamérica: Winnefeld," *El Universal* (Mexico City), 19 February 2011, A1, A4.

10　Quoted in Bernd Debusmann, "Among Top US Fears, a Failed Mexican State," *International Herald Tribune*, 10-11 January 2009, 2. Also see Diana Washington Valdez, "US Military Report Warns 'Sudden Collapse' of Mexico Is Possible," *El Paso Times*, 13 January 2009, http://www.elpasotimes.com.

11　See the report of an interview that Cemex's Lorenzo Zambrano gave to the Spanish daily *El País* in February 2011, "Si se pierde Monterrey ante el crimen, lo demás estará perdido," *Crónica* (Mexico City), 22 February 2011, 12.

12　Ginger Thompson, "US Is Widening Its Role in Mexico's Drug War," *New York Times*, 7 August 2011, 1, 8.

13　Robert D. McFadden, "Army Doctor Held in Fort Hood Rampage," *New York Times*, 5 November 2009, http://www.nytimes.com/.

14　Colin Freeze, "Video Evidence Shows Details of Homegrown Terrorism Plans," *Globe and Mail*, 20 October 2009. The intended targets were the Toronto Stock Exchange, the local offices of the Canadian Security Intelligence Service (CSIS), and Canadian Forces Base Trenton, over one hundred kilometres east of the city.

15　See, for one estimate, James Kirchick, "The Homegrown-Terrorist Threat: It Can Happen Here, and It Is Happening Here," *Commentary* 130, 2 (February 2010): 16-20.

16　Alden, *Closing of the American Border*, 129.

17　Edward Alden and Bryan Roberts, "Are US Borders Secure? Why We Don't Know, and How to Find Out," *Foreign Affairs* 90 (July/August 2011): 19-26.

18　Quoted in John Ibbitson, "Obama's Message: Glory Days of Open Border Are Gone," *Globe and Mail*, 26 March 2009, A1, A15. Also see Allan Gotlieb, "We Need Borders without Boundaries," *Globe and Mail*, 2 April 2009, A15.

19　For a case premised on the exclusion of Mexico, see John Manley and Gordon Giffin, "A Table for Two, Not Three," *Globe and Mail*, 5 May 2009, A15.

20　Stephen M. Walt, *The Origins of Alliances* (Ithaca, NY: Cornell University Press, 1987), 1: "I define *alliance* as a formal or informal relationship of security cooperation between two or more sovereign states. This definition assumes some level of commitment and an exchange of benefits for both parties."

21　Insight into the changing context of Canada-US security debates in the half-decade preceding the accord can be found in Frederick W. Gibson and Jonathan G. Rossie, eds., *The Road to Ogdensburg: The Queen's/St. Lawrence Conferences on Canadian-American Affairs, 1935-1941* (East Lansing: Michigan State University Press, 1993).

22 See Christopher Conliffe, "The Permanent Joint Board on Defense, 1940-1988," in *The US-Canada Security Relationship: The Politics, Strategy, and Technology of Defense*, ed. David G. Haglund and Joel J. Sokolsky (Boulder, CO: Westview, 1989), 146-65.

23 See Dwight N. Mason, "The Canadian-American North American Defence Alliance in 2005," *International Journal* 60, 2 (Spring 2005): 385-96.

24 No one knows exactly how many such agreements have been reached. The most recent compilation, made by the BPG, lists at least 851 but mentions that some of these may no longer be operative. Bi-National Planning Group, *The Final Report on Canada and the United States (CANUS) Enhanced Military Cooperation* (Colorado Springs: Peterson Air Force Base, 13 March 2006), Appendix G.

25 According to the provisions of Article 13, once the treaty had been in force for twenty years, that is, as of 1969, "any Party may cease to be a Party one year after its notice of denunciation has been given to the Government of the United States of America": NATO, *NATO Handbook* (Brussels: NATO Office of Information and Press, 1995), 233-34.

26 See the special theme issue: Michel Fortmann, David G. Haglund, and Stéfanie von Hlatky, eds., "France's 'Return' to NATO: Implications for Transatlantic Relations," *European Security* 19 (March 2010): 1-142.

27 J.L. Granatstein, "NATO Drifts into Irrelevance," *Ottawa Citizen*, 11 August 2011.

28 Thom Shanker and Steven Erlanger, "Gates Delivers a Blunt Warning on NATO Future," *New York Times*, 11 June 2011, A1, A6.

29 NATO, *NATO Handbook: 50th Anniversary Edition* (Brussels: NATO Office of Information and Press, 1998), 396.

30 Short, at the time development minister in the Blair government, was apparently the first Western official to employ the concept, in a talk she gave at the Royal College of Defence Studies on 13 May 1998; see David Law, "Security Sector Reform in the Euro-Atlantic Region: Unfinished Business," in *Reform and Reconstruction of the Security Sector*, ed. Alan Bryden and Heiner Hänggi (Münster, Germany: Lit Verlag, 2004), 21-45.

31 The distinction between first- and second-generation SSR is drawn in Timothy Edmunds, "Security Sector Reform: Concepts and Implementation," Working Paper 86 (Geneva: Centre for the Democratic Control of Armed Forces, October 2002).

32 See Islam Yusufi, "Security Governance: Security Sector Reform in Southeast Europe," IPF Research Report (Budapest: Center for Policy Studies, 2004), 16.

33 Parts of this section and the one following it are based on my article "*Pensando lo imposible*: Why Mexico Should Be the Next New Member of the North Atlantic Treaty Organization," *Latin American Policy* 1 (December 2010): 264-83.

34 NATO, *NATO Handbook* (1995), 233-34.

35 Ibid. (emphasis added).

36 See Frédéric Bozo, "France and NATO under Sarkozy: End of the French Exception?" FIP Working Paper (Paris: Fondation pour l'Innovation Politique, March 2008).

37 On the concept of North American "identity," see Philip Resnick, "New Worlds, New Jerusalems: Reflections on North American Identities," *Norteamérica* 5, 1 (January-June 2010): 15-36; and Mauricio Tenorio Trillo, "On the Limits of Historical Imagination: North America as a Historical Essay," *International Journal* 61, 3 (Summer 2006): 567-87.

38 For the argument that North America is characterized by "regionalization" but *not* by regional identity, see Ann Capling and Kim Richard Nossal, "The Contradictions of Regionalism in North America," *Review of International Studies* 35 (2009): 145-65.

39 European Security and Defence Policy (ESDP) and Common Security and Defence Policy (CSDP).

40 Shannon O'Neil, "The Real War in Mexico: How Democracy Can Defeat the Drug Cartels," *Foreign Affairs* 88 (July/August 2009): 63-77, quoted at 64.

41 G. John Ikenberry, "The Rise of China and the Future of the West – Can the Liberal System Survive?" *Foreign Affairs* 87 (January/February 2008): 23-37, quoted at 24.

Conclusion

Continental Security – What Now?

JONATHAN PAQUIN AND PATRICK JAMES

As the contributors of this volume have illustrated through an examination of different topics from various research angles, North American security relations have had a rough ride since the early 2000s. The North American Free Trade Agreement partners have operated in a security environment that has been more complex and produced more irritants than the political environment that prevailed before 2001. This volume shows that 9/11 really was a game changer in North America: it exacerbated some of the differences in the interests, perceptions, and priorities of Canada, the United States, and Mexico; it caused political discontinuity in the North American integration process; and it curbed the idea of a North American community.

International Relations Theory and Continental Security

Among the questions considered in the different chapters was the following: Given the nature of the regional context, how do international relations theories help to explain the behaviour of North American states in the post-9/11 era?

From a realist standpoint, it is relatively easy to explain why continental security challenges have caused political discontinuity in the North American integration process. States have been promoting their own security, economic interests, and relative power, and this has made coordination a difficult task. Despite these imperatives, however, the alignment of Canada's and Mexico's security policies with those of the United States since 9/11 suggests that these countries have adopted a bandwagoning type of strategy as opposed to a more traditional balance-of-power approach. Whereas some realists would have expected Ottawa and Mexico City to come together to "balance" the hegemonic power of the United States at a time when that country was acting aggressively and had begun to decline relative to China, Canada and Mexico have in fact been working in isolation from each other most of the time, each conducting bilateral talks with the United States to strengthen its own alignment with Washington. In Canada's case, as Massie emphasizes, the "soft-balancing" position traditionally adopted by Ottawa – which has consisted in seeking counterweights to the United States and aimed at undermining US unilateralism, as illustrated by the decision to oppose the invasion of Iraq – did not guide Canada's continental security negotiations. Ottawa instead adopted a soft-bandwagoning posture toward the United States in the years following 9/11, which was eventually replaced by a harder brand of bandwagoning that corresponded with the election of Stephen Harper in 2006. This shift pleased continentalists in Canada who advocate systematic alignment with the United States for economic and security reasons.

In Chapter 2, Frank Harvey offers an interesting theoretical contribution that accounts for the decisions surrounding North American security relations by shedding light on one aspect of the homeland security dilemma, namely, public misperceptions of terrorist threats. His main contribution concerns the causes of such irrational fear. He challenges the conventional wisdom according to which fears are driven by risk entrepreneurs who deliberately overestimate the risk of terrorist acts, arguing that these fears are, in fact, endogenous to human nature and thus hardly controllable. Based on the literature on probability neglect, Harvey explains that the American public has had the tendency to disregard the low statistical probability of being hit by a terrorist attack because these attacks are usually unpredictable and uncontrollable, which explains the public's irrational reaction to such threats. And this is where the dilemma lies: US security policies are fashioned in response to the public's emotional fears rather than being based on statistical and rational analyses. Hence, the discrepancy between actual and perceived terrorist threats will likely persist among the US public, even if, as is improbable, risk entrepreneurs and the media suddenly stop overestimating terrorist threats. This theoretical contribution suggests that Canadian and Mexican officials should keep this cognitive bias in mind in future negotiations with

Washington on continental security measures if they hope to eventually achieve further integration.

How to Avoid Irritants in the Future

North America constitutes a unique asymmetrical setting. It is composed of one developing country and two advanced industrialized states, one of which is a global superpower. When 9/11 hit the United States, it made the asymmetrical nature of this environment more acute, which inevitably created political tensions between and among the three NAFTA partners. As Canadian Prime Minister Pierre Elliott Trudeau declared during a visit to the United States in 1969: "Living next to you is like sleeping with an elephant; no matter how friendly and even-tempered is the beast, one is affected by every twitch and grunt."[1] While this metaphor was used to characterize Canada-US political tensions in the 1960s, it is still accurate today, and probably describes not only Canada's feeling toward the United States but Mexico's as well. One could even argue that, following 9/11, the US elephant has not always been even-tempered and has done much more than twitch.

This leads to another important question that was addressed by some of our contributors: how can the tension between state autonomy and the search for greater regional cooperation be reconciled for the sake of better security relations? As was made quite clear by the essays in this volume, negotiations in which security demands collide with basic political and constitutional values result in sparks, frustration, and controversy. This is so because the three North American states do not share the same immigration and security policies and, more importantly, the same constitutions. We should not forget that these are three sovereign states, each a separate body politic.

Hence, Canada and Mexico have manoeuvred in troubled waters over the last decade, trying to maintain their political autonomy in the face of pressure from Washington to harmonize their security policies. Although, on paper, security and trade should be perfectly compatible with the help of monitoring and surveillance technologies, the harmonization process has created several problems at the political and institutional levels. Pressure from the United States to adopt common security pre-clearance, information sharing, and compatible immigration measures has sometimes collided with Canada's and Mexico's constitutional provisions. For example, the fact that the Canadian government ultimately bowed to Washington's demand that Canadian airlines share their passenger lists with the Department of Homeland Security – when flying over US airspace without landing or when flying point-to-point in Canada by going through US airspace – led to criticism by the Privacy Commissioner of Canada because this demand collided with the individual rights guaranteed by the Canadian Charter of Rights and Freedoms. As Paquin and Bélanger underline in Chapter 5, this particular case posed a real dilemma for the Canadian government because it opposed applying privacy rights to security measures.

Unless Ottawa, Washington, and Mexico City eventually agree to adopt a continental constitution, or unless Canada and Mexico come to the conclusion that constitutional principles should no longer stand in the way of security and economic integration, political disagreements and irritants will continue to arise; such effects are perfectly natural and hardly avoidable. That being said, the contributors to this volume have prescribed certain measures that could ease these tensions. First, the NAFTA partners must be able to put themselves in each others' shoes, otherwise future negotiations will stagnate. If Canada and Mexico fail to understand the US point of view toward homeland security and are unable to accept that the US government remains obsessed with security policies several years after 9/11, their economic priorities will come up against a wall. In this respect, Harvey recommends that Ottawa (and this applies to Mexico City as well) speak the language of Washington and promote a security agenda – as opposed to an economic one – designed to protect Canada's economic interests, "rather than a proactive economic agenda that will come across as competing with US security interests." Haglund, for his part, argues that one way to foster cooperation and reduce tensions between the NAFTA partners would be to further institutionalize their security coordination by integrating it into the transatlantic alliance. By including Mexico in NATO, Haglund boldly argues in Chapter 12, Canada and the United States would "embrace" the whole of their southern partner's security problems. This could lead to better cooperation and minimize security irritants.

Different Perception of Threats

Security issues, notably border security, have received higher priority in the United States than in Canada and Mexico. This can be explained by the fact that the United States was *the* target on 9/11, and that the trauma resulting from this tragedy was felt more deeply in the United States. As Harvey points out, Canadians and Mexicans claim to understand the risks of terrorist threats but they are only "outsiders looking in" and have never experienced this kind of trauma. This probably explains why many Canadian and Mexican officials believe that the US government exaggerates terrorist threats. In fact, the Canadian and Mexican governments probably felt that 12 September was as traumatic as 11 September when they realized that the US borders had been closed. The security measures unilaterally imposed by Washington following 9/11 created real panic in Ottawa and Mexico City and had negative impacts on commercial transactions. Regaining the pre-9/11 level of cross-border trade has thus been the paramount concern of the northern and southern neighbours of the United States since 2001.

All of this explains the willingness and readiness of these two states to negotiate political and administrative agreements with Washington, and, frankly, to make significant security concessions, in order to ease the bureaucratic burden at the borders in the midst of Washington's redefinition of its security priorities and norms. The Smart Border agreements, the Security and Prosperity Partnership (SPP), and the Beyond the Border Action Plan have all been part of a long chain of policy coordination whereby Canada and Mexico have aligned their security regulation norms with those of the United States in exchange for a reduction in transaction costs at the border. That being said, integrative measures promoted by Washington but unrelated to the improvement of trade flows at the border have clearly been less attractive to Ottawa and Mexico City. For instance, as Lagassé points out in Chapter 10, Canada has not shown the same interest in furthering defence integration with the United States as it has in border security issues. A deeper bilateral defence architecture has been unattractive to Canadian governments because it is unrelated to trade and would potentially be costly in terms of defence autonomy.

As this volume has also shown, the difference in the way the three NAFTA partners have articulated their interests and perceived terrorist threats is at the core of the political problems encountered in the management of continental security since 2001. It is quite clear that the three North American states are not facing the same fears: Washington fears Islamist terrorism, Ottawa fears a thicker US border, and Mexico City fears US unilateralism and further ostracism related to illegal immigration and drug trafficking. Without a common perception of the greatest threat, and without a common assessment of the causes of and solutions to other security-related issues that have become prominent over the last decade, such as illegal immigration and drug trafficking, it is unlikely that the integration process inaugurated with NAFTA in the 1990s will be pursued. As Charles Doran argues, these problems "seem to erect all kinds of new barriers to the free flow of goods and services between these countries."

Challenging Conventional Wisdom

It is commonplace to describe Canada-US relations as non-linkage relations because of the high level of complex interdependence that characterizes this dyad.[2] Linkage refers to coercion in one issue area as a form of retaliation for actions in another. In the case of Canada-US relations, linkage politics are difficult to achieve because of the level of economic and institutional integration, which greatly limits Ottawa's and Washington's control over sectoral agendas. As a result, the United States could hardly influence Canada's behaviour in one political domain by threatening to change its behaviour and preferences in another domain without harming itself.

This book partially challenges this argument by showing that linkage politics did, to a certain extent, come into play during continental security negotiations. In fact, the post-9/11 security context naturally linked security and trade. And because the three North American partners did not perceive threat in the same way, linkage politics necessarily came into play. Some important nuances must be noted here, however. The authors of the various chapters did not conclude that a coercive strategy was used by the hegemonic United States to blackmail its smaller partners, but rather that an implicit bargaining situation was involved whereby Washington made Canada's and Mexico's economic benefits dependent on the results of the security negotiations. Following 9/11, Washington had reached a point where no risk was acceptable and thus was reluctant to address trade impediments before settling border security issues. The Bush administration was willing to pay an economic price for its security, while both Canada and Mexico felt they had no choice but to offer security concessions to the United States. In the United States, the federal government spent hundreds of billions of dollars on new security apparatus, including the creation of the enormous Department of Homeland Security, with the sole objective of making the United States more secure. In Canada and Mexico, by comparison, important security investments were made largely because they were prerequisites for greater, faster cross-border trade with the United States.

Hence, linkage politics were probably more the result of the structural imperatives of the post-9/11 era than a coercive and calculated strategy undertaken by the Bush administration to extend its reach throughout North America. It was the structural dynamic that compelled the Canadian and Mexican governments to align some of their security policies with those of the United States in order to optimize trade relations. For instance, the signing of the Canada-US and the Mexico-US Smart Border agreements in 2001-02 and the SPP resulted from this logic of linkage politics. Even the institutional design of the SPP integrated this dynamic. The security and prosperity pillars of the SPP were communications vessels that probably facilitated trade-offs between governments.

Our empirical findings have shown, however, that linkage politics have ultimately had limited traction. For instance, the United States has been frustrated on multiple occasions during negotiations with its two NAFTA partners but has not threatened them with retaliatory measures. The US government failed to obtain compatible immigration security measures with Canada despite several attempts, and did not succeed in reaching a reciprocal "land pre-clearance" agreement to exchange customs and immigration officers at the Canada-US borders, a measure that would have significantly reassured the US government. Despite the asymmetrical level of power between the United States and Canada, therefore, complex interdependence has had the effect of limiting the ability of Washington to rely on linkage politics even if it wanted to.

Trilateral Institutionalism: A Failed Idea

As Athanasios Hristoulas emphasizes in Chapter 7, Mexico has been a vocal proponent of continental security for two main reasons. First, it pursued a trilateral approach following 9/11 in order to manage the negative perception in Mexico of a closer relationship with the US "hegemon." The inclusion of Canada in a trilateral process made Mexico's deeper integration with the United States more tolerable. Second, the Mexican government believed that by favouring a trilateral approach, it could address the issue of migration in a broader framework and thus move the controversial issue of Mexican migrant workers outside the bilateral and confrontational dynamic with the United States. It must be added here that the Mexico-US corner of the North American triangle has been marked by a minimal level of cooperation at the border because of a lack of mutual trust between American and Mexican law enforcement officers. Washington has considered Mexican officials insufficiently effective in law enforcement and Mexico City has often distrusted Washington's unilateralism over security regulations. Moreover, as Isabelle Vagnoux points out in Chapter 8, the political rhetoric in Washington and the semantic overstretch of the words "security" and "terrorism" have played against Mexico's attempts to foster greater cooperation with Washington in order to find a solution to the problem of illegal immigration.

Despite Mexico's support for trilateralism, the Canadian government has never been a proponent of this approach. As Stephen Clarkson explains in Chapter 6, instead of relying on a trilateral strategy to counter US power during the security negotiations that took place in the years following 9/11, successive Canadian governments were not really interested in seeing Mexico as part of the continental security process, pointing out that Mexico faced different problems that had nothing to do with what was at stake in Canada-US relations. Even the SPP trilateral forum showed that, because of their respective interests and internal political constraints, the political space of North American leaders was not always aligned. As a result, this trilateral forum was quickly overshadowed by the imperative of bilateral relations. Trilateralism ended up being a sort of double competitive bilateral forum within the SPP instead of a trilateral dialogue. This problem prevented deeper integration at the institutional level. As Paquin and Bélanger show in Chapter 5, the SPP, which was the only trilateral initiative launched since 2001, failed partly because of this problem. Moreover, Canada's desire to avoid giving rise to trilateralism was probably reinforced with the election of Stephen Harper's Conservative government. The new prime minister revived the project of a bilateral security perimeter by signing the Beyond the Border Action Plan with the United States in 2011, leaving Mexico isolated.

Trilateral institutionalism also failed because the three governments have pushed for administrative agreements, as opposed to a legally binding regime of cooperation, in order to have the political flexibility to achieve as much coordination as possible without having to deal with legislative oversights. The downside of such administrative agreements, however, is that they are hardly sustainable over time since they depend on the political will of elected executives who come and go. As the SPP has shown, sustainability of a cooperative trilateral regime is difficult to achieve without legally embedded cooperation. These factors may explain the low level of trilateral institutionalism since 2001.

The Continental Security Perimeter

Stephen Harper's accession to power in 2006 rekindled the debate over the North American security perimeter, a concept that had been rejected in Ottawa under previous Liberal governments. As Justin Massie suggests, the Conservative government, which seems to be uninhibited when it comes to the issue of greater security policy integration with the United States, has aligned its policies more closely with those of that country, including in the area of continental security, to assure its southern neighbour of Canada's status as a reliable partner. For the Harper government, progress on the security perimeter ultimately means greater trust between the two countries, and possibly an increase in Canadian exports to the United States.

The 2011 Beyond the Border agreement signed by Ottawa and Washington was perceived as a way to accelerate the integration process by moving the common security regulation measures from the border to the continental frontier. This action plan is ambitious and somewhat risky for Canada, however. Its implementation requires that Canada increase its alignment with US security regulations on a broad variety of issues – including an exit information system at the border and a compatible electronic system of visa-exempt nationals – and that it adopt the same standards to fight cybercrime. Interestingly, the action plan makes no provision for the adoption by the US government of any Canadian standard. Harmonization is clearly a one-way process here. Of course, one could argue that the United States can legitimately expect that the size of its economic market will naturally lead the Canadian government to adopt its norms. This nonetheless raises political questions that will lead those who buy into the peripheral dependence approach to conclude that Canada is more dependent than ever on the United States.

In signing this action plan, Canada's aim is to provide as many "mirror security measures" as possible, with the main objective of facilitating cross-border trade. By doing so, the Canadian government is gambling that the Department of Homeland Security will soften its security restrictions on goods at the border, but this remains to be seen.

Final Thoughts: Priority Combinations

When reflecting upon North American relations in the new security environment created by 9/11, it becomes clear that some combinations of actors have been impacted more than others. It would be fair to say that, overall, trilateral relations have played a limited role in these developments. Consider, in that vein, the collapse of the Security and Prosperity Partnership. On the other hand, the policy dynamics for each actor on an individual basis (Canada, Mexico, and the United States) and two of the three pairings (Canada/US and US/Mexico) have been greatly affected by the events of 9/11. All of this tends to reinforce two points about how policy comes into being.

First, policy shifts for each state individually reinforce the ongoing importance of domestic politics. Numerous examples of how internal considerations enabled and constrained policy initiatives at varying points for each government are found in this book. Second, the two dyadic relationships that matter most – as opposed to the trilateral relationship or the one dyadic relationship that did not change much – are those that pertain to the continental hegemonic power in relation to its border states.

Given these two observations, scholars and practitioners of different stripes will see their views confirmed in this study of recent and contemporary security relations in North America. Realists will see the persistence of power politics, while scholars who emphasize strategic interaction will point to the importance of domestic politics. In the final analysis, post-9/11 security policy in North America must be viewed as one that reflects self-interest and the continuing relevance of power politics.

NOTES

1   Department of Foreign Affairs and International Trade Canada, "Canada and the World: A History, 1968-1984: The Trudeau Years," http://www.international.gc.ca/.
2   Robert O. Keohane and Joseph S. Nye Jr., *Power and Interdependence*, 4th ed. Toronto: Pearson, 2012 [1977].

Bibliography

Abelson, Donald E. *American Think Tanks and Their Role in US Foreign Policy.* London and New York: Macmillan and St. Martin's Press, 1996.

–. *A Capitol Idea: Think Tanks and US Foreign Policy.* Kingston and Montreal: McGill-Queen's University Press, 2006.

–. "From Policy Research to Political Advocacy: The Changing Role of Think Tanks in American Politics." *Canadian Review of American Studies* 25, 1 (1995): 93-126.

Abelson, Donald E., and Duncan Wood. *People, Security and Borders: The Impact of the WHTI on North America.* Ottawa: Fulbright Foundation, 2007.

Abizaid Bucio, Olga. *The Canada-Mexico Relationship: The Unfinished Highway.* Ottawa: FOCAL Policy Paper, October 2004.

Abu-Laban, Yasmeen, Radha Jhappan, and François Rocher, eds., *Politics in North America: Redefining Continental Relations.* Toronto: University of Toronto Press, 2007.

Ackleson, Jason, and Justin Kastner. "The Security and Prosperity Partnership of North America." *American Review of Canadian Studies* 36, 2 (2006): 207-32.

Adler, Katya. "Jordan Jihadis Vow to Fight to the End." BBC News, 19 September 2007. http://news.bbc.co.uk/.

Alden, Edward. *The Closing of the American Border: Terrorism, Immigration, and Security since 9/11.* New York: HarperCollins, 2008.

Alden, Edward, and Bryan Roberts. "Are US Borders Secure? Why We Don't Know, and How to Find Out." *Foreign Affairs* 90, 4 (July-August 2011): 19-26.

Allison, Scott T., and David M. Messick. "The Group Attribution Error." *Journal of Experimental Social Psychology* 21 (1985): 563-79.

Alper, D.K. "Trans-Boundary Environmental Relations in British Columbia and the Pacific Northwest." *American Review of Canadian Studies* 27, 3 (Autumn 1997): 359-83.

Andersen, Martin Edwin. "Beating Latin America's International Criminal Organizations." *Joint Forces Quarterly* 62 (3rd Quarter 2011): 81-88.

Anderson, Greg. "The Compromise of Embedded Liberalism, American Trade Remedy Law, and Canadian Softwood Lumber: Can't We All Just Get Along?" *Canadian Foreign Policy* 10, 2 (Winter 2003): 87-108.

Anderson, Greg, and Christopher Sands, eds. *Forgotten Partnership Redux.* Amherst, NY: Cambria Press, 2011.

–. *Negotiating North America: The Security and Prosperity Partnership.* Washington, DC: Hudson Institute, White Paper Series, 2007.

Andreas, Peter. "Borderless Economy, Barricaded Border." *NACLA Report on the Americas* 33, 3 (November-December 1999): 14-21.

Andreas, Peter, and Thomas J. Biersteker. *The Rebordering of North America: Integration and Exclusion in a New Security Context.* New York: Routledge, 2003.

Argitis, Theophilos, and Andrew Mayeda. "Obama Agrees to Perimeter Security with Canada to Bolster Trade." *Bloomberg Business Week,* 12 December 2011.

Ayres, Jeffrey, and Laura Macdonald. "Democratic Deficits and the Demise of the Security and Prosperity Partnership of North America: The Role of Civil Society." In *North America in Question: Regional Integration in an Era of Political Economic Turbulence,* ed. Jeffrey Ayres and Laura Macdonald, 334-60. Toronto: University of Toronto Press, 2012.

"Bachmann: US-Mexico Border Wall OK." *Austin Daily Herald,* 16 August 2011. http://www.austindailyherald.com/.

Baglole, Joel. "Washington Is Urging Canada to Increase Military Spending." *Wall Street Journal,* 17 October 2002, A16.

Bailey, John. "Combating Organized Crime and Drug Trafficking in Mexico: What Are Mexican and US Strategies? Are They Working?" In *Shared Responsibility,* ed. Eric Olson, David A. Shirk, and Andrew D. Selee, 327- 46. Washington, DC: Woodrow Wilson International Center for Scholars, 2010.

Balthazar, Louis, Guy Laforest, and Vincent Lemieux, eds. *Le Québec et la reconstruction du Canada, 1980-1992: Enjeux et perspectives.* Québec: Septentrion, 1991.

Baril, Maurice. "Canadian Defence Force: This Institution's Future." *Vital Speeches of the Day* 66, 12 (1 April 2000): 357-60.

Barnes, Fred. "How Bush Decided on the Surge." *Weekly Standard* 13, 20 (4 February 2008).

Barrett, John, and Douglas Ross. "The Air-Launched Cruise Missile and Canadian Arms Control Policy." *Canadian Public Policy* 11, 4 (1985): 711-30.

Bassili, John N. "Traits as Action Categories versus Traits as Person Attributes in Social Cognition." In *On-line Cognition in Person Perception,* ed. John N. Bassili. Hillsdale, NJ: Lawrence Erlbaum, 1989.

Bélanger, Louis. "Governing the North American Free Trade Area: International Rule Making and Delegation in NAFTA, the SPP, and Beyond." *Latin American Policy* 1, 1 (2010): 22-51.

Bélanger, Louis, Ivan Bernier, and Gordon Mace. "Canadian Foreign Policy and Quebec." In *Canada among Nations 1995: Democracy and Foreign Policy,* ed. Maureen Appel Molot and Maxwell A. Cameron, 119-43. Ottawa: Carleton University Press, 1995.

Bélanger, Louis, Andrew Cooper, Heather Smith, Claire Turenne Sjolander, and Robert Wolfe. "Most Safely on the Fence? A Roundtable of a 'Canadian' Foreign Policy after 9/11." *Canadian Foreign Policy* 11, 1 (Spring, 2004): 97-118.

Bell, Dean C. *Canadian–United States Army Interoperability in the Age of Modularity.* Fort Leavenworth, KS: School of Advanced Military Studies, United States Army Command and General Staff College, 2005.

Benítez-Manaut, Raul. "Mexican Security and Defense Doctrines: From the 19th to the 21st Centuries." *Creating Community in the Americas,* no. 9 (November 2002): 1-4. http://www.wilsoncenter.org/.

–. "Sovereignty, Foreign Policy, and National Security in Mexico, 1821-1989." In *Natural Allies? Canadian and Mexican Perspectives on International Security,* ed. Hal Klepak, 57-87. Ottawa: Carleton University Press; FOCAL, 1996.

Bercuson, David J. "A Defence Policy to Serve Canadian Interests." *Fraser Forum* (May 2004): 4-5.

Bernard-Meunier, Marie. "The 'Inevitability' of North American Integration?" *International Journal* 60 (2005): 703-11.

Bhagwati, Jagdish, and Alan S. Blinder. *Offshoring of Jobs: What Response from US Economic Policy?* Cambridge, MA: MIT Press, 2009.

Bi-National Planning Group. *The Final Report on Canada and the United States (CANUS) Enhanced Military Cooperation.* Colorado Springs: Peterson Air Force Base, 13 March 2006.

Bland, Ben, and Girlfa Shivakumar. "Beijing Flexes Muscles with South China Sea Challenge to Indian Ship." *Financial Times,* 2 September 2011.

Bland, Douglas L. "Institutionalizing Ambiguity: The Management Review Group and the Reshaping of the Defence Policy Process in Canada." *Canadian Public Administration* 30, 4 (1987): 527-49.

Bondi, Loretta. *Beyond the Border and across the Atlantic: Mexico's Foreign and Security Policy Post-September 11th.* Washington, DC: Center for Transatlantic Relations, 2004.

Bordeleau, Daniel. "Ottawa Commande des F-35." Radio-Canada, 29 March 2011.

Bothwell, Robert. *Canada and the United States: The Politics of Partnership.* Toronto: University of Toronto Press, 1992.

Bow, Brian. *The Politics of Linkage: Power, Interdependence, and Ideas in Canada-US Relations.* Vancouver: UBC Press, 2009.

Bozo, Frédéric. "France and NATO Under Sarkozy: End of the French Exception?" FIP Working Paper. Paris: Fondation pour l'Innovation Politique, March 2008.

Brodie, Janine. "Mobility Regimes: Reflections on the Short Life and Times of the Security and Prosperity Partnership of North America." Paper presented at the Annual Meeting of the International Studies Association, 17-21 February 2010, New Orleans, Louisiana.

Bryden, Alan, and Heiner Hänggi, eds. *Reform and Reconstruction of the Security Sector.* Münster, Germany: Lit Verlag, 2004.

Burke, Jason. *The 9-11 Wars.* London: Allen Lane, 2011.

Burney, Derek H. "Our Free Trade Priorities Needn't Include Mexico – There's a Lot of Canada-US Issues Crying Out for Attention." *Globe and Mail,* 7 April 2008, A13.

Bush, Richard C. *The Perils of Proximity: China-Japan Security Relations.* Washington, DC: Brookings Institution Press, 2010.

Byers, Michael. "Canadian Armed Forces under United States Command." *International Journal* 58, 1 (Winter 2002-03): 89-114.

–. "Cold Peace: Arctic Cooperation and Canadian Foreign Policy." *International Journal* 65, 4 (Autumn 2010): 899-912.

Callinicos, Alex. *The New Mandarins of American Power: The Bush Administration's Plans for the World.* Cambridge: Polity, 2003.

Cameron, Maxwell A., and Brian Tomlin. *The Making of NAFTA: How the Deal was Done.* Ithaca, NY: Cornell University Press, 2000.

Campbell, Bruce. "Standing Committee on International Trade." *House of Commons,* No. 058, 1st Session, 39th Parliament, 26 April 2007.

Campbell, Keith W., and Constantine Sedikides. "Self-Threat Magnifies the Self-Serving Bias: A Meta-Analytic Integration." *Review of General Psychology* 3, 1 (1999): 23-43.

Canada. Department of Foreign Affairs and International Trade Canada (DFAIT). "Foreign Direct Investment Statistics." http://www.international.gc.ca/.

Canada. Department of National Defence. "Canada and United States Amend NORAD Agreement." News release, 5 August 2004.

–. *Canada First Defence Strategy.* Ottawa: Department of National Defence, 2008.

–. *Canada's International Policy Statement: A Role of Pride and Influence in the World. Defence.* Ottawa: Department of National Defence, 2005.

–. *Framework for Enhanced Military Cooperation among North American Aerospace Defense Command, United States Northern Command, and Canada Command.* September 2009. http://www.cpcml.ca/publications2012/ 091002-EnhancedFrameworkNAMilitaryCooperation.pdf.

Canada. Governor General. "Strong Leadership. A Better Canada." Speech from the Throne, 16 October 2007. http://dsp-psd.pwgsc.gc.ca/collection_2007/gg/ SO1-1-2007E.pdf.

Canada. Privy Council Office. *Securing an Open Society: Canada's National Security Policy.* Ottawa: Pricy Council Office, April 2004.

Canada Border Services Agency. "The Canada Border Services Agency's Arming Initiative." March 2011. http://www.cbsa-asfc.gc.ca/.

Canada Command and United States Northern Command. *Canada-US Civil Assistance Plan (CAP).* 14 February 2008. http://www.northcom.mil/.

Canada-US Project. *From Correct to Inspired: Blueprint for Canada-US Engagement.* Ottawa: Carleton University, 19 January 2009.

Canadian Association of Defence and Security Industries. *Canada's Defence Industry: A Vital Partner Supporting Canada's Economic and National Interests.* Ottawa: Canadian Association of Defence and Security Industries, 2009.

Canadian Security Intelligence Service. "Economic Espionage: Conducting Business in the International Marketplace." Ottawa: Canadian Security Intelligence Service, 1999.

Canadian Trade Commissioner Service. *Canada's Defence Industries.* Ottawa: Government of Canada, 2005.

Capling, Ann, and Kim Richard Nossal. "The Contradictions of Regionalism in North America." *Review of International Studies* 35 (2009): 145-65.

Carter, Ralph G., and James M. Scott. *Choosing to Lead: Understanding Congressional Foreign Policy Entrepreneurs.* Durham, NC: Duke University Press, 2009.

Castañeda, Jorge G. "El principio de No Intervención." In *Obras Completas,* vol. 1, *Naciones Unidas,* ed. Jorge G. Castañeda. Mexico: IMRED-El Colegio de Mexico, 1995.

–. *Ex Mex: From Migrants to Immigrants.* New York: New Press, 2007.

Cave, Damien. "Better Lives for Mexicans Cut Allure of Going North." *New York Times,* 6 July 2011.

Chrétien, Jean. *My Years as Prime Minister.* Toronto: Vintage Books, 2008.

Cimon, Yan. *Capacités et collaboration.* Montreal: École des Hautes Études Commerciales, 2006.

Cimon, Yan, and Louis Hébert. *How Networks Matter: Insights from Armed Forces Collaborative Activity.* Quebec: Faculté des sciences de l'administration, Université Laval, 2009.

Citizenship and Immigration Canada. "Backgrounder – Immigration Information Sharing Treaty." 12 December 2012. http://www.cic.gc.ca/.

Clarke, Richard A. *Against All Enemies: Inside America's War on Terror.* New York: Free Press, 2004.

–. *Your Government Failed You: Breaking the Cycle of National Security Disasters.* New York: Harper Perennial, 2009.

Clarkson, Stephen. *Does North America Exist? Governing the Continent after NAFTA and 9/11.* Toronto: University of Toronto Press, 2008.

–. *Lockstep in the Continental Ranks: Redrawing the American Perimeter after September 11th.* 2002. http://homes.chass.utoronto.ca/~clarkson/publications/.

–. *Uncle Sam and Us: Globalization, Neoconservativism, and the Canadian State.* Toronto: University of Toronto Press, 2002.

Cody, Richard A., and Robert L. Maginnis. "Note to File – Coalition Interoperability: Abca's New Focus." *Canadian Army Journal* 10, 1 (2007): 86-90.

Conliffe, Christopher. "The Permanent Joint Board on Defense, 1940-1988." In *The US-Canada Security Relationship: The Politics, Strategy, and Technology of Defense,* ed. David G. Haglund and Joel J. Sokolsky. Boulder, CO: Westview, 1989.

Conservative Party of Canada. *Stand Up for Canada: Conservative Party of Canada Federal Election Platform 2006.* Ottawa: Conservative Party of Canada, 2006.

Cooper, Andrew F. *Canadian Foreign Policy: Old Habits and New Directions.* Scarborough, ON: Pearson Education, 1997.

Cooper, P.C., K. McKay, and S.J. Murray. "Digital Interoperability." *Army Doctrine and Training Bulletin* 6, 1 (2003): 40-45.

Cosmides, Leda, John Tooby, and Robert Kurzban. "Perceptions of Race." *Trends in Cognitive Sciences* 7, 4 (April 2003): 173-79.

Covarrubias, Ana. "No intervención *versus* promoción de la democracia representativa en el sistema interamericano." In *Sistema interamericano y democracia. Antecedentes históricos y tendencias futuras,* ed. Arlene B. Tickner, 51-64. Bogotá: CEI-Ediciones Uniandes-OEA, 2000.

Covello, Vincent T., Peter M. Sandman, and Paul Slovic. *Risk Communication, Risk Statistics, and Risk Comparisons: A Manual for Plant Managers.* Washington, DC: Chemical Manufacturers Association, 1988. http://www.psandman.com/.

Critchlow, Donald T. *The Brookings Institution, 1916-1952: Expertise and the Public Interest.* Dekalb: Northern Illinois University Press, 1985.

D'Aquino, Tomas. "Security and Prosperity in the Canada–United States Relationship: Two Sides of the Same Coin." Address to the Conference of Defence Associations and the CDA Institute Conference on Defence and Security, March 2011. Calgary: Canadian Defence and Foreign Affairs Institute, 2011. http://www.cdfai.org/.

Daudelin, Jean. "The Trilateral Mirage: A Tale of Two North Americas." Paper prepared for the Canadian Defence and Foreign Affairs Institute. Ottawa: Carleton University, May 2003.

David, Charles-Philippe, ed. "De la SDN à l'ONU: Raoul Dandurand et la vision idéaliste des relations internationales." *Études Internationales* 31, 4 (December 2000): 641-762.

Davis, Jeff. "Harper Hits Mark with Border Security Message." *The Embassy,* 25 February 2009, 3.

Debusmann, Bernd. "Among Top US Fears, a Failed Mexican State." *International Herald Tribune,* 10-11 January 2009.

DeMuth, Christopher. "Think-Tank Confidential: What I Learned During Two Decades as Head of America's Most Influential Policy Shop." *Wall Street Journal*, 11 October 2007.

Dewitt, David, and John Kirton. *Canada as a Principal Power.* Toronto: John Wiley and Sons, 1983.

Doern, Bruce, and Brian Tomlin. *Faith and Fear: The Free Trade Story.* Toronto: Stoddart, 1991.

Donneur, André, and Valentin Chirica. "Immigration et sécurité frontalière: Les politiques canadienne et américaine et la coopération bilatérale." In *Le Canada dans l'orbite américain: La mort des théories intégrationnistes?* ed. Albert Legault. 15-40. Quebec City: Les Presses de l'Université Laval, 2004.

Doran, Charles F. *Forgotten Partnership: US-Canada Relations Today.* Baltimore: Johns Hopkins University Press, 1984.

–. "Power Cycle Theory and Global Politics." *International Political Science Review* 24, 1 (January 2003): 13-49.

–. *Systems in Crisis.* Cambridge: Cambridge University Press, 1991.

Doubler, Michael D. *Operation Jump Start: The National Guard on the Southwest Border, 2006-2008.* Arlington, VA: National Guard Bureau, Office of Public Affairs, Historical Services Division, 24 October 2008. http://www.nationalguard.mil/.

Drezner, Daniel W. *All Politics Is Global: Explaining International Regulatory Regimes.* Princeton, NJ: Princeton University Press, 2007.

Dumbrell, John, and Axel R. Schäfer, eds. *America's "Special Relationships": Foreign and Domestic Aspects of the Politics of Alliance.* London: Routledge, 2009.

Dunn, Timothy J. *The Militarization of the US-Mexico Border, 1978-1992.* Austin: CMAS Books, University of Texas, 1996.

Eayrs, James. *In Defence of Canada: Growing Up Allied.* Toronto: University of Toronto Press, 1980.

Edmunds, Timothy. "Security Sector Reform: Concepts and Implementation." Working Paper 86. Geneva: Centre for the Democratic Control of Armed Forces, October 2002.

Edwards, Lee. *The Power of Ideas: The Heritage Foundation at 25 Years.* Ottawa, IL: Jameson Books, 1997.

Escobar, Veronica. "All Quiet on the Southern Front." *New York Times,* 5 October 2011.

Fallows, James. "Declaring Victory." *Atlantic Monthly,* September 2006. http://www.theatlantic.com/.

Fantino, Julian. "Le F-35 Essentiel." *Cyberpresse,* 15 August 2011. http://www.lapresse.ca/.

Fargher, John S.W. Jr. "Defense Contract Management in Multinational Programs." *National Contract Management Journal* 15, 2 (1982): 1-14.

Fergusson, James G. *Canada and Ballistic Missile Defence 1954-2009: Déjà Vu All Over Again.* Vancouver: UBC Press, 2010.

–. "The Return of Ballistic Missile Defence." *On Track* (Autumn 2010). 36-38.http://www.cdainstitute.ca/images/ontrack15n3.pdf.

Finklea, Kristin M., William J. Krouse, and Mark A. Randol. *Southwest Border Violence: Issues in Identifying and Measuring Spillover Violence.* CRS Report for Congress R41075, 25 January 2011.

Fischhoff, Baruch, Roxana Gonzalez, Deborah A. Small, and Jennifer S. Lerner. "Judged Terror Risk and Proximity to the World Trade Center." *Journal of Risk and Uncertainty* 26, 2-3 (2003): 137-51.

Flaherty, The Honourable James. *The Budget in Brief 2008.* 16 February 2008. http://www.budget.gc.ca/2008/pdf/brief-bref-eng.pdf.

Flynn, Stephen E. *America the Vulnerable: How Our Government Is Failing to Protect Us from Terrorism.* New York: HarperCollins, 2004.

Foreign Affairs and International Trade Canada. "Minister MacKay Meets with Mexican Secretary of External Affairs in Halifax, Nova Scotia." Ottawa: Foreign Affairs and International Trade Canada, 23 May 2007.

Fortmann, Michel, and David G. Haglund. "Canada and the Issue of Homeland Security: Does the 'Kingston Dispensation' Still Hold?" *Canadian Military Journal* 3, 1 (Spring 2002): 17-22.

Fortmann, Michel, David G. Haglund, and Stéfanie von Hlatky, eds. "France's 'Return' to NATO: Implications for Transatlantic Relations." *European Security* 19 (March 2010): 1-142.

Foster, Kenneth, David Bernstein, and Peter Huber, eds. *Phantom Risk: Scientific Inference and the Law.* Cambridge, MA: MIT Press, 1993.

Fox Piven, Frances. *The War at Home: The Domestic Costs of Bush's Militarism.* New York: New Press, 2004.

Frank, Mark G., and Thomas Gilovich. "The Dark Side of Self and Social Perception: Black Uniforms and Aggression in Professional Sports." *Journal of Personality and Social Psychology* 54 (1988): 74-83.

Freeze, Colin. "Man Who Forced Grounding of Aeromexico Flight Sent to US" *Globe and Mail,* 1 June 2010.

–. "Video Evidence Shows Details of Homegrown Terrorism Plans." *Globe and Mail,* 20 October 2009.

Friesen, Shaye K., and Andrew N. Gale. "Slaying the Dragon: The Future Security Environment and Limitations of Industrial Age Security." *Canadian Military Journal* 11, 1 (2010): 32-37.

Frum, David, and Richard Perle. *An End to Evil: How to Win the War on Terror.* New York: Random House, 2004.

Fumento, Michael. *Science under Siege: Balancing Technology and the Environment.* New York: William Morrow, 1996.

Gal-Or, Noemi. "The Future of Canada-Mexico Relations according to Canada's International Policy Statement." *Nueva época* 11 (Summer 2006): 2.

Gatehouse, Jonathon. "Why the Canadian Military Isn't Ready for a War." *Maclean's*, 30 September 2002, 16.

Gibson, Frederick W., and Jonathan G. Rossie, eds. *The Road to Ogdensburg: The Queen's/St. Lawrence Conferences on Canadian-American Affairs, 1935-1941.* East Lansing: Michigan State University Press, 1993.

Gilbert, Daniel T. "If Only Gay Sex Caused Global Warming: Why We're More Scared of Gay Marriage and Terrorism than a Much Deadlier Threat." *Los Angeles Times*, 2 July 2006.

–. *Stumbling on Happiness.* New York: Vintage Books, 2007.

–. "Thinking Lightly about Others: Automatic Components of the Social Inference Process." In *Unintended Thought,* ed. James S. Uleman and John A. Bargh, 189-211. New York: Guilford Press, 1989.

Gilbert, Daniel T., and Patrick S. Malone. "The Correspondence Bias." *Psychological Bulletin* 117 (1995): 21-38.

Gilbert, Daniel T., Brett W. Pelham, and Douglas S. Krull. "On Cognitive Busyness: When Person Perceivers Meet Persons Perceived." *Journal of Personality and Social Psychology* 54, 5 (May 1988): 733-40.

Gilley, Bruce. "Middle Powers during Great Power Transitions: China's Rise and the Future of Canada-US Relations." *International Journal* 66, 2 (2011): 245-64.

Gilpin, Robert. *War and Change in World Politics.* Cambridge: Cambridge University Press, 1981.

Gladman, Brad W. "Strengthening the Relationship: NORAD Expansion and Canada Command." *Journal of Military and Strategic Studies* 9, 2 (Winter 2006/ 2007).

Glassner, Barry. *The Culture of Fear: Why Americans Are Afraid of the Wrong Things.* New York: Basic Books, 1999.

Goldenberg, Eddie. *The Way It Works: Inside Ottawa.* Toronto: McClelland and Stewart, 2006.

Gordon, Wendell. "A Case for a Less Restrictive Policy." *Social Science Quarterly* 56, 3 (December 1975): 485-91.

Gorman, Christine. "The Science of Anxiety." *Time* 159, 23 (10 June 2002). http://www.time.com/.

Gotlieb, Allan. "No Access, No influence." *National Post*, 3 December 2003, A18.

–. "The Paramountcy of Canada-US Relations." *National Post*, 22 May 2003, A20.

–. "We Need Borders without Boundaries." *Globe and Mail*, 2 April 2009, A15.

Government of Canada. *Beyond the Border: A Shared Vision for Perimeter Security and Economic Competitiveness. Action Plan.* Ottawa: Public Works and Government Services Canada, 2001.

–. "Security and Prosperity Partnership of North America – Report to Leaders."
     June 2005. http://www.spp-psp.gc.ca/.
–. "Security and Prosperity Partnership of North America: Secure North America
     from External Threats." http://www.spp-psp.gc.ca/eic/site/spp-psp.nsf/eng/
     00055.html.
–. "Terms of Reference for the United States–Canada Regulatory Cooperation
     Council." 3 June 2011. http://canada.usembassy.gov/.
Govtrack. "H.R. 6061 (109th): Secure Fence Act of 2006." http://www.govtrack.us/.
Granatstein, J.L. "NATO Drifts into Irrelevance." *Ottawa Citizen,* 11 August 2011.
–. *Who Killed the Canadian Military?* Toronto: HarperCollins, 2003.
Griffin Cohen, Marjorie, and Stephen Clarkson. "Introduction: States under
     Siege." In *Governing under Stress: Middle Powers and the Challenge of Globaliza-
     tion,* ed. Stephen Clarkson and Marjorie Griffin Cohen, 1-11. London: Zed
     Books, 2004.
Grigorescu, Alexandru. "East and Central European Countries and the Iraq War:
     The Choice between 'Soft Balancing' and 'Soft Bandwagoning.'" *Communist
     and Post-Communist Studies* 41, 3 (2008): 281-99.
Gruber, Lloyd. *Ruling the World: Power Politics and the Rise of Supranational Institu-
     tions.* Princeton, NJ: Princeton University Press, 2000.
Haglund, David G. "Canada and the Sempiternal NATO Question." *McGill Inter-
     national Review* 5 (Spring 2005): 15-23.
–, ed. *Over Here and Over There: Canada-US Defence Cooperation in an Era of Interop-
     erability.* Kingston, ON: Queen's Centre for International Relations, 2001.
–. *"Pensando lo imposible:* Why Mexico Should Be the Next New Member of the
     North Atlantic Treaty Organization." *Latin American Policy* 1 (December 2010):
     264-83.
–. "The US-Canada Relationship: How 'Special' Is America's Oldest Unbroken
     Alliance?" In *America's "Special Relationships": Foreign and Domestic Aspects of the
     Politics of Alliance,* ed. John Dumbrell and Axel R. Schäfer, 60-75. London:
     Routledge, 2009.
Haglund, David G., and Michel Fortmann. "Canada and the Issue of Homeland
     Security: Does the Kingston Dispensation Still Hold?" *Canadian Military Jour-
     nal* 3, 1 (2002): 17-22.
Haglund, David G., and Stéphane Roussel. "Escott Reid, the North Atlantic Treaty,
     and Canadian Strategic Culture." In *Escott Reid: Diplomat and Scholar,* ed. Greg
     Donaghy and Stéphane Roussel, 44-66. Montreal: McGill-Queen's University
     Press, 2004.
Haglund, David G., and Joel J. Sokolsky, eds. *The US-Canada Security Relationship:
     The Politics, Strategy, and Technology of Defense.* Boulder, CO: Westview, 1989.

Hale, Geoffrey E. "'In the Pipeline' or 'Over a Barrel'? Assessing Canadian Efforts to Manage US-Canadian Energy Interdependence." *Canadian-American Public Policy* 76 (February 2011): 1-44.

Halper, Stefan A., and Jonathan Clarke. *America Alone: the Neo-Conservatives and the Global Order.* New York: Cambridge University Press, 2004.

Hamill, Ruth, Timothy D. Wilson, and Richard E. Nisbett. "Insensitivity to Sample Bias: Generalizing from Atypical Cases." *Journal of Personality and Social Psychology* 39 (1980): 578-89.

Hamilton, David L. "Causal Attribution Viewed from an Information Processing Perspective." In *The Social Psychology of Knowledge,* ed. Daniel Bar-Tal and Arie W. Kruglanski. Cambridge: Cambridge University Press, 1988.

–. "Dispositional and Attributional Inferences in Person Perception." In *Attribution and Social Interaction: The Legacy of Edward E. Jones,* ed. John M. Darley and Joel Cooper, 99-114. Washington, DC: American Psychological Association, 1998.

Hamm, Bernd, ed. *Devastating Society: The Neo-Conservative Assault on Democracy and Justice.* London: Pluto Press, 2005.

Hansen, Birthe, Peter Toft, and Anders Wivel. *Security Strategies and American World Order: Lost Power.* New York: Routledge, 2009.

Harper, Stephen. "A Departure from Neutrality." *National Post,* 23 May 2003, A18.

–. "Liberal Damage Control: A Litany of Flip-Flops on Canada-US Relations." *Policy Options* (June-July 2003): 5-7.

Hart, Michael. *From Pride to Influence: Towards a New Canadian Foreign Policy.* Vancouver: UBC Press, 2008.

–. "Lessons from Canada's History as a Trading Nation." *International Journal* 58, 1 (2002-03): 25-42.

–. *A Trading Nation: Canadian Trade Policy from Colonialism to Globalization.* Vancouver: UBC Press, 2002.

Hartfiel, Robert Michael. "Planning without Guidance: Canadian Defence Policy and Planning, 1993-2004." *Canadian Public Administration* 53, 3 (2010): 323-49.

Hartung, Sharon, Blaize Homer Reich, and Izak Benbasat. "Information Technology Alignment in the Canadian Forces." *Canadian Journal of Administrative Sciences* 17, 4 (2000): 285-302.

Harvey, Frank P. *The Homeland Security Dilemma: Fear, Failure and the Future of American Insecurity.* New York/London: Routledge, 2008.

–. "The Homeland Security Dilemma: Imagination, Failure and the Escalating Costs of Perfecting Security." *Canadian Journal of Political Science* 40, 2 (2007): 283-316.

Hathaway, Oona A. "Treaties' End: The Past, Present, and Future of International Lawmaking in the United States." *Yale Law Journal* 117, 7 (2008): 1236-72.

He, Kai. "Institutional Balancing and International Relations Theory: Economic Interdependence and Balance of Power Strategies in Southeast Asia." *European Journal of International Relations* 14, 3 (2008): 489-518.

Heider, Fritz. *The Psychology of Interpersonal Relations.* London: Lawrence Erlbaum Associates, 1958.

Heine, Steven J., and Darrin R. Lehman. "The Cultural Construction of Self-Enhancement: An Examination of Group-Serving Biases." *Journal of Personality and Social Psychology* 72, 6 (1997): 1268-83.

Helliwell, John J. *How Much Do Borders Matter?* Washington, DC: Brookings Institution Press, 1998.

Heredia, Blanca. "La política y reforma económica: Mexico, 1985-2000." In *Chile-Mexico: Dos fransiciones frente a frente,* ed. Carlos Elizondo, 169-92. Mexico: Fonda de Cultura Economica, 2002.

Hernández, J. Jaime, and Silvia Otero. "Lucha anticrimen es por Norteamérica: Winnefeld." *El Universal* (Mexico City), 19 February 2011, A1, A4.

Hester, Annette. *Canada as the "Emerging Energy Superpower": Testing the Case.* Calgary: Canadian Defence and Foreign Affairs Institute, 2007.

Heulsemeyer, Axel. *Globalization in the Twenty-First Century: Convergence or Divergence?* Basingstoke, UK: Palgrave Macmillan, 2003.

Hirshhorn, Dan. "Perry: May Need Troops in Mexico." *Politico,* 18 November 2010. http://www.politico.com/.

Hobson, Sharon. "Risk-Bound Rewards: Canada's Defence Industry." *Jane's Information Group,* 20 October 2008.

Hollman, D.F. *NORAD in the New Millennium.* Toronto: Canadian Institute of International Affairs, 2000.

Holmes, John W. "Shadow and Substance: Diplomatic Relations between Britain and Canada." In *Britain and Canada: Survey of a Changing Relationship,* ed. Peter Lyon, 105-20. London: Frank Cass, 1976.

Homer-Dixon, Thomas. "The Rise of Terrorism." *Foreign Policy* 128 (January-February 2002): 52-62.

Hristoulas, Athanasios. "Algo Nuevo, Algo Viejo." *Foreign Affairs Latinoamerica* 10, 1 (2010): 34-42.

Hughes, David. "Nato Transformation US, Canadian, French Military Officials Agree Nato Must Change, but Funding Is Limited." *Aviation Week and Space Technology* 159, 16 (2003): 78-79.

Ibbitson, John. "Obama's Message: Glory Days of Open Border Are Gone." *Globe and Mail,* 26 March 2009, A1, A15.

–. "Shunning Missile Shield Could Be a Grave Error." *Globe and Mail,* 12 October 2006, A6.

Ikenberry, G. John. *After Victory: Institutions, Strategic Restraint, and the Rebuilding of World Order after Major Wars.* Princeton, NJ: Princeton University Press, 2001.

–. "The Rise of China and the Future of the West – Can the Liberal System Survive?" *Foreign Affairs* 87 (January/February 2008): 23-37.

–. *Strategic Reactions to American Preeminence: Great Power Politics in the Age of Unipolarity.* Washington, DC: National Intelligence Council, 28 July 2003.

Ikenberry, G. John, Michael Mastanduno, and William C. Wohlforth. "Introduction: Unipolarity, State Behavior, and Systemic Consequences." *World Politics* 61, 1 (2009): 1-27.

Industry Canada. "Industrial Regional Benefits." http://www.ic.gc.ca/.

James, Patrick, and Mark Kasoff, eds. *Canadian Studies in the New Millennium.* Toronto: University of Toronto Press, 2008.

James, Patrick, Nelson Michaud, and Marc J. O'Reilly, eds. *Handbook of Canadian Foreign Policy.* Lanham, MD: Lexington Books, 2006.

Jang, Brent. "US Wants Passenger Data for All Sun-Seeker Flights." *Globe and Mail,* 11 October 2007.

Janigan, Mary. "An Open Border?" *Maclean's,* 24 September 2001, 42-43.

Jockel, Joseph T. *Canada in NORAD 1957-2007: A History.* Montreal and Kingston: McGill-Queen's University Press, 2007.

–. "Five Lessons from the History of North American Aerospace Defence." *International Journal* 65, 4 (Autumn 2010): 1013-23.

–. *No Boundaries Upstairs: Canada and the United States, and the Origins of North American Air Defence, 1945-1958.* Vancouver: UBC Press, 1987.

Jockel, Joseph T., and Joel J. Sokolsky. "Renewing NORAD – Not if Not Forever." *Policy Options* (July-August 2006): 53-58.

Joffe, Josef. "Defying History and Theory: The United States as the 'Last Superpower.'" In *America Unrivaled: The Future of the Balance of Power,* ed. G. John Ikenberry, 155-80. Ithaca, NY: Cornell University Press, 2002.

Johnson, Joel T., John B. Jemmott III, and Thomas F. Pettigrew. "Causal Attribution and Dispositional Inference: Evidence of Inconsistent Judgments." *Journal of Experimental Social Psychology* 20, 6 (1984): 567-85.

Jones, Edward E. *Interpersonal Perceptions.* New York: W.H. Freeman, 1990.

Jones, Edward E., and Keith E. Davis. "From Acts to Dispositions: The Attribution Process in Person Perception." In *Advances in Experimental Social Psychology,* vol. 2, ed. Leonard Berkowitz, 219-66. New York: Academic Press, 1965.

Jones, Edward E., and Dan McGillis. "Correspondent Inferences and the Attribution Cube: A Comparative Reappraisal." In *New Directions in Attributional Research,* vol. 1, ed. John H. Harvey, William Ickes, and Robert Kidd. New York: Erlbaum, 1976.

Jones, Edward E., and Richard E. Nisbett. "The Actor and the Observer: Divergent Perceptions of the Causes of Behavior." In *Attribution: Perceiving the Causes of Behavior,* ed. Edward E. Jones, D.E. Kanouse, H.H. Kelley, R.E. Nisbett, S. Valins, and B. Weinder. Morristown, NJ: General Learning Press, 1972.

Kagan, Robert, and William Kristol. *Present Dangers: Crisis and Opportunity in American Foreign and Defense Policy.* San Francisco: Encounter Books, 2000.

Kahneman, Daniel, Paul Slovic, and Amos Tversky, eds. *Judgment under Uncertainty: Heuristics and Biases.* London: Cambridge University Press, 1982.

Kaplan, Fred. "The Post-9/11 Military." *Slate,* 2 September 2011.

Keating, Tom. *Canada and World Order: The Multilateralist Tradition in Canadian Foreign Policy,* 2nd ed. Don Mills, ON: Oxford University Press, 2002.

Kelley, Harold H. "Attribution Theory in Social Psychology." In *Nebraska Symposium on Motivation,* ed. David Levine, 192-238. Lincoln: University of Nebraska Press, 1967.

–. *Causal Schemata and the Attribution Process.* Morristown, NJ: General Learning Press, 1972.

–. "The Processes of Causal Attribution." *American Psychologist* 28 (1973): 107-28.

Keohane, Robert O. *After Hegemony: Cooperation and Discord in the World Political Economy.* Princeton, NJ: Princeton University Press, 1984.

Keohane, Robert O., and Joseph S. Nye Jr. *Power and Interdependence,* 4th ed. Toronto: Pearson, 2012 [1977].

Kirchick, James. "The Homegrown-Terrorist Threat: It Can Happen Here, and It Is Happening Here." *Commentary* 130 (February 2010): 16-20.

Klepak, Harold P. *Natural Allies? Canadian and Mexican Perspectives on International Security.* Ottawa: Carleton University Press, 1996.

Kluger, Jeffrey. "How Americans Are Living Dangerously." *Time,* 26 November 2006, http://www.time.com/.

Kovacic, William E., and Dennis E. Smallwood. "Competition Policy, Rivalries, and Defense Industry Consolidation." *Journal of Economic Perspectives* 8, 4 (1994): 91-110.

Krauthammer, Charles. "The Unipolar Moment." *Foreign Affairs* 70, 1 (1990/1991): 23-33.

Krull, Douglas S. "On Partitioning the Fundamental Attribution Error: Dispositionalism and the Correspondence Bias." In *Cognitive Social Psychology: The Princeton Symposium on the Legacy and Future of Social Cognition,* ed. Gordon B. Moscowitz, 211-27. Mahwah, NJ: Lawrence Erlbaum Associates, 2001.

Lachance, Daniel J.L., Joe T. Fernandes, Tim R. Gushue, Andrew B. Godefroy, and Lisa Moulton. *Projecting Power: Trends Shaping Canada's Air Force in the Year 2019.* Trenton, ON: Canadian Forces Aerospace Warfare Centre, 2009.

Lagassé, Philippe. "Canada, Strategic Defence, and Strategic Stability," *International Journal* 63, 4 (Autumn 2008): 917-37.

–. "A Maritime NORAD?" *SITREP: Journal of the Royal Canadian Military Institute* 64, 5 (November-December 2004): 10-12.

–. "A Mixed Legacy: General Hillier and Canadian Defence, 2005-2008." *International Journal* 64, 3 (Summer 2009): 605-23.

–. "Northern Command and the Evolution of Canada-US Defence Relations." *Canadian Military Journal* 4, 1 (Spring 2003): 15-22.

Lagassé, Philippe, and Paul Robinson. "Reviving Realism in the Canadian Defence Debate." Martello Paper 34. Kingston, ON: Queen's Centre for International Relations, 2008.

Laqueur, Walter. *The New Terrorism: Fanaticism and the Arms of Mass Destruction.* Oxford: Oxford University Press, 1999.

Larson, Deborah Welch, and Alexei Shevchenko. "Status Seekers: Chinese and Russian Responses to US Primacy." *International Security* 34, 4 (2010): 63-95.

Law, David. "Security Sector Reform in the Euro-Atlantic Region: Unfinished Business." In *Reform and Reconstruction of the Security Sector,* ed. Alan Bryden and Heiner Hänggi, 21-43. Münster, Germany: Lit Verlag, 2004.

Leblanc, Daniel. "Market Forces Will Determine Distribution of Boeing Benefits, PM Says; Ottawa's Decision Not to Interfere Thwarts Fortier's Efforts to Boost Share for Quebec." *Globe and Mail,* 27 January 2007.

Lennox, Patrick. *At Home and Abroad: The Canada-US Relationship and Canada's Place in the World.* Vancouver: UBC Press, 2009.

Lerhe, Eric. "Will We See a Maritime NORAD?" *Journal of Military and Strategic Studies* 9, 2 (2006/07).

Lerner, Melvin. *The Belief in a Just World: A Fundamental Delusion.* New York: Plenum Press, 1980.

Lesser, Ian, Bruce Hoffman, John Arquilla, David Ronfeldt, and Michele Zanini. *Countering the New Terrorism.* Santa Monica, CA: Rand Corporation, 1999.

Létourneau, Charles. *L'influence canadienne à travers les opérations de paix, 1956 à 2005.* Montréal: CEPES/UQAM, 2006.

Leyton-Brown, David. "Managing Canada? United States Relations in the Context of Multilateral Alliances." In *America's Alliances and Canadian-American Relations,* ed. Lauren McKinsey and Kim Richard Nossal, 162-79. Toronto: Summerhill Press, 1988.

Linville, Patricia W., and Edward E. Jones. "Polarized Appraisals of Out-Group Members." *Journal of Personality and Social Psychology* 38 (1980): 689-703.

Litman, Todd. "Terrorism, Transit and Safety." *Toronto Star,* 27 July 2005.

Lusztig, Michael. *The Limits of Protectionism: Building Coalitions for Free Trade.* Pittsburgh, PA: University of Pittsburgh Press, 2004.

Macdonald, Laura. *Adapting to a New Playing Field? Civil Society Inclusion in the Hemisphere's Multilateral Processes.* Ottawa: FOCAL Policy Paper, 2000.

Mandel-Campbell, Andrea, and Ken Warn. "Security Puts Strain on Nafta Partners: Border Controls." *Financial Times,* 16 October 2001.

Manley, John, and Gordon Giffin. "A Table for Two, Not Three." *Globe and Mail,* 5 May 2009, A15.

Mann, James. *Rise of the Vulcans: The History of Bush's War Cabinet.* New York: Viking, 2004.

Manning, Bayless. "The Congress, the Executive and Intermestic Affairs: Three Proposals." *Foreign Affairs* 55 (January 1977): 306-24.

Martin, Paul. *Hell or High Water: My Life in and Out of Politics.* Toronto: McClelland and Stewart, 2008.

Mason, Dwight. "The Canadian-American North American Defence Alliance in 2005." *International Journal* 60, 2 (2005): 385-96.

Massie, Justin. "Canada's (In)dependence in the North American Security Community: The Asymmetrical Norm of Common Fate." *American Review of Canadian Studies* 37, 4 (2007): 493-516.

–. "Making Sense of Canada's 'Irrational' International Security Policy: A Tale of Three Strategic Cultures." *International Journal* 64, 3 (2009): 625-35.

Massie, Justin, and Stéphane Roussel. "The Twilight of Internationalism? Neocontinentalism as an Emerging Dominant Idea in Canadian Foreign Policy." In *Canada in the World: Internationalism in Canadian Foreign Policy,* ed. Heather A. Smith and Claire Turenne Sjolander, 36-52. Don Mills, ON: Oxford University Press, 2013.

McCaffrey, Barry, and Robert Scales. *Texas Border Security: A Strategic Military Assessment.* Texas Department of Agriculture, September 2011. http://mccaul.house.gov/.

McCaul, Michael. "Border Security." Congressman Michael McCaul's Official Website. http://mccaul.house.gov/border-security/.

McCombs, Brady. "Border Boletín: Poll Shows Lukewarm Support for More Border Walls." *Arizona Daily Star,* 14 July 2011. http://azstarnet.com/.

McCombs, Brady, and Tim Steller. "Border Seen as Unlikely Terrorist Crossing Point." *Arizona Daily Star,* 7 June 2011.

McDonald, George. *The Canada First Defence Strategy – One Year Later.* Calgary: Canadian Defence and Foreign Affairs Institute, 2009.

McDonough, David S. "Canada, NORAD, and the Evolution of Strategic Defence." *International Journal* 68, 3 (Summer 2012): 768.

McFadden, Robert D. "Army Doctor Held in Fort Hood Rampage." *New York Times,* 5 November 2009. http://www.nytimes.com/.

Meacher, Michael. "The War on Terrorism Is Bogus." *Guardian,* 6 September 2003.

Mercer, Jonathan. *Reputation and International Politics.* Ithaca, NY: Cornell University Press, 2006.

Mexico. The NAFTA Office of Mexico in Canada. "Trade Intelligence: Statistics." Mexican Ministry of Economy, Underministry of International Trade Negotiations. http://www.nafta-mexico.org/.

"Mexico Would Support Shift to Security Perimeter with US and Canada." Canadian Press, 2 February 2002.

Meyer, Carl. "Promised Strategy to Bolster Defence Industry Cautiously Welcome." *Embassy*, 8 June 2011.

Michaud, Nelson. "Souveraineté et sécurité: Le dilemme de la politique étrangère dans l'après 11 septembre." *Études internationales* 33, 4 (December 2002): 647-65.

Micklethwait, John, and Adrian Wooldridge. *The Right Nation: Conservative Power in America.* New York: Penguin Books, 2004.

Migration Policy Institute. "Customs and Border Protection Commissioner Alan Bersin Addresses MPI." 14 October 2010. http://migrationpolicy.podbean.com/.

Miller, Dale T., and Michael Ross. "Self-Serving Biases in the Attribution of Causality: Fact or Fiction?" *Psychological Bulletin* 82, 2 (1975): 213-25.

Mintz, Alex, and Karl DeRouen Jr. *Understanding Foreign Policy Decision Making.* Cambridge: Cambridge University Press, 2010.

Mitchell, Paul T. "A Transformation Agenda for the Canadian Forces: Full Spectrum Influence." *Canadian Military Journal* 4, 4 (2003): 55-62.

Moens, Alexander. "'Lessons Learned' from the Security and Prosperity Partnership for Canadian-American Relations." *American Review of Canadian Studies* 41, 1 (2011): 53-64.

Moens, Alexander, and Rafal Domisiewicz. *European and North American Trends in Defence Industry: Problems and Prospects of a Cross-Atlantic Defence Market.* Ottawa: Department of Foreign Affairs and International Trade, April 2001. http://www.international.gc.ca/arms-armes/assets/pdfs/ moens_domisiewicz2001.pdf.

Monson, Thomas C., and Mark Snyder. "Actors, Observers, and the Attribution Process: Toward a Reconceptualization." *Journal of Experimental Social Psychology* 13 (1977): 89-111.

Morris, Julian, ed. *Rethinking Risk and the Precautionary Principle.* Oxford and Boston: Butterworth-Heinemann, 2000.

Morton, Desmond. "Defending the Indefensible: Some Historical Perspective on Canadian Defense." *International Journal* 42, 4 (1987): 627-44.

Mowle, Thomas H., and David H. Sacko. "Global NATO: Bandwagoning in a Unipolar World." *Contemporary Security Policy* 28, 3 (2007): 597-618.

Mueller, John. "A False Sense of Insecurity?" *Regulation* 27, 3 (Fall 2004): 42-46.

–. *Overblown: How Politicians and the Terrorism Industry Inflate National Security Threats, and Why We Believe Them.* New York: Free Press, 2006.

–. "Response." *Terrorism and Political Violence* 17, 4 (2005): 523-28.

–. "Six Rather Unusual Propositions about Terrorism." *Terrorism and Political Violence* 17, 4 (2005): 487-505.

National Drug Intelligence Center. "Situation Report: Cities in Which Mexican DTOs Operate within the United States." 11 April 2008. http://www.justice.gov/archive/ndic/pubs27/27986/27986p.pdf.

NATO. *NATO Handbook*. Brussels: NATO Office of Information and Press, 1995.

–. *NATO Handbook: 50th Anniversary Edition*. Brussels: NATO Office of Information and Press, 1998.

NAV CANADA. "NAV CANADA and the 9/11 Crisis." Newsroom – Backgrounder, http://www.navcanada.ca/.

Nisbett, Richard, and Lee Ross. *Human Inference: Strategies and Shortcomings of Social Judgment*. Englewood Cliffs, NJ: Prentice Hall, 1980.

NORAD, NorthCom, and CanadaCom. *Tri-Command Vision*. 12 March 2010. http://www.northcom.mil/.

Nossal, Kim Richard. "America's 'Most Reliable Ally'? Canada and the Evanescence of the Culture of Partnership." In *Forgotten Partnership Redux: Canada-US Relations in the 21st Century*, ed. Greg Anderson and Christopher Sands, 375-404. Amherst, NY: Cambria Press, 2011.

–. "Canadian Foreign Policy after 9/11: Realignment, Reorientation, or Reinforcement." In *Foreign Policy Realignment in the Age of Terror*, ed. Leonard Cohen, Brian Job, and Alexander Moens, 20-34. Toronto: Canadian Institute of Strategic Studies, 2002.

Nossal, Kim Richard, Stéphane Roussel, and Stéphane Paquin. *International Policy and Politics in Canada*. Toronto: Pearson Education, 2011.

Nye, Joseph S. *The Future of Power*. New York: Public Affairs, 2011.

–. "Transnational Relations and Interstate Conflicts: An Empirical Analysis." *International Organization* 28, 4 (1974): 961-96.

Ojeda, Mario. "La realidad geopolítica de México." *Foro Internacional* 17, 1 (July-September 1976): 1-9.

Olson, Eric. "Six Key Issues in United States–Mexico Security Cooperation." Washington, DC: Woodrow Wilson International Center for Scholars, July 2008. http://www.wilsoncenter.org/sites/default/files/six_issues_usmex_security_coop.pdf.

O'Neil, Shannon. "The Real War in Mexico: How Democracy Can Defeat the Drug Cartels." *Foreign Affairs* 88 (July/August 2009): 63-77.

Organization of American States. "Inter-American Convention against the Illicit Manufacturing of and Trafficking in Firearms, Ammunition, Explosives, and Other Related Materials." OAS Department of International Law, 14 November 1997. http://www.oas.org/.

Otero, Silvia. "Crecen las 'Zonas de Riesgo' para EU." *El Universal* (Mexico City), 19 February 2011, A2.

Pape, Robert A. "Soft Balancing against the United States." *International Security* 30, 1 (2005): 7-45.

Paquin, Jonathan. "Canadian Foreign and Security Policy: Reaching a Balance between Autonomy and North American Harmony in the 21st Century." *Canadian Foreign Policy* 15, 2 (2009): 99-108.

Park, Bernadette, and Myron M. Rothbart, "Perception of Out-Group Homogeneity and Levels of Social Categorization: Memory for the Subordinate Attributes on In-Group and Out-Group Members." *Journal of Personality and Social Psychology* 42 (1982): 1051-68.

Passel, Jeffrey, and D'Vera Cohn. *A Portrait of Unauthorized Immigrants in the United States.* Washington, DC: Pew Hispanic Center, 14 April 2009. http://pewhispanic.org.

Pastor, Robert A. "North America's Second Decade." *Foreign Affairs* 83, 1 (January/ February 2004): 124-35.

Patry, Bernard. *Partners in North America: Advancing Canada's Relations with the United States and Mexico. A Report of the Standing Committee on Foreign Affairs and International Trade.* Ottawa: House of Commons, December 2002.

Paul, T.V., and Norrin Ripsman. *Globalization and the National Security State.* Oxford: Oxford University Press, 2010.

Pauly, Louis W. *Who Elected the Bankers? Surveillance and Control in the World Economy.* Ithaca, NY: Cornell University Press, 1997.

Pearson, Lester B. "The Development of Canadian Foreign Policy." *Foreign Affairs* 30, 1 (October 1951): 17-30.

Pettigrew, Thomas F. "The Ultimate Attribution Error: Extending Allport's Cognitive Analysis of Prejudice." *Personality and Social Psychology Bulletin* 5 (1979): 461-76.

Pew Hispanic Center. "The Mexican-American Boom: Births Overtake Immigration." 14 July 2011. http://www.pewhispanic.org.

Pipes, Daniel. *Militant Islam Reaches America.* New York: W.W. Norton, 2002.

Pollack, Kenneth M. *The Threatening Storm: The Case for Invading Iraq.* New York: Random House, 2002.

Posen, Barry R. "Command of the Commons: The Military Foundation of American Hegemony." *International Security* 28, 1 (2003): 5-46.

Potter, Evan H. "Canada and the World: Continuity and Change in Public Opinion on Aid, Trade, and International Security: 1993-2002." *Études internationales* 33, 4 (December 2002): 697-722.

Preble, Christopher. *Exiting Iraq: Why the US Must End the Military Occupation and Renew the War against al Qaeda.* Washington, DC: Cato Institute, 2004.

Press-Barnathan, Galia. "Managing the Hegemon: NATO under Unipolarity." *Security Studies* 15, 2 (2006): 271-309.

Preston, Julia. "Mexican Immigration to US Slowed Significantly, Report Says." *New York Times,* 23 April 2012. .

Project for the New American Century. "Letter from the Project for the New American Century to the Honorable William J. Clinton, President of the United States." 26 January 1998. http://www.newamericancentury.org/.

–. *Rebuilding America's Defenses: Strategy, Forces and Resources for a New Century.* Washington, DC: Project for the New American Century, September 2000.

Public Safety Canada. "Seminar Proceedings: Perimeter Security and the Beyond the Border Dialogue: Perspectives from the PNW-Western Canada Region." Summary of remarks made by Chris Gregory. Border Policy Research Institute, Western Washington University, Bellingham, 20 June 2011.

Putnam, Robert D. "Diplomacy and Domestic Politics: The Logic of Two-Level Games." *International Organization* 42, 3 (Summer 1988): 427-60.

Quattrone, George A., and Edward E. Jones. "The Perception of Variability within In-Groups and Out-Groups: Implications for the Law of Small Numbers." *Journal of Personality and Social Psychology* 38 (1980): 141-52.

Resnick, Philip. "New Worlds, New Jerusalems: Reflections on North American Identities." *Norteamérica* 5, 1(January-June 2010): 15-36.

Ricks, Thomas. *Fiasco: The American Military Adventure in Iraq.* New York: Penguin, 2006.

Robertson, Colin. "Advancing Canadian Interests with the US." *The Embassy,* 4 May 2011.

–. *"Now for the Hard Part": A User's Guide to Renewing the Canadian-American Partnership.* Strategic Studies Working Group, Canadian International Council and Canadian Defence and Foreign Affairs Institute, February 2011. http://www.cdfai.org/PDF/Now%20for%20the%20Hard%20Part.pdf.

–. "Taking the Canada-US Partnership to the Next Level." *Policy Options* 32 (2011): 76-81.

Rodrigue, Isabelle. "Bouclier antimissile." *Le Droit,* 13 January 2006, A6.

Ropeik, David, and George Gray. *Risk: A Practical Guide for Deciding What's Really Dangerous in the World around You.* New York: Harvard University Center for Risk Analysis/Houghton Mifflin Company, 2002.

Rose, Gideon. "Neoclassical Realism and Theories of Foreign Policy." *World Politics* 51, 1 (1998): 144-72.

Ross, Andrew, and Kristin Ross, eds. *Anti-Americanism.* New York: New York University Press, 2004.

Ross, Lee. "The Intuitive Psychologist and His Shortcomings: Distortions in the Attribution Process." In *Advances in Experimental Social Psychology,* vol. 10, ed. Leonard Berkowitz, 173-220. New York: Academic Press, 1977.

Ross, Michael, and Garth Fletcher. "Attribution and Social Perception." In *Handbook of Social Psychology,* vol. 2, ed. G. Lindzey and E. Aronson, 73-122. New York: Random House, 1985.

Roussel, Stéphane. "The Blueprint of Fortress North America." In *Fortress North America? What Continental Security Means for Canada*, ed. David Rudd and Nicholas Furneaux, 12-19. Toronto: Canadian Institute of Strategic Studies, 2002.

–. "Pearl Harbor et le World Trade Center. Le Canada face aux États-Unis en période de crise." *Études internationales* 33, 4 (2002): 667-95.

Saltzman, Ilai Z. "Soft Balancing as Foreign Policy: Assessing American Strategy toward Japan in the Interwar Period." *Foreign Policy Analysis* 7, 1 (2011): 1-20.

Sands, Christopher. *The Canadian Gambit: Will It Revive North America?* Security and Foreign Affairs Briefing Paper. Washington, DC: Hudson Institute, 2011.

Savage, Luiza Ch. "Ditch the Sombreros. Should Ottawa Quit a Continental Strategy and Go Back to One-on-One with the US?" *Maclean's*, 16 April 2008, 29.

Savoie, Donald. *Power: Where Is It?* Montreal and Kingston: McGill-Queen's University Press, 2010.

Schauer, Frederick F. *Profiles, Probabilities and Stereotypes.* Cambridge, MA: Belknap Press of Harvard University Press, 2003.

Schneier, Bruce. *Beyond Fear: Thinking Sensibly about Security in an Uncertain World.* New York: Copernicus Books, 2003.

–. "The Psychology of Security." 18 January 2008. http://www.schneier.com/.

Schweller, Randall L. "Bandwagoning for Profit: Bringing the Revisionist State Back In." *International Security* 19, 1 (1994): 72-107.

–. *Deadly Imbalances: Tripolarity and Hitler's Strategy of World Conquest.* New York: Columbia University Press, 1998.

–. "Unanswered Threats: A Neoclassical Realist Theory of Underbalancing." *International Security* 29, 2 (2004): 159-201.

Selee, Andrew. "Overview of the Merida Initiative." Washington, DC: Woodrow Wilson International Center for Scholars, May 2008. http://www.wilsoncenter.org/sites/default/files/overview_merida_initiative.pdf.

Shanker, Thom, and Steven Erlanger. "Gates Delivers a Blunt Warning on NATO Future." *New York Times*, 11 June 2011, A1, A6.

Shirk, David. "Law Enforcement and Security Challenges in the US-Mexican Border Region." *Journal of Borderlands Studies* 18, 1 (Fall 2003): 1-24.

"Si se pierde Monterrey ante el crimen, lo demás estará perdido." *Crónica* (Mexico City), 22 February 2011, 12.

Sky Island Alliance. "New Poll: Americans Support Greater Investment in Ports of Entry – Not Border Walls." 14 July 2011. http://www.skyislandalliance.org/misc/SIA%20Border%20Poll%20Press%20Release.pdf.

Slovic, Paul. "Perception of Risk." *Science* 236 (1987): 280-85.

–. *The Perception of Risk.* London: Earthscan Publications, 2000.

Smith, James A. *The Idea Brokers: Think Tanks and the Rise of the New Policy Elite.*
New York: Free Press, 1991.

Smythe, Elizabeth. *Multilateralism or Bilateralism in the Negotiation of Trade-Related
Investment Measures.* Canadian-American Public Policy. Orono: Canadian-
American Center, University of Maine, 1995.

Sokolsky, Joel J. "Realism Canadian Style: National Security Policy and the Chrétien Legacy." *Policy Matters* 5, 2 (June 2004): 1-44.

–. "A Seat at the Table: Canada and Its Alliances." In *Canada's Defence: Perspectives
on Policy in the Twentieth Century,* ed. B.D. Hunt and R.G. Haycock, 145-62.
Toronto: Copp Clark Pitman, 1993.

Sokolsky, Joel J., and Philippe Lagassé. "Suspenders and a Belt: Perimeter and
Border Security in Canada-US Relations." *Canadian Foreign Policy* 12, 3 (2005/
2006): 15-30.

Spencer, Robert A. *Canada in World Affairs: From UN to NATO (1946-1949).* Toronto: University of Toronto Press, 1959.

Staples, Steven. *Missile Defence: Round One.* Toronto: Lorimer, 2006.

Steger, Debra P. "Institutions for Regulatory Cooperation in 'New Generation'
Economic and Trade Agreements." *Legal Issues of Economic Integration* 39, 1
(2012): 109-26.

Stein, Janice G. *Choosing to Cooperate: How States Avoid Loss.* Baltimore: Johns Hopkins University Press, 1993.

Stein, Janice Gross, and Eugene Lang. *The Unexpected War: Canada in Kandahar.*
Toronto: Viking Canada, 2007.

Stephenson, Alan. "Securing the Continent: Where Is NORAD Today." Strategic
Studies Working Group Papers. Ottawa: Canadian International Council and
Canadian Foreign Affairs and Defence Institute, November 2011.

Stiglitz, Joseph. "The True Cost of 9/11." *Slate,* 1 September 2011.

Stockholm International Peace Research Institute (SIPRI). "The Arms Industry."
http://www.sipri.org/.

Stone, James C. "Doubling the Size of the Defence Budget: The Economic Realities of Strategy 2020." PhD dissertation, Royal Military College of Canada,
2004.

Storrs, K. Larry. *Mexico–United States Dialogue on Migration and Border Issues,
2001-2005.* CRS Report for Congress RL32735, 2 June 2005.
http://www.fas.org/sgp/crs/row/RL32735.pdf.

Studer-Noguez, Isabel. *Ford and the Global Strategies of Multinationals: The North
American Auto Industry.* New York: Routledge, 2002.

Sunstein, Cass R. "Fear and Liberty." *Social Research* 71, 4 (2004): 967-96.

–. *The Laws of Fear: Beyond the Precautionary Principle.* New York, NY: Cambridge
University Press, 2005.

–. "Probability Neglect: Emotions, Worst Cases, and Law." *Yale Law Journal* 112, 1 (October 2002): 61-107.

–. "Terrorism and Probability Neglect." *Journal of Risk and Uncertainty* 26, 2-3 (2003): 121-36.

Tajfel, Henri. "Experiments in Intergroup Discrimination." *Scientific American* 223 (1970): 96-102.

Tajfel, Henri, and John C. Turner. "An Integrative Theory of Intergroup Conflict." In *The Social Psychology of Intergroup Relations*, ed. W.G. Austin and S. Worchel. Monterey, CA: Brooks/Cole, 1979.

–. "The Social Identity Theory of Intergroup Behaviour." In *Psychology of Intergroup Relations*, ed. S. Worchel and W.G. Austin. Chicago: Nelson-Hall, 1986.

Tajfel, Henri, M.G. Billig, R.P. Bundy, and Claude Flament. "Social Categorization and Intergroup Behaviour." *European Journal of Social Psychology* 2 (1971): 149-78.

Tasseron, Jeff. "Facts and Invariants: The Changing Context of Canadian Defence Policy." *Canadian Military Journal* 4, 2 (Summer 2003): 19-30.

Taylor, Donald M., and Janet R. Doria. "Self-Serving and Group-Serving Bias in Attribution." *Journal of Social Psychology* 113 (1981): 201-11.

Taylor, Donald M., and Vaishna Jaggi. "Ethnocentrism in a South Indian Context." *Journal Cross-Cultural Psychology* 5, 2 (1974): 162-72.

Tenorio Trillo, Mauricio. "On the Limits of Historical Imagination: North America as a Historical Essay." *International Journal* 61, 3 (Summer 2006): 567-87.

Tetlock, Philip E. "Social Psychology and World Politics." In *Handbook of Social Psychology*, ed. Daniel Gilbert, Susan Fiske, and Gardner Lindzey. New York: McGraw-Hill, 1998.

Thompson, Ginger. "US Is Widening Its Role in Mexico's Drug War." *New York Times*, 7 August 2011, 1, 8.

Thompson, John H., and Stephen J. Randall. *Canada and the United States: Ambivalent Allies*. 4th ed. Athens: University of Georgia Press, 2008.

Trope, Yaacov. "Identification and Inferential Processes in Dispositional Attribution." *Psychological Review* 93 (1986): 239-57.

–. "Uncertainty-Reducing Properties of Achievement Tasks." *Journal of Personality and Social Psychology* 37 (1979): 1505-18.

Tucker, Michael. *Canadian Foreign Policy: Contemporary Issues and Themes*. Toronto: McGraw-Hill Ryerson, 1980.

US. Department of Homeland Security. "Testimony of Secretary of Homeland Security Janet Napolitano before the Senate Homeland Security Committee, Southern Border Violence: Homeland Security, Threats, Vulnerabilities and Responsibilities," 25 March 2009. http://www.dhs.gov/.

–. "U.S. Border Patrol Nationwide Apprehensions by Sector, Fiscal Year 1992-2012." http://cbp.gov/xp/cgov/border_security/border_patrol/usbp_statistics/usbp_fy12_stats/.

US. Department of State. "Country Reports: Western Hemisphere Overview." In *Country Reports on Terrorism, 2005.* Washington, DC: Office of the Coordinator for Counterterrorism, April 2006.

US. Department of State, Office of the Coordinator for Counterterrorism. "Country Reports: Western Hemisphere Overview," in *Country Reports on Terrorism 2010.* Washington, DC: Department of State, 18 August 2011. http://www.state.gov/documents/organization/170479.pdf.

US. Department of Transportation, Research and Innovative Technology Administration. "Border Crossing/Entry Data: Quick Search by Rankings." http://www.bts.gov/.

US. General Accounting Office. *Defense Industry: Consolidation and Options for Preserving Competition.* Report to Congressional Committees GAO/NSIAD-98-141. Washington, DC: United States General Accounting Office, 1 April 1998.

US. Government Accountability Office. *Secure Border Initiative: DHS Needs to Follow Through on Plans to Reassess and Better Manage Key Technology Programs.* Report to the Congress GAO-10-840T. Washington, DC: United States Government Accountability Office, 17 June 2010.

–. *Secure Border Initiative: SBInet Planning and Management Improvements Needed to Control Risks.* Report to the Congress GAO-07-504T. Washington, DC: United States Government Accountability Office, 2 February 2007.

–. *Various Issues Led to the Termination of the United States-Canada Shared Border Management Pilot Project.* Report to the Congress GAO-08-1038R. Washington, DC: Government Accountability Office, 2008.

US. House of Representatives. "Joint Subcommittee Hearing: Mérida Part Two: Insurgency and Terrorism in Mexico." Washington, DC: Committee on Homeland Security – Subcommittee on Oversight, Investigations and Management, 4 October 2011.

–. "Subcommittee Hearing: A Call to Action: Narcoterrorism's Threat to the Southern U.S. Border." Washington, DC: Committee on Homeland Security – Subcommittee on Oversight, Investigations and Management, 14 October 2011. http://homeland.house.gov/.

US. Joint Forces Command. *The Joint Operating Environment 2008: Challenges and Implications for the Future Joint Force.* Suffolk, VA: United States Joint Forces Command, 2008. http://www.jfcom.mil/newslink/storyarchive/2008/JOE2008.pdf.

US. Office of National Drug Control Policy. *National Southwest Border Counternarcotics Strategy.* Washington, DC: Office of National Drug Control Policy, June

2009. http://www.whitehouse.gov/sites/default/files/ondcp/policy-and-research/swb_counternarcotics_strategy09.pdf.

US. White House. "Fact Sheet: The Secure Fence Act of 2006." Office of the Press Secretary, 26 October 2006, http://georgewbush-whitehouse.archives.gov/.

–. "Joint Statement by President Bush, President Fox, and Prime Minister Martin: Security and Prosperity Partnership of North America." Washington, DC: Office of the Press Secretary, 23 March 2005.

–. "President Discusses Border Security and Immigration Reform in Arizona." Office of the Press Secretary, 28 November 2005. http://georgewbush-white-house.archives.gov/.

–. "Smart Border: 22 Point Agreement. US-Mexico Border Partnership Action Plan." http://georgewbush-whitehouse.archives.gov/.

–. *Strategy to Combat Transnational Organized Crime*, 25 July 2011. http://www.whitehouse.gov/.

–. *United States–Canada Beyond the Border: A Shared Vision for Perimeter Security and Economic Competitiveness. Action Plan.* December 2011. http://www.whitehouse.gov/.

US-Mexico Binational Council. *US-Mexico Border Security and the Evolving Security Relationship: Recommendations for Policymakers.* Washington, DC: Center for Strategic and International Studies, April 2004. http://csis.org/files/media/csis/pubs/0404_bordersecurity.pdf.

Uslaner, Eric M. "The Democratic Party and Free Trade: An Old Romance Restored." *NAFTA: Law and Business Review of the Americas* 6 (Summer 2000): 347-62.

Valdez, Diana Washington. "US Military Report Warns 'Sudden Collapse' of Mexico Is Possible." *El Paso Times,* 13 January 2009. http://www.elpasotimes.com.

Valle, Eduardo. "¿Arde México?" *El Universal* (Mexico City), 19 February 2011, A9.

Von Hlatky, Stéfanie, and Jessica N. Trisko. "Sharing the Burden of the Border: Layered Security Cooperation and the Canada-US Frontier." *Canadian Journal of Political Science* 45, 1 (2012): 63-88.

Vonk, Roos. "Trait Inferences, Impression Formation, and Person Memory: Strategies in Processing Inconsistent Information about Persons." In *European Review of Social Psychology,* vol. 5, ed. Wolfgang Stroebe and Miles Hewstone, 111-49. Chichester, UK: Wiley, 1994.

Walker, Stephen G., and Akan Malici. *US Presidents and Foreign Policy Mistakes.* Stanford, CA: Stanford University Press, 2011.

Walker, Stephen G., Akan Malici, and Mark Shafer, eds. *Rethinking Foreign Policy Analysis: States, Leaders, and the Microfoundations of Behavioral International Relations.* New York and London: Routledge, 2011.

Waller Meyers, Deborah. "Does 'Smarter' Lead to Safer? An Assessment of the Border Accords with Canada and Mexico." *International Migration* 41, 4 (December 2003): 5-44.

Walt, Stephen. "Alliance Formation and the Balance of Power." *International Security* 4, 9 (Spring 1985): 3-43.

–. "Alliance Formation in Southwest Asia: Balancing and Bandwagoning in Cold War Competition." In *Dominoes and Bandwagons: Strategic Beliefs and Great Power Competition in the Eurasian Rimland,* ed. Robert Jervis and Jack Snyder, 51-84. New York: Oxford University Press, 1991.

–. "Keeping the World 'Off-Balance': Self-Restraint and US Foreign Policy." In *America Unrivaled: The Future of the Balance of Power,* ed. G. John Ikenberry, 121-54. Ithaca, NY: Cornell University Press, 2002.

–. *The Origins of Alliances.* Ithaca, NY: Cornell University Press, 1987.

–. *Taming American Power: The Global Response to US Primacy.* New York: W.W. Norton, 2005.

Waltz, Kenneth N. "Structural Realism after the Cold War." *International Security* 25, 1 (2000): 5-41.

Weaver, R. Kent. "The Changing World of Think Tanks." *PS: Political Science and Politics* 22, 2 (September 1989): 563-78.

Wohlforth, William C. "The Stability of a Unipolar World." *International Security* 24, 1 (1999): 5-41.

Woodward, Bob. *Bush at War.* New York: Simon and Schuster, 2002.

–. *State of Denial: Bush at War, Part II.* New York: Simon and Schuster, 2006.

Yetiv, Steve A. *Explaining Foreign Policy: US Decision-Making in the Gulf Wars,* 2nd ed. Baltimore: Johns Hopkins University Press, 2011.

Yusufi, Islam. "Security Governance: Security Sector Reform in Southeast Europe." IPF Research Report. Budapest: Center for Policy Studies, 2004.

Zakaria, Fareed. "Transcript: Unrest in the Arab World; US Budget Battles." CNN, 6 March 2011. http://transcripts.cnn.com/.

Contributors

Donald E. Abelson is professor of political science, director of the Canada-US Institute, and director of the Centre for American Studies at Western University.

Louis Bélanger is professor of political science and director of the Institut des hautes études internationales (HEI) at Université Laval.

Stephen Clarkson is professor of political economy at the University of Toronto.

Yan Cimon is associate professor at the Faculty of Business Administration at Université Laval.

Charles F. Doran is the Andrew W. Mellon Professor of International Relations at the School of Advanced International Studies, Johns Hopkins University.

David G. Haglund is professor of political science at Queen's University and co-editor of the *International Journal*.

Frank P. Harvey is associate dean research and university research professor of international relations at Dalhousie University.

Athanasios Hristoulas is professor of international relations and director of Canadian Studies at the International Studies Department of Instituto Tecnológico Autónomo de México (ITAM).

Patrick James is Dornsife Dean's Professor of International Relations and director of the Center for International Studies at the University of Southern California.

Philippe Lagassé is associate professor at the Graduate School of Public and International Affairs of the University of Ottawa.

Justin Massie is assistant professor of political science at the Université du Québec à Montréal (UQAM).

Jonathan Paquin is associate professor of political science and director of the International Peace and Security Program at Université Laval.

Mark Paradis is a doctoral student in the Political Science and International Relations Program at the University of Southern California.

Isabelle Vagnoux is professor of American studies at Aix-Marseille Université, LERMA, France.

Index

Printed and bound in Canada by Friesens
Typeset using PressBooks.com and PDF rendering by PrinceXML
Copy editor: Francis Chow
Proofreader: Joanne Muzak
Indexer: Noeline Bridge